WITHDRAWN
UTSA LIBRARIES

RENEWALS 458-4574

Studies in Central and Eastern Europe

Edited for the International Council for Central and East European Studies by **Roger E. Kanet**, University of Miami, USA

Titles include:

Stanislav J. Kirschbaum (*editor*)
CENTRAL EUROPEAN HISTORY AND THE EUROPEAN UNION

Stephen Velychenko (*editor*)
UKRAINE, THE EU AND RUSSIA
History Culture International Relations

Studies in Central and Eastern Europe
Series Standing Order ISBN 978–0–230–51682–3 hardcover
(*outside North America only*)

You can receive future titles in this series as they are published by placing a standing order. Please contact your bookseller or, in case of difficulty, write to us at the address below with your name and address, the title of the series and the ISBN quoted above.

Customer Services Department, Macmillan Distribution Ltd, Houndmills, Basingstoke, Hampshire RG21 6XS, England

Globalization and Regionalization in Socialist and Post-Socialist Economies

Common Economic Spaces of Europe

Edited by

John Pickles
Earl N. Phillips Distinguished Professor of International Studies
University of North Carolina at Chapel Hill, USA

© Editorial matter, selection and introduction © John Pickles 2008
All remaining chapters © respective authors 2008

First published 2008 by
PALGRAVE MACMILLAN

Palgrave Macmillan in the UK is an imprint of Macmillan Publishers Limited, registered in England, company number 785998, of Houndmills, Basingstoke, Hampshire RG21 6XS.

Palgrave Macmillan in the US is a division of St Martin's Press LLC, 175 Fifth Avenue, New York, NY 10010.

Palgrave Macmillan is the global academic imprint of the above companies and has companies and representatives throughout the world.

Palgrave® and Macmillan® are registered trademarks in the United States, the United Kingdom, Europe and other countries.

ISBN-13: 978–0–230–52213–8 hardback
ISBN-10: 0–230–52213–0 hardback

This book is printed on paper suitable for recycling and made from fully managed and sustained forest sources. Logging, pulping and manufacturing processes are expected to conform to the environmental regulations of the country of origin.

A catalogue record for this book is available from the British Library.

Library of Congress Cataloging-in-Publication Data

Globalization and regionalization in socialist and post-socialist economies : common economic spaces of Europe / edited by John Pickles.
p. cm.—(Studies in Central and Eastern Europe)
Includes index.
ISBN-13: 978–0–230–52213–8   ISBN-10: 0–230–52213–0
1. Europe, Eastern – Economic conditions – 1989– 2. Europe, Central – Economic conditions – 1989– 3. Former Soviet republics – Economic conditions. 4. Post-communism. I. Pickles, J. (John)
HC244.G565 2009
330.947—dc22   2008037193

10 9 8 7 6 5 4 3 2 1
17 16 15 14 13 12 11 10 09 08

Printed and bound in Great Britain by
CPI Antony Rowe, Chippenham and Eastbourne

Contents

List of Figures

List of Tables

List of Abbreviations

ADB	Asian Development Bank
ASEAN	Association of South East Asian Nations
ATM	Automated Teller Machine (bankomat)
AVAS	Autoritatea pentru Valorificarea Activelor Statului (Romania: Authority for State Assets Recovery – the privatization agency)
BOFIT	Bank of Finland Institute for Economies in Transition
BRIE	Bulgarian Romanian Interuniversity Europe
CE	Central Europe
CEE	Central and Eastern Europe
CEEC	Central and Eastern European Countries
CIA	Central Intelligence Agency
CIS	Commonwealth of Independent States
CMEA	Council of Mutual Economic Assistance
COMECON	Council for Mutual Economic Assistance
CR	Concentration Ratio
CZ	Czech Republic
D	Germany
DDT	Dichlorodiphenyltrichloroethane (insecticide)
DGPA	Directorate-General for Protection and Anti-Corruption
DKMT	Danube–Körös–Mureş–Tisza
EBRD	European Bank for Reconstruction and Development
EC	European Community
ECB	European Central Bank
ECU	European Currency Unit
EU	European Union
EU-15	Refers to the 15 countries in the European Union before the expansion on 1 May 2004, when eight Central and Eastern European countries as well as Cyprus and Malta joined the organization. They are Austria, Belgium, Denmark, Finland, France, Germany, Greece, Ireland (Republic of), Italy, Luxembourg, Netherlands, Portugal, Spain, Sweden, and the United Kingdom
EU-27	Austria, Belgium, Bulgaria, Cyprus, the Czech Republic, Denmark, Estonia, Finland, France, Germany, Greece, Hungary, Ireland, Italy, Latvia, Lithuania, Luxembourg, Malta, The Netherlands, Poland, Portugal, Romania, Slovakia, Slovenia, Spain, Sweden, and the United Kingdom
ECE	East Central Europe

EMU	Economic and Monetary Union
ERM-2	Exchange Rate Mechanism
EU	European Union
FDI	Foreign Direct Investment
FSB	Federalnaya Sluzhba Bezopasnosti (Russia: Federal Security Service; FSK successor since 1995)
G7	Group of Seven
G8	Group of Eight
GDP	Gross Domestic Product
GNI	Gross National Income
GUS	Główny Urzad Statystyczny (Polish: Central Statistical Office)
IFC	International Finance Corporation
GPW	Warsaw Stock Exchange (Giełda Papierów Wartościowych)
GSNKh	*Guberniia Sovnarkoz* (Russia: Provincial Economic Council)
HH index	Herfindahl-Hirschman index
HRK	Rectors' Conference (Germany)
ICCEES	International Congress of Central and East European Studies
IFI	International Financial Institutions
IMF	International Monetary Fund
IOSCO	International Organization of Securities Commissions
IPO	Initial Public Offering
IRFS	International Financial Reporting Standards
JETRO	Japan External Trade Organization
KGB	Komitet Gosudarstvennoy Bezopasnosti (Committee for State Security, former USSR)
LT	Lithuania
Mostorg	Moscow Trade Agency
MS	Member State(s)
MSNKh	Moscow Sovnarkhoz (a local branch of VSNKh)
NATO	North Atlantic Treaty Organization
NBP	Narodowy Bank Polski (National Bank of Poland)
NEP	New Economic Policy
NMS	New Member States
NNI	New Neighbourhood Instrument
OECD	Organization for Economic Cooperation and Development
PL	Poland
RECEP	Russian European Centre for Economic Policy
R&D	Research and Development
RGAE	Russian State Archive of the Economy
RSFSR	Russian Soviet Federated Socialist Republic
SK	Slovakia
SME	Small and Medium-sized Enterprise
TACIS	Technical Assistance for the Commonwealth of Independent States (EU)

USSR	Union of Soviet Socialist Republics
UNCTAD	United Nations Conference on Trade and Development
VPK	Komissiya Soveta Ministrov SSSR po voenno-promyshlennym voprosam, or Voenno-promyshlennaia komissiia (Russia: Military Industrial Commission)
VSNKh	Supreme Council of the National Economy (Russia)
WERI	World Economy Research Institute (Poland)
WTO	World Trade Organization

Acknowledgements

This volume is the second of two I have edited in this series dealing with the changing economic spaces and practices of post-socialist Europe. *State and Society in Postsocialist Economies* appeared earlier this year and addressed the changing roles played by state and societal actors in shaping contemporary post-socialist economic landscapes. *Globalization and Regionalization in Socialist and Post-Socialist Economies: Common Economic Spaces of Europe* focuses on the interweaving of general processes of economic internationalization, harmonization and integration *with* the complexities produced by the parallel and linked processes of regionalization, localization and adaptation. In various ways, the chapters in this volume question assumptions about contemporary European integration and broader processes of globalization, and they do so from the perspective of both earlier experiences of economic internationalization and from a diverse range of contemporary perspectives on the building of common European economic spaces. The authors come from nine countries. Together their topics and approaches reflect the growing diversity of perspectives on the practices of socialist and postsocialist economies.

I would like to thank Bob Jenkins for his help in editing the preliminary manuscripts, Christian Sellar for assistance with some translation issues and Leon Pickles for help with indexing. Roger Kanet has been a wonderful supporter of this project and has offered constructive comments at every stage. I would also like to thank the anonymous reviewers who provided useful comments and suggestions on all the chapters.

Palgrave editors, Gemma D'ArcyHughes and Amy Lankester-Owen, and their production staff (especially Vidhya Jayaprakash) of Newgen Imaging in Thiruvanmiyur, Chennai, India, have been exemplary in their attention to detail and in keeping the project on schedule, even as it was interrupted at my end by various other commitments and demands.

Finally, thanks to the authors who have responded positively to the demands of repeated revision and updating, turned around chapters and queries with speed and borne the delays in the overall project with good humour.

JOHN PICKLES
July 2008

Preface by General Editor

When the International Council for Central and East European Studies (ICCEES) was founded at the first international and multidisciplinary conference of scholars working in this field, held in Banff, Alberta, Canada, on 4–7 September 1974, it was given the name International Committee for Soviet and East European Studies (ICSEES). Its major purpose was to provide for greater exchange between research centres and scholars around the world who were devoted to the study of the USSR and the communist states and societies of Eastern Europe. These developments were the main motivation for bringing together the very different national organisations in the field and for forming a permanent committee of their representatives, which would serve as an umbrella organization, as well as a promoter of closer co-operation. Four national scholarly associations launched ICSEES at the Banff conference: the American Association for the Advancement of Slavic Studies (AAASS), the National Association for Soviet and East European Studies in Great Britain (NASEES), the British Universities Association of Slavists (BUAS), and the Canadian Association of Slavists (CAS).

Over the past three decades six additional Congresses have been held: in Garmisch-Partenkirchen, Germany, 1980; Washington, USA, 1985; Harrogate, UK, 1990; Warsaw, Poland, 1995; Tampere, Finland, 2000; and Berlin, Germany, 2005. The next Congress is scheduled for 2010 in Stockholm, Sweden. The original four national associations that sponsored the first congress have been joined by an additional seventeen full and six associate member associations, with significantly more than a thousand scholars participating at each of the recent congresses.

It is now a little over three decades since scholars felt the need to coordinate the efforts in the 'free world' to describe and analyse the Communist political systems, their societies and economies, and East-West relations in particular. Halfway through this period, the Communist system collapsed, the region that was the object of study was reorganized, and many of the new states that emerged set out on a path of democratic development, economic growth, and, in many cases, inclusion in Western institutions. The process turned out to be complex, and there were setbacks. Yet, by 2004, the European Union as well as the North Atlantic Treaty Organization had welcomed those post-Communist states that had met all of the requirements for membership. Not all of the applicant states achieved this objective; but the process is ongoing. For this reason, perhaps even more than before, the region that encompassed the former Communist world demands study, explanation, and analysis, as both centripetal and centrifugal forces are at work in each state and across the region. We are most fortunate that the community of scholars addressing these issues now includes many astute analysts from the region itself.

ROGER E. KANET

Notes on Contributors

Mary Schaeffer Conroy, University of Colorado at Denver, Denver, CO, USA. *Europe Our Common Home in the Pharmaceutical Industry? The Soviet Pharmaceutical Industry and European Houses during the NEP*. Mary Schaeffer Conroy received her Ph. D. from Indiana University in 1964. She is the author of *Peter Arkad'evich Stolypin: Practical Politics in Late Tsarist Russia* (Westview Press, 1976); *In Health and In Sickness: Pharmacy, Pharmacists and the Pharmaceutical Industry in Late Imperial, Early Soviet Russia* (East European Monographs, 1994); and *The Soviet Pharmaceutical Business During Its First Two Decades, 1917–1937* (Peter Lang, 2006); and editor of and contributor to *Emerging Democracy in Late Imperial Russia* (University Press of Colorado, 1998). She has contributed articles and chapters on politics and civil society in Imperial Russia and on disease and health care in Imperial and Soviet Russia to journals and compilations.

Peter Haiss, Europe Institute, Vienna University of Economics and Business Administration and **Natalie Chou**, Institute of European Studies, Vienna. Peter R. Haiss is a lecturer at the Vienna University of Economics and Business Administration, Vienna, Austria, and is with the Project and Corporate Finance Austria Department of Bank Austria Creditanstalt, Member of UniCredit Group. His major research interests are the finance-growth-nexus and financial sector transition in Central & Eastern Europe, including bond markets and foreign direct investment. Natalie Chou was a graduate student at the Institute of European Studies, Vienna, Austria and at the University of Pennsylvania, USA, during the research project. Her major research interests are bond markets and Asian financial markets.

Stefan Hedlund, Uppsala University Uppsala Sweden. *The Property Rights Hurdle: Reconciling EU and Russian Traditions*. Stefan Hedlund is professor of Soviet and East European Studies. Before his appointment at Uppsala University in 1990, he was Associate Professor of Economics at Lund University, with a specialization in development economics. Up until the fall of the Berlin Wall, his research was mainly focused on the Soviet-type economic system. Since then, he has worked extensively on problems relating to attempted economic transition. His present research revolves around neo-institutional theory and problems of path dependence. His most recent publication is *Russian Path Dependence* (Routledge, 2005).

Rustem Khaziev, Bashkir State University, Ufa, Russia. *Factories of the 'Red Bourgeoisie' in the Urals during the NEP: Data and Analysis*. Rustem Khaziev is in the Department of History, Bashkir State University. He has published articles on economic reform in the Urals including in *Ekonomicheskaja istorija Ezhegodnik* and is author of *Poslednie iz mogikan: krasnye kuptsy epokhi nepa': Materialy i dokumenty ob ural'skikh kommersantakh 1921–1928 godov.* (The Last of the Mochicans: Red Businessmen in the Epoch of the NEP': Material and Documents about Urals Businessmen.) Ufa: Rio Bashgy, 2003.

Ken Morita, (Professor, Faculty of Economics, Hiroshima University, Japan) 1–12-2 Mukainada Shin-machi, Minami-ku, Hiroshima, Japan 734–0055. Tel: +81–82-286–5511 and **Yun Chen**, (Associate Professor, School of International Relations and Public Affairs, Fudan University, China). Dr. Ken **Morita** is a professor in the faculty of Economics at Hiroshima University, Japan and is one of the leading international scholars in the field of Transition and Development Studies. Between 1982 and 1984 he was the Special Economic Advisor for the Ambassador of the Japanese Embassy in Warsaw, Poland, and has spent the intervening years in various academic and research posts in Japan and Poland. Dr. Yun **Chen** is an associate professor in the school of International Relations and Public Affairs at Fudan University, China and is one of the leading young international scholars in the field of Transition and Development Studies. Between 2002 and 2004 she was a Doctoral Researcher in the School of Economy at Fudan University, and since 2002 has held several research positions in China and Japan including a Research Fellow in the Japan Research Center at Fudan University.

Elżbieta Mirecka is a senior researcher at the Wrocław School of Banking, Wrocław, Poland. She has published numerous articles on structural reform, banking and capital markets, and globalization and financial stabilization.

Ştefania Panaitescu is in the Faculty of Economic Sciences, University of Oradea, Bihor, Romania. Her research focuses on EU accession policies and their impacts on Romania. 3–5, Armatei Romane street, 410087 Bihor, Romania.

John Pickles is the Earl N. Phillips Distinguished Professor of International Studies ad Professor of Geography at the University of North Carolina at Chapel Hill. His main research interests are in regional economic transformation in eastern Europe, ethnicity, violence and economic change, and critical theory and cultural studies. He has published numerous articles in these fields, as well as several monographs, the most recent of which are *A History of Spaces: Cartographic Reason, Mapping, and the Geo-Coded World* (Routledge 2004), *Environmental Transitions: Transformation and Ecological Defence in Central and Eastern Europe* (with Petr Pavlinek. Routledge 2000), *Theorizing Transition: The Political Economy of Post-Communist Transformations* (edited with Adrian Smith, Routledge 1998), *Bulgaria in Transition* (edited with Krassimira Paskaleva, Phillip Shapira, and Boian Koulov, Ashgate 1998),

Ground Truth: The Social Consequences of Geographical Information Systems (edited Guilford Press, 1995), and *Phenomenology, Science, and Geography: Space and the Social Sciences* (Cambridge University Press, 1985). He is currently working on the integration of central and east European apparel production networks into EU and broader global value chains.

Steven Rosefielde, UNC Economics. *Contingent Property Rights: The Cost to the EU of Russia's Accession.* Steven Rosefielde is Professor of Economics, University of North Carolina, Chapel Hill. His most recent books include *Russia in the 21st Century: The Prodigal Superpower* (Cambridge UP, 2005), *Masters of Illusion: American Leadership in a Media Age* (Cambridge UP, 2006), and *Russian Economics from Lenin to Putin* (Blackwell, 2006).

Ksymena Rosiek, Department of Industrial and Environmental Policy, Cracow University of Economics. Ksymena Rosiek has been teaching at the Krakow University of Economics since 2002, in the Department of Industrial and Environmental Policy. She teaches courses on economy of environmental protection, sustainable development, financial instruments in environmental protection, and methods for the valuation of industrial and non-productive projects. She is currently completing a doctoral thesis on 'The Role of Foreign Sources of Financing Environmental Ventures in Poland'.

Hans-Heinrich Rieser, Hechingen, Germany and Christoph **Waack**, Leibniz-Institute of Regional Geography, Leipzig, Germany and Hans-Heinrich **Rieser**, Dr. phil., was born in 1953. At the Tuebingen Eberhard-Karl-University he studied Geography, Mathematics and Social and Economic History. On basis of a partnership contract he studied 1977/1978 for one year at the Babes-Bolyai-University in Cluj-Napoca in Romania. After exam he worked as assistant at the Institute of Geography in Tuebingen and as Regional Geographer on Southeast Europe. The main aspects of his work are at present transitions items and cross border cooperation. Christoph **Waack** (born 1966), Dr rer.nat, is currently working as a researcher at the Leibniz-Institute of Regional Geography, Leipzig. In 1997–2000 he worked as a research assistant and lecturer at the Institute for Geography at the University of Tuebingen. He published a study on divided border towns in Eastern Europe.

Anna Zachorowska-Mazurkiewicz, *The Influence of European Integration on the Institutional Situation of Women in Labour Market in Poland.* Anna Zachorowska-Mazurkiewicz is an Assistant Professor at Jagiellonian University in Krakow, Poland. She works in the Institute of Economics and Management. She received her M.A. in economics from University of Economics in Katowice, Poland and Ph.D. from Jagiellonian University. She has recently published a book on women in labour market 'Kobiety i instytucje' (Katowice: Slask, 2006). Her research interests centre on gender, globalization and European integration.

Katarzyna Żukrowska, Professor dr hab., Warsaw School of Economics, Head of International Security Department, Dean of Socio-Economic College. Affiliation: EADI, IPRA, EuPRA. Expert works for UN, NATO, OECD, EU. Interests: systemic transformation, international economic and political relations, European integration, defense economics. Supervision of four doctorates and 37 master thesis. Total number of publications 344, what includes: 31 books, 143 chapters, 124 articles and 46 reviews. Most recent publications: K. Żukrowska, M. Grącik (ed.) *Bezpieczeństwo międzynarodowe. Teoria i praktyka, (International Security. Theory and Practice)* 2006; K. Żukrowska (ed.) *Unia Europejska i USA wobec wyzwań globalnych, (European Union and the USA confronted with global challenges)* 2006; K. Żukrowska (ed.) *Europe and the Complex Security Issues,* 2005; K. Żukrowska, A. Konarzewska (ed.), *External Relations of the European Union – Determinants, Casual Links, Areas,* 2004; K. Żukrowska, R. Orsi, V. Lavrac *Fiscal, Monetary and exchange rate issues of the Eurozone Enlargement. A Report,* 2004; K. Żukrowska, H-D. Jacobson (ed.) *Policy Advice in the Process of the Eurozone Enlargement: Markets and Policies. A Report,* 2004; J. Ziemiecki, K. Żukrowska, *Konkurencja a transformacja w Polsce. Wybrane aspekty polityki gospodarczej, (Competition and transformation In Poland. Selected issues of economic policy).* 2004.

1
Globalization and Regionalization in Socialist and Post-Socialist Economies

John Pickles

> A day will come when all the nations of this continent, without losing their distinct qualities or their glorious individuality, will fuse together in a higher unity and form the European brotherhood. A day will come when the only battlefield will be the marketplace for competing ideas. A day will come when bullets and bombs will be replaced by votes. (Victor Hugo 1849, quoted in http://europa.eu/abc/12lessons/lesson_12/index_en.htm)

The common spaces of Europe

The year 1989 remains a complex signifier, capturing as it does the diverse hopes and desires of a wide range of 'Europeans'. For the Czech dissidents, the 'return to Europe' was both a strategic claim to sustain the Velvet Revolution and a real belief that post-War collectivism had been an interruption of the historical development of the market, democracy and civil society. For neoliberals, the 'return to Europe' was an inevitable correction away from the misguided path of planned economy and its 'road to serfdom' and back to the natural economy of free markets.[1] For Altvater, the ending of communist regimes in a matter of weeks or months in 1989 signalled the success of desire on the part of state socialist citizens for the lifestyle and consumption goods they had come to know through television, sourcing and tourism.[2]

In this process, international financial institutions (IFIs) such as the World Bank (WB), International Monetary Fund (IMF) and European Bank for Reconstruction and Development (EBRD) pursued the broader goals of international financial and investment interests to open these fledgling market economies to the global capitalist economy. For the World Bank, 'The successful integration of transition countries brings benefits for the world economy – above all, by opening up almost a third of the world's population and a quarter of its land mass.'[3] While admitting that: 'As transition proceeds, many countries may indeed face adjustment costs', the World Bank envisaged that the net outcome of these changes would be overwhelmingly positive.[4] As it argued,

> The rapid integration of the global economy in recent decades springs from the widespread recognition that economies invariably achieve more working with each other – exchanging goods, capital, and ideas – than acting alone. The failure of the Soviet ideal of 'socialism in one country' is further confirmation, if any were needed, of this simple truth.[5]

In all of these perspectives, the geostrategic interests of the turn (back) to Europe necessitated a defensive politics of engagement and linkage with the economies of Western Europe against any possible domestic *nomenklatura* retreat or external Russian intervention. It was in this geostrategic moment that the European Union acted to consolidate the democratic gains of the turn by opening access to EU institutions and support through the Enlargement and Accession process. Victor Hugo's prescient comment about the future of a unified Europe that preserves its distinctive qualities and glorious individuality became the model for the creation and extension of the European Union.

This notion of a common European space arose under the specific conjuncture of post-War reconstruction and the strong sense that economic crisis can lead to political instability and conflict. A common European economic space would, from this perspective, be a guarantor against any further rise of fascism, first by integrating the economies of national systems and second by generating common economic development goals that would create social and regional cohesion. Economic integration would, in turn, be a guarantor of political freedoms and enable the deepening of democracy not only within the national states of Europe but also in the transnational structures of the European Union. From Common Market to Common Political Project to Common Currency and Monetary Union was thus a staged project that linked economic development with broader goals of regional political stability (Table 1.1). Both could occur only through the production of a common economic space.

This common economic space was always intended to be built from national structures with their already territorialized economies and polities, and, if any level of political consensus was to be achieved in each of the future Member States, issues of national identity and political autonomy had to be considered. A political strategy of *unity with difference* was, as a result, a foundation stone of the European project from its inception; the gradual articulation of the coal and steel industries to create interdependencies and avoid future opportunities for rivalry; the forging out of the coal and steel community of a broader Common Market that linked and expanded regional capacities and comparative advantages; new opportunities to expand in scale and rationalize standards and procedures in production, logistics, and markets; the forging of a transnational regional structure of economy, politics and identity with its own structures of government, the capacity to make and enforce laws and, increasingly, the ability to regulate the common space through the instruments of customs unions, open borders and new outer-border surveillance regimes; and now the gradual expansion of the EMU and the forging of a common currency regime for the expanded EU-27.

These processes of regional integration have been achieved through a diverse and complex series of technical instruments by which common logics, rules and practices have been forged in and by the transnational institutions of the European Commission, the European Parliament and the European Court. While the goals of the EU have been expansive and ambitious, particularly with its bold decision to integrate the former socialist states of Central and Eastern Europe after 1989, the mechanisms for achieving these goals have been more quotidian. It has been through a myriad of technical reports, committees, instruments, regulations and initiatives that the actual process of regional economic harmonization has been achieved.

This truly is a continental revolution; a slow, painstaking adjustment of the micro-practices of everyday economies to specific and common standards, norms and regulations across a region of 27 countries. 'Harmonization' in this context has always been a political and an economic project. Regional economic systems and actors are to be harmonized to enable greater levels of economic efficiency, scope for new forms of organization, scales of enterprises and flexibilities and mobilities in business and for workers. And the process was always intended to achieve precisely what the term also means: the harmonization of regional economies that in the past have been built and run as structures of state power in conditions of intense colonial and modern inter-state rivalry. Harmonization was a well chosen term and, in the chapters of this book, we see how this double meaning – technical adjustment and regional integration – are now being brought about in the New Member States.

Table 1.1 Europe's mission

Europe's mission in the twenty-first century is to
• provide peace, prosperity and stability for its peoples; • overcome the divisions on the continent; • ensure that its people can live in safety; • promote balanced economic and social development; • meet the challenges of globalization and preserve the diversity of the peoples of Europe; • uphold the values that Europeans share, such as sustainable development and a sound environment, respect for human rights and the social market economy.

Source: European Union. *Europa: Europe in 12 Lessons* [http://europa.eu/abc/12lessons/lesson_1/index_en.htm].

Of course, the project of a unified Europe has also unfolded at the very time that the national and regional economies have themselves experienced the massive and transformative effects brought about by the globalization of economic organizations and practices. Globalization has both sustained the project of European expansion and driven the arguments for the economic efficiency and competitiveness of a common European economic space. But, especially in the past two years, it has also begun to change the terms of the debate. George Brown's Report from the Exchequer about *Global Europe* and Peter Mandelson's adoption of the broad principles of *Global Europe* have begun to recast in interesting and important ways how the structure and practices of a common economic space are being thought.[6] In this unfolding debate, the challenge for the EU and its new postsocialist Member States is precisely one of articulating its longstanding commitments to a common economic space and community, with all the infrastructural investments to support extended and integrated regional production and financial networks this entails, with the challenges of a deregulated, highly competitive global economy in which price and cost differentials potentially undermine the goal of a high-value regional system.

The dialects of a common economic space

This book is about the relationship between these processes of regionalization and globalization, and the ways in which each plays itself out in concrete institutions and places. That is, it deals with the dialectic relationship between the specificities of particular local and regional conditions and economies and the general integration and harmonization of economic systems.

How do we understand these projects of integration and harmonization? How do we understand them as cultural projects rather than as linear and inexorable developmental projects? Many authors have sought to inscribe in postsocialist transitions the logic of 'return to Europe', to a norm of economic and political practice distorted under a statist and collectivist agenda. In this model of transitology, transition from communism was a natural development towards capitalism and liberal democracy, to the 'End of History'. The current project of framing a Europe of the regions is refracted in important ways by a more general history of Europe as a common space of culture and peoples. Here the 'cultural heritage' of common ancestries, beliefs and values continues to underpin a notion of what it is to be European, whether in terms of long *durees* of imperial bonds (the Holy Roman Empire), religious belief (the Roman Catholic Church) or Enlightenment values of individual freedom and the benign role of the state as guarantor of those rights. The Second World War, following directly on the heels of the war to end all wars and the Great Depression, was also a determining imperative for a new articulation aimed at forging a new transnational Europe, a Europe of the states, in which a common space of values, political structures and economic flows was to be the guarantor of political stabilization and economic development, 'a feeling of kinship between Europeans.'[7]

However, the authors in this collection ask more difficult questions. All are intrigued in one way or another by the ways in which actual political economic transitions occur.[8] While they each focus on the process of integration and harmonization into broader global processes, they do so with an attentive eye on the difference that the goals, practices, institutions and norms of the actors involved make in shaping those broader processes.

In this sense, the chapters in this book each attempt to tease out of the processes of global economic integration the intricate details in which the concrete economies of particular places are shaped by, and in turn shape, those processes and outcomes. That is, the chapters seek in different settings to elaborate the specific roles played by the embeddedness of social and economic networks, the role of social interests and the effects of untraded interdependencies in shaping the actual practices and outcomes of the economy.

Many of the problems associated with models of a clear-cut break with the communist past and a uniform path of transition that would rapidly lead states from their former centralized and planned economic system to a liberalized free market economy have been the focus of much research in social science over the past 20 years. In particular, Grabher and Stark have argued forcefully that it is not as easy as many commentators have assumed to create capitalism by design through the creation of a few key institutional and structural transformations.[9] A second set of criticisms has focused more explicitly on the spatial and temporal diversity of transition. Karl and Schmitter stressed the importance of identifying different kinds of transition, not only in Southern and Eastern Europe, but also in other contexts such as Latin America.[10] Because neoliberal approaches undervalue the embeddedness of transformation, it has become particularly important to develop contextual, place and time-specific accounts of what Pickles and Smith called 'actually existing transitions'.[11] A third criticism, noted for example by Bradshaw and Stenning, is that the neoliberal approach has failed sufficiently to recognize the human costs of transition.[12] While the World Bank appears to accept that transition can have unequal consequences, it nevertheless remains rooted to a model of 'development' that appears not to allow for the possible sustainability of alternative economic practices and political structures.[13]

One of the most interesting dimensions of the changing experience of transition that people have encountered over the last decade has been the very varied positions that governments have chosen to adapt to a broadly similar set of external global circumstances. The extent to which states have chosen to implement macroeconomic policy instruments designed to introduce a free market have varied greatly.[14] The social support mechanisms that have been created to support the losers from such policies have also been extremely variable in scope, implementation and effect.[15] The result has been a richness and diversity of experience that reflects real differences in the ways in which people and governments have sought to grapple with the implications of transition for their own conditions. It is the interpretation and representation of such diversity and difference that lie at the heart of these emerging geographical accounts of transition.

The 'switching' between Soviet-style and capitalist modernities was swift and deep, although the actual transformations that followed 1989 have, for many, been long-drawn-out and painful. The collapse of the *ancien regime* unleashed new class processes and intense struggles to secure access to and control over the resources of the state and economy. Transition was experienced increasingly as loss of foundations, a decay of old truths, and uncertainty about future meanings and material prospects. Class struggles over the production and allocation of social surplus reshaped relations between town and country and core–periphery, thus launching a massive shifting of capital among social groups and regions, particularly in the cities. Wealth and power shifted away from party officials (the *nomenklatura*) and into the hands of new groups of private owners, in ways that were both speedy and surprisingly visible. Geographical shifts occurred in investment patterns as former 'social' industry policies that allocated employment to peripheral regions were abandoned in favour of capital concentration in the prime cities of Berlin, Prague, Bratislava, Budapest, Sofia, etc. As farmers struggled to adjust to new conditions of disinvestments and land restitution, new social elites consolidated their control over dachas, hotels, banks and factories.

The working class was caught in these struggles and, as they had been under state socialism, some found their interests tenuously and uncomfortably aligned with managers and new owners while others found their livelihoods destroyed overnight. Unlike socialist production politics, postsocialist production relations increasingly fell under the absolute control of postsocialist managers and owners, often backed by finance capital and political 'families'. These insurgencies of the middle class mobilized discourses of a broader public, often backed by one party or another, to dismantle the remnant powers and privileges of earlier leaders and class factions. In the process they unleashed a simultaneous deepening and weakening of the political process. In many cases, economic competition for resources was played out through electoral politics and struggles for the control of the state, with a consequent loss of popular confidence in both old and new political leaders and the necessity or opportunity of organizing integration processes on new grounds and through new arguments.

When Jacques Chirac released the draft constitution for the EU in February 2003, it was Poland that objected to the lack of explicit mention of the common Christian heritage of European peoples. Clearly, the return to Europe meant something quite different for Poland than it did for the Western states, whose own experience of postsocialist transition has been the opening of labour markets, rapid influxes of immigrants, and the emergence of multicultural societies. Throughout Eastern and Central Europe the 'return to Europe' has symbolized not only a geopolitical reunification, but also a return to a cultural hearth of common traditions and values.

In both 'returns' the history of state socialism *and* the paths taken in transition away from state ownership and control of the economy have shaped the ways in which regional and local economies have embedded themselves in broader-scale institutions and processes. Here the idea of a universal experience of transition from Eastern and Central European state socialist to Western democratic capitalist models is replaced by what Kalb et al. called 'a more diffuse and pluralistic notion of post-communist transformation'.[16] In this view, transformation processes have been shaped by the complex geographies of regional ecology, economic and sociopolitical variation across the region, and place and region have as much shaped the transformation as they are being reworked by it. These are 'conjunctures of local and wider forces which cannot be logically derived from universal theoretical models such as communism, capitalism and democracy, but which are nevertheless part and parcel of the general process of transformation of one mode to another'.[17] These hidden histories are about the lives and places of people throughout the region working to maintain coherent traditions, negotiate new demands and contribute to individual and collective prosperity in whatever ways they could.

Globalization and pan-European geographies

The one signifying event since 1989 that marks postsocialist transition in Central and Eastern Europe in a similar way took place in 2004. This was the year in which the first group of postsocialist states was admitted into the EU (Poland, Czech Republic, Slovakia, Hungary, Estonia, Latvia, Lithuania, and Slovenia). It may also mark the end, practically, of 'postsocialism' as a discursive strategy for dealing with transformation in the region. With increasing rapidity the region is being 'EU-ized' and one consequence is that the concerns and problems to be addressed are changing. The EU itself describes this process of transition:

> Soon after the fall of the Berlin Wall in 1989, the European Community quickly established diplomatic relations with the countries of Central Europe. It removed long-standing import quotas on a number of products, extended the Generalised System of Preferences (GSP) and, over the next few years, concluded Trade and Cooperation Agreements with Bulgaria, the former Czechoslovakia, Estonia, Hungary, Latvia, Lithuania, Poland, Romania and Slovenia.
>
> In the meantime, the European Community's Phare Programme, created in 1989, set out to provide financial support for the countries'

efforts to reform and rebuild their economies. Phare soon became the world's largest assistance programme in Central Europe, providing technical expertise and investment support.

During the 1990s, the European Community and its Member States progressively concluded Association Agreements, so called 'Europe Agreements', with ten countries of Central Europe. The Europe Agreements provide the legal basis for bilateral relations between these countries and the EU.

In fact, much of the work of transition in the Applicant States prior to 2004 was devoted to meeting the chapter requirements of the *acquis communautaire*. These dealt with such issues as institutional transparency, legal and regulatory frameworks and forms of governance, environment, economy and well-being that had to be met before any country could be admitted to the EU. The technical needs and financial investments needed to meet these demands were huge and many governmental and non-governmental resources were devoted full-time to ensuring that they were met, although, as authors in this volume show, there were at times also countervailing efforts to limit their success. This was also true in the second tier of Applicant States who joined the EU in 2007 (Romania, Bulgaria). As a result, there has been a large literature on enlargement, particularly on issues of governance and administration, and a great deal of interest in the ways in which European integration seems to be occurring on at least two other fronts.

The first is the fact that the process of enlargement has been made particularly difficult for Western Europe by the large-scale transnational immigration, asylum seeker and migrant labour streams from Eastern and South-Eastern Europe. These have occurred in conjunction with a wider immigration stream and globalization of Western Europe from former colonial areas, particularly from North and West Africa. From the Schengen Agreements to humanitarian aid and training programmes in Austria to rights of asylum throughout the EU, member states have attempted to deal with the scale of migrant streams in a variety of ways. The situation became particularly acute in countries such as Austria and Italy, as war in the former Yugoslavia and economic and political collapse in Albania generated enormous pressures from migrants and asylum seekers on those governments. The subsequent peacekeeping and state-building projects at the heart of Europe forced Europeans to address fundamental issues of ethnicity and citizenship that postsocialism had wrought. Here postsocialist theories of transition 'meet' postcolonial theories of global Europe and multicultural societies. In this meeting, deep social and political rifts have emerged and new patterns of employment and residence have come much more clearly into focus across Europe.[18]

The second form of integration has to do with economic integration. The EU has supported various forms of outsourcing of assembly production to the countries of Eastern and South-Eastern Europe since the early 1980s. More recently, and particularly under pressure from the WTO regulations, the EU adopted a series of trade liberalization measures and accompanying incentives that have supported the relocation of industrial production and foreign direct investment in the region.[19] Most of this investment has been outsourcing of assembly production known as outward processing. Its growth in the 1990s has been nothing short of phenomenal, particularly in agro-processing, clothing, textiles and shoes, and more recently in automobiles.[20] Foreign direct investment has been of particular importance in more highly capitalized industries with an existing capacity for export production, and – as several essays in this volume show – increasingly in financial and service industries.[21]

Globalization and regionalization in postsocialist economies

The chapters in this volume address the common challenges faced by countries trying to transform the state socialist economic model through the introduction of market forces. Central to the experience of economic transformation was the move from state-dominated to market-initiated economic activity. In this transition there has been a significant alteration in the role of the state. While in state socialism the party-state was the planner of economic priorities and organizer of production, in the transformation to market economies the state has decreased its active economic role. Privatization and the growth of non-state economic actors have transformed exchange relations and market forces have come to dominate the setting of economic priorities and organization of production. In each of these contexts, globalization and regionalization represent two distinct processes in tension. On the one hand, national and international standards and norms have been harmonized as democratic and market principles have resulted in increasingly common institutions and practices, whether by the enlargement of corporate investments (such as international banking and bond systems) or by the harmonization of local institutions and practices to those of transnational organizations (such as the EU). On the other hand, while in some sectors, such as banking and bond markets, harmonization has created increasingly common spaces of regulation and practice, in other cases postsocialist transformation has produced important and interesting forms of regional differentiation that further shape distinct geographies of Europe. These regional formations pose challenges for how we are to understand the continuing projects of building common economic spaces of Europe.

The next four chapters focus on tendencies towards globalization and harmonization of economic practices, whether through historical case studies of foreign investment and internationalizing of the economy during the NEP in Russia or through comparative analyses of bond markets and foreign direct investment in postsocialist Europe and market socialist China. The subsequent chapters turn to case studies drawn primarily from Poland, Romania, and Russia to illustrate the diversity of regional experiences produced by the opening and harmonizing of postsocialist economies after 1989 and the important ways in which processes of economic globalization are always mediated by regional systems of economy, politics, and history.

Globalization and the emergence of common economic spaces

In Chapters 2 and 3, **Khaziev** and **Conroy** illustrate the fundamental importance of thinking historically and sectorally about these broader issues of state, society and economy as global and regional processes interact to reframe economic lives. In their wonderful accounts of the factories of the 'red bourgeoisie' in the Urals during the NEP and of the articulation and integration of European capital into the Russian pharmaceutical industry during the NEP, they demonstrate the dangers of overlooking the historical articulations of Soviet economic practices with broader global institutions and capital when trying to understand contemporary processes of economic investment and integration. In particular, they illustrate the value of industry and enterprise-level analyses and the opportunities afforded this work by the recent opening of Soviet archives.

The new opportunities that came with the establishment of the New Economic Policy (NEP) in the Russian Soviet Federated Socialist Republic (RSFSR) in 1921 have attracted considerable attention from Russian and Western scholars interested in the rejuvenation of the Russian economy and society in 1921–1929. In his chapter, Khaziev describes private businesses in the Urals during the 1920s NEP and analyses newly available statistics about private manufacturing in the Ural region. In parallel with Conroy's findings, Khaziev suggests the need to see state socialist economies as complex social and political structures that may have important implications for the ways in which we understand and interpret contemporary transformations in economic systems.

Conroy has been able to use newly accessible Russian archival materials and trade journals of the period to examine the interaction, during the NEP, of core Soviet pharmaceutical enterprises with West European houses in three areas: (1) trade, (2) investment and joint ventures and (3) transfers of technology and intellectual property through training abroad, industrial espionage and reverse engineering. State-owned Soviet industry and privately owned West European houses operated in ways that Cold War historiography both overlooked and was unable to see because of closed archives. For this volume, the implications are instructive and indicate the need for much more careful evaluation of the ways in which 'closed economies' were already articulated with global production and financial networks.

In their chapter, **Morita** and **Chen** examine Japanese Foreign Direct Investment (FDI) in the Polish and Chinese economies. Japanese investments in Poland remained small relative to FDI from other countries, with a pattern of concentration in the automotive industry, particularly in products supplying foreign automakers in other European countries. In contrast, Japan is one of the largest investors in China, which is a major destination for Japanese FDI. The Chinese share of Japan's FDI peaked in the mid-1990s and has rebounded strongly since a recent low in 1999. The authors argue that these changes are sensitive to Chinese government policy, particularly the regional growth strategies encouraging FDI. A major difference in motivation of Japanese investment in China compared with Poland is an orientation to the domestic market. In China, the Japanese FDI is also heavily weighted toward automobile manufacturing, but the goal is production for the domestic market rather than export to other production facilities. Their comparative analysis thus highlights the significant differences in the ways in which state policy and domestic market conditions are influencing the patterns and processes of FDI in each region.

Haiss and **Chou's** analysis of the emerging bond market in three Eastern and Central European (ECE) countries and three Asian countries further pursues this important work on comparative transitions, with a particular focus on the role of the state and domestic conditions. The chapter shows that there is great variation within both regions in the mix of equity, credit and bond markets. Market capitalization remains poorly developed in ECE countries, with a relatively balanced split between bond and credit markets dominating financial markets. In contrast, financial markets in the Asian economies are dominated by credit and equity markets, while bond markets remain poorly developed.

Regionalization and the diversity of economic lives

If 1989 marks a temporal shift in the political economy of a broader postsocialist economic space, Poland signals the problem with such kinds of generalization and the value of thinking more regionally. Long histories of overseas migration, powerful émigré influence in countries such as the United States and the unique economic role of remittance economies in sustaining forms of political independence at home combined with longstanding sustained trade union opposition to the Communist Party in ways that have shaped a distinct transitional experience for the Polish economy and its insertion into the common economic spaces of a broader postsocialist Europe. In this regard, **Rosiek's** chapter on the Polish coal industry demonstrates the importance of understanding the organizational structure of the economy under state socialism, and in particular the role of heavy industry in central planning. Through an account of the industry in the 1960s and 1970s, she shows how the combination of large-scale and diverse production systems in an economy dominated by state-owned heavy industry (especially coal mining and coal-based energy industry) has had an important impact on the path of economic reform ever since. Liberalization of these commanding heights industries in the 1990s was more contested than in economies with a broader mix of industrial sectors or dominated by agro-processing or lighter manufacturing. Consequently, strong state intervention and centralized industrial policy were sustained during the reform period and changes in the structure and ownership of production resulted in large-scale unemployment and social unrest. One result was an economy with high levels of energy and raw materials consumption.

More recently, efforts have focused on the need to develop high-tech and competitive industries in the context of a broader EU-27, and these are currently negotiating the challenges brought by new roles for the state, the scale of public subsidies and the competitive capacities of the broader regional production networks in which enterprises increasingly operate. Despite these changes, the contribution of industry to GDP declined by nearly 45 per cent between 1990 and 2003, and, despite policy prescriptions aimed at the development of innovative and competitive economic activity, the expected shift from low to high technologies did not occur between 1995 and 2003.

Mirecka shows how these emerging financial structures and institutions in ECE are affecting the ways in which banking has developed in Poland. State socialist central banking systems and early reforms in the 1980s to allow some degree of independence for banks from the state were insufficient to substantially restructure the industry. As a result, by 1989, banking was far from the service industry it had become in Western Europe. After 1989 and through the 1990s, bank privatization and new laws and regulations governing investment and currency exchange have attracted foreign investment, new banks have been established and several domestic banks have been restructured under foreign ownership. As a result, the Polish banking system has been the target of state and EU regulatory reforms as accession and state policy seeks to regularize and harmonize Polish banking with West European banking norms. Long dominated by state agencies and direct subventions to industry, the Polish banking system – like so many throughout the region – has presented serious challenges to regulators. This chapter documents this changing policy environment and shows how the legacies of the state banking system articulate with the demands of new international norms and increasingly foreign-owned banks. The specific conditions of the Polish economy have been particularly important; there is a strong legacy of poor service, saving rates are low and enterprise reform is difficult. The result has been contraction and concentration in the industry and, as a result, the role of foreign-owned banks has increased rapidly. As Mirecka shows, between 1993 and 2005, the proportion of foreign-owned banks in the economy grew from 11.5 per cent to 80 per cent. However, as the banking system has been integrated into the broader financial systems of the EU, the peculiarities of Poland's banking history continue to shape the services provided and the outlook of customers.

The ways in which globalization and regional integration also generated forms of social resistance to EU accession is illustrated by **Zachorowska-Mazurkiewicz's** chapter on women in the labour market in Poland. She begins by outlining the position of women in the labour market during state socialism, which was characterized by high rates of female labour force participation and an official ideology of equality. Despite these characteristics, feminization of certain occupations (e.g. childcare and healthcare) took place, women were concentrated in occupations with other women and a persistent wage gap existed between genders. With transformation to the market, labour force participation decreased for both men and women; increased feminization of occupations occurred; and the gender wage gap shrank. As Poland began the EU accession process in the late 1990s, there occurred a major adjustment of laws and institutions to EU requirements. Despite these changes, there has not been significant improvement in the employment status of women. Unemployment among women is higher than among men, particularly at middle levels of educational achievement, and the gender wage gap did not appreciably change in the second half of the 1990s. Thus, in the short run, at least, adoption of EU standards did not produce a noticeable improvement in the labour force status of women.

Żukrowska addresses the potential for Poland to join the Economic and Monetary Union (EMU), the joint currency and monetary policy zone within the EU. She reviews the key EMU 'convergence criteria' (price stability, interest rates, budget deficits and public debt controls, along with policy approaches for meeting these criteria). While Poland has made a number of steps toward meeting the criteria, a key obstacle to Poland's success in joining the EMU is the ongoing state budget deficit. Unlike the former Member States, political integration for the new Member States meant that no opting out was to be allowed. Thus, they have had to agree to be prepared to face competition in the EU market, to shoulder all membership obligations, and all this without the option of opting out of the EMU if circumstances require it. Żukrowska demonstrates how Poland has prepared to join the EMU, and provides a comparative analysis with the results achieved by the other new Member States. The chapter shows, in particular, that many of the assumptions made in preparing strategies for East Central European economies to join the EU and EMU were based on theories which are difficult to apply to former closed economies. The author argues that these policies assume a division between developed and developing economies, a policy of slow opening to international markets, state aid for the incubation of businesses and currency appreciation while the economy catches up with EU norms. However, recent evidence suggests that such assumptions prove correct only in some specific economies, but do not apply well to others.

In her essay on Romania, **Panaitescu** offers an overview of the criteria for EU membership and the process of negotiation that was applied to ECE. In the Romanian case, social and political struggles over reform shaped the path of economic harmonization and integration during accession negotiations. Following the signing of the Accession Treaty in Luxembourg, successive Romanian governments failed to vigorously pursue structural reforms in the economy and delayed implementing the administrative and legal reforms to which they committed. In particular, policies pursued between 2000 and 2004 by the centre-left government during accession negotiations promised reforms in Brussels but delayed them at home. The chapter focuses on these political struggles over economic liberalization and evaluates the role and importance of European Union leverage through the special safeguard clauses the EU has insisted upon even after the signing and ratification of the Treaty. Panaitescu argues that the reforms undertaken by the Romanian government after 1996 set the stage for a decision by the EU to bring Romania into the accession process. As negotiations evolved, the EU included 'safeguard clauses' designed to delay Romanian (and Bulgarian) accession from 2007 to 2008 should it become necessary. In the end, the imperative for accession overwhelmed the scepticism of Brussels, convergence criteria were not met, but accession with monitoring and potential future penalties went ahead.

If some unintended consequences of harmonization of banking systems with EU norms has been bank concentration, contraction and foreign ownership, parallel challenges have faced New Member States as previously existing regional economies are transformed by the new geographies and policies required by Brussels. In a fascinating comparative study of the effects of regional policies on Romania's border economies, **Rieser** and **Waack** show how the consequences of accession are influenced by the complex structures of historical and contemporary relations across particular borders. With EU membership in 2007, Romania gained open borders with Hungary and Bulgaria, while being forced to tighten its borders with Ukraine, Moldova, and Serbia and Montenegro (now Serbia). Border policy in the postcommunist period has reflected the general processes of decentralization across the political economy. Former centralized controls were relaxed, and in some areas strong local initiatives were developed to promote cross-border cooperation; for example, as institutionalized in the Danube-Körös-Mureş-Tisza Euroregion linking Romania, Hungary, and Serbia. The presence of ethnic minorities, particularly Hungarians, in each country strengthened these initiatives. In other areas, local initiatives were weaker and agreements on the creation of Euroregions have been more difficult. The area of the Danube bridge crossing between Romania and Bulgaria at Giurgiu-Rousse shows the need for external assistance and pressure where local ties are weak. As a result, the authors are able to show how EU policies are being mobilized to encourage and support projects of cross-border integration on each of Romania's international borders, while also exploring the consequences of the deepening of regional synergies and longer-term economic development along some of the border areas.

Another 'border' question of immense importance is the question of Russia. The role of Russia in the region has become particularly important and EU policy towards the common economic spaces of Europe has been strongly influenced by the changing fortunes of the Russian economy. The challenges facing Russia in its economic transformation, the longer legacy of state socialism, the lack of consensus on the need for market institutions, and the distance from EU expansion have all contributed to the uniqueness of the Russian model.

Two chapters by **Hedlund** and **Rosefielde** problematize the notions of economic integration and harmonization occurring between Russian and EU economies. Each provides a broader historical reading of the political economy of Russia, arguing that integration and alignment of finance and production networks face many more challenges than are commonly recognized.

Following the eastward expansion of the European Union in the spring of 2004, the relationship between Russia and the EU has tumbled to a post-Soviet low. In his chapter, **Hedlund** turns to this deterioration in the relations between the EU and Russia, and suggests that this is due not to 'democratic backsliding', the war in Chechnya or even superpower hangover, but rather to what he calls the 'property rights hurdle'; fundamentally incompatible institutions of and commitments to distinct property regimes. The continued absence in Russia of a state that is able and willing to act as a credible enforcer of contracts and property rights poses serious questions for future efforts to deepen regional economic networks and forge the common economic space with the EU. If this hurdle cannot be overcome, the relationship will remain marked by serious conflicts and misunderstandings.

Rosefielde pushes even farther, suggesting that contingent property rights function as a pillar of Russia's Muscovite authoritarian state and that this places the Kremlin at loggerheads with EU social democracy, with its own understanding of property rights founded on private assets and the rule of contract law. The incompatibility of property rights may not preclude Russia's integration into European production and trade networks or even EU accession, but he argues they do provide early warning of a stormy marriage, a risk exacerbated by the Kremlin's increasing pugnacity, EU dithering and fitful involvement in CIS regime change, particularly in Ukraine.

Conclusion

If the world is flattening, as authors like Tom Friedmann would have us believe, it is doing so in ways that are also generating new and complex forms of regional difference and articulation. Postsocialist economies were themselves both hegemonic and not monolithic. As state power exercised collective *nomenklatura* control over the appropriation and distribution of social surplus, local, regional, and institutional actors challenged and reshaped these appropriative strategies, reworked forms of collective ownership, sustained longer traditions of collective regulation, and forged minor chords through which individual lives could be sustained and lived.

The great transformations in this articulated hegemony that emerged particularly in the late 1980s opened the economies of state socialism to the diversity of forms and practices that had come, by that time, to constitute rapidly globalizing systems and institutions of economic life. The opening was, as a result, also a tidal wave of structural adjustments and private ventures, many of which tied the reforming economies of Central and Eastern Europe directly into the broader European economy. Agro-processing industries expanded their reach across the region and quickly standardized products, production processes and quality control. The banking and bond markets similarly adjusted the structures of state socialist systems to the needs of their international investors.

However, in these sectors of the economy, and in others, the concrete practices of transformation generated far more complex regional outcomes and new forms of regional association than this story of structural adjustment and economic harmonization might imply. The result has been a 20-year process of economic change in which new geographies of the common economy have emerged. The common economic spaces of Europe, in this regard at least, remain a project of the regions and, judging by the socioeconomic conditions of life in many of those regions, they also remain a basic challenge for policymakers and individuals struggling to adjust to new complex mixes of regional economic growth and decline.

Perhaps this tension is nowhere more evident today than in Russia, where the globalizing of Moscow occurs alongside massive economic wealth creation from oil rents while large parts of the country experience economic involution resulting from the crushing effects of collapsing infrastructure, population decline from interregional migration, and the re-emergence of a strong patrimonial state. In the coming years, the common project of economic integration, if it occurs at all, will certainly occur through the production of regionally and sectorally differentiated lives.

Notes

1   F.A. Hayek *The Road to Serfdom* (London: New York 2001).
2   E. Altvater, *The Future of the Market: An Essay on the Regulation of Money and Nature* (London: Verso 1993).
3   World Bank, *World Development Report 1996: From Plan to Market* (New York and Oxford: Oxford University Press 1996) p. 132.
4   *ibid.* p. 132.

5   *ibid.* p. 140.
6   G. Brown. *Global Europe: Full Employment Europe* (London: UK Department of the Treasury 2005): http://www.hm-treasury.gov.uk/media/2/A/global_europe_131005.pdf; P. Mandelson. Global Europe. http://ec.europa.eu/trade/issues/sectoral/competitiveness/global_europe_en.htm
7   http://europa.eu/abc/12lessons/lesson_12/index_en.htm
8   J. Pickles and A. Smith (eds) *Theorising Transition: The Political Economy of Post-Communist Transformations* (London: Routledge 1998).
9   A. Smith, and A. Swain, 'Regulating and Institutionalising Capitalisms: the Micro-Foundations of Transformation in Central and Eastern Europe' in *Theorising Transition: The Political Economy of Post-Communist Transformations*, Pickles, J. and Smith, A. (eds) (London: Routledge 1998).
10 Karl T.L. and Schmitter P.C. (1991) 'Modes of Transition in Latin America, Southern and Eastern Europe' *International Social Science Journal* 128(43) pp. 269–284.
11 Pickles, J. and Smith, A. (Eds) (1998) *Theorising Transition: The Political Economy of Post-Communist Transformations.* London: Routledge.
12 Bradshaw, M.J. and Stenning, A.C. (2001) 'The Progress of Economic Transition in East Central Europe' in *Transition, Cohesion and Regional Policy in Central and Eastern Europe* Bachtler, J., Downes, R. and Gorzelak, G. (eds), London: Ashgate.
13 World Bank (1996) *World Development Report 1996: From Plan to Market.* New York and Oxford: Oxford University Press.
14 Dunford, M. (1998a) 'Differential Development, Institutions, Modes of Regulation and Comparative Transitions to Capitalism: Russia, the Commonwealth of Independent States, and the former German Democratic Republic' in *Theorising Transition: The Political Economy of Post-Communist Transformations*, Pickles, J. and Smith, A. (eds), London: Routledge.
15 Hall, D.E. and Danta, D. (2000) *Europe Goes East: EU Enlargement, Diversity and Uncertainty*, London: The Stationery Office.
16 Kalb et al. (1999: 11).
17 Kalb, D., Svasek, M. and Tak, H. (1999) 'Approaching the 'New' Past in East-Central Europe' *Focaal* 33 pp. 9–23.
18 A Rainnie, A. Smith and A. Swain (eds) *Work, Employment and Transition: Restructuring Livelihoods in Post-Communism* (London: Routledge 2002).
19 R. Begg, J. Pickles and A. Smith, 'Cutting it: European Integration, Trade Regimes and the Reconfiguration of East-Central European Apparel Production', *Environment and Planning A* 2002.
20 J. Pickles and R. Begg 'Ethnicity, State Violence, and Neo-Liberal Transitions in Post-Communist Bulgaria' Special Issue of *Growth and Change: Ethnicity, violence, and regional change* 31(2), Spring, 2000: 179–210.
21 P. Pavlínek, and A. Smith, 'Internationalization and Embeddedness in East-Central European Transition: The Contrasting Geographies of Inward Investment in the Czech and Slovak Republics' *Regional Studies* 32(7) 1988: 619–638.

2
Factories of the 'Red Bourgeoisie' in the Urals during the NEP

Rustem Khaziev

Introduction

The opportunities that came with the establishment of the New Economic Policy (NEP) in the Russian Soviet Federated Socialist Republic (RSFSR) in 1921 have attracted considerable attention from Russian and Western scholars interested in the rejuvenation of the Russian economy and society between 1921 and 1929.[1] Although several major works focus on this period, in whole or in part, they do not help us understand how the small businessmen and traders (the so-called *Nepmen*) that Alan Ball refers to as 'Russia's last capitalists'[2] actually implemented the economic innovations at the local level, far from officials in Moscow. This chapter describes private businesses in the Urals during the 1920s NEP and analyses the newly available statistics about private industry manufacturing in the Ural region: the changing number of participants during the NEP; their placement in various categories depending on the size and nature of their operations; and the value of their production and sales. In so doing, it provides a detailed case study of the ways in which these alternative economic innovations were constructed and sustained for a time alongside the deepening state collectivization projects, and how the party state reacted to the successes of these freelancing capitalists – the 'Red Bourgeoisie'.

These events may seem specific to Russia and indeed to a particular area of Russia almost eight decades ago. Nevertheless they are relevant to developments in post-Soviet Russia and to the current relationship between East Central European states and post-Soviet Russia. The government dominated the economy of Late Imperial Russia but a lively private sector also operated. Although the Russian economy lagged behind Western Europe, the lag was not enormous. A surprising amount of entrepreneurship and private enterprise continued in Soviet Russia during the 1920s NEP. However, the Soviet government's attempt to substitute its visible hand for the invisible hand of the market distorted the economy. The distortions increased in ensuing decades. This helps to explain the difficulties post-Soviet Russia has had in recreating its pre-Soviet economic system. It also explains why most states in East Central Europe turned their backs on the Soviet economic model in the interwar period, orienting their economies toward Western Europe, and – in part – why they rejected the Soviet economic model as well as the Soviet political system in the past two decades.

Who were the 'Red Bourgeoisie'?

Small producers and traders were criminals during the period of War Communism. With the beginning of the NEP their activities became legal. However, it was one thing to decree that production and trading by individuals was now permitted by law and another for men and women to acquire funding and the wherewithal to establish production units and shops. Soviet citizens needed consumer goods and services after the economic collapse, hyperinflation, grain requisitions, transportation breakdowns and illegal black market activities of the civil war that followed the strains of the World War and the revolutions of 1917. But the private sector of the socialist economy, legalized by the Bolsheviks in 1921, did not become evident immediately. It was difficult – financially, politically and psychologically – for former and new businessmen and women, merchants, shopkeepers, travelling salesmen, dealers and other 'Red Bourgeoisie' to establish the trading firms, the small and medium-scale factories, the stalls at the bazaar, the pubs (*tractiry*), the restaurants, the barber shops and so forth, that gradually emerged during the NEP era. Understandably, the business community worried about how the Soviet government would respond to their activities. Indeed, from the start state officials had ambivalent attitudes toward the new businesses and intended the new private businesses to be only temporary agencies for recovery of the socialist economy. From the beginning, then, the 'Red Bourgeoisie' were in a very shaky and, in some cases, untenable position.

Disappointed that the public welcomed the new bourgeoisie, as they abandoned War Communism and implemented the New Economic Policy, the Bolsheviks simultaneously legalized private businesses and frantically attempted to discredit the private owners. In the minds of the public, the image of NEPmen (and women) was associated with the selling of luxury goods without ration cards or queueing; with courteous assistants in small shops and large shops in trading arcades that became core shopping centres in provincial capitals; with an abundance of 'tasty food' (*vkusnosti*) and delicacies on counters reminiscent of a long-forgotten 'tsarist period'; with a business culture that appreciated comments, ideas, and suggestions from consumers that might enable the firm or office to better serve the masses on a supply and demand basis. For the Communist Party it was a sad reality that workers, peasants and ordinary citizens admired the new business people for achieving much with limited economic resources.[3]

Party and government prosecutors vigorously conducted an 'anti-NEPmen' campaign to counteract the positive effects brought by the free markets they had allowed to flourish in the 1920s. Before the October Revolution, the Bolsheviks had lambasted the rapacious, exploiting bourgeoisie. During the NEP, party and government officials labelled the new business people the 'Red Bourgeoisie,' the 'Detritus of the Soviet State' and 'well-fed men in striped trousers with greasy grins, releasing rings of cigarette smoke'. These caricatures were intended as preventive inoculation for Soviet society to blunt the influence of the NEPmen.[4] Ironically, these tragicomic cartoons of the so-called 'turbid scum of socialism' are to be found not only when looking at party and government attacks on NEPmen in the 1920s but also in post-Soviet Russia. A recent example was the arrest, conviction and incarceration in 2005 of one of the richest post-Soviet businessmen, oil oligarch Mikhail Khodorkovsky. The same fate that befell the NEPmen – rapid fall from owners of successful businesses to prison – also befell some of their historical descendants, who operated in the emerging Russian market of 1992–2006. The latter were labelled 'canoes' (*chelnoki*), oligarchs, 'filthy-rich' businessmen and the like.

The NEPmen who rose to be seen as the Olympians of the non-state economic sector in the 1920s were a motley social group that included pre-revolutionary merchants, millers, salesmen, managers (that is, persons who had certain skills in commercial activity), and also homemakers, soldiers' widows and soldiers' wives (*soldatki*), soldiers demobilized from the Red Army (*krasnoarmeitsy*), 'terminated' employees of state and non-state offices, special settlers (*spetsposelentsy*) who – as unreliable 'class elements' – were sent away from Moscow, St. Petersburg and other big cities in the Urals and Siberia, underemployed and dismissed workers, job-seekers from the countryside, and even Communists and government officials who combined their party-state service (*partgossluzhba*) with illegal commerce.[5]

Although party and government officials needed the NEPmen's business acumen, their innate suspicion and hostility to the 'Red Bourgeoisie' led them to impose many limitations on their activities. The NEPmen were excluded from standing for election and many lost their voting rights; they were barred from teaching in the schools and their children were prohibited from attending schools that were open to children of the 'proletarian population'; they were not allowed to open independent newspapers, to serve as recruits or volunteers in the Red Army, become members of trade unions, creative unions, youth and women's organizations, or to enter state employment at any level or in any capacity.[6]

Labour weekdays of private businessmen in the Urals during 1921–1929

Although easy and quick money was a lure, between 1921 and 1929 most Ural businessmen were focused on furthering industrialization. The 'Red

Bourgeoisie' did not consider profit exclusively as a means of satisfying their personal needs. Their initial savings and part of their incomes were invested in new equipment and their employees by providing incentives in the form of differential wages, cash bonuses and premiums for good work.

From the beginning, they faced two major hurdles: the economic destruction of the War and the many restrictions imposed by various *upolnomochemymi organami* (sanction bodies), particularly the *Rabkrin* (The Workers' and Peasants' Inspectorate). Fierce fighting in the Urals during the civil war in 1918–1919 had destroyed industrial buildings and equipment, the value of money deteriorated, and increasingly large capital investments in material and labour were needed to resume operations.

The conditions that followed the catastrophe of 1917–1921, and the brazen discrimination by government authorities against 'exploiters of other people's labor',[7] prevented potential lessees from setting up enterprises such as mills, leather-processing plants, oil-processing plants, furniture factories and painting shops. The denationalization process was also inhibited by a lack of skilled specialists in provincial and republican state offices in the Urals with the elementary expertise to sign the documents needed to transfer property from the state to private businessmen. For example, because 7 per cent of previously signed contracts had not been ratified or put into operation, in September 1921 the Yekaterinburg *Gubekonomsoveschanie* (Provincial Economic Committee) ordered that leasing of enterprises be temporarily stopped. A special committee formed in the same year concluded that the Ural GSNKh (*Guberniia Sovnarkoz* or Provincial Economic Council) had an apparatus that was too weak and ineffective to solve the problems of leasing. In outlying regions some officials simply did not know what legal and economic requirements there were for leasing property to 're-entry-businessmen'. Local bureaucrats were afraid of 'wasting the people's property' and complained that VSNKh (The Supreme Council of the National Economy) 'limited itself only to sending general instructions and the typical draft contracts'.[8] These initial problems with denationalization were exacerbated by the opinion, held by some officials, that the new businessmen were decadent bourgeoisie. Local officials seriously feared the withdrawal of supervision over the activities of the new owners, considering their expansion 'catastrophic for the dictatorship of the proletariat'. But, additionally, the Ural GSNKh reacted against the 'capitalists' because 'supervision over rented enterprises is not actually exercised because of the lack of technical resources'.[9]

Because of limitations on industrial enterprises, private capitalists did not want to invest in factory production. Very often the producers, willing to exploit this or that industrial entity, did not have enough working capital. Businessmen were also deterred by the harsh conditions of leasing which required that they had to pay to the state from 10 to 20 per cent of their production for a period of from two to six years.[10] Understandably, it was largely the former owners who most often sought licences for industrial production. Besides economic rewards, such as recouping their finances and getting dividends from the reactivated enterprises, these industrialists were often motivated by a desire to revive the businesses they had originally created and often knew down to the slightest details. Heavy taxes, administrative restrictions on credit and difficulties in purchasing raw materials and hiring a workforce were, however, serious impediments to taking back the 'factory business'.

Others who had amassed money from trade deals remained reluctant to start up industrial enterprises. For these people, low levels of profitability and large economic and bureaucratic expenses blocked the flow of 'hot money' – money earned more quickly by operations through middlemen from trade to industry.

On this issue, R. Arskii has hypothesized two reasons for the preponderance of trade in the private capitalist sector. First, during the period of nationalization big industrialists could save practically nothing. This contrasted with traders who managed to hide part of their goods and money from requisition. Second, the circulation of capital in industry was always less than in trade, and this was especially true during the period of the NEP.[11] An open letter called the 'Ten Commandments of the Trader' emphasized that 'with the lack of circulating capital,' overhead expenses leapt 'sky-high' compared with 'the pre-war period'. Arskii theorizes that this was why NEPmen mainly focused on trade instead of production.[12]

The result was that private capital could not play a significant role in the revival of industry in the Soviet Union; the niche for the development of non-socialist enterprises was simply too narrow. Instead, private investment in industry was limited to branches that were of little importance to the state or its cooperatives, and to enterprises of local importance leased to private capitalists on an *ad hoc* basis.

The majority of NEPmen–businessmen produced technologically simple, non-labour-intensive and immediately profitable, popular consumer goods. In 1925 private production units amounted to 32 per cent of the total consumer goods produced in the country.[13] The state restricted the shift of big enterprises into the hands of the 'Red Bourgeoisie' and, as a result, businesses were small. But even when it was possible to make a profitable industrial item, the lessees were hindered by the prevailing interest rates and limited access to credit. The paucity of rubles in circulation and the difficulties facing those who were not bureaucrats in getting loans significantly slowed business development. An example of this problem was the production of millstones in 1925 by S. L. Sturkovich. This was 'an undertaking' in which he was 'experienced', although the venture was 'a bit ambitious commercially', requiring capitalization of 43,693 rubles of which 71.5 per cent came from 'his own circulation capital of 31,240 rubles' and 28.5 per cent from 'the circulation capital' of 'others'.[14]

S. L. Sturkovich was an ambitious, dynamic entrepreneur. He lived in Leningrad and had an office in Sverdlovsk and a factory in the same region. In 1922, having received back his former property and having invested some money in it, Sturkovich soon found himself on the verge of bankruptcy. He experienced serious failure in 1924 when, with the aim of developing the business,

> he began to build a plant at the Mramorskaya Station on the Perm Railway. He could not finish the plant because of shortage of funds...Building the plant ate the most part of S. L. Sturkovich's money and led him to a critical financial position. In October 1924 S. L. Sturkovich's company was declared insolvent...In January 1925 a public auction to sell Sturkovich's property was announced.[15]

By May 1926, Sturkovich had managed to settle the critical financial position of his company:

> at present the old plant is functioning producing millstones, oil-stone circles, grinding stones...crushed and ground emery, ground graphite and magnetite. Thirty workers with an engineer specialist at the head are employed. Installation of a new sixty-horsepower steam engine as well as...a second stove, that will increase the production of the plant, are slated. At present the plant produces forty-five pairs of millstones of different dimensions and up to 600 oil-stones [at a sum of]...up to 15 thousand rubles. According to the responses, the quality of the products is satisfactory. The enterprise is working under pressure and its products enjoy significant popularity.[16]

The adaptability and survival of firms like Sturkovich and Co. was extremely disconcerting to the Bolsheviks. In Bashkortostan in the summer of 1921, fearing the development and strengthening of private capital, all enterprises were classified into viable (those staying under the operative administration of the state) and those which had a negative balance. People deciding to take up business could only count on the lease of 'stagnant objects' from the second group.[17] The Chelyabinsk *gubispolkom* also introduced 'antiNEP' restrictions, issuing a special regulation about the organization of private enterprises of minor and handicraft industries. The system of strictly limiting employees was borrowed from the arsenal of War Communism:[18] no more than 20 employees to a business with mechanical equipment and no more than 40 employees in companies without mechanical equipment.

Special attention was paid to the political reliability of those competing to possess a mill, a shop, a department, etc. The ruling of Chelyabinsk *Gubekonomsoveshchaniye* from 9 September 1921 prohibited the return of factories and other immovable property to former owners who had fled with Kolchak's Army[19] or who were identified 'as activists against the Soviet regime'.[20] Private owners who became adversaries of the working class and peasants after the revolution, but then felt contrite and eager to earn their living and to work for the sake of the Soviet state, were relegated to the category of politically unreliable citizens.[21]

Borrowing the bugaboo of irreconcilable classes and the antirevolutionary activity of *miroedov* (capitalists), a number of skilled 'dispossessed' businessmen, who according to the mandate committee of GSNKh had not passed the test for loyalty to the Communist regime, were barred from the possibility of operating legally in the market. The government's attitude toward 'Russian capitalism' was expressed graphically by an effigy of a 'gigantic coffin', which was brought to demonstrations to symbolise the death of capitalists and capitalism and by a movie, *The Death of the Nepmen*, which depicted how capitalists were sentenced to be executed and, although their sentences were sometimes postponed, often disappeared.[22] When the authorities not only closed down illegal commercial operations, but also introduced at every opportunity fines on the flimsiest of pretexts and confiscated surplus revenues by sanctions and taxes, few attempted to compete by entering the black market.

By the beginning of 1922, most of the leased enterprises in the industrial regions of Ufa and Chelyabinsk provinces were mills.[23] The situation was the same in other regions of the Urals. The Ural NEPmen controlled one-third of all enterprises leased by the end of 1921 and they were very small.[24] The situation changed little the following year. During 1922 only 6 per cent of industrial enterprises in Chelyabinsk province were transferred to private lessees.[25] The concept that NEPmen represented a 'gross evil' was widespread among officials, and industrialists and the general population were generally hostile to them. In some districts of Chelyabinsk province people proudly claimed that they were not familiar at all with the phenomenon of 'leasing private property'.[26] And in March 1923 the Perm GSNKh organized the process of 'leasing mills' with such restrictions that it was extremely difficult[27] to transfer them to private persons.[28]

In order to create favour able economic conditions for state and cooperative enterprises, employees in private businesses were meticulously monitored to ensure that their social welfare was protected. The result was that the size of private enterprises was further constrained. On average each private enterprise in Chelyabinsk Province had 13 employees, while state industrial enterprises had 42.[29] In Orenburg Province, in autumn 1925, on average 70 per cent of enterprises leased by 'Red Bourgeoisie' employed only three or fewer workers, whereas only 0.4 per cent of state enterprises employed 30 or fewer workers.[30]

Tax and credit policies were also used to prevent private capital from maturing and 'threatening' state enterprises. Besides different payments (the industrial tax, the building rent, etc.), NEPmen were forced to pay lump sums that resembled the contribution fines of the 1918–1920s. For example, in January 1923 the Chelyabinsk *gubispolkom* announced the introduction of the civil tax to restore agriculture. Payments amounted to 150 rubles for the workers and employees, 500 rubles for minor businessmen and 5,000 rubles for the renters using employed labour.[31] The increased tax burden coincided with new restrictions aimed to undermine the growth of private owners in the industrial–handicraft production of oil.[32] The result was that by the summer of 1925 the rate of private lease development in Chelyabinsk Province lagged well behind other areas of the entire Soviet Union, 'comprising a motley crew. The latter only partly consist of skilled traders; generally they are newcomers – former clerks, the unemployed and people who have never been in trade.'[33]

State enterprises dominated industrial production throughout the Urals as it did in the rest of the Soviet Union. But due to the fact that there was a developed system of producing semi-finished materials in small industrial workshops for the big metallurgical plants, the percentage of privately leased enterprises was greater in the Urals than in the country as a whole.[34] Thus, the higher percentage of NEPmen industrial producers in the Ural economy can be explained by the existence of the cooperation between these workshops and plants and not by any especially protective measures taken by state officials or by any tolerance on their part for private enterprise.

In some branches, especially food, private capital managed to dominate state and cooperative enterprises. Thus, the number of private enterprises grinding cereals exceeded the number of state enterprises (by dozens) and cooperative ones (by several times).[35] A large part of the capital of NEPmen in the Urals in 1924 was concentrated in three sectors: flour – 17.5 per cent; textiles – 9 per cent; and chemical and metal processing – 5 per cent.[36] However, these types of enterprises amounted to only 26.5 per cent of the one-third (31.5 per cent) of non-state judicial persons involved in food, light, chemical and heavy industries. These compensated for the goods deficit, but in 'non-strategic' products. Thus, penetration of a few 'big bugs' (5 per cent) into the scientific industry was not considered dangerous, especially as they were under constant state control.

Suspicions and antipathy exhibited by the Soviet populace toward the flourishing of the 'Red Bourgeoisie' while a significant number of workers and peasants were foundering pushed the government to curb the economic activity of NEPmen so that they were not dangerous to socialism. By the spring of 1923, the balance of state and private owners' interests in the Urals was nine to one; government and cooperatives controlled 89.9 per cent of industrial enterprises, while private businessmen controlled only 10.1 per cent.[37]

During 1925, the industrial department of Perm *Ispolkom* (Provincial Executive Committee) signed licences for only 22 enterprises, nine of which belonged to private owners, including two former owners. Almost half of the enterprises (twelve) were from 'the frozen fund'[38] and their reactivation required solid material investments. By lending to develop the dilapidated industrial sites, the industrial section of Perm *Ispolkom* wished to restore several industrial enterprises in the region through the investments of private owners. For the main owner – the state – it was profitable to lease non-liquid entities for a set term, entities that even under unsuccessful reconstruction, to say nothing of those that were profitable and stable, could be returned at any moment.

Government protection of state economic subjects, which were guarded administratively and aided by economic discounts, provided an environment conducive to growth. In the Urals, state industry subordinate to district authorities grew 160 per cent during the fiscal year 1923/24 to 1924/25, and 234 per cent during 1925/26. In the cooperative industry the figures for the given years were 209 per cent and 284 per cent, and in the private sector 123 and 139 per cent.[39]

NEPmen, reacting quickly to the political and economic needs of consumers, searched for more profitable ways of investing their acquired experience and money. They gradually left factory production, which was illiquid and too expensive compared with trade. As a result, the number of 'Red Bourgeoisie' leasing large-scale (*tsenzovye*) enterprises in the Urals diminished significantly. From 1923 to 1925/26 the number of large-scale enterprises leased by Nepmen was reduced by 1.5–2 times, declining on average by 5 to 10 per cent each year.[40] Beginning in the summer of 1924 'the mass closure of enterprises and the return of their licenses' took place in the Votsk Autonomous region.[41] From the second half of 1924/25 'some legally working private enterprises' liquidated themselves in neighbouring Siberia.[42]

Businesses in troublesome and less profitable industries were the first to disappear, especially compared with those in more profitable trade in the industrial centres of the country. In 1924 in Sverdlovsk, one of the largest Ural cities, 'the large industrial bourgeoisie' amounted to 5.4 per cent of the total of 'all non-laboring elements,' which amounted, in turn, to 14.4 per cent in the city.[43] Owners of small enterprises predominated. 'Exploiters of labor' amounted to no more than 2 per cent of the 'non-labouring' elements in the city of Sverdlovsk. Close and distant relatives of businessmen were also sometimes involved in family business, but only in small numbers (from 3 per cent in industry to 10 per cent in trade). The situation was different in rural areas, where the number of family hands surpassed the number of owners.[44]

According to the data of the Sverdlovsk Society of Mutual Credit, by the end of 1925 leading positions in the local business community were held by 'retailers' (65 per cent), handicraft specialists (16 per cent) and 'industrialists' (11 per cent).[45] In two years the number of 'industrialists' was reduced almost by half to about 7 per cent, while the number of less oppressed handicraft specialists increased up to 25 per cent.[46] It was they who formed the category of 'minor industrialists' who, 'at the same rate' as the traders, opted for three times more licences in 1926 than in 1925 in the Ural region.[47] This increase was significant given that fines and legal prosecution threatened every businessman who attempted to mask industrial production under handicraft activity to gain illegal profits.[48]

According to the report prepared by Sverdlovsk Exchange for the All-Russian Congress of Exchange Trade in 1926, the circulation of capital in the private factory sector in the Ural region amounted to 8 per cent of all private capital in circulation. The Central Statistical Administration (*Tsentral'noe Statisticheskoe Upravlenie*) graded enterprises according to their scale during the period 1921–1929. A *tsenzovoe* enterprise was a large plant with at least 30 employees. During the NEP, most of these types of enterprises were retained by the state after being nationalized and few were leased by individuals.

Russian historians usually describe 1926–1928, the end of the NEP, as the first years of 'reconstruction' (*rekonstruktsiia*). The party and government bodies isolated businessmen and prevented them from reconstructing large-scale private enterprises. They treated private enterprise as a 'temporary element in a transitional period'. Thus, on average, one in 19 large-scale (*tsenzovye*) private enterprises had only 19 workers. Private owners managed 60,100 small-scale private enterprises employing 72,921 people in total.[49] The material output of these small enterprises comprised '1.8 per cent of gross output and 0.5 per cent of goods' in the Chelyabinsk region between 1926 and 1929.[50] In 1927/28, non-socialist industry amounted to 16.4 per cent of the overall capital in the Soviet Union.[51]

Despite these small numbers, the Bolshevik regime labelled the new businessmen 'bourgeois *otrod'e*'. The term *otrod'e* [offspring] is a pejorative slang term referring to people who are the actual or historical successors of someone or something reprehensible. The Soviet state called private capitalists of the NEP period *otrod'em*, even though very few actually were holdovers from the Old Regime, because the government considered the business people of the 1920s to be as exploitative and evil as those in imperial Russia. The term '*otrod'e*' was particularly used when Stalin launched his assault on the 'Red Bourgeoisie' and the local officials who supported the limited autonomy they had because they helped the Soviet economy recover.

In general, the government's attitude toward industrial capital during the period 1921–1929 was conflicting. Realizing the need to legalize private business to develop the socialist economy, the government kept accusing 'NEPmen-vampires' of being alien to the working class of the Soviet state. In some cases the government's criticism of the 'new industrialists' was fair and justified and found agreement among some of the NEPmen themselves. The Glazov *Rynochnyi Komitet* (Market Committee) announced in the bulletin prepared on 16 April 1925 for the city financial inspection that in private industrial enterprises 'using employed labor' it is rare that workers get dismissal subsidies, payments for days off, the percentage of social insurance due them, etc.[52]

On the other hand, the government overlooked 'Red Bourgeoisie' businesses implementing some socially detrimental practices, such as illegal dismissals of workers, violations of working conditions and extension of the working day. In such cases, the government appeased the irritation of 'scandalized workers', angry with the actions of the businessmen, by making excuses about the objective difficulties from which private owners suffered. This decision to favour businessmen is explained by the desire of the *Bashsovnarkhoz* administration in 1923 to get rid of 'the useless ballast' of stagnant enterprises that only private owners were equipped to take over and which would improve the general economic situation in the region.[53]

The favours shown to NEPmen were considered by the government to be temporary concessions and the practice of shaking a big stick at 'counter-revolutionaries' illustrated that they were only temporary signs of unity between Soviet power and private capital. There was never a fear that the tolerant attitude by the party elite to private owners, traders and NEPmen producers would lead to the renaissance of market economy. Bolsheviks never lost faith in the 'fierce, vehement, life-and-death struggle between capitalism and communism'.[54]

Industrial enterprises of Ural businessmen from 1921 to 1929

According to statistical analysis

Soviet historians, who for decades have criticized the NEPmen's profit motive, substantiated their conclusions by materials taken from party and state archives. Most of these were typical documents reflecting the official view of the struggle between private capital and Soviet power. A unique collection of private files about Ural businessmen found in RGAE (the Russian State Archive of the Economy)[55] enables us to fill in some of the gaps in the study of industrial activity of private businessmen in 1921–1929 in one of the largest regions of Russia.

These scattered materials, which have been systematized by the author of this chapter, belong to the Ural–Siberian Office of the 'Credit-Bureau'. It was one of the local branches of 'The First Russian Company Certifying Credits' in Moscow in 1922. In spite of the fact that the company director and, from 1924, the auction company 'Credit-Bureau' was *Narodnyi komissariar vnutrennei torgovli* (Narkomat of Home Trade), this company had business that was closely connected with commercial espionage. The *Narkomats* (People's Commissariats) were analogous to ministries in European governments of the 1920s. Some Soviet government *Narkomats* guarded (*bliuli*) their own narrow departmental (*vedomstvennost'*) interests. They accepted current events or the requirements of party functionaries, who increased or lowered the economic potential of private capital in the national economy. This was not the case with the enterprise called the 'Credit-Bureau'.

Operating on a self-supporting basis, the 'Credit-Bureau' employed almost 16,000 staff and non-staff agents to gather information about private businessmen or economic commercial subjects for their clients. Solid and solvent clients from a number of state and commercial banks and from companies of mutual credit who applied to the 'Credit-Bureau' demanded good service and a meticulous and responsible attitude from the commission. The increasing cost to their own enterprises of using unreliable information about the private enterprises resulted in the creation of a system that included numerous cross-checks, through various channels, of the information disseminated. In the home market the procedures of the 'Credit-Bureau' – professionally monitoring active individual businessmen and different kinds of property of juridical persons and granting loans to support and develop their business – created a vast and reliable database about Russian businessmen.[56] The information preserved in the Ural–Siberian office file of 'Credit-Bureau' enables us to study the activity of 653 people connected with business. Of these, 61 businessmen were either individual or joint owners of 49 industrial enterprises, differing in size and power. The analysis that follows is based on this population of 653 business people and the 61 private businessmen in these 49 private enterprises.

Production by NEPmen between 1921 and 1929 concentrated on four areas of specialization and accounted for 58 per cent of labour and capital investments. Other production (42 per cent) included various commercial enterprises, such as sewing coats, caps and men's and women's clothes; production ranging from sausages to household ware and the simplest kinds of metal, barrels and boxes, and consumer goods.

With competition greater than in other market segments, the spread of confectionery enterprises (28 per cent) can be explained by certain advantages of this kind of business: the volume of the local market traditionally consuming sweets and providing constant demand for this produce; quick return on investments; simple technologies required for baking; small capital used to purchase and exploit simple equipment which did not require additional skills and training. Three other industries, leather (15 per cent), soap producing (9 per cent) and wood-processing (6 per cent), were determined by historical factors – the traditional representation of this business in the region and by geography – the natural resources and convenient location of the Urals for these types of industries.

The greatest diversification of business enterprises was in two cities: Sverdlovsk and Ufa. Although Sverdlovsk and Ufa were similar in the types and mix of private enterprises (food, chemical, wood-processing and leather ones), there were differences between the cities in the number of businessmen represented in the market. This allowed for a high degree of city rivalry for customers, who then had the opportunity of choosing goods according to their price and quality.

Choosing between a popular, widespread operation or a less attractive one (which offered little consumers needed) was made on the basis of the simplest economic analysis: expected expenses and expected (min.–max.) income. These took into account the availability of one's own raw materials, the policy of the government agencies that acutely needed goods, sales requests and the solvency of customers.

Of course, there were people who took a risk by starting workshops modelled on existing enterprises or renovated their former businesses, which had been confiscated and which they were now leasing. But why did such local employers fearless or recklessly – without risk assessment – revive businesses? Their outlook emerged from the doubt and depression they had experienced as a result of the Bolsheviks' War Communism policies and anti-business ideology. Private capital did not aspire to the 'avant-garde role' of renewing the economic mechanism of the Soviet regime, as many officials in Moscow and in the hinterlands asserted. The NEPmen and NEPwomen did not go into business 'to create favour able prerequisites for the growing efficiency of socialist production, the basis for multiplying goods and services available to the working people of the socialist society'. The NEPmen and NEPwomen were concerned with elementary survival. Of course their business activities also raised the living standards of the populace. The NEPmen dominated in very narrow, local economic spheres. However, some of them reaped profits and incomes equal to those of state enterprises. Local private capitalists struggled during the NEP to revive their businesses in order to support themselves and their families. To ensure their survival, the 'Red Bourgeoisie' made all sorts of practical accommodations, organizing their businesses with whatever materials and opportunities were 'at hand'.

As for commercial preferences in enterprises producing food products, the undeniable leader of the most popular regional confectionery business was Perm. It turned out that there was a sort of boom in the Ural capital of gingerbread, biscuits, sweets etc., while the baking of cakes and candies amounted to 60 per cent of the city production, and local businessmen were unwilling to start other kinds of enterprises. The factory run by the Perm citizen Isaac Davidovich Liberman, living at Communist Street number 78, offered consistent and competitive production of sweets under the trademark 'Renome'. Starting his business in 1923, I. D. Liberman had, by the beginning of 1927, 'a license of the first category (*pervyi razriad*).'[57] Liberman's enterprise was small. But he was a successful entrepreneur. He realized all his production 'on the spot.' The business had a consistent monthly circulation of 3,000 to 4,000 rubles and a positive balance.[58] In Nizhnii-Taghil, there were equal numbers of confectionery businesses (34 per cent) and leather enterprises (32 per cent), while all the other industries put together amounted to 34 per cent. Private capital was not concentrated in the same way in other Ural regions, although some did specialize in particular industrial and handicraft products.

The comparative analyses of production in branches of industry in the Ural region during the initial NEP period of 1921–1924 and during the period of 1925–1929 illustrate how the NEPmen, 'these sharks', gradually turned 'into poor people', as E. A. Preobrazhensky described the process.[59] The comparative analyses also illustrate how 'movement forward by creeping inertia' (*mobilizatsionno-inertsionnom*) occurred in the development of private businesses in the Soviet Union of the NEP despite government attempts to choke them off through increasing punishments.

In trying to survive between 1925 and 1929, the 'Red Bourgeoisie' had to solve two main problems simultaneously. First, they found themselves legally limited in expressing themselves politically and in economic activity, and so they attempted to adapt peacefully to the gloomy reality. Second, they had to respond quickly to the commercial challenges thrust on them by their fellow businessmen and businesswomen. Competition in reacting to the changing demands of consumers stimulated production and expanded investments into profitable undertakings. While competition declined between 1925 and 1929, the initial period of 1921–1924 was characterized by increasing competition among business pioneers, with visible proliferation of confectionery and leather enterprises.

The beginning of tax pressure and state confiscations coincided with the diversification of industry caused by this strong competition in the market. If in 1921–1924 only two main kinds of production were developing, beginning in 1925 the number of enterprises as well as the types of goods increased. Between 1925 and 1929, with the elimination of deficits, the market became satiated with higher quality produce and proposals for more types of production of these items. Demand, however, remained unchanged. Contraction of the market was reflected in: bankruptcies and shutdowns of many private enterprises; reorientation of declining production into spheres that were more beneficial; increases in usurious interest rates on loans; and high rates of profit of some businesses, which increased rapidly both in amount and as a percentage of equity capital. Additionally, during the second half of the NEP, inhospitable government policies negatively affected private capital. The government claimed that political emergencies necessitated repression of the NEPmen, and at times there were show-trials of NEPmen. The government suppressed the market economy by lawless, bureaucratic, discriminatory actions against the 'Red Bourgeoisie'.

Consequently, the years 1925–1929 saw a significant reduction of enterprises that had been leaders between 1921 and 1924. Enterprises in the confectionery industry decreased from 43 per cent to 9 per cent and in the leather industry from 22 per cent to 5 per cent. Meanwhile, less popular industries increased from 35 per cent to 43 per cent. Thus, between 1925 and 1929 two qualitatively different but interrelated and contradictory processes were at work: 1) a spurt of business activity beginning in 1921, an economic wave brought about by economic liberalization; and then 2) the NEP reaching its peak legally, with attendant decrease and liquidation of private capital.

Data on the 49 enterprises illustrate a number of factors that determined the success of private Ural business between 1921 and 1929. At first, in the notes recorded by Ural–Siberian 'Credit-Bureau' office agents there emerged a generally positive estimate of the NEPmen-producers' business status. The responses of the businessmen were graded according to a four-tier scale: 'excellent', 'good', 'satisfactory' or 'bad', and they show that most of the respondents judged their status to be excellent, good or satisfactory. Seventy 4 per cent were satisfied with their position. About 53 per cent of producers had successful businesses, about 21 per cent had satisfactory ones and only 26 per cent suffered financially.

The classification of producers into two age groups shows greater participation in business among citizens in the 20 to 40-year-old age group (84 per cent) and less participation among citizens older than 40 (16 per cent). The non-state sector of the economy was represented both by businessmen who had pre-revolutionary trade experience and by their young competitors who, for the first time after October 1917, realized the details of what the Komsomol denigrated as 'money-grubbing'. Thus, the ablest group of the population, aged 20 to 40, constituted the working core of the industrialists surveyed.

The above data closely correspond to the data concerning the successfulness of business operations among these age groups. As might be expected, more than 60 per cent of producers in the first age group (20 to 40-year-olds) had excellent or good businesses, while in the second age group this figure did not surpass 40 per cent. However, since young producers were bigger risk-takers, the 20 to 40-year-olds also suffered more financial problems than those in the older group. Business operations depended on many factors, but it turned out that the most crucial factor in having a successful business was what is commonly known as 'the safe rear'. Analysing operations of 49 businessmen, we found a direct correlation between success in business and marital status. The data we have processed showed that married NEPmen were much more successful and effective in business than their bachelor colleagues. Married businessmen constituted the highest number of successful persons – 60 per cent – and only 10 per cent of married businessmen suffered financially. Almost 50 per cent of bachelor NEPmen producers were mere outsiders in business, none of them reached the top, and a few more than 20 per cent of bachelors had stable businesses.

The inertia of business development in 1925–1929 is also evident in the data of Ural producers for these years. The economic position of Ural industrialists declined in the final stages of the NEP and as the government continued attacking market relations in the national economy. After 1925, the proportion of formerly successful businessmen was almost halved, from 64 per cent to 33 per cent, and the enterprises of the 'private capitalists' diminished more than seven times, from 67 per cent to 9 per cent. The fact that the status of successful businessmen changed least of all (it decreased from 18 per cent to 16.6 per cent) once again proves that the government's aim was not to crush separate individuals but to undermine private capital on a mass scale. This capital mostly consisted of middle NEPmen, who were destroyed by taxes and other administrative punishments. However, those businessmen who deeply penetrated the economic structure of the country were not exterminated quickly when the state destroyed the NEP. It was necessary for the government to make a business operation as difficult as possible and then finally to 'kill' it like the 'animals' fed before Christmas, as E. A. Preobrazhenskii remarked.[60]

The 'Credit-Bureau' data portrays NEPmen producers as mostly a creative social stratum between 1921 and 1929. In spite of administrative barriers and the sometimes deserved public condemnation and severe punishments meted out to businessmen for stealing, engaging in criminal affairs and other deviant activities, they operated as partners in the economic triad of the country (state, cooperative and private economic subjects). NEPmen did not wish to get parity in rights with state and cooperative producers, but only to participate in economic activities that were legal and acceptable to the Soviet state. However, the rational economic orientation of the 'Red Bourgeoisie' on profits, together with their apparent idleness, which caused irritation and disapproval on the part of the population, significantly politicized the history of 1921–1929 and, as a result, the myth that the 'the newly rich' were objectionable and must be suppressed took root in a number of NEP documents mostly written by state authorities. The historical–statistical analysis of 'Ural bourgeoisie' enables us, with more objectivity, to restore the social portrait of NEPmen–producers and understand the basic principles of businessmen's legal activity in 1921–1929.

Conclusion

The methodology of historical–statistical analysis, which has not been used widely enough either in Russian and or foreign historiography, has impelled us to conclude the following. Ural businessmen rejected the uncertainty of starting new businesses because they were not confident that private business, permitted in 1921, would last for a long time. The data accumulated confirms that the attitude of private capitalists to their businesses was mostly constructive. This capital also played a positive economic role in the development of the national economy of the country. In most cases, NEPmen–industrialists affirmed that they wanted a normal commercial partnership with the state and rational taxation. They suffered and failed because of punitive confiscations. Nepmen hoped and attempted to adjust themselves to circumstances. Their desire to stay the course, to possibly postpone the liquidation of their business, resulted from basic economic and emotional considerations – the need to provide for their families, moral–ethical commitments, the need to repay loans and recoup personal finances, and regret for the time and labour they had expended. But they also may have been motivated by a vague faith that Soviet officials would tolerate businessmen who accepted the Communist regime and were loyal to Soviet power.

The Soviet government, however, regarded the NEPmen, and particularly the small group of NEPmen–industrialists, as a social force which could have only a limited existence, which could be 'allowed to exist' during a declared period of compromise. The government's success in prohibiting private enterprise and preserving the concept of the businessmen's economic guilt emphasizes that the NEP was only a transient stage on the path to socialism, a short-lived period of peace between labour and capital that resulted due to the political will of party administrators, who in turn were pressured by society as a whole and the 'Red Bourgeoisie' specifically. The compromise between the market and the socialist way of production could not be eternal. But while it lasted it was quite real because of the pent-up demand of the population for goods that the socialist sector could not produce. This forced the state to allow, to a greater or lesser degree, businessmen who refrained from getting involved in politics to exist temporarily on the economic field. The terms and the forms of cooperation of Soviet power with private capital under the conditions of compromise precipitated political struggles inside the party administration. But the divergence of opinions within the party hierarchy did not influence the fundamental fate of the undesirable market in general.

The alliance of the Soviet power with 'the submissive bourgeoisie' or with the newly born 'Red merchants', even if planned for a long time, was temporary. First, the New Economic Policy, which provided much freedom for economic initiative, brought about private 'antisocial elements' that were little controlled and frightened the party. They were called the 'creeping restorers of capitalism', which imperceptibly would destroy embryonic socialism from the inside. Second, the NEP enterprises, being more economically profitable than the distribution system of the tough state government, were more resistant to administrative controls. They promised more expensive and undesirable goods, but they were permitted as a temporary lifejacket for the state to preserve its power.

The history of the first years of Soviet Russia's existence was characterized by the opposition of various social forces, impelling the socialist government to choose between War Communism or a system such as the NEP. The cost of the struggle was in the dimensions of economic trade-offs, the creation of a state regime that accepted the controlled 'Red Private Owner' and protected his rights. For the Bolsheviks, NEP was a crisis measure to save one-party power. In case the system evolved into something more than NEP, such as true economic liberalism, it was always possible for the state to intrude and return things to their initial position. Under the obvious or hypothetical threat of 'democratic socialist development' taking root,[61] state power could return to the already familiar 'War Communism' type of administration that finally took place in the late 1920s.

Although this chapter has dealt with the foundations of the Soviet economic system, it has also described measures that were replicated in East Central Europe in the late 1940s. The ways in which these economic theories were implemented created serious challenges first in the Soviet Union and then in Eastern Europe. Restructuring and liberalizing these collective economies have been fraught with difficulties in both regions, as the following chapters illustrate.

Notes

1   See, for example, V. A. Shishkin, *Vlast'. Politika. Ekonomika. Poslerevoliutsionnaia Rossiia (1917–1928)* [Power, policy and economy in post-revolutionary Russia, 1917–1928] (St. Petersburg: Dmitrii Bulanin, 1997); L. I. Borodkin and E. I. Safonova, 'Gosudarstvennoe regulirovanie trudovykh otnoshenii v gody nepa: formirovanie sistemy motivatsii truda v promyshlennosti' [The government regulation of labour relations in the NEP years: shaping the system to motivate industrial workers] in L. I. Borodkin, ed. *Ekonomicheskaia istoriia: Obozrenie,* 5 [Economic History: Review] (Moscow: Moskovskii gosudarstvenyi universitet, 2000), 23–46; E. G. Gimpelison, *NEP i sovetskaia politicheskaia sistema: 20-e gody* [The NEP and the soviet political system: 20th year] (Moscow: Institut rossiiskoi istorii RAN, 2000); E. G. Gimpelison, *NEP: Novaia ekonomicheskaia polotika Lenina-Stalina. Problemy i uroki (20-e gody XX v.) [The NEP: The new economic policy of Lenina-Stalina. The Problems and lessons (the 20th years of XX century)]* (Moscow: Sobranie, 2004); Ch. E. Clark, *Uprooting Otherness: The Literacy Campaign in NEP-era Russia* (Selinsgrove: Susquehanna University Press; London: Associated University Presses, 2000); O. J. Bandelin, *Return of the NEP: The False Promise of Leninism and the Failure of Perestroika* (Westport, CT: Praeger, 2002); N. A. Grik, *Sovetskaia ekonomicheskaia politika v 1921–1933 gg.: kriticheskii analiz* [Soviet economic policy, 1921–1933 (Critical analysis)] (Tomsk: Tomskii gosudarstvenyi universitet, 2002); L. N. Liutov, *Obrechennaia reforma: promyshlennost' Rossii v epokhu NEPa* [The doomed reform. Russian industry of the NEP period] (Ul'ianovsk: Ul'ianovskii gosudarstvenyi universitet, 2002); *Rossiia nepovskaia* [Russia during the NEP], in S. A. Pavliuchenkov, ed. *Rossiia nepovskaia* (Moscow: Novyi khronograf, 2002); J. Hessler, *A Social History of Soviet Trade: Trade Policy, Retail Practices, and Consumptions, 1917–1953* (Princeton: Princeton University Press, 2004); M. Sch. Conroy, *The Soviet Pharmaceutical Business During Its First Two Decades (1917–1937)* (AUS. Series IX, History, 202; New York: Peter Lang, 2006).
2   A. M. Ball, *Russia's Last Capitalists: The Nepmen, 1921–1929* (Berkeley: University of California Press, 1990).

3   R. A. Khaziev, *'Poslednie iz mogikan: krasnye kuptsy epokhi nepa': Materialy i dokumenty ob ural'skikh kommersantakh 1921–1928 godov* [Last of the Mohicans: red merchants of the NEP period: Material and the documents about the Ural merchants, 1921–1928.] (Ufa: Bashkirskii gosudarstvenyi universitet, 2003), pp. 5–6.

4   On the negative impact of the Bolshevik regime's satirical and cartoon campaign against the NEPmen, see I. B. Orlov, ' 'Novaia burzhuaziia' v satire 20-h gg.' ['New bourgeoisie'] in S. Sekirinsky, ed. *Istoriia Rossii XIX-XX vekov: Novye istochniki ponimaniia* [XX century Russian history] (Moscow: Moskovskii obschestvenyi fond, 2001), pp. 230–236; idem, 'Obraz nepmana v massovom soznanii 20-h gg.: mify i real'nost' [The image of nepmen in twentieth century mass consciousness: myths and reality], *Novyi istoricheskii vestnik* [New history bulletin], 1 (2002) 29–42; idem, 'Grimasy nepa' v istoriko-revoliutsionnom fil'me 1920-kh godov' ['Grimasy nepa' in historical and revolutionary film in 1920], *Otechestvennaia istoriia* [National history], 6 (2003) 21–30; L. N. Liutov, *Simbirskoe-Ul'ianovskoe Povolzh'e v gody nepa. (Ekonomika regiona). Uchebnoe posobie* [Simbirskoe – Ulianovskoe Povolzhie in the years of Nep (regional economy)] (Ul'ianovsk: Simbirskia kniga, 2005), photo, p. 53.

5   For a general survey of the literature on private capital during the NEP era, see E. V. Demchik, *Chastnyi kapital v gorodakh Sibiri v 1920-e gg.: ot vozrozhdeniia k likvidatsii* [Private capital in Siberia's cities, 1920: from rebirth to liquidations] (Barnaul: Izdatel'stvo Altaiskogo gosudarstvenogo universiteta, 1998); E. V. Demchik, 'Chastnyi capital i gosudarstvennaia vlast' v Sibiri: dialog serediny 1920-h gg.' [Private capital and state power in Siberia: dialogue about the mid-1920s] in B. A. Skubnevskii and V. N. Razgon, eds. *Predprinimateli i predprinimatel'stvo v Sibiri* [Businessmen and enterprise in Siberia], 3 (Barnaul: Izdatel'stvo Altaiskogo gosudarstvenogo universiteta, 2001), pp. 91–105; U. En'iuan', 'Nepmany, ikh kharakteristika i rol' [The Nepmen, their character and role], *Otechestvennaia istoriia* [National history], 5 (2001) 78–87; V. E. Bondyrev, 'Dvoistvenyi kharakter NEPa v otnoshenii chastnika' [The double character of the NEP in terms of private capital], *Istoriia gosudarstva i prava: Federal'nyi zhurnal: nauchno-pravovoe izdanie* [History, state and right: scientifically and legal publishing], 1 (2002) 15–21; Hessler, *Social History*, pp. 103–132, 141, 167, 169, 171; *'Bybliki dlia pespubliki': istoricheskii profil' nepmanov* [Bagels for a republic: a historical profile of nepmen], in R. A. Khaziev, ed. (Ufa: Bashkirskii gosudarstvenyi universitet, 2005) passim; Conroy, pp. 78, 82, 90–91, 96–98, 116–117, 141, 143–145.

6   R. A. Khaziev, *'Poslednie iz mogikan: krasnye kuptsy epokhi nepa'* [Last of the Mohicans: red merchants of the NEP epoch], p. 18.

7   On this problem see I. V. Narskii, *Zhizn' v katastrofe: Budni naseleniia Urala v 1917–1922 gg.* [Life in catastrophe: Everyday life of the people of the Urals, 1917–1922] (Moscow: ROSSPEN, 2001).

8   *Ural'skii rabochii* [The Urals worker, newspaper], 2 (12 January 1922) 3.

9   Ibid.

10 A. V. Shafikova, 'Pervyi god raboty promyshlennosti Bashkirii v usloviiakh novoi ekonomicheskoi politiki' [The first year of work in Bashkir industry under the New Economic policy] in M. B. Aimalov, ed. *Bashkortostan v pervoi polovine XX veka: maloizvestnye stranitsy istorii* [Bashkortostan in the first half of twentieth century: a little-known page of history] (Ufa: Vostochnyi universitet, 1997), p. 69.

11 R. Arskii, *Kak borot'sia s chastnym kapitalom* [What is a fight against the private capital?] (Leningrad: Priboi, 1927), pp. 4, 22.

12 Ts. M. Kron, *Chastnaia torgovlia v SSSR (po materialam Soveta S'ezdov Birzhivoii torgovli)* [Private trade in the USSR (On material from the Soviet Congress on exchange trade)] (Moscow: Vsesoiuznyi Sovet S'ezdov Birzhivoii torgovli, 1926), pp. 81–90.

13 V. P. Timoshenko and A. E. Bedel', *Opyt ispol'zovaniia inostrannykh investitsii v khoziaistvennom razvitii strany* [The experience of the use of foreign investment in national economic development] (Ekaterinburg: Institut istorii ural'skogo otdelenia RAN, 1997), p. 29.

14 Khaziev, 'Poslednie iz mogikan: krasnye kuptsy epokhi nepa' [Last of the Mohicans: red merchants of the NEP epoch], p. 65.

15 Ibid., pp. 64–65.

16 Ibid., p. 66.

17 A. V. Shafikova, 'Osobennosti razvitiia promyshlennosti BASSR v gody NEPa' [The particularities of the development of BASSR industry in the years of the NEP], in S. F. Kasimov and M. Kh. Nadergulov, eds. *Aktual'nye voprosy istorii i literatury Bashkortostana* [Real questions about the history and literature of Bashkortostan] (Ufa: Bashkirskaia Entsiklopediia, 2002), p. 156.

18 According to the ruling of VSNKh of 29 November 1920 all industrial enterprises with more than five workers with the mechanical engine and more than 10 without it were expropriated. See *Sobranie uzakonenii i rasporiazhenii raboche-krest'ianskogo pravitel'stva RSFSR* [Holdings of the legal documents and transcripts of the Worker and Peasant Government *RSFSR*], 93 (1920), article 512.

19 The Urals, finding itself in the epicentre of the struggle between the Red Army and its adversaries, was one of the concentrations of owners who actively supported anti-Bolshevik forces during the Civil War. According to the special ruling of VSNKh, all the property of 'the revolutionary enemies' supporting Kolchak was forcibly nationalized. See *Postanovleniia i rasporiazheniia Sovetskoi vlasti Ufimskogo revkoma* [The resolutions and transcripts of the Soviet authorities of the revolutionary committee of Ufa], 4 (24 September 1919) 1.

20 *Cheliabinskaya oblast' 1917–1945 gg. Sbornik dokumentov i materialov* [The Chelyabinsk region, 1917–1945. A collection of documents and materials] in P. G. Agaryshev and A. P. Finadeev, eds, *Arkhiv-Khranitel' Vremeni: Istoriia Arkhivnoi Sluzhby Cheliabinskoi Oblasti V Dokumentakh, Vospominaniiakh, Fotografiiakh* [Archive, the Protector of Time. History of the archival service of the Chelyabinsk Region through documents, memories, photographs] (Cheliabinsk: Iuzhnoural'skoe knizhnoe izdatel'stvo, 1998), pp. 76–77.

21 At the dawn of Soviet power capitalists were classified as 'cultured' (submissive) and 'non-cultured' (non-submissive). The latter were doomed to political and economic oblivion. This principle functioned without changes during the NEP. See V. I. Lenin, *Ocherednye zadachi sovetskoi vlasti* (PSS) [The next goals of Soviet power], 5th edn, 36 (Moscow: Gosudarstvennoe izdatel`stvo poloticheskoi literatury, 1962), p. 305.

22 This picture was exposed at the exhibition organized by the Painters' Unity in 1922. See I. B. Orlov, ' 'Grimasy nepa' v istoriko-revoliutsionnom fil'me 1920-kh godov' ['Grimasy nepa' in historical and rvolutionary film, 1920], *Otechestvennaia istoriia* [National history], 6 (2003) 24.

23 *Ural'skii rabochii* [Ural workers, newspaper], 2 (12 January 1922) 3.

24 *Ural'skii rabochii* [Ural workers, newspaper], 68 (4 December 1921) 2.

25 Ob'edinenyi gosudarstvennyi arkhiv Cheliabinskoi oblasti (OGACHO) [The United State Archive of the Chelyabinsk region], f. 77, op. 1, d. 690, l. 6.

26   OGACHO, f. 77, op. 1, d. 690, l. 6.

27   Under the pretext of ensuring safety of food in the Soviet Union, Narkomfin of RSFSR ruled that local committees to confiscate mills from 'private leasees' should be organized and regional departments of home trade were to prefer mills staying in state hands before 'leasing them privately'. See Tsentral'nyi gosudarstvennyi arkhiv Udmurtskoi Respubliki (TsGAUR) [The Central State Archive of the Republic of Udmurtiay], f. 121, op. 1, d. 18, ll. 2, 8.

28   *Zvezda* (Perm) [The Star, newspaper], 57 (17 March 1923) 3.

29   OGACHO, f. 77, op. 1, d. 690, l. 6.

30   See *Otchet o deiatel'nosti Orenburgskogo gubernskogo ispolnitel'nogo komiteta Soveta rabochikh, krest'ianskikh, kazach'ikh i krasnoarmeiskikh deputatov s 1. 10. 1924 po 1. 10. 1925 g.* [Report on the activity of the Orenburg revolutionary executive committee of workers, peasants, cossacks and red guard deputies] (Orenburg: Gubispolkom, 1925), p. 125.

31   *Ezhenedel'nyi biulleten' otdela upravleniia Cheliabinskogo gubispolkoma* [Weekly bulletin of the division of management of the Chelyabinsk revolutionary committee], 1 (12 January 1923) 1.

32   In the circular, published by Narkomfin of RSFSR on 9 February 1927, local financial institutions were categorically prohibited from giving credits to private oil-mills. See TsGAUR, f. 70, op. 3, d. 10, l. 29.

33   *Cheliabinskaya oblast'. 1917–1945 gg.* [The Chelyabinsk region, 1917–1945], p. 105.

34   See *Kon'iunkturnyi obzor khoziaistva Urala za 1925–1926 gg.* [The current review of Ural economy, 1925–1926] (Sverdlovsk: Tipografiai Granit, 1927), p. 40.

35   *Osnovnye voprosy ekonomiki SSSR v tablitsakh i diagrammakh. Kontrol'nye tsifry na 1927/28 g. i sravnitel'nye dannye za 1913, 1924/25, 1925/26 i 1926/27 gg.* [The main questions of the economy of the USSR in tables and diagrams. The control figures in 1927/1928 and comparative data in 1913, 1924/25, 1925/26 and 1926/27] in B. A. Gukhman, ed. (Moscow: Izdatel'stvo Kommunisticheskoi Akademii, 1928), tables 6–14.

36   See *Ural'skii torgovo-promyshlennyi spravochnik* [The Ural trade-industrial reference book] (Perm: Permkniga, 1924), pp. 174–178, 218–219, 221, 226–231.

37   V. S. Nemchinov, *Narodnoe khoziaistvo Urala (ego sostoianie i razvitie)* [The national economic of the Urals (condition and development)] (Ekaterinburg: Uralkniga, 1923), p. 29.

38   Gosudarstvennyi arkhiv Permskoi oblasti (GAPO) [The State archive of the Perm region], f. 423, op. 1, d. 247, l. 2.

39   *Kon'iunkturnyi obzor* [The current review], p. 40.

40   Ibid., p. 42.

41   *'Sovershenno sekretno': Lubianka–Stalinu o polozhenii v strane (1922–1934 gg.)* ['Strictly confidential': Lubyanka–Stalin about conditions in the country (1922–1934)], in N. M. Peremyshlennikova and L. P. Kolodnikova, eds, 2 (Moscow: Institut rossiiskoi istorii RAN, 2001), p. 125.

42   E. V. Demchik, *Chastnyi kapital v gorodakh Sibiri v 1920-e gg.* [Private capital in Siberia's cities, 1920: from rebirth to liquidations], p. 119.

43   *Gorod Sverdlovsk. Istoriko-ekonomicheskii ocherk* [The City Sverdlovsk. Historical–economic essay] (Sverdlovsk: Izdanie Ural'skogo oblastnogo ispolnitel'nogo komiteta, 1924), p. 28.

44   Ibid., pp. 28–30.

45   Gosudarstvennyi arkhiv Sverdlovskoi oblasti (GASO) [The State Archive of the Sverdlovsk region], f. 156, op. 1, d. 83, l. 17.

46   GASO, f. 156, op. 1, d. 83, l. 17.

47 GASO, f. 241, op. 2, d. 2953, l. 74.
48 The ruling of *Sovnarkom* (Council of People's Commissars) from 21 May 1928, combining the former institutional rulings about industrialists, introduced sanctions up to imprisonment for 'businessmen setting up private capitalist enterprises under the mask of industrial cooperative organizations'. See *Zakony o chastnom kapitale (sbornik zakonov, postanovlenii, raz'iasnenii i instruktsii)* [The laws about the private capital (Collection of the laws, resolutions, explanations and instruction)] in B. S. Mel'tsman and B. E. Ratner, eds (Moscow: Gosfinansy, 1929), pp. 8–9, 12.
49 GASO, f. 156, op. 1, d. 50, ll. 197–198.
50 *Chelyabinskaya oblast'. 1917–1945 gg.* [Chelyabinsk region, 1917–1945], p. 123.
51 N. Riauzov, *Vytesnenie chastnogo posrednika iz tovarooborota* [Displacing the private go-between from the trade turnover] (Moscow: Gosudarstennoe planovo-khoziastvennoe izdatel'stvo, 1930), p. 13.
52 TsGAUR, f. 54, op. 1, d. 17, l. 4.
53 *Deyatel'nost' BTsSNKh* [The activity of *BTsSNKh*] (Ufa: BashSNKh, 1923), pp. 3–5.
54 Lenin, *Politicheskii otchet Central'nogo komiteta RKP (b), 27 marta: XI s'ezd RKP (b), 27 marta – 2 aprelia 1922 g.*, (PSS), 5th edn, 45 (Moscow: Gosudarstvennoe izdatel'stvo politicheskoi literatury, 1964), p. 95.
55 See for example Rossiiskii gosudarstvennyi arkhiv ekonomiki (RGAE) [The Russian State Archive of Economy], f. 7624, op. 4, dd. 899–912. For more details see also Khaziev, *'Poslednie iz mogikan: krasnye kuptsy epokhi nepa'* [Last of the Mohicans: red merchants of the NEP era], pp. 3–310, which includes archaeographic analysis of the 450 documents, with an introduction and footnotes.
56 Khaziev, *'Poslednie iz mogikan: krasnye kuptsy epokhi nepa'* [The last of the Mohicans: red merchants of the NEP era], pp. 3–4.
57 During the NEP licences of the first and second categories were attached to small-scale enterprises; licences of the third and fourth categories were attached to medium-scale ones and licences of the fourth and fifth categories were attached to large-scale enterprises.
58 Ibid., p. 170.
59 See L. Pellikani, 'Kollektivistskaia antiekonomika' [The collectively anti-economic], *Socializm budushego* [Socialism of the future], 3 (1992) 62.
60 Ibid.
61 Bandelin, *Return of the NEP*, p. 25.

3
Europe – Our Common Home? Russian–European Pharmaceutical Relations during the 1920s

Mary Schaeffer Conroy

Introduction

This chapter is part of a larger study on the Soviet pharmaceutical industry, a fairly neglected industry but one requiring a high level of scientific research and one that is integral to healthcare. Here we look at the industry during the NEP, the period of the 'New Economic Policy' and particularly the relationship between the core Soviet industry and Western European houses.

Although this study focuses on the Russian pharmaceutical industry and its dealings with Western European pharmaceutical houses in the third decade of the 20th century – some 80 to 90 years ago – nevertheless the study is germane to issues about free trade, the market system, globalization, and Europe as a common space that are being debated at the present time. There are studies of trade between Soviet Russia and Germany in general and in the railway sector during the 1920s.[1] But the nature of the pre-Soviet and early Soviet pharmaceutical industry and its interaction with counterparts in Europe has been little investigated. The Imperial Russian government hovered over the pharmaceutical industry. Still the industry was based on market principles and carried on brisk trade with French, German and Swiss houses before World War I. Trade was disrupted during the war and during the Russian Civil War but revived during the 1920s. Russian pharmaceutical trade also was robust with the United States before the Great War, continued during it to some extent, faltered during the Civil War and then picked up during the 1920s, despite lack of diplomatic relations between Russia and the United States, a story that is beyond the purview of this chapter.[2] The organization of the Russian pharmaceutical industry before the Soviet period and its integration into the global economy appeared conducive to growth. Thus, zeroing in on the Soviet pharmaceutical industry in the 1920s enables us to compare private enterprise in economics and healthcare with the Soviet socialist variant. It also helps us to evaluate the impact of globalization and pan-European cooperation on an industry and consumers.

The Soviet government, having emerged victorious from attempts to unseat it during the civil war of 1917/18–21, officially established the NEP in March 1921 to jump-start the economy which was in disarray after six years of war. The food-producing sector, which had exported heavily to Western Europe in the late nineteenth and early twentieth centuries, was in dire straits. To facilitate recovery, the Bolshevik-dominated Soviet government encouraged peasants to farm and sell their produce by abandoning the punitive measures of 'War Communism', 1917/18–21 (requisitioning peasant produce and attempting to force peasants into collective and state farms) and by giving the peasants incentives – a flat tax on grain that was partially commuted to a money tax in 1924. Above and beyond that the government allowed peasants to sell products on the open market for whatever consumers would pay.

The remainder of the Soviet economy was divided into key sectors labelled the 'Commanding Heights' and small-scale production and trade. Shops and production units under the latter classification were leased back to private individuals, known as *kustari* or NEPmen. Newly accessible archival materials have allowed us to see how this retail economic sector produced and disseminated staples like clothing, food and household goods[3] and provided entertainment.[4] The Government allowed some entrepreneurialism which benefited citizen-consumers. However, it regulated and heavily taxed small-scale producers and traders, as it did lessees of pharmacies, in order to maintain control over the economy. The 'Commanding Heights' comprised heavy industry, banking and the money supply, foreign trade, and communications. The Government retained close control over these sectors. Newly accessible archival materials have yielded small studies of a few, such as banks and the money supply.[5]

The core Soviet pharmaceutical industry also was part of the 'Commanding Heights'. There were no studies of the Soviet pharmaceutical industry when I began investigating the subject 15 years ago. Since then, new works on the pharmaceutical sector in Ukraine and Belarus have recently appeared.[6] But more are needed. The Soviet pharmaceutical sector is worthy of attention for two main reasons. First, this study expands research on scientific and technological transfers within Europe.[7] Second, the Soviet pharmaceutical sector was a key element in one of the first experiments in government-planned, state-managed healthcare. Without pharmaceuticals there can be no effective preventive medicine or treatment. Government control over pharmaceutical production and distribution has been touted as a panacea for both cost overruns and shortages of pharmaceuticals. Thus it is instructive to examine how well the government-controlled core Soviet pharmaceutical industry operated.

New Russian-language works on demography document significant diminution of infectious diseases like smallpox, diphtheria and typhoid during the 1920s. Dysentery was halved. However, typhus, measles, scarlatina and whooping cough hit at nearly the same rates as in 1913 and cases of malaria far exceeded 1913 rates.[8] In the 1920s smallpox and diphtheria were curbed by inoculation and typhoid and dysentery by vaccination coupled with better sanitation. Vaccines were made in separate institutes in Soviet as in Tsarist Russia. Therefore, Soviet scientists and vaccinators, hygiene education and improvements in sanitation were containing some infectious diseases. However, there were weak links in the chain. The production of vaccines depends upon reagents and other pharmaceuticals. So do sanitary measures. Continuing problems from typhus, whooping cough and malaria raise a red flag about the availability of disinfectants, soap, insecticides, antiseptics – in other words about the robustness and efficacy of the Soviet pharmaceutical industry. This concern is given weight by Christopher Kobrak, specialist on the German pharmaceutical house, Schering. He notes that, although Russia was placed seventh in terms of production and consumption of pharmaceuticals by the latter part of the NEP, 1925–1928, per capita use of drugs in the Soviet Union during this period was below that of Brazil, Spain, Argentina, and Mexico. Additionally, the leader – the United States – outperformed the Soviet Union 22 times and the next four countries, England, Germany, France and Japan, with far smaller populations, outpaced the Soviet Union two to four times.[9] So, while medical personnel, hospitals, clinics, and hygiene education improved in the USSR in the 1920s, the Soviet pharmaceutical industry apparently had flaws. What were they?

This chapter seeks to answer those questions by comparing the core Soviet pharmaceutical industry that produced half or more of drugs and other pharmaceuticals used in the Soviet Union in the 1920s with key Western European pharmaceutical companies. The latter were negatively impacted by World War I but rebounded by developing new products, opening new markets, and economizing, in other words by classic market-oriented methods. The core Soviet pharmaceutical industry, in contrast, was under state management. It was part of the experiment to create an economy in the Soviet Union of the 1920s that was more scientific than one at the mercy of market cycles. Since the Soviet Union was rife with disease in 1921, an effective pharmaceutical industry was imperative. This chapter explores the Soviet pharmaceutical experiment of the NEP period, mainly with regard to Western European contacts, to ascertain whether it was more or less successful than its neighbours.

The pre-Soviet pharmaceutical industry and competitors

Before the opening of the archives, Soviet historians claimed that their pharmaceutical industry was backward. In reality, although there was a dearth of pharmacies in rural areas, city dwellers were well served and the Russian pharmaceutical industry was on a par with the American industry of that era. In the late nineteenth and early twentieth centuries, the hundred or so pharmaceutical enterprises that operated in the Russian Empire lagged behind Swiss and German houses in the production of the new chemically synthesized medicines because these houses had a head start and German companies, in particular, patented their synthetics. Russia lacked indigenous sources of cocaine, a local anaesthetic, and quinine, necessary to quell the symptoms of malaria, Russia's main communicable disease.[10] Additionally, the opium grown in the Russian Empire and the seaweed available on Russian shores for iodine, crucial as a disinfectant for water as an antiseptic and to prevent goitre, did not have high enough levels of active ingredients to satisfy the pharmacopoeia. Thus, these botanical products, chemically synthesized medicines such as aspirin and fine medical equipment were imported. Otherwise the Russian Empire was rich in medical botanicals, which also were lucrative exports. Russia had a monopoly on Santonin, the main treatment for roundworms in humans and hogs at that time. Russian pharmacologists did noteworthy research on hormones. Vaccines, antitoxins and serums for protection for some diseases were produced in separate institutes. Russia had made headway in inoculating the populace against smallpox and against other infectious diseases, as the low civilian death rate during World War I proved.[11] However, anti-malaria measures lagged.

Domestic pharmaceutical houses supplied half or more of the medicines, soap and toiletries used in the Empire. By 1912, Schering's branch in Russia produced ether, tannin, iodine, bromides and urotropin (a disinfectant and Schering exclusive from 1894) for the Russian market,[12] but Russian houses also produced chemicals which had been imported before World War I. The war spurred pharmaceutical production. Russians increased output of iodine, potassium, toluol (an important ingredient in salicylic acid, used in turn for aspirin and also for explosives), salicylic acid and other drugs and produced some medical items they had not produced before, both by requisitioning German factories and by reverse engineering. Thus, although Russia lost important pharmaceutical companies in Poland during World War I,[13] the war also benefited the pharmaceutical industry and consumers.

The Civil War of 1917/18–21, however, was totally destructive. During that war nationalization of pharmaceutical factories, replacing their owners and managers with party loyalists rather than capable businessmen, coupled with neglect of these facilities; fall-off in production of medicinal botanicals; and severed international trade links laid low the Russian pharmaceutical industry. On the retail end, *apteki* and *aptekarskie magaziny* (pharmacies and 'drug stores') also fell on hard times, being reduced to about a third of their 1917 numbers. Medicines were distributed through informal channels. Abuse of drugs escalated.[14] As late as the summer of

1923, epidemics of malaria raged and typhus, other fevers, typhoid, cholera and venereal disease remained rampant. Only remnants of pharmaceuticals were on hand. They were the products of foreign firms, such as CIBA, Parke-Davis, Hoechst, Reidel and Merck; products of foreign factories that had operated in Russia prior to 1917 – Roche, Bayer, Schering and Farbwerke; products of the Warsaw factory Spiess; and products of nationalized Russian enterprises – Ferrein, Saturn and Pashkevich.[15]

Russian citizens were in a desperate medical situation in 1921 and domestic pharmaceutical companies and pharmacies could not provide adequate succour. Pharmaceutical companies in Switzerland, France and Germany also languished after World War I. The main manufacturing plant of the Swiss firm Hoffmann-La Roche, located in a town just across the German border, 'was closed down by German authorities' during World War I, causing the company 'enormous difficulties. The loss of its Russian market was especially devastating'.[16] The firm had established a presence in Russia in 1896 when Iozef Aronstamm, a Petersburg pharmacist, took it upon himself to purvey Roche products such as cough syrup. The endeavour was given Hoffmann's blessing when he attended the International Medical Congress in Moscow in 1898. Aronstamm subsequently established agencies and warehouses in Moscow, Riga, Vilnius, Warsaw and Odessa. By 1909 Russia accounted for 21 per cent of Roche's turnover. The firm was nationalized in 1919. Aronstamm tried to get it back after the German–Russian rapprochement in Locarno in 1922 but was unsuccessful. He re-established his branch in Riga in 1921.[17] 'The firm was saved from collapse', according to Renate Riedl, 'by transformation into a public limited (joint stock) company, established in 1919 with a capital stock of 4 million Swiss francs', and research breakthroughs by the firm's leading pharmacologist on an amino acid later used to treat Parkinson's disease, Vitamin C and a drug used for cardiac complications in surgery. But these developments were realized in the 1930s and later.[18] The Swiss firms CIBA, Sandoz and Geigy formed a cartel in 1918 to counter the new German cartel IG Farben and competed by developing washable mothproofing products and later DDT. CIBA specifically pioneered the first synthetic cardiovascular agent Coramine in 1924 and 'gained recognition in the field of hormonal therapy'. Although hormone research had begun before World War I, major breakthroughs did not occur until the 1930s.[19]

The French pharmaceutical industry was dominated by small companies that had developed out of pharmacies. The French greatly relied on German products. During the war they faced shortages of labour and raw materials. They were helped by British supplies, such as urotropin and lanolin, but these were cut off in 1918. In the 1920s suggestions on beefing up the industry included patenting pharmaceuticals, as was the German practice, and limiting trade names to 15 years. Larger companies like Poulenc and Usines de Rhone argued that patenting would be beneficial; smaller houses protested that it would limit their initiative to bring out new drugs. In the 1920s, French companies 'aimed to satisfy the public's demand for proprietary preparations ... such as laxatives, cough medicines, tonics and balsams' and focused on emerging markets in South America and the Far East, realizing the cachet of a Paris address. Firms protested the government's attempt to regulate proprietary medicines, to interfere in partnerships between pharmacists and businessmen, and feared that the system of national health insurance introduced in 1928 would limit their freedom on drug pricing. But only in the mid-1930s did more government interference come.[20]

The German company Schering had established a presence in Russia in 1906 to acquire Russian-made turpentine (made from dry distillation of wood) for a key Schering product, synthetic camphor. In the 1920s Schering faced hurdles as great as those confronting Farmatrest/Gosmedtorgprom. Malnutrition and tuberculosis racked Berlin, the company headquarters. The company suffered from monetary inflation; sequestration of its plant and intellectual property in Britain, Russia and in the United States; loss of markets; competition from foreign houses; competition within Germany from the conglomerate IG Farben, which included Bayer, Hoechst and other chemical giants; and the financial slump that affected Germany in 1925–1926 before the Great Depression hit.[21] Schering's merger with Kokswerke, the coal mining and coke conglomerate, with operations in Silesia, was a mixed blessing. Schering contributed more to Kokswerke than it appeared to receive in return. Schering's management made policy mistakes – costly increases in office and sales staff, poor acquisitions, and so forth.[22]

Schering determinedly surmounted these difficulties. The firm did participate in trading consortia, which were given credits by private lending German and Dutch institutions that were guaranteed 60 per cent by the German government. However, Schering, like other firms, had to take care of the remaining 40 per cent.[23] In its day-to-day operations, Schering was independent of the government until after 1933, when in seeking government aid it became more and more curtailed by taxes, limits on imports, accounting regulations, and restrictions on dividends and testing with animals, not to mention the more familiar, notorious rules on Jewish members of its board, executive and research staff.[24] Before that, through arranging return of 80 per cent of its American property and concentrating on the American market, developing new products, focusing on hormonal research, establishing branches and affiliates around the world, and joining a camphor cartel and an iodine cartel, Schering restored its fortunes. In the 1920s it held 50 per cent of the market for synthetic camphor in the United States (the major market in the world at the time) and was an important player in photography as well as pharmaceuticals. Although Kobrak concedes that Schering's financial records were less than transparent, he considers it profitable and financially solid through the 1930s.[25]

In sum, Western European pharmaceutical houses bounced back by shrewd application of capitalist methods. What methods would the state-owned Soviet pharmaceutical industry use?

The Soviet pharmaceutical industry

During the 1920s NEP the core Soviet pharmaceutical industry was a trust, first called Farmatrest and after 1924, when the production and trading arms were united, Gosmedtorgprom. As part of the 'Commanding Heights', the core pharmaceutical industry was in the jurisdiction of VSNKh (or the more pronounceable Vesenkha), the Supreme Council of the National Economy. Headquartered in Moscow, during the NEP the core industry was composed of only seven, then five, and finally six of the largest and most important pre-revolutionary pharmaceutical factories. Eighty or so lesser pharmaceutical enterprises were under regional management following nationalization. But, although limited in terms of enterprises, Farmatrest/Gosmedtorgprom dominated the Soviet pharmaceutical industry.[26] The Ukraine fought for and won some pharmaceutical independence during the NEP.[27] However, through locking in local Pharmacy Administrations, Farmatrest/Gosmedtorgprom supplied the bulk of pharmaceuticals to pharmacies and clinics throughout the Union.[28] For example, in 1924 Farmatrest supplied about 60 per cent of aspirin, salicylate preparations, sulphuric ether, sodium iodide and terpinhydrate.[29] Thus, the core Soviet pharmaceutical industry was large scale. Would this and control by the central government be a help or a hindrance?

Like other major industries in the Soviet Union of the 1920s, Farmatrest/Gosmedtorgprom was hybrid, part extension of the government, part operating on its own resources. Vesenkha imposed ambitious production and financial plans on Farmatrest/Gosmedtorgprom. The pharmaceutical trust sent back quarterly reports. Well before the Five-Year plans for the entire Soviet economy began in 1927–1928, therefore, the core pharmaceutical industry was planned and managed by the central government. Its financing also partly came from the government. The trust received basic capital from the nationalized enterprises and operating capital from the State Bank and State budget allocations.[30] Factory administrators considered the trust's budgets inadequate. They were in the low millions during the early NEP, as compared with military budgets of 300 to 400 million rubles. Further, monies allocated were not always received fully or in time.[31] But, as an economic hybrid, the core pharmaceutical industry also was allowed to raise revenue from domestic and foreign sales of its wares and from rationalization procedures. Would this system enable the industry to be robust and effective? Would government backing plus smart day-to-day direction make the Soviet trust as successful as its European competitors – and in accordance with Socialist ideology make it more advanced?

Trade: imports and government limitations

During the NEP, Soviet–European pharmaceutical trade resumed pre-1914 configurations. Russia imported raw materials and finished goods she could not produce and exported medicinal botanicals which were plentiful. As often as not Government domination thwarted the industry.

Imports superseded exports during the first years of the NEP. Imports of quinine were of the utmost necessity for tens of thousands stricken with malaria in 1921 and 1922, with the figure escalating to ten million in the summer of 1923. Quinine does not cure malaria but only mitigates the symptoms. Nevertheless, in the 1920s, before Germany produced a synthesized version of the drug (which Soviet scientists copied),[32] quinine was the only remedy available. Russia could not produce this drug domestically and by June 1923 stores of quinine had run out.[33] Farmapravlenie, the Board that ran Farmatrest, estimated that it was necessary to import 130,000 kilos of quinine, if only half the sick received a bare minimum (*golodnaia norma*) dose of 20 grams.[34]

Iodine was another crucial product Soviet Russia had trouble producing. In 1922 Farmatrest imported 4,500 kilograms of iodine and in 1923, 1,675 kilograms. The trust also requested sulphur, caffeine (a stimulant), rubber goods, alkaloid opiates, thermometers, syringes, ampoules and chemical vessels. Imports from Berlin and Riga between August 1922 and May 1923 amounted to approximately 717,000 gold rubles.[35]

The Riga connection raises interesting questions. Riga was the capital of the new independent state of Latvia, which had emerged from Lifland, a province of the former Russian Empire. Some 27 pharmaceutical-related manufactories had existed in tiny Lifland.[36] Imperial Moscow, though, had been the hub of the pharmaceutical industry with 32 factories. The biggest and best formed the core Soviet pharmaceutical industry; others existed in other parts of the USSR. Lifland/Latvia had been overrun by troops during the Great War and the Civil War. Moscow had not been a theatre of war during either conflict. Why then purchases in Riga? Were these from Hoffmann-La Roche, from Riga companies, or was the city an entrepôt?

In any case, at the end of 1923 about 100 raw botanical and chemical materials were lacking for Soviet state factories No. 2, 4, 8, and 13,[37] formerly owned by the Union of Zemstvos, Schering, Ferrein and Allen and Hansburys. Farmatrest informed the Department of Foreign Trade in Vesenkha that the industry needed 30,000 kilograms of iodine from England, 50,000 kilograms of barium from England and Germany, 240,000 kilograms of nut gall from England and Germany, 21,000 kilograms of soap from France and Italy, and 5,000 kilograms of potassium sulphoguiacol (probably a water-soluble form of guaiacol, first produced by Roche) from Germany. Additionally, 65 boilers and other pieces of equipment 'from abroad' were 'necessary for the production' of codeine, aspirin and other items 'in the factories of Gosmedtorgprom'. Estimated cost was 1,632,254 gold-backed rubles.[38]

In some respects Farmatrest's requests were not inordinate. In 1937, the United States, with a population similar to the USSR, estimated that it needed to import 1,000 pounds (about 450 kilograms) of Santonin, 260,000 pounds (about 118,316 kilograms) of belladonna leaves and roots, and approximately the same amount of ergot of rye (some from Russia).[39] Further, the cost of Farmatrest's imports was minimal compared to the five million Finnish marks in gold allocated by the Soviet government (Sovnarkom) to the Finnish Communist Party for 'propaganda and educational activities' in Finland and abroad in 1920, at the height of the Civil War.[40]

However, although medicines and disinfectants were basic medical necessities, as with consumer goods,[41] Vesenkha strictly controlled import credits for Farmatrest.[42] The Supreme Council of the National Economy could be parsimonious, although it was sometimes generous. In the matter of quinine imports, the representative of Gosmedtorg, undoubtedly at the prompting of Vesenkha, informed the epidemiological section of the Commissariat of Health that 'the purchasing power of the population' must be taken into account and 'from the commercial side' there could not 'be imported a greater amount of quinine than' could 'be sold and preserved in the warehouses of Gosmedtorg'. Thus, instead of 130,000 kilos of quinine government officials decided to import only 75,000 kilos.[43] On the other hand, by May 1924, large amounts of other products had been imported, mainly from Germany. These included 200 kilograms each of the febrifuges aminopyrine and antipyrine; 100,000 dozen ampoules of Neosalvarsan (against venereal disease); 1,000 kilograms of the disinfectant Protargol; 5,000 kilograms of quinine from Holland and Germany, plus other items, for a total of 604,000 rubles.[44]

Still, the core pharmaceutical industry estimated that it would need 35 imports to fulfil the five-year government-mandated production plan for 1924–1929. These included sublimate (16,000 kilograms for the fourth year and 32,000 kilograms for the fifth); ten metals, such as lead, bismuth, zinc and nickel; seven partially manufactured items, such as aniline (1,000 kilograms were estimated for the first year rising to 6,000 in the fifth); p-nitrophenol (probably for disinfectants) and dimethylamine (for petroleum refining, detergents, and organic synthesis); and 18 raw materials such as bromine, sulphuric acid, ammonia and French or American turpentine.[45]

Soviet Russia's need to import turpentine, made by the process of dry distillation of wood, indicated how far the pharmaceutical industry had deteriorated during the Civil War. This is why Schering came to Russia in 1906. Moreover, a small-scale producer (*kustar'*), Engineer Moshkin, was able to produce synthetic camphor itself. He sold it to Farmatrest between 1922 and 1924,[46] emphasizing that small, autonomous production units are often more flexible and innovative than large ones.

Farmatrest, in contrast, had to jump through bureaucratic hoops. Even when benign, the multiplicity of bureaucrats hovering over Farmatrest complicated sourcing. Importing was done both by the Trade Representative of Vesenkha (*Torgovyi predstavitel'* or *Torgpredstvo*) in Berlin and by Gosmedtorg, the trading arm of the pharmaceutical industry.[47] In September 1923, wares for the pharmaceutical industry from Germany worth 500,000 gold rubles were signed for by both agencies.[48] Financing was similarly splintered. One hundred thousand gold rubles were available to Farmapravlenie for purchases in 1924, partly through a loan from Vesenkha and partly from Farmapravlenie's own resources. Sometimes Gosmedtorg bought on credit.[49] Interestingly, payment for trips abroad and imports was sometimes made in American dollars.[50]

The plethora of government agencies and their penchant for thoroughly discussing every order and permit to go abroad held up decision-making and acquisition of raw materials. For example, in 1923 one Rotenburg, a buyer for Farmapravlenie, had to delay his buying trip to Germany because he had not received the requisite papers.[51] Excessive bureaucracy annoyed higher officials themselves. In 1924 Vesenkha fumed that sharing foreign trade activities with the Commissariat of Foreign Trade and multiple authorities in charge of imports slowed up orders badly needed by pharmaceutical factories.[52]

Both Soviet trade representatives and Gosmedtorg were penurious in purchasing foreign supplies for the pharmaceutical industry.[53] For example, in January 1924, the RSFSR Trade representative (*torgpredstvo*) attempted to buy iodine in London. Schering claimed it had monopoly rights to receive raw iodine for Russia, because the firm had owned a factory in Russia before the October Revolution. The Russian Trade Representative countered that Schering no longer owned its factory, since the Soviet government had nationalized it; therefore the firm could claim no monopoly. The RSFSR *torgpredstvo* also informed Farmatrest that, after the first payment, Russia would be able to get wares on credit, avoiding London's demand for payment in sterling.[54] In May 1924, the Berlin branch of Gosmedtorg advised Farmapravlenie it could probably purchase quinine, cocoa butter, theobromine (diuretic and nerve stimulant) and caffeine more cheaply in Holland than in Germany – because of the financial crisis in Germany and also because of temporarily poor relations between Germany and the USSR. Other pharmaceutical products could be bought cheaply in England and France; microscopes could be obtained on favourable terms in Austria.[55] In May 1924 Vesenkha administrators, representatives from the chemical industry and Farmatrest administrators averred that contracts with Italy, locking Russia into orders for industrial and agricultural products at seven million rubles a year, were too expensive and perhaps should be discontinued.[56]

However, these hard-nosed business practices sometimes sabotaged the industry. The merger of Farmatrest and Gosmedtorg in 1924 made Gosmedtorgprom 'the largest organization in the Soviet Union for production and trade in medicines, surgical instruments and other forms of health products'.[57] Vesenkha continued to curtail imports, however, hampering the industry. At a Production Conference held in September 1925, representatives of Farmapravlenie lamented that the pharmaceutical factories under its jurisdiction had fulfilled their plan by only 34 per cent, to a great extent because of inadequate buildings and equipment. Gosmedtorgprom was not able to remodel because of its 'strained financial condition' (*napriazhenie finansovogo sostoianiia*) and also because in 1925/1926 'foreign equipment' that had been ordered 'was not received' due to a 'delay in getting [import] licenses' from Vesenkha.[58] Shortages of raw materials choked production. In 1926 the Union of Moscow State Factories for Basic Chemical Production, in the jurisdiction of the Moscow Sovnarkhoz (MSNKh—a local branch of Vesenkha), informed Gosmedtorgprom that 'until receiving potassium from abroad, dispensing of nitrous acid' would 'not be done'. Although production of sulphuric acid would continue fully according to the 1925–1926 plan, production of nitrite was to be contracted by 50 per cent and production of lead salt by 60 per cent. Gosmedtorgprom was able to deliver only 50 per cent of the contracted amount of nitrous acid to the Electric Trust and seven per cent of the contracted amount of this substance to a second purchaser. Gosmedtorgprom had to stop all deliveries of nitrous acid to Mostorg (Moscow Trade Agency) until 'supplies of potassium' were 'received' when 'production would continue...according to contracts'.[59]

To put this problem in context, it must be noted that Russia produced 75,000 puds of potassium during World War I![60] During the production year 1926/1927, Gosmedtorgprom's reports continued to complain that shortfalls in manufacture were caused by 'interrupted supplies of raw materials' and 'foreign apparatus [that] were not received'. Production of silver and mercury preparations was lower than in the previous year.[61]

The government sabotaged the industry in other ways. While denying Farmatrest the wherewithal to modernize, Vesenkha encouraged a prosperous German to lease and remodel a Soviet pharmaceutical factory. In April 1924 the Concession Commission in Vesenkha informed Gosmedtorgprom in a 'secret missive' that 'German citizen G. F. Briuk' requested use of Moscow Chemical–Pharmaceutical Factory No. 5, the former 'Standart', which had been leased to a private individual during the first half of the NEP and now was 'in the jurisdiction of the Lease Administration of the Moscow [department] of Vesenkha'. Vesenkha approved, asserting that there appeared to be no 'competition with the state [pharmaceutical] industry'. The German proposed spending about 180,000 gold rubles to install refrigerators, steam boilers and drying chambers to produce patented preparations and reagents, work up medicinal herbs for export and distribute them to 'the borderlands, where there' were 'limited staff to serve the sick', and produce chemicals such as phenol, benzol, toluol, vinegar acid and sulphuric acid.[62]

Briuk's proposal might have benefited Soviet consumers. But Gosmedtorgprom viewed it as a threat and thus temporized. Vesenkha asked for a response in 30 days. Eight months later, on 30 December 1924, the industry informed the Concession Commission that it did 'not consider the proposal of Briuk solid and interesting for the USSR'. Yet in the end Gosmedtorgprom capitulated to the Supreme Council of the National Economy.[63]

Pharmaceutical industry leaders were realistic about the benefits and the dangers of imports to the growth of their industry. Some ideologues[64] argued that large wholesale firms made fantastic profits importing items from abroad that were made in the Soviet Union and, as a consequence, the Foreign Trade Commissariat should raise tariffs to support domestic industry. Industry stalwarts A. Aluf, S. Mar and F. A. Ferrein (probably a relative of the pre-Soviet pharmaceutical industrialist Vladimir Karlovich Ferrein), debated the new tariff schedules of 1924 with more common sense. They emphasized that, while Farmatrest and Aniltrest produced some items that were imported, the imported items were cheaper. Other substances – such as quinine – were not produced in Russia. In both cases, high tariffs constituted a tax on the sick. Similarly, the realists acknowledged that *kustar'* industries produced some substances – most notably iodine – more cheaply than Gosmedtorgprom and Aniltrest, thus requiring retention of small-scale competitors for a time.[65] Ferrein, in particular, argued that the Soviet pharmaceutical industry would be importing some basic raw and finished products for the foreseeable future.[66]

The Soviet government did not agree, however. In preparation for the First Five-Year Plan, inaugurated in 1927–1928, the Government cut imports, taking a toll on the industry and on consumers alike. Unlike the shortages resulting from lowered industrial prices in 1926–1927,[67] in the pharmaceutical sector there were shortages of tannin (used as an astringent and styptic and also in the leather industry) the year before and it was import cuts in 1926–1927 that caused 'severe insufficiencies of quinine, surgical instruments, and medical equipment'. To cope with the deficit of equipment, the industry established repair workshops.[68] In 1927 the Soviet government placed prohibitive tariffs not only on luxury items like perfume, eau de cologne, pomade and cosmetic soap but on crucial medicinal items. Tariffs on cocaine were raised from 6 rubles and 30 kopeks per kilogram in 1924 to 30 rubles per kilogram in 1927. Tariffs on bromine and iodine were doubled. Duties on medical instruments were raised from 74 kopeks per kilogram in 1924 to 1 ruble and 50 kopeks per kilogram in 1927. Only quinine and its salts were entirely exempted from customs duties, indicating ongoing eruptions of malaria, hence desperate need for these items.[69]

Tsarist customs duties had focused on swelling government coffers. They often hurt the pharmaceutical industry but benefited consumers.[70] Now the pendulum swung in the opposite direction. The Soviet government's tariff hikes on iodine, cocaine and medical instruments protected nascent Soviet production of these items but they hurt citizens because domestic production did not cover need. 'Cocaine is produced inside the country', a leading Soviet pharmaceutical journal noted in 1928, 'but in insufficient amounts and it is not certain whether it needs to be imported from abroad'.[71] The same was true of iodine and medical instruments. By 1927–1928 most medical instruments were produced in fairly large state enterprises, two new ones being established in 1926 and 1927.[72] However, total output of Soviet medical instruments satisfied only 60 to 70 per cent of need. Moreover, according to one Soviet commentator, Soviet X-ray, electrical and complex laboratory equipment were 'of the simpler variety' and did not meet standards required 'for improving medical help, for the progress of scientific thought in medicine'.[73] The conclusion we can draw is that government management was frequently detrimental to the Soviet pharmaceutical industry and did not benefit Soviet consumers either.

Trade: exports and economic realities

Despite a chart reproduced by Christopher Kobrak, expert on Schering, showing no Soviet pharmaceutical exports,[74] the USSR did try to balance pharmaceutical imports with exports of medicinal botanicals. International market fluctuations and insufficient botanicals on hand, as well as too much bureaucracy, hampered this endeavour. The core Soviet pharmaceutical industry used the same methods as its competitors in capitalist economies to increase sales.

In the early part of the NEP exports were sluggish. In 1923 and 1924, Russia sold only 3,860 tons of plant materials in contrast to the more than 30,000 tons exported in 1913.[75] Cash-flow problems on the part of foreign buyers, particularly Germany, impeded exports. In 1924 the Berlin office of Gosmedtorg glumly reported that 'the severe money crisis in the country did not give a favourable perspective for the established activity…in medicinal plants'.[76] A plethora of agencies also complicated and slowed Soviet exports. The Commissariat of Foreign Trade, along with Vesenkha, supervised exports.[77] The Russian Republic People's Commissariat of Agriculture was involved when medicinal plants were exported and so was the Russian Republic Commissariat of Health.[78]

A further impediment was lack of plant products. Liquorice root, used as an expectorant, a laxative and to coat pills, had long been one of Russia's most lucrative exports.[79] In the 1920s and 1930s liquorice was one of America's main pharmaceutical imports. Early in the NEP, Gosmedtorg sourced from small-scale producers for this and other botanicals. In 1923, Gosmedtorg contracted with the Administration of the Tersk Central Agricultural Industrial and Credit Cooperative to 'prepare for Gosmedtorg in 1923, 50,000 puds of *solodkovyi koren'* (liquorice root)…clean…to the standards of the foreign market'. A pud being 36 pounds, this was an enormous amount. According to a similar agreement (*Soglashenie*) in March 1924, Ivan Petrovich Karelin, an inhabitant of the small Volga mercantile town of Myshkin in Tver' Province, promised to prepare 'buckthorn (*Krushiny lomkoi*)...to the amount of three wagons—about 800 puds—for the price of one ruble, 25 kopeks per pud...gathered in the spring...well-dried, cleaned...without any kind of mixture, fully answering the requirements of the foreign market'.[80]

Sales of Santonin, desperately needed by the American livestock industry as a worm treatment, faltered during the NEP for political reasons.[81] Efforts to export other botanicals, however, gradually became more sophisticated and somewhat more successful. Gosmedtorgprom concentrated on increasing the collection and cultivation of medicinal botanicals so that 'in case of war or blockade...there would be no risk...of insufficient medicaments' and strove to increase exports of botanicals to help the Soviet Union achieve a favourable trade balance and conserve its 'gold supply'.[82] In 1924 the Soviet Union's main botanical exports were lycopodium (club moss), Spanish fly, liquorice root and lime-blossoms.[83] They were carried in German and Italian as well as Soviet ships, plying routes from Hamburg to Shanghai and docking not only in Leningrad and Murmansk but also in Riga and Revel, ports of newly independent Latvia and Estonia.[84]

In the second half of the NEP, export goals remained difficult to achieve. The agencies involved in foreign trade had multiplied. Not only Gosmedtorgprom but Khimfarmtorg, Ukr[aine]medtorg, Sel'skosoiuz and four other agencies exported botanicals.[85] Industry analysts averred that eight exporters resulted in 'disorganization' and 'disorder'.[86] Also, they disparaged the quality, consistency and packaging of Soviet exports, which were not, as yet, up to international standards.[87] Because of these problems, during the 1924–1925 operating year Russia exported less than two-thirds – 65 per cent – of the amount of plants exported in 1913.[88]

Table 3.1 Purchasers of soviet botanicals (approximate)

	1924/1925	1925/1926
Germany	43 per cent	33.1 per cent
United States	28 per cent	43.4 per cent
England	21 per cent	4.3 per cent
France	3.5 per cent	18.5 per cent
Austria	1 per cent	0 per cent
Estonia	0.1 per cent	0 per cent
Latvia	0 per cent	0.2 per cent

Source: Compiled from *Kratkii otchet o rabote Gosmedtorgproma za 1925/26 operats. god* (Moscow, April 1927), p. 22.

Nevertheless, West European houses (and American ones) imported sizable amounts of certain Soviet botanicals in 1924–1925[89] and 1925–1926,[90] as the following Table 3.1 shows.

Still, in 1925–1926, the Soviet Union's botanical exports, now showcasing buckthorn, did not meet government-mandated targets. Only about 40 per cent of the Foreign Trade Commissariat's goal of 612,000 rubles was realized. Lack of success again was attributed to problems in the international market – low orders and low prices' and 'competition from other countries which themselves collected and cultivated medicinal plants' as well as to too much bureaucracy – disagreements on the part of a whole range of organizations ... in the preparation of medicinal plants in the internal market and in selling them abroad' complicated exporting.[91] During the operating half-year, October 1926 to June 1927, the pharmaceutical export plan, mainly for liquorice, lycopodium and buckthorn, was fulfilled by only 45 per cent. Only 358,483 rubles were realized instead of the 790,000 rubles projected in the plan, for the same reasons as before.[92]

To increase export revenues, Gosmedtorgprom, like a conglomerate in a capitalist economy, attempted to enlarge its supply pool and to improve the quality of its botanical exports. The first action plan involved acquiring the Santonin Factory in Chimkent (which belonged to the Kazakh Autonomous Republic) and a liquorice factory in the Urals. Although much liquorice came from Turkestan,[93] the Liquorice Factory was located in the Ural Mountains.[94] The privately owned Chimkent Santonin Factory had been seized by workers during the civil war and then nationalized by the government of Turkestan. It was transferred from the jurisdiction of the Turkestan *Sovnarkhoz* (local economic council) to Vesenkha in 1921. In 1923 the enterprise was proclaimed a corporation called the Santonin Trust.[95] In 1924 part of Syr-Dar'ia and Semipalatinsk oblasts were transferred to the Kazakh Republic and with the territory came the Santonin Factory Trust. The Kazakh ASSR received 60 per cent of the profits and 40 per cent went to the USSR Treasury.[96] The Chimkent factory increased in importance when it began to manufacture tannin; nicotine from *makhorka*, a strong native tobacco; and Anabasine, thus reducing imports of these items.[97] Analogous to capitalist monopolies, Gosmedtorgprom took control of the Chimkent factory in 1927–1928, naming it for Felix Dzerzhinskii, newly deceased head of Vesenkha and the Cheka (early Soviet political police).[98] The Kazakh Chemical Trust was liquidated in 1931.[99]

Gosmedtorgprom's second strategy for increasing export revenues was to guarantee the quality of medicinal botanicals.[100] The trust employed six plenipotentiaries to supervise cultivation and collection in Leningrad, Voronezh, Rostov-on-Don, Kiev, Odessa, and the Caucasus.[101] Additionally, the industry standardized key plant products. This was important, for lack of standardization, particularly in cardiac remedies, could be fatal, as an article on proper production of Digitalis and other products made from foxglove (Digitoxin, Digitalein, Gitalin, etc.), translated from the German and reproduced in a Ukrainian trade journal, reminded pharmacists in 1926.[102]

The Standardization Commission in the USSR Commissariat of Foreign Trade (Narkomtorg) included S. Ia. Shiutte, Director of the Chemical Division of the Administration of Foreign Operations of Narkomtorg, as chair; nine professors and plant specialists; the chair of the Bureau of Standardization in the USSR Commissariat of Trade; and two other officials – chairs of the Russian Republic commissariats of agriculture and health.[103] The commission standardized 71 plants organized into three groups – most marketable, less marketable and barely marketable.[104] It published an 86-page booklet giving instructions for obtaining and packaging botanicals and warned about methods to falsify them.[105]

Three other publications appeared in 1927 to encourage individuals and groups to cultivate and collect medicinal botanicals. One, an encyclopaedia of 236 pages with 64 illustrations, described a hundred or more plants, their useful parts, geographical location, applications, importance, amounts used domestically and for export, average prices, a 'yes' or 'no' check list as to whether they should be collected and an extensive bibliography.[106] A group of Leningrad botanists published a small, specialized handbook. One of two authors, appropriately named Monteverde, was Chief Botanist at the Botanical Garden in Leningrad, established by Peter the Great and still in existence. Another author was a professor at Leningrad University.[107] A third manual, similar to a business text in a capitalist economy, discussed the balance between 'manufacturing prices (*zagotovitel'nye tseny*)' and 'overhead (*nakladnye*) expenditures', counselling that the former would be 'correct and, consequently, normal, if overhead expenses would be lower ... the more would be guaranteed success of manufacture and most of all export'. The book cited percentages of sales costs for 20 plant materials, emphasizing that local costs included packaging, storage, rail rates, local railroad taxes and insurance, and noted that costs 'from the base to the ship' included customs duties, insurance, packaging for ocean transport and 'other'.[108]

These books, the establishment of quality control and acquisitions illustrate how the Soviet pharmaceutical industry used business methods akin to those of its Western European competitors. Complete success eluded the industry, however, because of international as well as domestic factors.

Direct investment on the part of Europeans and joint ventures

The Soviet industry needed investment to modernize. Fortunately, despite loss of Russian properties through nationalization, foreign pharmaceutical firms were eager to invest and establish joint ventures in the Soviet Union. Here Soviet pharmaceutical executives exercised a modicum of autonomy and made some faulty decisions. They declined proposals from German and Japanese investors for spurious as well as sensible reasons but enthusiastically accepted a questionable proposal from an American entrepreneur.

Despite strong trade links with Germany in the 1920s and good relations with the Berlin office of Gosmedtorg, in 1923 and 1924, Farmapravlenie rejected several German proposals. These included a project from Schering for a concession to produce iodine in Russia, a proposal from the German firm Leo to produce lead and tin tubes for cosmetics and some pharmaceutical preparations and a proposition from Khemishe Industryi Konstern [sic] 'to organise a factory in Leningrad or Moscow to produce aromatic substances for perfume...soaps, oils'.[109] Farmapravlenie turned down Schering because it had an offer from a syndicate to produce iodine in a lake in the Aspheron Peninsula of the Caucasus that supposedly had greater potential and another for Beiuk-Shor near Baku which reputedly contained 20,000 puds of iodine.[110] As for the lead and tin tubes, Farmapravlenie researched pre-war production and discovered that, although some tubes of this sort had been imported, a firm called Fol'ga, in Libau, and the Butyrskaia factory in Moscow both made the tubes. Farmapravlenie believed the Butyrskaia factory could fully supply the one million tubes that Farmatrest needed annually.[111]

The Moscow State Archive of the Economy in Moscow details proposals from Hoshi Pharmaceuticals, Ronzo Iod and other Japanese firms in the autumn of 1923 and winter of 1924 to build factories which would produce alkaloids of opium and also iodine in Chita, Vladivostok and other areas of the Soviet Far East. Vesenkha approved the proposals but Farmapravlenie rejected them for two reasons. The first was incredible – that Farmatrest could produce a sufficiency of the opiates in the Chimkent Santonin factory and in Moscow from Turkestan poppies. The second objection was curiously altruistic – that the proposed production was cover for illegal export of opium to China and the narcotics also could be used by Koreans and Chinese working in Soviet Siberia.[112]

Whereas German and Japanese initiatives sometimes got short shrift, Soviet executives were keen about American proposals despite lack of diplomatic relations between the two states.[113] Some, like those with Armand and Julius Hammer's Allied Drug and Chemical Company and the Moness Chemical Company, were shields for channelling funds from Moscow to the American Communist Party.[114] The joint venture between Farmapravlenie and E. Virgil Neal's firms, Tokalon and International Consolidated Chemical Corp., signed in January 1924, reflected the Soviets' awe of 'Americanism' as well as Neal's charisma and his superior negotiating and entrepreneurial skills because, although Tokalon's cosmetics and perfumes had high quality, the USSR had plenty of these items and Neal's medicines were of dubious value.[115]

Chemicals and biologicals: advancing the USSR by all means necessary

During the second half of the NEP, the Soviet pharmaceutical industry began to concentrate on production of biologicals, an area in which some pre-Soviet Russian pharmaceutical firms had excelled, and also on synthetic pharmaceuticals. Medical researchers began investigating the use of sex hormones for rejuvenation in the 1880s. In the 1890s they realized the importance of the thyroid gland and the problems iodine deficiency could cause.[116] Russians had a track record on biologicals. A. V. Pel' and P. P. Kravkov, in the nineteenth century, and Liubov' Nikolaevna Lavrova, an early twentieth-century graduate of the Women's Pharmacy School founded by one of the first women pharmacists in Russia, Antonina Boleslavna Lesnevskaia, all did cutting-edge research on hormones.[117]

By 1925–1926 Gosmedtorgprom was producing Urotropin and by 1927 Atophan, both Schering products on which the firm held patents through the 1930s.[118] Gosmedtorgprom also produced Pantopon, a Roche product. The Soviet industry used underhanded as well as legitimate methods, including sending scientists abroad for technical training, industrial espionage and reverse engineering, to reproduce these and other drugs.

Training abroad

The archives document how, in 1928, Farmapravlenie, Gosmedtorgprom's Administrative Board, dispatched six Soviet pharmacy specialists from the Karpov (former Ferrein) Factory, the Salicylate Factory, the Derzhinskii Factory in Chimkent, the Semashko (former Keler) Factory, the Medical Instruments Factory, and Farmapravlenie to Merck and other German factories for periods up to three and a half months to study methods of producing generic products such as reagents, salicylic acid, tannin, guaiacol and medical instruments. Payment for some trips was in American dollars.[119]

Industrial espionage

Earlier, the industry had used industrial espionage to clone drugs. Soviet representatives in Germany, and sometimes the Red Army, funnelled drawings and technical information back to Moscow in 'top secret' correspondence. For example, in June 1924 the Secret Organ of the Commissariat of Health forwarded to Gosmedtorgprom materials gathered by the Soviet representative of the Commissariat of Health in Germany, which described the Villi (Willi) Salge firm's method for obtaining iodine, one of the items that the USSR desperately needed. Detailed drawings of apparatus were included.[120] In 1925 the Red Army sent Gosmedtorgprom 'secret' information on methods and apparatus used to produce aspirin in the Bayer Factory in El'berfel'd. Included in the packet of materials was a handmade pencil sketch of the apparatus.[121] In 1928 Nisenman, Chair of the Administration (*Pravlenie*) of Gosmedtorgprom, sent two drawings and 36 pages of German text describing production of synthetic ether oils to a Comrade Fel'dman at the State Scientific Chemical–Pharmaceutical Institute. Comrade Fel'dman, however, opined that the material had 'little value since it' consisted 'nearly exclusively of excerpts from works or articles in journals...the drawing also' was 'taken from a popular book'.[122] In 1926 a German 'chemical–pharmaceutical' specialist applied to work in the USSR but there is no certainty as to how useful he was.[123]

Reverse engineering

The Soviet pharmaceutical industry also produced items ambiguously listed under the rubric of 'new production of formerly imported items', some of which were said to be 'patented'. More properly they probably were ethical or proprietary medicines – the 'strengthening substance' Phytin, the cough syrups Sirolin and Pertussin, a children's food supplement Mal'ton, and so on. British firms also replicated foreign proprietary medicines in the 1920s – but by licensing.[124] There are no records of Soviet firms obtaining licences. However, since industry journals published formulae for 'New [Foreign] Medical Substances',[125] perhaps these were in the public domain. On the other hand, the Soviet pharmaceutical industry might have been guilty of intellectual piracy.

In any case, in addition to Urotropin, in 1925–1926 the Karpov Factory began 'new production' of cocaine, Antifebrin, iodoform and a few other medicines 'heretofore imported'.[126] Interestingly, in 1924, one Butkevich noted the antibacterial properties of penicillium, used from 1893 by A. Wehmer to produce citric acid, but, unfortunately, this did not lead to the production of Soviet penicillin.[127]

In 1927 the industry claimed production of Pantopon (a Roche product); Dionin and Stypticin [sic]; the hormone products Adrenalin, Mammin, Ovarin and Tyreoidin; and the antivenereal Novosal'varsan, Ferratin, Osarsol, Pepsin, Tannalbin and Diuretin.[128] Information on how 'the factories of Gosmedtorgprom organised' this 'new production of formerly imported items' was not disclosed.[129]

Soviet replication of hormone preparations reflected Russian pioneering and continued research. In 1926, for example, the Ukrainian pharmacy journal, *Khimiko-farmatsevticheskii vestnik*, reviewed a text published in Dorpat, newly independent Estonia, about new hormone preparations, including ovarian preparations.[130] With regard to hormone preparations, the Soviet industry matched European houses and was in advance of some, such as CIBA, that concentrated on hormone research – progesterone, the ovarian hormone Estradiol and testosterone – only in the 1930s.[131]

Other products probably were reproduced through reverse engineering. Five new preparations were advertised in 1927 which were intended to compete with foreign products. Three were 'standardised cardiac preparations', Adonilen, Diginorm and Gitalin,[132] said to have been developed at the Scientific Chemical–Pharmaceutical Institute in Moscow, the institute Boris Nikolaevich Saltykov, revolutionary pharmacist from Tsarist times, created in 1922 from the research laboratory at the former Ferrein Factory where he began working in 1892.[133] Diginorm 'R' was the Soviet equivalent of Digipurat and Gitalen, the Soviet equivalent of Digalen; both were made from the leaves of foxglove. Adonilen was made from *Adonis vernalis*.[134] Biokhinol' (exported under the spelling 'Bijochinol') and Bismutogvi 'were two new antisyphilitic preparations made partly from heavy metal bismuth'. Simpler than Novosal'varsan, like the cardiac preparations, they were developed at the Scientific Chemical Pharmaceutical Institute in 1926.

Results

By the end of the NEP Gosmedtorprom's factories had increased output. The Karpov (former Ferrein) Factory alone produced 89 inorganic preparations, 14 mercury preparations, 71 reagents, 116 galenical preparations – extracts, infusions, oils, salves – two kinds of soap, including medicinal green soap and ten 'dosed preparations'.[135] An experimental iodine station was being built near Baku.[136]

Total output of pharmaceuticals increased in comparison with the start of the NEP (though not in comparison with the Imperial period), as Table 3.2 shows.

Table 3.2 Products: in kilograms for chemical–pharmaceuticals; in dozens for perfume, cosmetics and soap

	1923	1923	1924/1925	1925/1926	1927	1927
Mercury	1,940					40,000
Iodine, bromine	116	1,454	45,797	73,177	42,530	100,000
Alkaloids	50	761	1,754	2,997	2,342	4,000
Salicylic	2,408		80,296	143,162	117,675	200,000
Disinfecting	7,032	8,211	111,804	159,653	57,691	220,000
Novarsol/ Novosalvarsan	30		192		502	1,000
Soap, perfume, cosmetics	10,539	31,526	686,592	1,258,655		

Source: Author compilation from Archives and Medical Literature cited in notes 136–139.

The first column lists Farmatrest products for the first three months of 1923. The second column for 1923 cites Farmatrest's sales. These must have come from imports or stores on hand.[137] Two years later we note progress. From 1925 to 1926 production of basic necessities increased, on average, one and a half times.[138] However, some reports inflated output. The first column for 1927 cites Gosmedtorgprom production for the first nine months.[139] The second column for 1927 uses approximate (*do*) production figures. At this time, Farmatrest was said to produce 95 per cent of chemical–pharmaceutical products and 50 per cent of galenical preparations used in the Soviet Union. Alkaloids included morphine, codeine, dionin, heroin, papaverine, stiptitsin, papaverin and cocaine. Additionally, this report listed sulphuric acid barium for X-rays at 'about' 18,000 kilograms—one-third of the 50,000 kilograms imported from Germany and England in the industry's barren year of 1923. The 'approximately' 1.2 million kilograms of mineral (inorganic) salts produced included sulphuric and chloride salts of caustic soda, calcium, copper and zinc, as well as potassium. Absence of potassium had accounted for 5,000 kilograms of imports in the dark days of 1923. Production of hormone preparations (Adrenalin, ovarin, mammin, tireoidin) amounted to 'about' 1,000 kilograms a year. Production of dosed substances – ampoules, pills and capsules – amounted to a respectable 50,000 kilograms.[140] But, even given the custom of 'storming' during the fourth quarter, the statistics in the second 1927 column are dubious.

Admittedly, there were signs of progress. The first nitrogen factory in Russia was constructed and a new superphosphate plant was being planned in 1927.[141] Production of iodine increased, although unevenly. In 1926 the Experimental Factory established by Gosmedtorgprom at Beiuk-Shor near Baku, on the Caspian Sea, produced 16 kilograms of crystallised iodine from waters rising from drilled oil wells every 24 hours.[142] Total production of iodine at Baku fell to 333 kilograms in 1926 because of too much rain.[143] The iodine facility near Arkhangel'sk produced 225 kilograms in 1925 but only 180 kilograms in 1926, also due to poor weather: 'the summer was rainy and windy, but without storms, tearing out the seaweed and scattering it on shore'.[144] In 1928, Feodor A. Ferrein admitted that iodine obtained from the drilled waters at Beiuk-Shor was 'insufficient for constructing a large factory' and that '[E]xperiments on the Black Sea do not give a clearer picture' although he was hopeful that eventually 'the Union' would be 'free from imports of iodine'.[145]

At the very end of the NEP, some price cuts, as in a market economy, signalled increased output and did not result in shortages. In 1927 prices were low for salicylate preparations, Novosal'varsan, papaverine and Pantopon,[146] because of 'improved production' and 'increased availability'. In June 1927 tablets of Atofan (a clone of the Schering trademarked Atophan to combat rheumatic conditions, produced from 1913[147]) and Bromural, heretofore imported, were available in sufficiency so prices for them were lowered. In

1928 F. A. Ferrein averred that, although valerian root, bilberries, sage, chamomile and some other important botanicals were in short supply and fish oil production was down because the plan for the Fishing Trust cut production, nevertheless, domestic production of pure benzol and toluol met the needs of the Soviet Union.[148]

In 1928, the Salicylate Factory in Moscow increased production of sodium salicylate by 50 per cent by replacing antiquated aluminium equipment with copper. This, in turn, enabled the factory to double production of salicylic acid. In the shop that produced aspirin, installation of foreign equipment in December 1927 raised production from 25 to 30 per cent. With better equipment, two workers were able to produce and package 14,000 kilograms of pure preparations per month, compared with the 3,000 to 4,000 kilograms produced by six to eight workers in 1924.[149]

The quality of Soviet products began to improve during the second half of the NEP. Analytical laboratories in factories and in the central warehouse checked wares to see whether they adhered to standards established by the Pharmacopoeia. The cases of rejection (*reklamatsiia*) of defective wares by purchasers were slightly less – 25.8 per cent in 1925–1926 versus 26.6 per cent in the previous year – although that may have been the result of shortages of some items.[150]

'Rationalization' of production also occurred during the 1926–1927 operating year. Packaging was shifted from the Semashko Factory, new buildings were erected at some of the six Moscow factories, and some new machinery was installed. Dwellings had been constructed for workers at some of the factories, although allotted space was quite small.[151] A great achievement was that, in the operating period October 1926 to June 1927, the Central Surgical Warehouse succeeded in producing some items of medical furniture and quartz lamps, heretofore imported, as well as 'dental chairs and drills, prepared earlier by *kustari*'.[152]

On the other hand, Gosmedtorgprom's financial situation was still somewhat shaky in 1926–1927, despite administrators' insistence, again, that finances were 'fully stable'. On the plus side, the number of (state) shareholders increased, payroll costs fell because the number of workers declined by 16 per cent due to 'liquidation of independent commercial activity at the Semashko Factory', and '*nakladnye*' (overhead costs) were less. Offsetting these gains, costs for raw materials and fuel rose, exports were lower than hoped, due to insufficient orders and competition from other countries, and revenue from domestic sales fell.[153]

Some products given publicity, such as 'Sekakornin', a standardized preparation of Sporyn'ia, made from parasites collected from roses, used in obstetric practice, and a major pre-Soviet export, seem to have been little produced.[154] More seriously, at the end of the NEP, despite increased output, the core, state-run pharmaceutical industry still did not satisfy Soviet citizens' needs. There were still serious shortages in pharmacies and in institutes due to deficits of packaging and distribution problems as well as production shortfalls. In 1927 the chief industry journal emphasized that shortages at the pharmacy were 'documented by letters, even from individuals, from various regions of the Union, requesting that they be sent the most basic and necessary medicines, which had not arrived in their regions'.[155] Ukrainian pharmacists complained that 'for whole months' pharmacies 'cannot receive sufficient amounts of preparations such as sodium chloride...and many others'[156] A. Aluf, old pharmacist and former Menshevik Internationalist who had reluctantly supported the Bolsheviks in 1918, lamented at the end of the NEP that the pharmaceutical industry he had helped to nationalize had not lived up to its expectations. Although 'chemical and pharmaceutical production' were 'in the hands of the government, for the most part working according to a fixed plan', he opined that 'rational [that is dosed or packaged] medicines' were 'distributed to an insignificant degree in Russia'.[157] The Bacteriological Institute in Ufa complained of shortages of equipment and basic materials throughout the NEP,[158] complaints that coincide with the evidence on low per capita use of pharmaceuticals cited by Christopher Kobrak in the introduction.

Conclusions

By the end of the NEP the core Soviet pharmaceutical industry unquestionably had advanced. It produced greater quantities of some pharmaceuticals and some were of higher quality. Much of the progress was due to interaction with European houses. The Soviet pharmaceutical industry also relied on apparatus imported mainly from Germany. The industry was integrated into the world market. There were minuses coming from market fluctuations, but there were pluses coming from the industry's monopoly on Santonin and near monopoly on crucial medicinal botanicals such as liquorice root. In sum, the Soviet pharmaceutical industry's relationship with European pharmaceutical houses during the 1920s emphasized how important globalization and pan-European cooperation were to the restoration of the industry and to consumers in the USSR and abroad. Put another way, the Soviet pharmaceutical industry's interaction with European companies validates the benefits of globalization.

The industry's experiences at home, on the contrary, provide a case study of how a country's economic system and political policies can impede an industry. The Soviet government's ownership of the pharmaceutical industry was a hindrance as much as a help. The industry had advanced chiefly by implementing business practices similar to those employed by its European counterparts but its advance was not commensurate with theirs. Consolidation of key pre-Soviet pharmaceutical factories did not result in synergies. The compartmentalization and dysfunction of the Soviet economy, although these problems are not elaborated on in this study, thwarted domestic sourcing, production and distribution. Farmapravlenie, the administrative board that ran Farmatrest day-to-day, made mistakes on its own. At times, the trust also was beholden to government gold. However, bureaucrats' controls and policies frequently curtailed Farmatrest. Exogenous Soviet officials were obsessed with fiscal rectitude and blocked the pharmaceutical industry's attempts to acquire materials and modern equipment. The greater agility of *kustari* operations allowed several to be more successful than the core industry. Admittedly, large privately owned enterprises can be as bureaucratic as any government operation. But from Kobrak's statistics, by the end of the 1920s, autonomous European (and Japanese and American) pharmaceutical factories outperformed government-dominated Soviet ones.

By the end of the NEP, Soviet factories had moved forward, as compared with their low status at the outset of the NEP (though not necessarily to their pre-Soviet status) by applying traditional capitalistic business methods. However, they still lacked supplies, important items like iodine were still inadequate, and citizens periodically suffered from lack of basic items, partly because of distribution problems. Soviet pharmaceutical R&D was problematic. Some Soviet products were probably produced illegally. Soviet scientists claimed to improve the foreign products they cloned. They did do original research on botanicals and hormones. Nevertheless, imitation of West European products indicated some dependency in R&D.

Most important was the situation for consumers. Statistics on the use of pharmaceuticals per capita in the Soviet Union were skewed by distribution problems in rural areas, a topic not covered in this chapter.[159] Nevertheless, Western European citizens filling prescriptions had more alternatives than those in the Soviet Union. Because there were many small French companies catering to consumers and the German pharmaceutical industry was 'fragmented' (Kobrak's term), consumers were not unduly affected by fluctuations in any one firm. 'Though one of the largest producers in Germany', Kobrak notes, 'Schering's sales were only a tiny fraction of the world and German production, and even German exports'. Schering's total sales were 'less than one half of one percent of worldwide production and only four percent of Germany's'.[160] Since the Soviet core pharmaceutical industry monopolized production and distribution, consumers were heavily affected by import restrictions and the industry's production and distribution shortfalls.

How the fortunes of the core pharmaceutical industry affected demographics is unclear.[161] In the 1920s, before the advent of sulfa drugs and antibiotics, cures for major diseases were still lacking. Gerald Grob documents that individuals with strong constitutions were able to withstand certain diseases. Other diseases abated spontaneously. Still others depended greatly on diet, vaccination and sanitation measures.[162] It must be reiterated, however, that the last factors were connected with pharmaceuticals. Finally, the story was not finished in the 1920s. In the 1930s bactericides increased life expectancy dramatically. In the USSR, according to new archival information, in 1938–1939 life expectancy for men was 44 years and for women 49.7 years.[163] Famine in 1932 and 1933 and child mortality had principally torpedoed life-expectancy statistics. Nevertheless, following the NEP, Soviet government policies were more inhospitable to the pharmaceutical sector. Lack of chemicals resulting from overly aggressive exporting slashed pharmaceutical production; price hikes and distribution problems impacted consumers at the pharmacy. Lack of vitamins, insecticides, disinfectants, febrifuges, anaesthesia, antiseptics and other pharmaceuticals must have contributed to low life expectancy.

Notes

1   See Hélène Seppain, *Contrasting US and German Attitudes to Soviet Trade, 1917– 1991: Politics by Economic Means* (New York: St. Martin's press, 1992) and Anthony Heywood, *Modernizing Lenin's Russia: Economic Reconstruction, Foreign Trade and Railways* (Cambridge: Cambridge University Press, 1999).

2   See Mary Schaeffer Conroy, 'Russian-American Pharmaceutical Relations, 1900– 1945', *Pharmacy in History*, 46(4) (2004) 143–166.

3   For example, see J. Hessler, *A Social History of Soviet Trade* (Princeton: Princeton University Press, 2004); A.M. Ball, *Russia's Last Capitalists: The NEPmen, 1921– 1929* (Berkeley: University of California Press, 1990); R.A. Khaziev, ed., *Bubliki dlia respubliki: istoricheskii profil Nepmenov* [Bagels for the Republic: An Historical Profile of the NEPmen] (Ufa: Bashkir State University Press, 2005).

4   D.J. Youngblood, *Movies for the Masses: Popular Cinema and Soviet Society in the 1920s* (Cambridge: Cambridge University Press, 1992).

5   Y. Goland, 'Currency Regulation in the NEP Period', *Europe-Asia Studies*, 46(8) (1994) 1251–1296.

6   For Ukraine see M.L. Siatinia, *Istoriia farmatsii* [History of Pharmacy] (L'viv: [no publisher cited], 2002) and for Belarus, e-articles by Tat'iana Petrishche, Medical Institute of Vitebsk.

7   The 'Tensions of Europe' (or TOE) project was brought to my attention by Dr Dagmara Jajesniak-Quast, now of the Zentrum fur Zeithistorische Forschung Potsdam. TOE is headquartered at the Technical University Eindhoven, The Netherlands.

8   A. Vishnevskii, *Demograficheskaia modernizatsiia Rossii, 1900–2000* [The Demographic Modernization of Russia] (Moscow: Novoe izdatel'stvo, 2006), pp. 261–262.

9   C. Kobrak, *National Cultures and International Competition: The Experience of Schering AG, 1851–1950* (Cambridge: Cambridge University Press, 2001) pp. 157, 369.

10   See M.S. Conroy, 'Malaria in Late Tsarist Russia,' *Bulletin of the History of Medicine*, 56(1) (1982) 41–55.

11   S.G. Wheatcroft and R.W. Davies, 'Population,' in R.W. Davies, M. Harrison and S.G. Wheatcroft, eds, *The Economic Transformation of the Soviet Union, 1913–1945* (Cambridge University Press, 1994) p. 62.

12   Kobrak, *National Cultures*, p. 48.

13 M.S. Conroy, *In Health and In Sickness: Pharmacy, Pharmacists and the Pharmaceutical Industry in Late Imperial, Early Soviet Russia* (Boulder: East European Monographs, 1994) pp. 137–161, 162–174; 320–393. For toluol and explosives see also Conroy, *The Soviet Pharmaceutical Business during Its First Two Decades, 1917–1937* (New York: Peter Lang, 2006) p. 27.

14 Conroy, 'Abuse of Drugs other than Alcohol and Tobacco in the Soviet Union', *Soviet Studies*, 42(3) (1990) 447–480.

15 Conroy, 'Health Care in Prisons, Labour and Concentration Camps in Early Soviet Russia, 1918–1921', *Europe-Asia Studies*, 52(7) (2000) 1257–1274; Conroy, *The Soviet Pharmaceutical Business*, pp. 47–73. See also I. I. Levinshtein, compiler, *V. S. N. Kh., Farmatrest: Ukazatel' predpriiatii i tovarnyi katalog* [The All Russian Council of the National Economy, Farmatrest: An Index of Enterprises and A Catalog of Wares] (Moscow: Tipografiia 'Tsustran' 1922) pp. 62–90.

16 R. Riedl, 'A Brief History of the Pharmaceutical Industry in Basel', in J. Libenau, G. J. Higby and E. C. Stroud, *Pill Peddlers: Essays on the History of the Pharmaceutical Industry* (Madison, WI: American Institute of the History of Pharmacy, 1990), p. 56.

17 K. Ammann, 'Istoriia shveitsarskoi farmatsevticheskoi kompanii v vostochnoi evrope (1900–1950). F. Hoffmann-La Roche AG v S. Peterburge i varshave' [A History of a Swiss Pharmaceutical Company in Eastern Europe (1900–1950). F. Hoffman-LaRoche in St. Petersburg and Warsaw]', in I.V. Narskii, ed., *Gorizonty lokal'noi istorii Vostochnoi evropy v XIX-XX vekakh* [Horizons of the Local History of Eastern Europe in the 19th–20th Centuries] (Cheliabinsk: Izdatel'stvo 'Kamennyi poias', 2003) pp. 124–128.

18 Riedl, 'A Brief History', pp. 57–58.

19 Riedl, ibid., pp. 64–65, 67–69.

20 M. Robson, 'The French Pharmaceutical Industry, 1919–1939', in Libenau et al., *Pill Peddlars*, pp. 109–115.

21 Kobrak, *National Cultures*, pp. 51–141.

22 Kobrak, ibid., pp. 187–191.

23 Kobrak, ibid., pp. 156–158.

24 Kobrak, ibid., pp. 217–254.

25 Kobrak, ibid., pp. 105, 116, 118–121, 124, 148, 151–156, 160, 178, 183–200.

26 L. Gartsshtein, 'Proizvodstvennaia rabota Gosmedtorgprom'a' [The Industrial Work of Gosmedtorgprom], *Khimiko-farmatsevticheskii zhurnal* [Chemical–Pharmaceutical Journal], 2(10–12) (1924) pp. 13–15.

27 Details in Conroy, *The Soviet Pharmaceutical Business*, pp. 117–120.

28 Rossiiskii Gosudarstvennyi Arkhiv Ekonomiki [Russian State Archive of the Economy, hereafter RGAE], f. 871, op. 1, d. 11, Contracts with local Aptekoupravleniia [Pharmacy Administrations], 1923–1924, unnumbered *listy*.

29 Gartsshtein, 'Proizvodstvennaia', p. 13.

30 Capital from the sequestered enterprises amounted to about 7 million rubles. Farmatrest received 1,000 million (inflated) rubles when it was separated from Glavkhim and some materials and fuel from Glavkhim amounting to 4½ million rubles (RGAE, f. 1840, op. 1, d. 19, p. 26 of the Trust's financial report). Farmatrest received credit from the State Bank (20,000 million rubles in December 1921 and 60,000 million rubles in March 1922), which charged 8 per cent interest, and had a line of credit with the Banking Department of Vesenkha (20,000 million rubles for 1½ to 2 months at 24 per cent interest per month and 1 per cent commission. In 1923 Farmatrest received a long-term loan of 9 million rubles (RGAE, f. 1840, op. 1, d. 19, l. 14 ob. and p. 24 of the trust's annual report).

31   RGAE, f. 1840, op. 1, d. 19, ll. 12, 12 ob., 14, 14 ob., 15, 18, 19.
32   Conroy, *The Soviet Pharmaceutical Business*, p. 221.
33   RGAE, f. 8140, op. 1, d. 24, l. 71.
34   RGAE, f. 871, op. 3, d. 13, ll. 2, 3, 4.
35   RGAE, f. 8140, op. 1, d. 24, l. 18, 26; f. 871, op. 3, d. 20, l. 2; f. 871, op. 3, d. 16, l. 9.
36   In 1913 Liflandskaia *Gubernaia* [Lifland Province] – roughly Latvia – was highly developed, with 12 chemical factories (some highly capitalized), three soap and perfume firms, 12 factories producing dyes, dry distillation of wood and coal, as well as other factories; *Khimicheskoe delo v Rossii* [The Chemical Business in Russia] (Odessa: Tipografiia 'Poriadok', 1913), cols. 161–163, 190–191, 252–253.
37   RGAE, f. 8140, op. 1, d. 34, ll. 16–17 ob.
38   RGAE, f. 871, op. 3, d. 17, ll. 73, 75, 76, 76 ob., 77, 78.
39   D.B. Worthen, *Pharmacy in World War II* (New York: Haworth Press, 2004) p. 80.
40   R. Pipes, *The Unknown Lenin* (New Haven: Yale University Press, 1996) p. 83.
41   R. Lewis, 'Foreign Economic Relations', in Davies, Harrison, and Wheatcroft, *The Economic Transformation*, p. 203.
42   RGAE, f. 871, op. 3, d. 3, l. 8.
43   RGAE, f. 871, op. 3, d. 13, ll. 2, 3, 4.
44   RGAE, f. 871, op. 3, d. 17, ll. 76, 78.
45   RGAE, f. 871, op. 3, d. 37, ll. 23–30.
46   RGAE, f. 8140, op. 1, d. 19, ll. 56–57 ob. In 1924 Gosmedtorgprom (the new name of the core pharmaceutical industry, now merged with its trading arm) stopped purchasing camphor from Moshkin because it was more expensive than foreign camphor. RGAE, f. 8140, op. 1, d. 29, l. 143.
47   RGAE, f. 871, op. 3, d. 17, l. 43.
48   RGAE, f. 871, op. 1, d. 11, no numbers on list, contract 1.
49   RGAE, f.871, op. 3, d. 17, l. 43.
50   RGAE, f. 871, op. 1, d. 28, l. 4, ll. 40, 29.
51   RGAE, f. 8140, op. 1, d. 24, ll. 18--28 (71–92).
52   RGAE, f. 871, op. 3, d. 17, l. 43.
53   Kobrak, *National Cultures*, pp. 157–158.
54   RGAE, f. 871. op. 3, f. 20. l. 2.
55   RGAE, f.871, op. 1, d. 28, l. 45. Theobromine, an alkaloid derived from the cacao bean, was used as a diuretic and nerve stimulant.
56   RGAE, f.871, op. 3, d. 20, l. 62.
57   *Kratkii ocherk deiatel'nosti 'Gosmedtorgproma'* [A Brief Sketch of the Activity of 'Gosmedtorgprom'] (Moscow: Tipografiia 'Gosmedtorgprom'a' Krivokolennyi pereulok, 12 [the printing press of the old V.F. Ferrein Pharmaceutical Company], 1927) p. 6.
58   ibid., pp. 13, 17–18. Apparently Vesenkha had given out too many licences in the first quarter of the year and was forced to withhold permissions during the rest of the year.
59   RGAE, f. 871, op. 3, d. 93, ll. 1, 2.
60   Original citation in Conroy, *In Health and in Sickness*, p. 342; note 192, p. 607.
61   Some important raw materials absent included tannin from nut gall (*chernil'nykh oreshkakh*), alkaloids from opium, sublimate and calomel from mercury, green soap made from vegetable oil, castor oil from the *kleshchevina* plant, and vinegar anhydride made from vinegar acid potassium. Aktsionernoe

Obshchestvo 'Gosmedtorgprom': *Kratkii otchet o rabote Gosmedtorgproma za 1925/26 operats. god.* [The Stock Company 'Gosmedtorgprom': A Short Report About the Work of Gosmedtorgprom for the 1925/26 Operating Year] (Moscow: Tipografiia 'Gosmedtorgprom[sans the genitive] (1927) pp. 6–7, 9.

62   RGAE, f. 871, op. 3, d. 37, ll. 1, 2, 4, 6, 7, 8, 11–12.

63   RGAE, f. 871, op. 3, d. 37, l. 13, 13 ob..

64   L. Gartsshtein, 'Narkomvneshtorg i torgovlia medikamentami [The People's Commissariat of Foreign Trade and trade in Medicaments]', *Khimiko-farmatsevticheskii zhurnal*, [no vol. number cited] 2 (5) (1924) 5–6.

65   S. Mar, 'K voprosu o 'nozhnitsakh' v farmatsevticheskom dele[On the Issue of 'Discrepancies' in the Pharmaceutical Business]', *Khimiko-farmatsevticheskii zhurnal*, [no vol. number cited] 1 (4) (1924) 4–6.

66   F. Ferrein, 'Tamozhnye tarify i ikh znachenie dlia khimiko-farmatsevticheskoi promyshlennosti [Customs Tariffs and Their Significance for the Chemical-Pharmaceutical Industry]', *Khimiko-farmatsevticheskii zhurnal,*, 10–12 [8–9] (1924) 9–11.

67   Davies and Khlevnyuk, 'Gosplan', in Davies, Harrison, Wheatcroft, *The Economic Transformation of the Soviet Union*, p. 34.

68   *Kratkii otchet o rabote Gosmedtorgproma za oktiabr'–iiun' 1926–27 oper. god* [A Short Report About the Work of Gosmedtorgprom for the October to June 1926–27 Operating Year] (Moscow: Tipografiia 'Zaria kommunizma', 1927) pp. 22, 25, 27.

69   Duties on mercury preparations shot up 266 per cent; those on bromine, iodine, and their compounds were raised 222 per cent; duties on salts containing silver were raised 200 pe cent; duties for adrenaline were raised 147 per cent; those for cocoa oil, ether oil and cocaine were raised 111 per cent, 400 per cent, and 490 per cent, respectively. High duties were placed on alkaloids produced in the USSR, an improvement over the 1924 tariff which imposed high duties on alkaloids even if they were not produced in the USSR. Prohibitively high import duties were imposed on cosmetics and perfumes and also on medical instruments. The reason for the rise in import duties was 'to protect domestic industry', but undoubtedly increasing state revenues also was a consideration. I. Bychkov, 'Oblozhenie poshlinami importnykh medtovarov [Taxation by Customs Duties of Imported Medical Wares]', *Khimiko-farmatsevticheskii zhurnal*, 7(43) (1927) 10–11.

70   Conroy, *In Health and In Sickness*, pp. 165–168.

71   'V Ukrmedtorg', [In the Ukrainian Medical Sales Office], *Farmatsevticheskii zhurnal* [Pharmaceutical Journal], 1(10) (1928) 578.

72   RGAE, f. 8009, op. 2, d. 126, l. 100. For details see Conroy, *The Soviet Pharmaceutical Business*, p. 115.

73   I. Ia. Bychkov, 'Farmatsevticheskaia promyshlennost': Proizvodstvo meditsinskikh instrumentov i priborov v SSSR [The Pharmaceutical Industry: Production of Medical Instruments and Apparatus in the USSR]', *Khimiko-farmatsevticheskii zhurnal*, 6(12) [60] (1928) 7.

74   Kobrak, *National Cultures*, p. 369.

75   Shass and Satsyperov, *Lekarstvennye i lekarstvenno-tekhnicheskie rasteniia SSSR, sbor, kultura, pererabotka i eksport* [Medicinal and Medical–Industrial Crops in the USSR, Collection, Cultivation, Processing and Export] (Moscow, 1927), pp. 13, 141.

76   RGAE, f. 871, op. 1, d. 28, ll. 5, 7, 40, 45.

77   S. Ia. Shiutte and E. Iu. Shass, *Gosudarstvennyi Standart eksportnogo lekarstvennogo i lekarstvenno-tekhnicheshkogo syr'ia, offitisal'nyi tekst s prilozheniiami, sostavlennymi direktorom Khimicheskogo Direktora S. Ia. Shiutte i Gosudarvennym brakerom*

po leksyr'iu E. Iu. Shass [The State Standard of Exported Medicinal and Medical–Industrial Raw Materials, An Official Text with Applications, Compiled by the Director of the Chemical Directory, S. Ia. Shiutte, and the State Inspector for Medical Raw Materials, E. Iu. Shass] (Moscow: Narkomtorg SSSR, 1927). Addresses of London and Paris branches in above, p. 73.

78 For the last three agencies see E. Iu. Shass, *Gosudarstvennyi standart eksportnogo lekarstvennogo i lekarstvenno-tekhnicheskogo syr'ia* [The State Standard of Exported Medicinal and Medical–Industrial Raw Materials] (Moscow: Izdatel'stvo Narkomtorg SSSR, 1927), pp. 4–5.

79 See Conroy, *The Soviet Pharmaceutical Business*, pp. 19, 59, 82–83.

80 RGAE, f. 871, op. 1, d. 11, no list number, between agreement 5 and agreement 8 in file.

81 Conroy, *The Soviet Pharmaceutical Business*, pp. 101–102.

82 Shass and Satsyperov, *Lekarstvennye rasteniia*, p. 12.

83 RGAE, f. 871, op. 1, d. 28, ll. 5, 7, 40, 45.

84 RGAE, f. 871, op. 1, d. 28, l. 45, 60 ob, 61, 64 ob.

85 *Kratkii Ocherk Deiatel'nosti Glavnoi Khimicheskoi i Farmatsevticheskoi Kontory Gostorga 'Khimfarmtorg'*, [A Brief Sketch of the Activity of the Chief Chemical Office of the State Trading Agency 'Khimfarmtorg'] (Moscow: [no publisher cited], 1926), pp. 11–13.

86 Shass and Satsyperov, *Lekarstvennye rasteniia*, p. 142.

87 Ibid., pp. 13, 76–82.

88 Ibid., p. 157.

89 *Kratkii otchet o rabote Gosmedtorgproma za 1925/26 operats. god*, p. 22.

90 Ibid., p. 22.

91 Ibid., pp. 21–22. The exact amount was 39.5 per cent.

92 *Kratkii otchet ... za oktiabr'-iiun' 1926–27 oper. god.*, p. 26.

93 Lyman D. Wilbur, 'Surveying Through Khoresm: A Journey Into Parts of Asiatic Russia Which Have been Closed to Western Travelers Since the World War', *The National Geographic Magazine*, 41(6) (1932) 757.

94 A.A. Utin, *Istoriia chimkentskogo khimiko-farmatsevticheskogo zavoda im. F. E. Dzerzhinskogo* [A History of the Chimkent Chemical–Pharmaceutical Factory Named for F. E. Dzerzhinskii] (Chimkent: Biuro tekhnicheskoi informatsii, 1958), pp. 37–38.

95 Utin, *Istoriia*, pp. 35–37.

96 Ibid., p. 37.

97 Utin, *Istoriia chimkentskogo khimiko-farmatsevticheskogo zavoda*, pp. 38–42.

98 *Kratkii otchet o rabote Akts. O-va 'Gosmedtorgproma' za 1927–28 op. god.* [A Short Report About the Work of the Stock Company 'Gosmedtorgprom' for the 1927–28 Operating Year] (Moscow: Mostipograph 'Zaria kommunizma', 1929), p. 9.

99 Utin, *Istoriia chimkentskogo khimiko-farmatsevticheskogo zavoda*, p. 49.

100 It should be noted that Russia standardized rhubarb in the seventeenth and eighteenth centuries, exporting only the best quality. C.M. Foust, *Rhubarb: The Wondrous Drug* (Princeton: Princeton University Press, 1992).

101 'Predpriiatiia Gosmedtorgproma', *Kratkii ocherk deiatel'nosti 'Gosmedtorgproma'*, [The Enterprises of Gosmedtorgprom, A Brief Sketch of the Activity of 'Gosmedtorgprom'], p. 13. Skublinskii was the plenipoteniary in charge of iodine production in Baku. Zemlinskii was in charge of medicinal plants in Leningrad, Chulkov occupied the post in Voronezh, Tsirlin in the Caucasus, Radilevskii in Kiev, Timchenko in Rostov-on-the-Don and Iakuner in Odessa.

102 R-r Rann, 'Chto dolzhen znat' farmatsevt pri prigotovlenii lekarstvennykh form iz naperstianki' [What the Pharmacist Must Know In the Preparation of Medicinal Forms From Foxglove], (translation of A.G. Fisher from *Pharmatzeutfiche Zeitung*, 20 (1926) 312), *Khimiko-farmatsevticheskii vestnik* [Chemical–Pharmaceutical News], 1(5–6) (1926) 6–9.

103 Shiutte and Shass, *Gosudarstvennyi standart*, p. 4. For details see Conroy, *The Soviet Pharmaceutical Business*, pp. 125–126.

104 Shiutte and Shass, *Gosudarstvennyi standart*, p. 3.

105 Shiutte and Shass, ibid., passim.

106 Shass and Satsyperov, *Lekarstevnnye rasteniia*.

107 N.A. Monteverde, et al. Sev. zap. oblastnaia torgovaia palata: Biuro Lekarstvennii, *Lekarstvennoe promyshlennoe syr'e: Rukovodstvo po standartizatsii* [The North-western Oblast' (Regional) Trade Office: Bureau of Medicinal and Medicinal Industrial Raw Materials: Guidelines for Standardization] (Leningrad: Tipografiia Tvorchestvo, 1927).

108 E. Iu. Shass, *Orientirovochnaia kal'kulatsiia nakladnykh raskhodov na eksportnoe leksyr'e po severo-zapadnoi oblasti* [The Approximate Calculation of Superimposed or Overhead Expenditures on Exported Raw Materials of the North-western Oblast'] (Leningrad: Publication of the author, 1927).

109 RGAE, f. 871, op. 3, d. 19, ll. 7–8.

110 RGAE, f. 871, op. 3, d. 37, l. 4.

111 RGAE, f. 871, op. 3, d. 19, ll. 4, 6, 6 ob.

112 For details see Conroy, *The Soviet Pharmaceutical business*, pp. 92–94.

113 W.A. Williams, *American-Russian Relations, 1781–1947* (New York: Octagon Books, 1971). On details of technological transfers for cash, see p. 210. For trade proposals to develop the Donets State Coal Trust in 1925, proposals and trade between the USSR and General Electric, Chase Manhattan Bank, Bethlehem Steel, Standard Oil, various engineering and other American firms during the 1920s, see pp. 177–228.

114 See H. Klehr, J. E. Haynes and F. I. Firsov, *The Secret World of American Communism* (New Haven and London: Yale University Press, 1995), pp. 26–29.

115 Full information in the author's manuscript biography of Neal.

116 M. Weatherall, *In Search of a Cure: A History of Pharmaceutical Discovery* (New York: Oxford University Press, 1990), pp. 84–89.

117 See Conroy, *In Health and In Sickness*, pp. 133–134.

118 See Kobrak, *National Cultures*, pp. 116–117 and Conroy, *The Soviet Pharmaceutical Business*, pp. 129–131 and note 117, pp. 302–303.

119 For details see Conroy, ibid., p. 128.

120 RGAE, f. 871, op. 3, d. 30.

121 RGAE, f. 871, op. 3, d. 56, ll. 1–7.

122 RGAE, f. 871, op. 3, d. 107, ll. 53, 55.

123 See Conroy, *The Soviet Pharmaceutical Business*, p. 129.

124 On production of these items by Beechams and other British firms in the inter-war period, see R.P.T. Davenport-Hines and Judy Slinn, *Glaxo: A History to 1962* (Cambridge: Cambridge University Press, 1992), p. 86. On Russian output of these products see *Kratkii ocherk deiatel'nosti 'Gosmedtorgproma'*, (1927) pp. 5, 10. Besides the 'patented' items cited, the USSR Commissariat of Health approved five others for production in the factories of Gosmedtorgprom.

125 For example, D. Shcherbachev, 'Obzor novykh sredstv' [A Survey of New Substances], *Khimiko-farmatsevticheskii zhurnal* [Chemical Pharmaceutical Journal], 1(4) (1924) 13–14; V. Izmail'skii, 'Khloraminy—novyi tip antiseptiki'

[Chloramines—A New Type of Antiseptics], ibid., p. 17; 'Frantsuzskie sal'varsonye preparaty' [French Salvarsan Preparations], loc. cit.; 'Tonephosphan,' loc. cit.; 'Sintez letsitina' [The Synthesis of Lecithin], loc. cit.; V.A. Izmail'skii, 'O Stovarsole i sal'varsanovykh preparatakh' [About Stovarsole and Salvarsan Preparations], 2(5), (1924) 14–16; A. Mogil'skii, 'Kolichestvennoe opredelenie khimicheskikh, farmatsevticheskikh i galenovykh preparatov' [Quantitative Determination of Chemical, Pharmaceutical and Galenical Preparations], *Khimiko-farmatsevticheskii zhurnal*, 2(5) (1924) 17.

126   *Kratkii otchet...za 1925/26 operats. god.*, p. 8. Urotropin was a Schering product, an internal disinfectant, first produced in 1913. Kobrak, *National Cultures and International Competition*, pp. 56, 364. Of course, Russia nationalized the Schering Factory in Moscow during World War I. However, since the product was said to be imported, it does not appear that it was produced in Russia from that time.

127   Vl. Saposhnikov, 'Limonnaia kislota i limonokisloe brozhenie' [Lemon Acid and Lemon-Acid Fermentation], *Khimiko-farmatsevticheskii zhurnal*, no. 6–7 (1924) 17–19.

128   *Kratkii ocherk deiatel'nosti 'Gosmedtorgproma'*, (1927) p. 4.

129   Ibid., pp. 4, 10.

130   'Retsenzii i referaty [Reviews and Synopses]', *Khimiko-farmatsevticheskii vestnik* (Odessa), no. 3–4 (1926) 23–24. The text reviewed was that by S. Loewl (Dorpat), *O novykh metodakh opredeleniia valorizatsii gormonykh preparatov* [About New Methods of Determining the Value of Hormone Preparations].

131   CIBA Limited, *The Story of the Chemical Industry in Basle* (Lausanne: Urs Graf Publishers, 1959) pp. 184–187. For general work on hormones in the 1930s, see Weatherall, *In Search of a Cure*, pp. 94–95.

132   *Kratkii ocherk diatel'nosti 'Gosmedtorgproma'* (1927) pp. 5–9.

133   'Khronika: k 35-letnemy iubileiu B. N. Saltykova' [Chronicle: The 35-Year Jubilee of B. N. Saltykov], *Khimiko-farmatsevticheskii vestnik* (Odessa), no. 3–4 (1926) 24.

134   *Kratkii ocherk deiatel'nosti 'Gosmedtorgproma'* (1927) pp. 8–9.

135   'Akts.-O-vo. "Gosmedtorgprom", *Gosudarstvennyi khimiko-farmatsevticheskii zavod imeni L. Ia. Karpova'* [The Stock Company 'Gosmedtorgprom,' The State Chemical–Pharmaceutical Factory Named for L. Ia. Karpov] (Moscow: Tipografiia 'Gosmedtorgprom'a', 1926), pp. 11–18.

136   *Kratkii otchet...za 1925/26 operats. god.*, p. 8.

137   RGAE, 871, op. 3, d. 16, l. 6.

138   Information *in Kratkii otchet...za 1925/26 operats. god.*, p. 6.

139   *Kratkii otchet...za oktiabr'-iiun' 1926–1927 oper. god.*, p. 8.

140   *Kratkii ocherk deiatel'nosti 'Gosmedtorgproma'* (1927), pp. 6–7.

141   M. S. Conroy, 'The Russian Pharmaceutical Industry in the Late Imperial, Early Soviet Period', in K. McDermott and J. Morison, *Politics and Society Under the Bolsheviks* (Basingstoke: Macmillan, 1999) p. 28.

142   *Kratkii ocherk deiatel'nosti 'Gosmedtorgproma'* (1927), pp. 10–11.

143   *Kratkii otchet...za oktiabr'-iiun' 1926–27 oper. god.*, p. 12.

144   S.I. Tilles, 'K istorii belomorskogo ioda' [On the History of White Sea Iodine], *Khimiko-farmatsevticheskii zhurnal*, 5(7) [43] (1927) 11.

145   F.A. Ferrein, 'Uspekhi v snabzhenii khimiko-farmatsevticheskoi promyshlen-nosti syr'em i polufabrikantami [Achievements in Supplying the Chemical–Pharmaceutical Industry with Raw and Partially Fabricated Materials]', *Khimiko-farmatsevticheskii zhurnal*, 6(22) [70] (1928) 5–6; iodine, p. 6.

146 This appears to have been no longer a Hoffmann-LaRoche product but a Soviet item, as were 'Aspirin' and 'Piramidon' in the mid-1920s. For the Soviet clones of the latter, formerly German-made products, see 'Otlichie original'nykh 'Aspirin'a' i 'Piramidon'a' ot preparatov, ikh zameniaiushchikh' [Distinctions of the Original 'Aspirin' and 'Pyramidon' from Preparations, Replacing Them], *Khimiko-farmatevticheskii vestnik* (Odessa), no. 7–8 (1926) 5.

147 Atophan was 'Schering's product against rheumatic conditions', Kobrak, *National Cultures*, pp. 56–57. See also p. 364. Again, although Russia nationalized the Schering Factory during World War I, since the product was said to be imported, it does not seem that it was produced by Schering in Russia.

148 Conroy, 'The Russian Pharmaceutical Industry', pp. 27–28.

149 Ia. Mazover, 'Gosudarstvennyi salitsilovyi zavod' [The State Salicylic Factory], *Khimiko-farmatsevticheskii zhurnal*, 6(12) [60] (1928) 9.

150 *Kratkii otchet...za 1925/26 operats. god.*, pp. 8, 9, 16.

151 *Kratkii otchet...za oktiabr'-iiun, 1926–27*, pp. 17–18.

152 Ibid., p. 27.

153 Ibid., pp., 12–13, 28–29, 8–9, 26, 32, respectively.

154 Ibid., pp. 5, 9.

155 L. Gartsshtein, 'Farmatsevticheskaia promyshlennost'. Torgovaia politika Gosmedtorgproma' [The Pharmaceutical Industry. Trade Policies of Gosmedtorgprom], *Khimiko-farmatsevticheskii zhurnal*, 5(3) [39] (1927) 9–10.

156 M.I. Iaroslav, 'Nuzhno li Ukraine svoe khimiko-farmatsevticheskoe proizvodstvo' [Does the Ukraine Need Its Own Chemical–Pharmaceutical Production], *Farmatsevticheskii zhurnal*, 2(2) (1928) 20–21.

157 A. Aluf, 'Ratsionalizatsiia lekarstvennykh form' [The Rationalization of Medicinal Forms], *Khimiko-farmatsevticheskii zhurnal*, 5(2) [38] (1927) 2.

158 Tsentralnyi Gosudarstvennyi Istoricheskii Arkhiv Respublika Bashkortostana [The Central State Historical Archive of the Republic of Bashkortostan], f. 1203, op, 2, d. 1, ll. 115, 115 ob., 146, 149, 148, 151–153.

159 For details see Conroy, *The Soviet Pharmaceutical Business*, pp. 139–148.

160 Kobrak, *National Cultures*, p. 151.

161 I am indebted to Professor, Dr Stephan Merl, University of Bielefeld, for this query.

162 G.N. Grob, *The Deadly Truth* (Harvard University Press, 2002), pp. 182–212 and passim.

163 Vishnevskii, *Demograficheskaia modernizatsiia Rossii, 1900–2000*, p. 264.

4

A Comparative Analysis of Japanese Foreign Direct Investment in Central Europe and China

Ken Morita and Yun Chen

Introduction

Generally speaking, transition economies face greater barriers than advanced industrialised economies in attracting inward foreign direct investment (FDI). In this chapter, we analyse the role of Japanese FDI in two transition economies (Poland and China) and make three main points. First, we investigate the motives and determinants of Japanese FDI in Central Europe and China and demonstrate how risk-averse investors make their decisions about investing in these higher-risk transition economies. Second, since avoiding risk is important to Japanese investors and Poland and China each represent relatively high-risk locations, we analyse what the implications of the scale of FDI are in each. Third, we examine some of the ways these countries are trying to alleviate risk and boost FDI. We focus particularly on what has been called the 'sovereign partnership approach'.[1]

Background

An overview: Central Europe and China

Since 1989, Poland and China have adopted contrasting approaches to reform. Poland adopted a radical approach to restructuring compared with the more gradual and earlier reforms of other Central European countries, such as Hungary. Hungary had initiated reforms in 1968 and adopted a more gradual approach after 1989. Chinese reforms also began early, with strong state management reforms being initiated at the end of 1978, with market socialism emerging gradually.

Table 4.1 reports basic indicators for the three countries. The scale of some of China's key indicators (such as population and Gross National Income

Table 4.1 Several basic indicators

	China	Poland	Hungary
Population (millions, 2003)	1,288.4	38.2	10.1
GNI (US$billion, 2003)	1,417	201	64
Per capita GNI (US$, 2003)	1,100	5,270	6,330
GDP growth rate (%, annual average, 1990–2003)	9.5	4.7	2.4
Value added as % of GDP (2003)	Agriculture 15 Industry 53 Services 32	Agriculture 3 Industry 31 Services 66	Agriculture 4 Industry 31 Services 65
Gini index	0.447 (2001) 0.376 (1992)	0.316 (1999) 0.272 (1992)	0.244 (1999) 0.279 (1993)
Life expectancy at birth (2002)	71	74	72
Population below the poverty line (national poverty line, %)	4.6 (1998)	23.8 (1993)	17.3 (1997)
Corruption Perception Index	3.4 (2004) 3.1 (2000)	3.5 (2004) 4.1 (2000)	4.8 (2004) 5.2 (2000)
Tax revenue % of GDP (1997)	4.9	35.2	32.5
Inward FDI (flow, US$ million, 2002)	52,700	4,119	857
Inward FDI (stock, US$ million, 2002)	447,892	45,150	24,416
High-technology exports % of manufactured exports (2002)	23	3	25
World Competitiveness Ranking	(2004) 31 (2005)	57 (2004) 57 (2005)	42 (2004) 37 (2005)

Sources: World Bank, *World Development Report*, annual, UNCTAD, *World Investment Report*, annual, Transparency International, *Global Corruption Report*, annual, IMD World Competitiveness Yearbook, annual.

GNI)) is so large that they dwarf those of these other two countries: 33.7 times and 127.6 times greater than Poland's and Hungary's respectively (in population), and 7 times and 22 times larger than Poland's and Hungary's (in GNI). However, China's per capita GNI was 5.8 times less than Hungary's and 4.8 times less than Poland's.

Japanese inward investment to China in 2002 was US$ 52.7 billion, to Poland it was US$ 4.1 billion, and to Hungary US$ 0.86 billion. Total FDI in 2002 amounted to US$ 447.9 billion (China), US$ 45.1 billion (Poland), and US$ 24.4 billion (Hungary). Per capita inward FDI stock in 2002 in

Poland and in Hungary was 3.3 and 7 times more respectively than in China.

Average GDP growth rates between 1990 and 2003 were 9.5 per cent per annum (China), 4.7 per cent (Poland) and 2.4 per cent (Hungary). The Gini coefficients in Poland (1999) and in Hungary (1999) were 0.316 and 0.244 respectively, reflecting moderate income disparity, but, by contrast, China's Gini coefficient (2001) reached 0.447, reflecting deepening income disparities across the country.

Agricultural and industrial value added as shares of GDP (2003) in China were much higher than in Poland and Hungary, but the Chinese service share was less. The high-technology component of Poland's manufacturing exports was only three per cent in 2002, far lower than Hungary's 25 per cent and China's 23 per cent share. Poland's competitiveness ranking was correspondingly inferior (57th in 2005), compared with China (31st) and Hungary (37th). By contrast, China has much less tax revenue as a proportion of GDP (4.9 per cent in 1997) than Poland (35.2 per cent) and Hungary (32.5 per cent).

The 2004 corruption perception index (10 being highly 'clean', 0 being highly 'corrupt') rates all three countries poorly. Out of 145 countries rated, China was ranked 71st with a corruption index of 3.4, Poland was 67th with 3.5, and Hungary was 42nd with 4.8.

Inward FDI in Central Europe and China

The Polish case

Delayed privatization and liberalization have been significant elements in sustaining Poland's high unemployment rate, its low competitiveness ranking, low levels of high-tech exports and low structural reform index score. On all these measures, Hungary and the Czech Republic are more efficient and have been more attractive for foreign investors.

Poland's economic performance between 2000 and 2005 has been uneven (Table 4.2). Real annual GDP growth is positive but low, ranging from 4 per cent in 2000 to 3.4 per cent in 2005. Unemployment is high (about 20 per cent), but has been declining as a result of out-migration and efficiency increases flowing with the government's 'second wave of restructuring'.[2]

GUS (annual) and WERI (semi-annual) data show that unemployment is significant in each voivodship (region) but with pronounced regional disparities among them. For example, between 1997 and 2003 unemployment rates in Mazowieckie increased from 7.3 to 15.1 per cent and from 19.7 to 30.6 per cent in Warminsko-mazurskie. Such high levels of unemployment have posed serious challenges for a government required to decrease its budget deficit to satisfy the Maastricht Convergence Criteria and implement new rounds of restructuring. Indeed, with a structural reform index score of 86 compared with scores for the Czech Republic and Hungary of 93

Table 4.2 Economic indicators of Polish economic performance

	2000	2001	2002	2003	2004	2005
Real GDP growth rate (%)	4.0	1.0	1.4	3.8	5.3	3.4
Inflation (CPI, %)	10.1	5.5	1.9	0.8	3.5	2.1
Unemployment rate (%)	15.1	19.4	20.0	20.0	19.1	18.1
Balance of payment (million US$)	−9,952	−7,166	−5,009	−4,599	−10,522	−4,364
Foreign deficit (million S$)	69,465	71,797	84,875	106,961	128,658	129,453
Foreign Exchange Reserves (million S$)	26,562	25,648	29,794	34,168	36,783	42,571
Budget deficit (percentage of GDP)	−2.2	−4.5	−5.4	−4.8	−3.9	−3.4

Sources: JETRO (Warsaw Office). World Economy Research Institute, *Poland: International Economic Report*, Annual; JETRO [Japan External Trade Organization], *Sekai to Nihon no Kaigai Chokusetsu Toushi* [Foreign Direct Investment of the World and Japan] (Tokyo, JETRO, Annual).

Table 4.3 Structural reform index

	1990	1991	1992	1993	1994	1995	1996	1997	1998	1999	2000
Bulgaria	0.19	0.62	0.86	0.66	0.63	0.61	0.57	0.67	0.79	0.79	0.85
Czech Rep.	0.16	0.79	0.86	0.90	0.88	0.82	0.82	0.82	0.90	0.90	0.93
Estonia	0.20	0.32	0.64	0.81	0.83	0.77	0.78	0.82	0.90	0.93	0.93
Hungary	0.57	0.74	0.78	0.82	0.83	0.82	0.82	0.87	0.93	0.93	0.93
Latvia	0.13	0.29	0.51	0.67	0.71	0.67	0.74	0.74	0.86	0.86	0.82
Lithuania	0.13	0.33	0.55	0.78	0.79	0.71	0.74	0.74	0.82	0.82	0.86
Poland	0.68	0.72	0.82	0.82	0.83	0.79	0.79	0.81	0.86	0.86	0.86
Romania	0.22	0.36	0.45	0.58	0.67	0.65	0.64	0.66	0.76	0.82	0.82
Slovakia	0.16	0.79	0.86	0.83	0.83	0.79	0.79	0.77	0.90	0.90	0.89
Russia	0.04	0.10	0.49	0.59	0.67	0.64	0.71	0.72	0.64	0.64	0.64

Sources: A. Aslund and A. Warner, 'The EU Enlargement: Consequences for the CIS Countries' in M. Dabrowski, B. Sley, and J. Neneman, eds, *Beyond Transition: Development Perspectives and Dilemmas* (Aldershot: Ashgate, 2004) p. 233.

(Table 4.3), by 2000 Poland had entered what we have referred to above as the 'second wave of restructuring'.[3]

Poland had experienced 'a significant increase in regional disparities between 1992 and 1996' and this pattern of regional differentiation has continued and deepened (Table 4.4), although at levels that are much smaller than in China (Table 4.5).[4] Privatization levels were also high in Poland in 1991, but by the end of 1990s they had declined to lower levels than other

Table 4.4   Regional GDPs (Poland)

	1986	1990	1991	1992	1995	1996
Average of top 5 over average of bottom 5	2.19	2.53	2.35	2.03	2.22	2.30

Sources: M. De Broeck and V. Koen, 'The "Soaring Eagle": Anatomy of the Polish Take-Off in the 1990s', IMF Working Paper (Washington DC: International Monetary Fund, 2000) p. 18.

Table 4.5   Regional GDPs (China)

	1955	1965	1975	1985	1995
Average of top 5 over average of bottom 5	4.95	4.15	5.82	4.38	4.57

Source: Authors' calculation.

Table 4.6   Private sector as share of GDP, 1991–1999 (%)

	1991	1992	1993	1994	1995	1996	1997	1998	1999
Poland	40	45	50	55	60	60	65	65	65
Czech Rep.	15	30	45	65	70	75	75	75	80
Hungary	30	40	50	55	60	70	75	85	80
Russia	5	25	40	50	55	60	70	70	70

Sources: EBRD (European Bank for Reconstruction and Development), *Transition Report* (London: European Bank for Reconstruction and Development, 2000).

Table 4.7   Private sector as share of industry production in China (%)

	1985	1990	1995	1997	2000
Private	3.06	9.76	29.44	36.36	62.57
State	64.86	54.61	33.97	25.52	23.53
Collective	32.08	35.63	36.59	38.11	13.90

Source: K. Nakagane, *Series Gendai Chugoku Keizai 1 – Keizai hatten to Taisei Ikou* [Series Contemporary Chinese Economy 1 – Economic Development and Systemic Transformation] (Nagoya: Nagoya University Press, 2002) p. 157.

countries, particularly Russia (Table 4.6). Over this period, China quickly caught up with Poland in the industrial sector (Table 4.7).

According to the 1997 EBRD *Transition Report*, Hungarian privatization was dominated by sales to outside owners, the Czech Republic by voucher privatization, Russia by voucher privatization and Poland by management and employee buyout. In Poland, only 18 per cent of firm privatization was achieved by sales to new owners, in part because of the limited financial capacity of the few large financially stable state-owned companies.[5]

General trends of inward FDI in Central Europe

Since the early 1990s, the patterns of inward FDI in Central Europe have not fundamentally changed. The Visegrad countries (Poland, Hungary and the Czech Republic) still account for 70 per cent of the total inward FDI (Table 4.8). Inward FDI stocks as a percentage of GDP have grown significantly in all three countries, but only Hungary has shown any significant growth in outward FDI investment as a percentage of GDP (Table 4.9).

Table 4.8   Inward FDI (stock) (US$ million, %)

	1985	1990	1995	2000	2001	2002
Central Europe (*)	49	2,841	31,980	98,137	119,969	145,794
Czech Rep		1,363	7,350	21,644	27,092	38,450
Hungary	49	569	11,919	19,804	23,562	24,416
Poland		109	7,843	34,227	41,031	45,150
Three countries' share of CE	100	71.8	84.8	77.1	76.4	74.1

(*)Central Europe here includes Albania, Bosnia and Herzegovina, Bulgaria, Croatia, the Czech Republic, Hungary, Poland, Romania, Serbia and Montenegro, Slovakia and Slovenia.

Sources: UNCTAD, *World Investment Report 2003.*

Table 4.9   Inward and outward FDI stocks as a percentage of GDP (%)

		1980	1985	1990	1995	2000	2001	2002
Czech Rep.	inward			3.9	14.1	42.1	47.4	54.8
	outward				0.7	1.4	2.0	2.1
Hungary	inward		0.2	1.7	26.7	42.5	45.4	38.2
	outward			0.6	1,1	4.4	8.4	7.3
Poland	inward			0.2	6.2	21.7	22.4	23.9
	outward			0.2	0.4	0.7	0.6	0.7
China	inward	3.1	3.4	7.0	19.6	32.3	33.2	36.2
	outward			0.7	2.3	2.4	2.7	2.9

Sources: UNCTAD, *World Investment Report 2003.*

Table 4.10   Major home countries of FDI in Poland (stock, actual) (%)

	1999	2000	2001	2002	2003
France	11.0	17.3	19.2	19.8	20.0
USA	14.7	16.1	14.7	14.2	12.5
Germany	17.3	12.9	13.4	12.8	12.1
Netherlands	9.2	9.2	8.6	9.5	14.2
Italy	9.1	7.5	6.6	6.0	5.5
UK	5.9	4.8	5.0	6.6	5.3
Total	100.0	100.0	100.0	100.0	100.0

Source: JETRO (Warsaw office).

The origin of FDI differs among receiving countries in Central Europe, but in all instances the EU is the principal supplier of FDI, with the main investors being Germany, France, the USA, The Netherlands, Italy and the UK (Table 4.10), and has largely been domestic market-seeking in orientation.[6] Although there has been considerable variation across countries, especially in recent years, such market-seeking behaviour is confirmed by UNCTAD's econometric study of 142 countries between 1980 and 1995, showing that the scale of the market in the host nation was a dominant reason for foreign direct investment, while low labour costs were important when the scale of the local market was small.[7]

Whether FDI and economic growth are causally related remains unclear.[8] In general, 'large markets and high-income markets attract more FDI',[9] although there is considerable temporal and spatial variation.

The Chinese economy

Since 2000, the Chinese economy has performed particularly well, with high real GDP growth rates, low rates of inflation, moderate rates of unemployment in urban areas and high levels of net foreign exchange reserves (Table 4.11). Budget deficits are below three per cent, but the most serious challenge caused by recent processes of transition and development has been the growth in income disparities. In the 1980s, these regional income disparities resulted from systemic differences between more centrally planning regions, with their traditional state-owned sectors, and more market-oriented regions with non-state-owned sectors. These were exacerbated by policy differences that support the coastal open strategy while maintaining traditional constraints on inland regions.

In 1990s, the all-fronts policy gradually reduced the importance of policies differentially favouring coastal regions, and at the end of 1992 a

Table 4.11 Economic indicators of Chinese economic performance

	2000	2001	2002	2003	2004	2005
Real GDP growth rate (%)	8.0	7.5	8.3	10.0	10.1	9.9
Inflation (CPI, %)	0.4	0.7	−0.8	1.2	3.9	1.8
Unemployment rate (%)	3.1	3.6	4.0	4.3	4.2	4.2
Balance of payment (million US$)	20,519	17,405	35,421	45,875	68,659	160,818
Foreign deficit (million S$)	145,730	170,110	171,360	193,634	228,600	281,050
Foreign Exchange Reserves (million S$)	165,574	212,165	286,407	403,251	614,500	821,514
Budget deficit (percentage of GDP)	−2.79	−2.58	−3.0	−2.5	−1.46	−1.64

Source: *Chinese Statistical Yearbook*, annual.

development zone boom occurred all over China with regions across the country competing for investment. Since January 1994 a series of tax and budget reforms were implemented, with then Prime Minister Zhu Rongji encouraging reforms in the financial and administrative systems that in turn led to deeper reforms in state-owned enterprises.

After the open door policy initiated in 1978, per capita income in both urban and rural areas increased rapidly, as did income disparities. The Gini coefficient for the whole of China increased from 0.341 in 1988 to 0.397 in 1999, reflecting disparities among regions, sectors, types of enterprises and between urban and rural areas. Since the 1990s, overall income disparities have deepened (World Bank Gini coefficients increased from 0.376 in 1992 to 0.403 in 1998 to 0.447 in 2001), but the disparities between urban and rural areas have deepened even further. 1999 statistics released by the National Statistical Office showed coefficients of 0.397 for the whole of China, with 0.3 within urban and 0.3361 within rural areas. In 2002, the income distribution research team of the Economic Research Institute in Chinese Social Science showed coefficients of 0.319 within urban areas and 0.366 within rural areas, and by March 2004 this same group had shown that coefficients for China as a whole had increased to 0.454.

Gini coefficients in urban areas increased from 0.16 in 1978 to 0.32 in 2000, although there were some years when inequality levels experienced particularly sharp increases; 1985 increases were chiefly due to reforms in wages and prices, the increases of 1988, 1993 and 1994 were mainly caused by inflation, and the 2000 increase was due to wage adjustment policy.

Table 4.12   Per capita income disparities of rural and urban area in China

	Ratio	Engel's coefficient	
	Urban / Rural	Rural	Urban
1978	2.57	67.7	57.50
1980	2.50	61.8	56.90
1985	1.86	57.8	53.31
1989	2.28	54.8	54.50
1990	2.20	58.8	54.24
1991	2.40	57.6	53.80
1992	2.58	57.6	53.04
1993	2.80	58.1	50.32
1994	2.86	58.9	50.04
1995	2.71	58.6	50.09
1996	2.51	56.3	48.76
1997	2.47	55.1	46.60
1998	2.51	53.4	44.66
1999	2.65	52.6	42.07
2000	2.79	49.1	39.44
2001	2.90	47.7	38.20
2002	3.11	46.2	37.68
2003	3.23	45.6	37.10
2004	3.12	47.2	37.10

Source: Chinese Statistical Yearbook 2005 and authors' calculation.

Gini coefficients in rural areas rose from 0.21 in 1978 to 0.35 in 2000 and interregional disparities in levels of inequality within rural areas also rose. These disparities were driven by geographical differences in industrial structure and factor endowments, as well as by the differential degrees of proximity to large urban areas and to the rapidly developing regions of the east (Table 4.12). In these regions, non-farm income has played a crucial role in village economic development and, in turn, has exacerbated income disparities among farming communities.

Regional per capita GDP disparities have also been significant, driven in particular by the remarkable expansion of Eastern incomes (see Table 4.13).

Table 4.13 Per capita GDP and disparity among three regions in China

	1980	1990	2000	2002	2003
Per capita GDP (yuan)					
East	598	2,240	11,334	14,363	18,931.4
Central	391	1,338	5,982	7,047	8,293.3
West	306	1,156	4,687	5,536	6,493.3
Ratio					
Central/East	0.65	0.60	0.53	0.49	0.44
West/East	0.51	0.52	0.41	0.39	0.34

Per capita GDP is in nominal.

Source: *Chinese Statistical Yearbook,* annual, and authors' calculation.

Taking per capita GDP in the East as the basis for an index of 100, 1980 coefficients for the Central and Western regions were 65 and 51 respectively and in 1990 they were 60 and 52. Since 1990, however, these disparities have deepened at a rapid rate; by 2000 the Central and Western regions had indices of 53 and 41, by 2002 they were 49 and 39, and in 2003 they were 44 and 34. For our present purposes, we turn now to ask how these disparities in China correlate with inward FDI.[10]

General Trends of Inward FDI in China

Inward FDI in China has expanded since Deng Xiaoping's Southern Journey was carried out in 1992. Actually, since the beginning of the 1990s, government policy allocating resources to particular regions and industries has shaped the levels and patterns of inward FDI and, by the late 1990s, had caused inward FDI to slow as government regulations were imposed against inward FDI (see Table 4.14). Over this period, the main investors remained largely unchanged (Table 4.15). The Hong Kong share of inward FDI decreased to around 30 per cent, although it remains the most important source of investment. FDI from the Virgin Islands is probably also investment linked to Chinese business networks with capital coming from Taiwan.

Chen, Chang and Zhang insist that FDI has 'been associated with phenomena such as ... the accelerating uneven development between the coastal and inland provinces [and] worsening income distribution',[11] findings that are also supported by Chen and Demurger, who have suggested that FDI might have been particularly important in creating regional disparities in those sectors and regions of the economy that have been most open to FDI.[12] For Tseng and Zebregs 'at the national and the provincial level, empirical studies have found a strong correlation between GDP and FDI inflow in China' with causality between the two running in both directions.[13] Empirical investigations of FDI effects in the Yangtze River Delta region between 1990 and 1995 have further suggested that FDI inflow had

Table 4.14   FDI inflows in China (flow)

	US$ million
1992	11,156
1993	27,515
1994	33,787
1995	35,849
1996	40,800
1997	44,236
1998	43,751
1999	40,319
2000	40,772
2001	46,846
2002	52,700
2003	53,505
2004	60,630
2005	60,320

Sources: UNCTAD, *World Investment Report*, Annual, *Chinese Statistical Yearbook 2005, Statistical bulletin of National Economy and Social Development in China 2005,* and authors' calculation.

Table 4.15   Major home countries of FDI in China (flow, actual) (%)

	1999	2000	2001	2002	2003	2004
Hong Kong, Macao, Taiwan	47.8	44.6	42.7	42.3	40.2	37.3
Hong Kong	41.3	38.9	36.3	34.8	33.9	32.2
Macao	6.4	5.6	6.4	7.5	6.3	5.1
Taiwan	3.2	3.7	4.6	5.2	8.4	10.3
ASEAN 10 countries	8.2	7.0	6.4	6.2	5.5	5.0
Singapore	6.6	5.3	4.6	4.4	3.8	3.3
Malaysia	0.6	0.5	0.6	0.7	0.5	0.6
Thailand	0.4	0.5	0.4	0.4	0.3	0.3
Philippines	0.3	0.3	0.4	0.4	0.4	0.4
Indonesia	0.3	0.4	0.3	0.2	0.3	0.2
Japan	7.4	7.2	9.3	7.9	9.4	9.0
USA	10.5	10.8	9.5	10.3	7.8	6.5
Virgin Islands	6.6	9.4	10.8	11.6	10.8	11.1
Cayman Islands	0.9	1.5	2.3	2.2	1.6	3.4
Europe	1.9	11.7	9.6	7.7	8.0	7.9
Total	100.0	100.0	100.0	100.0	100.0	100.0

Sources: China Statistical Yearbook, annual, JETRO Shanghai Center.

significant impacts on regional GDP growth rates and regional disparities for the years 1990 to 1992, although the effect did not continue after that.[14] The lack of a significant relationship between the two after 1992 seems to be explained by three main factors: (1) in the development boom that started with Deng Xiaoping's Southern Journey, FDI covered the entire region of the Yangtze River Delta; (2) overall inward FDI reduction in the second half of the 1990s affected the significance of the FDI impacts on GDP growth rates; and (3) an active non-state-owned sector, which did not itself receive FDI, contributed to the region's growth and disparity and hence reduced the significance of the FDI relationship.

Rapid economic growth has been particularly marked in some provinces (Table 4.16). For example, the regional distribution of FDI (as a percentage of national total) has been particularly concentrated in the Yangtze River Delta region, particularly Jiangsu province, whose share reached 25.1 per cent in 2004 (Table 4.16). While recent growth has been marked in all regions, growth in the Yangtze River Delta region in 2004 was 10.6 per cent (in population), 24.9 per cent (in GDP), 36 per cent (in the volume of trade), and 34.6 per cent (in actual inward FDI). In this sense, at least, the Yangtze River Delta region serves as the core of the Chinese economy, especially in regard to its international economic activities.

Table 4.16 Regional distribution of FDI inflow (percentage of national total)

	1998	1999	2000	2001	2002	2003	2004
The Bohai Rim Region	28.8	25.9	29.4	23.8	22.3	25.7	27.8
Beijin	7.9	4.3	5.7	3.9	3.3	5.2	4.1
Tianjin	5.9	3.9	5.7	3.0	2.5	2.7	3.6
Hebei	2.4	2.2	1.9	1.2	1.4	1.5	1.3
Liaoning	8.4	8.0	8.0	6.0	6.3	5.6	5.6
Shandong	4.2	7.5	8.1	9.7	8.7	10.8	13.2
Yangtze River Delta Region	29.3	30.4	32.3	39.7	42.7	45.9	42.1
Shanghai	11.2	10.0	10.2	10.7	10.8	9.3	7.6
Jiangsu	14.5	15.7	18.0	21.8	23.7	25.9	25.1
Zhejiang	3.5	4.7	4.0	7.2	8.1	10.7	9.4
South China Region	28.7	28.6	27.0	24.5	24.0	16.2	17.0
Guangdong	17.6	13.3	18.5	16.2	18.4	11.7	12.6
Fujian	9.6	11.8	7.2	7.2	4.7	3.7	3.5
Hainan	0.3	1.9	0.2	0.2	0.3	0.2	0.2
Guangxi	1.2	1.6	1.1	0.8	0.6	0.6	0.7
Other Regions	13.2	15.1	11.3	12.0	11.1	14.6	13.0
Total	100.0	100.0	100.0	100.0	100.0	100.0	100.0

Sources: China Statistical Bulletin of Foreign Economic Relations, annual, and *China Statistical Handbook,* annual, and authors' calculation.

In recent years, the main determinants of FDI have been relative wage rates, relative GDP, relative real exchange rates and the volume of exports and imports,[15] as well as the size of the domestic market, infrastructural improvements and open FDI policies, especially the establishment of Open Economic Zones.[16] FDI seems to be driven by both market-seeking and export-seeking behaviour.

Current Japanese Outward FDI[17]

Japanese FDI in Poland

Japan's economic relations with Poland have been relatively stable. In 2003, the ratio of Polish exports to Japan as a proportion of total Polish exports was only 0.2 per cent, compared to 68.8 per cent for the former EU 15 countries and 0.5 per cent for China. The import ratio of goods from Japan as a proportion of total Polish imports was also low at 1.9 per cent, compared with 61.1 per cent for the 15 former EU countries and 4.2 per cent for China. Cumulative Japanese FDI in Poland in 2002 was US$ 351 million (only 0.6 per cent of the total Japanese FDI), a proportion that has remained level over many years. In 2004, the largest providers of FDI into Poland were France (20.1 per cent), the USA (18.2 per cent), Germany (15.0 per cent) and The Netherlands (12.5 per cent) (Table 4.10).

Table 4.17 shows the stock amount of Japanese FDI in Poland.[18] Until the end of 1989, Japanese FDI in Poland was carried out by a single company, which had been established in August 1989. Japanese companies were thus seen to be largely inactive investors compared with US, (West) European and South Korean companies. In 1990–1991, eight Japanese companies made investments totalling US$ 3 million, but these were all sales rather than manufacturing enterprises. Subsequent investments remained modest

Table 4.17 Japanese FDI in Poland (stock)

Year	US$ 10,000
1996	83,000,000
1997	95,000,000
1998	148,000,000
1999	242,000,000
2000	361,600,000
2001	517,500,000
2002	351,800,000
2003	258,000,000
2004	362,300,000

Source: JETRO (annual).

until 1993–1994, in which year investments increased significantly with a total FDI of US\$ 12 million from Matsushita-Phillips for battery production, Marubeni for industrial boiler production, JT for Tobacco production and 26 other investors. At the end of October 1995, the Warsaw Office of JETRO found 30 Japanese FDIs with US\$ 3 million more than in the previous year. But, again, most of these were subsidiaries for sales promotion.

In 1996–1997, a second stage of growth in Japanese FDI seems to have occurred, lagging one or two years behind US and European FDI. A JETRO questionnaire circulated to 800 Japanese subsidiaries established in 18 European countries found that the most attractive country for Japanese FDI in Europe was the UK, followed by the Czech Republic, Slovakia, Poland and Hungary. In 1996–1997, Japanese full-scale manufacturing FDI began in Poland with several large investments. Until October 1996 total Japanese FDI in Poland involved 38 companies and US\$ 8.3 million. By June 1997, this had increased to 48 companies and US\$ 126.8 million. The majority was invested in the tertiary sector, although some full-scale manufacturing FDI from Isuzu, NK Poland, Chiyoda Corporation and Penta Ocean was beginning.

Japanese FDI in Poland was still very small. According to the then PAIZ (which counts only FDI above US\$ 1 million), Japanese cumulative FDI by the end of the first half of 1998 amounted to only 11 investments totalling US\$ 178 million and amounting to only 0.8 per cent of overall inward FDI in Poland. The most important FDI in 1998 was NSK RHP Europe-Nichimen with the Polish company FLT Iskra; this was the first Japanese FDI to participate in the privatization of a Polish company, holding 80 per cent of its shares.

These investments were part of a shift from market-seeking to export-seeking investments. A typical example of this shift was Bridgestone and Firestone Polska, established in Warsaw in November 1994 with an investment of 220,000 zlotys for sales promotion with Mitsui Co. and Benelux Mitsui Co. The sales promotion corporation was dissolved in July 1998 and a new corporation was established in collaboration with Stomil Poznan (a Polish state-owned tyre producer) with an investment of about US\$ 63 million to produce tyres for the European market. Since 1997–1998, Japanese FDI in Poland has become more concentrated in manufacturing, particularly in automobile parts production. These investments involved the expansion of existing establishments and the creation of greenfield sites linked to Toyota and geared to providing parts for automakers in France, the UK and Germany. Polish accession to the EU in 2004 has greatly enhanced the value and attractiveness of these kinds of investments.

Toyota chose to locate their parts production in Poland for several reasons. First, they received a ten-year exemption from corporation tax. Second, the Walbrzych Special Economic Zone offered several important advantages. The Zone is located only 100 kilometres from the German border and it has easy access to other parts makers in the region, high levels of unemployment among a large pool of employable and skilled workers and abundant subterranean water for industrial use. Third, the Legnica area was already dominated by German VW.[19]

After 1997–1998, the shift from market- to export-seeking investments became even clearer. Isuzu Motors Polska and Bridgestone/Firestone Polska began production in 1999. In the same year, with an investment of about one billion yen, Tokai Rubber Industries and Mitsui Co. established TRI Poland in a joint venture with Stomil Wolbrom to produce rubber products for automobiles. Sumitomo Electric also started to build automobile electric parts (wiring systems) in a Wielkopolskie factory in Rawicz. In 2000, NSK Iskra transferred their bearing production to Poland from the UK in order to expand production, and the Mitsubishi Corp. established MCTI Polska for transport, storage and communication. In August 2001, the Mitsui Corporation agreed to develop an industrial development area for Japanese investors in Zarow. The area was authorized as a Special Economic Zone and was expected to attract automobile parts-producing companies. In October 2001, the then Bank of Tokyo-Mitsubishi acquired a licence to open the first of the Japanese banks in Poland.

Four Japanese manufacturing companies began production in 2002, all of which were automobile parts producers. Toyota Motor Manufacturing produced transmission in the Walbrzych Special Economic Zone. Mitsuboshi Belting established MOI Tech Europe Sp in Pruszkow to provide timing belts to Japanese and European automobile manufacturers. Toyo Seal Industries started to produce rubber products in Tychy, and Toho Industrial began machinery and equipment production in Radom. This trend continued in 2003, with Japanese FDI in Poland focusing on automobile and related industries. Toyota Motor Industries Poland established a diesel engine factory in Jelcz-Laskowice with an investment of E200 million, supplying diesel engines to their UK factory. In 2003, Amatsuji Steel Ball founded a machine factory in Zarow and NGK Insulators opened a factory to supply non-refractory ceramic goods in Gliwice. Toyota Motor Manufacturing, in conjunction with PSA in Walbrzych, expanded its manual transmission production capacity and began producing gasoline engines for a new car to be manufactured in the Czech Republic. These Polish investments provided several advantages. With a working population in Central Europe of 18 million and regional unemployment rates of between 18 and 20 per cent, an abundant work force was available, wage rates and wage rate increases were modest, and the quality and skills of the labour force were good.[20]

As of May 2004, more than 100 Japanese FDI had been made in Poland, 34 of which were manufacturing for export to West European markets. Automobile and related industries were the most important of these, including 2004 investments by SANDEN (automobile-related products), DAICEL (automobile-related products), NTK (ceramic products), Fuji Seiko (cutting tools), Toyota Boshoku and Denso (engine-related components), Toyota Tsusho and Daiki Aluminium Industry (aluminium products), Tsubaki-Hoover (bearings) and Yagi Industries (bearings).[21] As of May 2005, the JETRO Warsaw Office reported that there were more than 110 Japanese FDI in Poland, of which 36 were manufacturing factories led by automobile and related industries.[22]

Japanese FDI in China

Since the open door policy of Deng Xiaoping, China has maintained close relations with the international economy. China's overall trade in 2001 was US$ 509.8 billion, US$ 620.8 in 2002, and US$ 851.2 in 2003, making the Chinese value of trade the fourth largest in the world after the USA, Germany and Japan.

In 2003, Japanese imports accounted for 18 per cent of China's total imports and exports to Japan accounted for 13.6 per cent of China's total exports. The main recipients of Chinese exports at that time were the USA (21.1 per cent), Hong Kong (17.4 per cent) and Japan, and Chinese imports came mainly from Japan, Taiwan (12 per cent), and South Korea (10.4 per cent). While Japanese overall trade amount declined, trade with China expanded, reaching US$ 133.6 billion in 2003, with a Japanese deficit of US$ 18 billion. In both imports and exports, the USA, China and South Korea are the primary trading partners with Japan.

Japanese inward FDI in China grew from 7.2 per cent of total inward FDI in 2000, to 9.3 per cent in 2001, 7.9 per cent in 2002, 9.4 per cent in 2003 and 9.0 per cent in 2004. By 2004, Japanese inward FDI in China ranked fourth after Hong Kong (31.3 per cent), the British Virgin Islands [*sic*] (11.1 per cent) and South Korea (10.3 per cent). The ratio of Japanese FDI in China to total

Table 4.18 Main host countries of Japanese outward FDI (2004, flow)

	US$ million*	Ratio (%)
Netherlands	8,058	22.7
USA	4,677	13.2
China	4,567	12.8
Cayman Islands	3,947	11.1
Oceania	1,869	5.3
UK	1,789	5.0
Panama	1,282	3.6
Thailand	1,184	3.3
Total	35,548	100.0

*reported base (in Japanese MOF).

Source: JETRO (2005).

Japanese outward FDI has also increased progressively from 2.0 per cent in 2000, 4.6 per cent in 2001, 4.8 per cent in 2002, 8.7 per cent in 2003, and 12.8 per cent in 2004, when Japan's ratio of FDI to overall outward FDI almost equalled that of the USA (13.2 per cent) (see Table 4.18).

Table 4.19 indicates the volume of Japanese FDI in China and Figure 4.1 shows the ratio of Japanese FDI in China to Japanese overall outward FDI

Table 4.19   Japanese FDI in China (flow)

Year	US$ million*
1996	5,131
1997	3,401
1998	2,749
1999	2,591
2000	3,680
2001	5,419
2002	5,298
2003	7,955
2004	9,162

*pledged base.

Source: JETRO, annual.

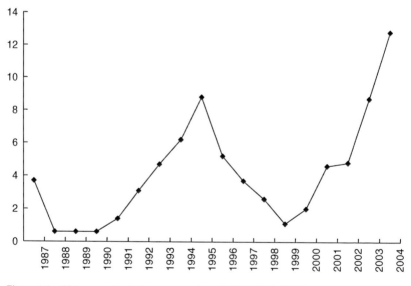

Figure 4.1   Chinese ratio to Japanese outward FDI (1987–2004)
Source: JETRO, annual.

between 1987 and 2004. Flow increased after 1992 to a peak of 8.8 per cent in 1995, followed by a decline to 1.1 per cent in 1999, until after 2000 when it again became significant. In the mid-1990s, Chinese government policies were particularly attractive for inward FDI in coastal and inland areas.

At the beginning of the 1990s, Japanese outward FDI to China was small (0.6 per cent in 1989 and 0.9 per cent in 1990) and concentrated on export activities in the North-East, particularly in Dalian. Such inward investment was supported by Chinese government policies that allowed foreign companies with more than 70 per cent of their production in export products to enjoy a 50 per cent tax exemption. With continued income growth in the urban areas, market-seeking FDI increased, particularly in industries such as telecommunication equipment, automobile and related electric machinery. The Dalian region still received the largest amount of FDI (US$ 1.19 billion at the end of 1992), followed by Shanghai (US$ 810 million), Shenzhen (US$ 555 million), Tianjin (US$ 367 million) and Beijing (US$ 121 million). Export-seeking FDI in Dalian was dominant at the time, although the manufacturing share of Japanese FDI in China in 1990 was less than non-manufacturing (46 per cent in manufacturing compared with 54 per cent in non-manufacturing). However, this situation changed quickly with large-scale FDI directed towards Shanghai in 1993–1994 and large-scale automobile FDI with Fuji Heavy Industries' decision in March 1998 to open a facility jointly with Guizhou Airlines in Guizhou province. With continued GDP growth, FDI expanded rapidly in the Yangtze River Delta, particularly in Shanghai and Jiangsu province, as investors sought market access through large-scale investments in the retail sector (notably with Yaohan in Wuxi and Jusco in Qingdao).

Japanese FDI in China declined rapidly in 1996, with the number of pledged FDI projects declining by 40.9 per cent and pledged amounts declining by 32.4 per cent over the previous year. There were several reasons for this decline, but two were of particular importance. Changes in Chinese government policies reduced the special benefits accorded FDI projects and Japanese companies reassessed the level of risk they bore in Chinese investments, resulting in much more risk-averse behaviour than had been the case earlier.[23]

Through the 1990s, many new FDI projects were undertaken in China. In automobiles, Tianjin Toyota Motor Engine (engine production) and Dongfeng Nissan Diesel Motor (truck and bus production) were established in 1996. In 1997, Tianjin Toyota Forging (forging production) and Tianjin Jinfeng Auto Parts (steering and propeller shaft production) were founded. And in 1998, Sichuan Toyota Motor (coaster production), Guangzhou Honda Motor (Accord and Odyssey production) and the cooperative agreement between Guizhou Yunque Motor and Fuji Heavy Industries (Rex production) were all initiated. However, as recession in the Japanese economy and difficulties in the Chinese economy (such as illegal tax payments, transfer pricing and difficulties in collecting payments) discouraged investors, the number and value of pledged investments started to decline year over year from 1997 to 1999 (with declines over the previous year respectively of 18.5 per cent and 33.7 per cent decline in 1997, 15.6 per cent and 19.2 per cent in 1998, and 2.6 per cent and 5.7 per cent in 1999). Thus, by the end of the decade, the situation had changed: restructuring in parent companies led to a re-evaluation of business commitments in China; frequent changes in China's institutions reduced the transparency of procedures under which companies operated; and the most obvious major projects for FDI had already been completed.[24]

Japanese FDI in China began to grow again in 2000, with the pledged number and amounts of investment over the previous year of 38.3 per cent and 42.0 per cent respectively. This expansion was influenced particularly by China's accession to WTO, the low cost of labour and high rates of economic growth. In 2000, Japanese automobile manufacturers' investments included Guangzhou Isuzu Bus (bus production), Tianjin FAW Toyota Motor (Vios production) and Shenyang Shenfei Hino Automobile Manufacturing (bus production).

The number and amount of pledged FDI in 2001 were 25.1 per cent and 47.3 per cent greater than in 2000 and seem to have been stimulated by corporate trends 'to expand production and to promote sales in China'.[25] Questionnaire research by JETRO in October 2001 found that, out of a total of 300 companies with plans to expand FDI, 287 intended to invest in China. These investments were planned in order to expand production and sales in the host countries (71.1 per cent), reduce costs (44.9 per cent), deal with the FDI of customers in Japan (24.7 per cent) and expand sales to third countries (18.8 per cent).[26]

The tendency to seek markets was particularly important for automobile and consumer electronics manufacturers. Sony, for example, started to produce a laptop computer in Jiangsu province in 2002. Toshiba also began to produce a laptop computer in Shanghai (at Pudong Jinqiao Processing Area) in 1998 and in Zhejiang province in 2002. In automobiles, Honda started Odyssey production in Guangzhou in April 2002, Toyota began Vios production in Tianjin in October 2002 and Nissan began Cefiro production in Hubei province in 2003. Mazda started Premacy and '323' production jointly with the FAW Group in Hainan province in 2001 and 2002. Interestingly, while the number of pledged FDI was 36.0 per cent greater in 2002 than in 2001, the value of investments was 2.2 per cent lower. The growing trend towards market-seeking was unchanged, particularly given the recent rapid expansion in the markets for automobiles in China. Honda, Toyota and Nissan all invested more in China, despite some market challenges in 2002 and 2003 resulting from difficulties with bill collection and fake products.

In 2003, the number and value of pledged FDI projects increased by 18.5 per cent and 50.2 per cent over the previous year. Japanese automobile manufacturers had established full-scale production and part-making facilities in China and were well positioned to take advantage of the rapid 'development of motorization in China'.[27] Toyota FDI was particularly active, signing a joint production contract with FAW in April 2003 and beginning Corolla production in February 2004 and Crown production in 2005.

In 2004, the number and value of pledged FDI were 6.1 per cent and 15.2 per cent greater than the previous year. Toyota began joint production of engines with Guangzhou Motors in February 2004 and with FAW (in Changchun) in March 2004, and they also started production and sales cooperation with Guangzhou Motors for the Camry. Honda began Cr-v production in a joint venture with Dongfeng Motors in April 2004 and Fit production in a joint undertaking with Guangzhou Motors in September 2004. Nissan also completed work on a factory in Guangzhou for joint production of the Sunny and Bluebird with Dongfeng Motors in May and Teana production in September. In the electrical and electronics industry, large-scale projects were completed, such as that by Matsushita Electric Industrial in the Matsushita Hangzhou Industrial Park in Zhejiang province, where companies were established for the precision processing of compressor parts and compressors for air conditioners.

In summary, the shift that occurred in 1995 in the goals of Japanese FDI in China from projects geared primarily towards export-seeking to ones focused more on local markets has had important impacts on the structure and orientation of foreign manufacturers. These investments have also had particularly important impacts in selected regions, most importantly in the regional accumulation of FDI in the Yangtze River Delta, particularly in Shanghai and Jiangsu province. After several years of reduced FDI flows, Japanese FDI in China expanded after 2000 as the strength of local markets began to play ever more important roles. Increases in GDP, institutional and infrastructural improvements and WTO accession each played an important role in investment decisions. Several problems with Chinese markets remained, particularly in sales; collecting payment remained challenging, obtaining clear and accurate information on market responses remained difficult, fake products undercut markets, there was little reliable information about potential suppliers and subcontractors and strict regulation remained in place preventing foreign companies building their own sales networks. For the more risk-averse Japanese companies, the huge potential of the Chinese market continues to be balanced by these limits on new investment.

FDI-Trade ratios and managerial resource disparities

Japanese FDI in Poland has remained small-scale and the motives for investing have shifted from ones that were predominantly market-seeking to ones that are more oriented to seeking export markets, particularly in automobile and related industries, and especially for markets in the EU. This shift was compounded by the weaker than expected results of restructuring policies and the freer than expected movement of goods resulting from EU accession. By contrast, Japanese FDI in China was originally oriented towards creating export platforms to supply larger Asian, European and American markets, but in time this has shifted to a more direct orientation towards the Chinese domestic market, especially in consumer electronics and automobile and related industries. This shift in orientation was also marked by a growing concentration of investment in manufacturing and increased regional accumulation of FDI in the Yangtze River Delta region, particularly in Shanghai and Jiangsu province. Again in contrast to Poland, Japanese FDI in China has been driven by the rapid and substantial increases in GDP brought about the successful gradual transition in the Chinese economy and by the institutional improvements that have accompanied China's entry into the WTO.

One major characteristic of Japanese FDI is the large scale of the FDI in consumer electronics and automobile and related industries. One determinant of the differences in Japanese FDI in Poland and in China may well be the disparity in available managerial resources. The importance of disparities in managerial resources in shaping industrial investment was originally suggested by Komiya (and even earlier by Penrose).[28] Komiya argued that managerial resources are 'the organization whose core is apparently made by a manager and is substantially for knowledge and experience of business management, for market standing shown by sales, material purchase and finance, by technological and specialised knowledge including marketing method, patent and know-how'.[29] Komiya also argued that FDI was driven by differences in profitability between economic activities in home and host countries, which were themselves caused by disparities in the accumulation of managerial resources between the countries concerned.

The FDI concentration index and trade linkage index confirm the importance of these disparities. To calculate the FDI concentration index, the numerator is calculated by dividing the annual amount of Japanese FDI in a particular country by the total amount of inward FDI for that year and the denominator is calculated by dividing the total amount of Japanese outward FDI by amount of worldwide outward FDI. The ratio of the numerator to the denominator is the FDI concentration index. When the ratio is more than one, Japanese FDI in the country is relatively larger than in other countries. Table 4.20 shows the FDI concentration index for Japan with China and Poland and demonstrates the much greater length of time and larger scale of China's receipts of Japanese FDI over Poland's shorter and smaller scale of FDI receipts.

Table 4.20 FDI concentration index

	China	Poland
1996	0.819	0.112
1997	1.626	0.092
1998	0.828	0.150
1999	0.424	0.312
2000	1.043	0.478
2001	0.790	0.161
2002	1.000	0.108
2003	1.826	0.087
2004	2.610	0.341

Index in Poland is calculated with accumulated amount.

Source: JETRO, annual and authors' calculation.

FDI activities are more sensitive than international trade to factors such as cultural and institutional norms and practices. As a result, comparative measures of FDI between specific countries are difficult to interpret. Instead, using the trade linkage index, we turn now to an examination of the strengths and weaknesses of international relations expressed by the scale of international trade. The trade linkage index is calculated by dividing Japanese exports to a particular country by total Japanese exports (the numerator) and by dividing the import volume from a particular country by total imports (the denominator). The ratio of the numerator to the denominator is the trade linkage index. When the ratio is greater than one, Japanese trade with a particular country is relatively larger than with other countries. Table 4.21 shows the trade linkage index of Japan with China and Poland. China consistently has indices of 2.5 to 2.8, while Poland consistently has indices of 0.2 to 0.3. In other words, China is a 'close' trading partner with Japan with strong international relations, while Poland remains a 'distant' partner with correspondingly weak international relations.

This trade index now allows us to scale comparative data on FDI between specific countries in ways that take into account the strengths and weaknesses of the international relations. To do this, we use the ratio of the FDI concentration index (the numerator) and the trade linkage index (the denominator), which we refer to as the FDI-trade index. When the ratio equals one, FDI relations between the two countries correspond with their international relations. When it is more than one, FDI relations between

Table 4.21 Trade linkage index

	China	Poland
1996	2.706	0.214
1997	2.671	0.221
1998	2.804	0.264
1999	2.747	0.272
2000	2.466	0.286
2001	2.679	0.293
2002	2.795	0.291
2003	2.845	0.297
2004	2.708	0.306

Source: JETRO, annual and authors' calculation; JETRO, *Boueki Toushi Hakusho* [Trade and Investment White Paper] (Tokyo, JETRO, Annual).

Table 4.22 FDI-trade index

	China	Poland
1996	0.303	0.523
1997	0.609	0.417
1998	0.295	0.568
1999	0.154	1.147
2000	0.423	1.671
2001	0.295	0.549
2002	0.358	0.371
2003	0.642	0.293
2004	0.964	1.114

Source: JETRO, annual and authors' calculation; JETRO, *Boueki Toushi Hakusho* [Trade and Investment White Paper] (Tokyo, JETRO, Annual) and author's calculation.

them are more active than expected from the scale of international relations, and when less than one FDI relations between them are less active than expected (Table 4.22). China consistently has an index of less than one (although the index in 2004 approached one), while in Poland the index exceeded one in 1999, 2000 and 2004. In these terms, FDI relations between Japan and China are weaker than measures of international relations would suggest, while Japanese FDI relations with Poland are, at times, stronger than measures of the strength of their international relations would suggest. Such comparative FDI-trade indexed data provides a different picture of the relative strengths of these relations from that given by the two indices separately; the scale of Japanese FDI in Poland is not as small as expected, while the scale of Japanese FDI in China is smaller than expected.

Risk-averse FDI: sovereign partnership approach

In comparative terms, the scale of Japanese FDI in Poland might not be small and in China it might not be large. Why, then, might these comparative differences occur? Part of the answer relates to the fact that Japanese FDI in Poland shifted from market-seeking to export-seeking in 1997–1998. Thus, for example, in December 1990 Toyota Motor Corporation established Toyota Motor Poland jointly with Nissho Iwai to import and sell automobiles. In the second half of 1998, Toyota and the Aisin Seiki group established a factory to produce transmissions for Yaris, exporting parts to the UK and France. However, Japanese FDI in Poland has not been without its problems, and these have also influenced the level of FDI. For example, the Daihatsu case negotiated throughout the 1980s and the Asahi Glass case at the beginning of the 1990s (both of which were prevented by Italian Fiat and British Pilkington respectively) have widely been recognized as examples of failed Japanese FDI resulting from weak international relations compared with their European competitors, above and beyond problems of macroeconomic instability and lack of government transparency. The bearing company FLT Iskra, for example, was taken over by the Japanese NSK and Nichimen in competition with the Swedish SKF, but the parent company experienced serious difficulties due to changes of government in Poland.

Japanese FDI in China has also been limited, particularly by risks connected with sales, such as collecting bills and undercutting from fake products, and by delays in legal and institutional reforms. The result has been tempered FDI and weak political relations or what some have referred to as a 'hot economy with cool politics'.

These and other underlying risks associated with financing and macroeconomic instability mean that large FDI investments, particularly in developing and transition economies, have been possible only because of parallel government efforts to provide insurance and share the risks associated with such investments. We end this paper with a discussion of some of the ways in which we might better understand this deeply imbricated role of the national and local state in maintaining the conditions for investment in situations in which international and global regimes and regularized institutions and norms have not fully developed.

As we have seen above, Japanese FDI in Poland has been constrained by problems arising from Poland's legal system, the poor quality of information and the high transaction costs associated with new investments in the country. In Coasian terms, these would seem to be indicators of market failure. However, as Keohane has insisted, approaching the issue in Coasian terms, when even one of the above three exists it is still reasonable to expect that governments would establish some organizational forms to sustain investment (what he refers to as an international regime among governments).[30] Although 'regimes themselves depend on conditions that are conductive to interstate agreements, they may also facilitate further efforts to coordinate policies to such an extent that even egoistic and self-interested governments may strive to cooperate' to provide the equivalent of a stable regime.[31]

International regimes have various definitions. For example, Ruggie defined a regime as 'a set of mutual expectations, rules and regulations, plans, organizational energies and financial commitments, which have been accepted by a group of states'.[32] Keohane defined international regimes as 'sets of implicit or explicit principles, norms, rules, and decision-making procedures around which actors' expectations converge in a given area of international relations'.[33] Along with Keohane, we regard 'regimes as largely based on self-interest' and 'incentives to form international regimes depend most fundamentally on the existence of shared interests'.[34] Such shared interests contribute to the maintenance and continuance of international regimes.

In the context of Japanese economic relations with China and Poland, there are four shared interests of particular importance to our analysis: (1) mitigating uncertainty, (2) reducing information collecting costs, (3) maintaining stability and (4) reducing transaction costs. In practice and until recently, Japanese relations with Poland and China seem to have had no common principles, norms, rules or decision-making procedures. Because Japanese companies are more risk-averse than US and West European ones, they have, as a result, reduced FDI pledges more quickly when imperfect information and large transaction costs existed.

In principle, establishing more stable international regimes should improve legal systems, eliminate imperfect information and reduce transaction costs, which in turn ought to provide the necessary conditions for risk-averse companies to be more active investors. However, in situations where an international regime has not yet been established, how is risk actually managed? Although we are not ready to explore fully such a difficult issue, by way of concluding we draw on a 'sovereign partnership' approach to illustrate one possible answer. The sovereign partnership approach expresses cooperation between sovereign states in terms similar to those of international regimes in which there is a partnership to protect economic rights and interests for both investor companies and host countries through bilateral and multilateral agreement among sovereign states. The benefits brought by a strong international regime are, in this approach, modelled bilaterally and multilaterally by state actors standing in for the relevant corporations and persons of the sovereign states. Relations among the parties are completely formal and independent in order to provide investing companies limited guarantees that are assumed to result from the fact that host governments are a party to the agreements. The sovereign partnership agreement can thus provide investor companies legitimate rights in host countries, avoiding the risks associated with being unlicensed or merely independent actors. In particularly risky host countries, investing companies cannot be given sufficient legitimate rights and so, in these situations, their home governments might take action to warrant respect for the mutual sovereignty of investing companies.

Dominant governmental organizations exercise, through sovereign partnership, leadership over subordinate organizations. They may, for example, assist in sorting out problems faced by businesses. The sovereign partnership seems to encourage expanded FDI in reforming economies, investments which are further expanded the more countries participate in the joint insurance system.[35]

Figure 4.2 is adapted from the work of McKinnon where the real interest rate, r, is plotted on the horizontal axis, and the real expected return, π, is plotted on the vertical axis. $R1$, $R2$ and $R2$ 'lie below and to the right of the 45-degree ray' because of the adverse selection and the incentive effect, showing that real expected return increases more slowly than real interest rate.[36]

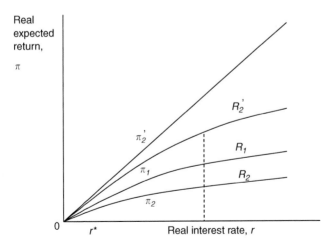

Figure 4.2 Expected returns and real interest rates

When insurance is introduced in such an economy by governmental agreement, what does it change? Being covered by insurance, financing 'gets to keep extraordinary profits without having to pay the full costs of unusually large losses from risky' investments.[37] As Figure 4.2 shows, risky barriers of investment R2 are reduced by insurance, which allows the expected return to be increased as expressed by its shift toward R2. Insurance thus works to strengthen international relations by providing stability and safety.

As we recognized in the previous section, it is difficult to say that Japanese economic relations with Poland are strong. Governmental relations remain relatively weak and this reduces expected returns from investment compared with expected costs caused by a risky environment. Such less active relations limit Japanese FDI in Poland.[38] By contrast, there are close trade relations between Japan and China. However, FDI relations between them are less close than their trade, in part because of the lower expected returns compared with expected costs associated with such risks as fake products.

Conclusion

Japanese FDI in Poland and China differs not only in degree, but in purpose. In Poland FDI firms have been focused more and more on export-seeking, while the main motive for Japanese FDI in China has been market-seeking. However, the work we have presented on the FDI concentration and trade linkage indices suggests that the relative significance of Japanese FDI in Poland and China might be the inverse of what might appear in the raw data, being relatively larger than expected for Poland and relatively smaller than expected for China.

Looking forward, and to the extent that Poland and China experience sustained macroeconomic growth and that each continues to adopt the more global standardized rules required respectively by EU and WTO accession, we will likely see more, not less, Japanese FDI in each country. However, we have also shown how, in this process, state policy and domestic market conditions quickly influence the patterns and processes of FDI in each region, particularly among risk-averse investors, and it is these state policy and domestic market conditions that can change quickly and have enormous impact on actual received FDI.

Notes

1   We focus our attention on the motives of Japanese FDI. Regarding the determinants of FDI, see, for example, H. Horaguchi, *Nihon Kigyou no Kaigai Chokusetsu Toushi* [Foreign Direct Investment of Japanese Companies] (Tokyo: Tokyo University Press 1992); E. Tomiyama, *Roshia Shijyou Sannyu Senryaku* [Entry Strategy for Russian Markets] (Kyoto: Minervashobo 2004). On the determinants of inward FDI in Poland, see, for examples, K. Morita and D. Stuglik, 'Japan's

Foreign Direct Investment in Poland: Current Situation and Determinants', *Economic Papers* 30 (Warsaw: Warsaw School of Economics, Institute for International Studies 2000), 98–113.

2   WERI (World Economy Research Institute), *Poland: International Economic Report*, Warsaw, Warsaw School of Economics, Annual, 1999/2000.

3   A. Aslund and A. Warner, 'The EU Enlargement: Consequences for the CIS Countries', in M. Dabrowski, B. Sley and J. Neneman, eds, *Beyond Transition: Development Perspectives and Dilemmas* (Aldershot: Ashgate, 2004) pp. 231–252. Aslund's explanation of the index indicates that the:

> formula is rather simple. The first element is 0.3 times EBRD's index for price liberalization and competition policy. The second element is 0.3 times EBRD's index for trade and foreign exchange liberalization. The third element is 0.4 times EBRD's index for large-scale privatization, small-scale privatization, and banking reform. Each index is normalized to reach a maximum of 1.   [A. Aslund, *Building Capitalism: The Transformation of the Former Soviet Bloc* (Cambridge: Cambridge University Press 2002)]

4   M. De Broeck and V. Koen, *The 'Soaring Eagle': Anatomy of the Polish Take-Off in the 1990s*, IMF Working Paper (Washington DC: International Monetary Fund, 2000). On income disparities in China, see: Y. Chen, *Chugoku no Keizai Kaihatsu to Chiiki Kakusa ni kansuru Jissho Kenkyu* [Empirical Study on Economic Development and Regional Differences: Examination on the City Cluster in Yangtze Delta] (PhD Dissertation, Hiroshima University, 2001); J. Knight and L. Song, *The Rural-Urban Divide Economic Disparities and Interactions in China* (New York: Oxford University Press, 1999); and World Bank, *China 2020 series: Sharing Rising Incomes: Disparities in China* (Washington DC: World Bank, 1997). Also see the following section on details of income disparities in China.

5   K. Morita, *Economic Reforms and Capital Markets in Central Europe* (Aldershot: Ashgate 2004).

6   EBRD, *Transition Report*, London, European Bank for Reconstruction and Development, Annual.

7   UNCTAD (United Nations Conference on Trade and Development), *World Investment Report* (Geneva: United Nations Conference on Trade and Development, Annual).

8   J. Mencinger, 'Does Foreign Direct Investment Always Enhance Economic Growth?' *Kyklos* 56(4) (2003) 491–508.

9   UNCTAD, 1998, p. 135.

10 However, we have no investigation of it here in this paper.

11 C. Chen, L. Chang and Y. Zhang, 'The Role of Foreign Direct Investment in China's post-1978 Economic Development', *World Development*, 23(4) (1995) 691–703.

12 Y. Chen and S. Demurger, 'Foreign Direct Investment and Manufacturing Productivity in China' (Paris: CEPII Research Project Report, 2002).

13 W. Tseng and H. Zebregs, 'Foreign Direct Investment in China: Some Lessons for Other Countries', IMF Policy Discussion Paper (Washington DC: International Monetary Fund 2002).

14 Y. Chen, *Chugoku no Keizai Kaihatsu to Chiiki Kakusa ni kansuru Jissho Kenkyu* [Empirical Study on Economic Development and Regional Differences: Examination on the City Cluster in Yangtze Delta] (PhD Dissertation, Hiroshima University 2001).

15 X. Liu, H. Song, Y. Wei and P. Romilly, 'Country Characteristics and Foreign Direct Investment in China: A Panel Data Analysis', *Weltwirtschaftliches Archiv*, 133(2) (1997) 313–329.

16   Tseng and Zebregs (2002).
17   As often indicated, even if they are actually Japanese companies' FDI in Poland, a substantial portion of them are recorded as European companies' FDI. It might be difficult to recognize correctly the actual Japanese FDI. This section is indebted to JETRO (annual) and Inagaki and the 21st China Research Institute (2005).
18   K. Morita, *Chuou no Keizai Kaikaku to Shouhin Sakimono Shijyou* [Economic Reforms and Commodity Futures Markets in Central Europe] (Tokyo: Tagashupan 2002).
19   *Chunichi Shinbun*, 5 November 1998.
20   JETRO, 2003, p. 331.
21   JETRO, 2005.
22   It showed a ratio of manufacturing (stock) was about 33 per cent, which was much less than the ratio of manufacturing (flow) in Japanese FDI in China of more than 80 per cent. Although it might be important to examine reasons for this, based upon distinguishing between flow and stock, we have no investigation here in this paper.
23   JETRO, 1998, p. 169.
24   JETRO, 2001, p. 164.
25   JETRO, 2002, p. 185.
26   JETRO, 2002, p. 186.
27   JETRO, 2004, p. 173.
28   R. Komiya, 'Direct foreign investment in postwar Japan' in P. Drysdale, ed., *Direct Foreign investment in Asia and the Pacific* (Canberra: ANU Press, 1972) p. 178 and E.T. Penrose, 'Foreign Investment and the Growth of the Firm', *Economic Journal*, 66(202) (1956) 220–235.
29   Komiya, p. 178.
30   R.O. Keohane, *After Hegemony: Cooperation and Discord in the World Political Economy* (Princeton: Princeton University Press, 1984).
31   Kehoane, p. 57.
32   J.G. Ruggie, 'International responses to technology', *International Organization*, 29(557–84) (1975) p. 570.
33   Keohane, p. 57.
34   Keohane, pp. 57, 97.
35   As a matter of course, when such an insurance system led by self-interest is well organized, no international framework is necessary. However, shared interest leading to the insurance function does not come from self-interest but from multinational integration and organization such as the EU and WTO. A sovereign partnership could be concluded between two countries, as mentioned earlier, but it remains unclear whether or not sovereign partnership is possible between Japan and China.
36   R. McKinnon, *The Order of Economic Liberalization: Financial Controls in the Transition to a Market Economy* (Baltimore: John Hopkins Press, 1991), as assumed by J.E. Stiglitz and A. Weiss, 'Credit Rationing in Markets with Imperfect Information', *American Economic Review*, 71 (1981) 393–410.
37   McKinnon, *The Order of Economic Liberalization*, p. 90.
38   It should be recognized that introduction of insurance in this paper's sense is a necessary condition to strengthen international relations.

5
Developing Emerging Bond Markets: Rationale and Choices in Central and Eastern Europe and Southeast Asia

Peter Haiss and Natalie Chou[*]

Introduction

In the emerging market economies of Europe and Asia parallel efforts are currently under way to develop bond markets. This chapter examines the similarities and differences in these efforts to build bond markets in selected emerging markets in Europe and Asia, specifically by comparing the Central and Eastern European (CEE) experience of Hungary, Poland and the Czech Republic with the South-East Asian experience of Thailand, Malaysia and Singapore. The chapter focuses on the general need for bond markets and the complex array of players and institutions on which their creation and success depends. The emergence of bond markets in transitional economies has only recently received scholarly attention, and then only focused on the generalities of bond markets.[1] In this chapter we try to fill this gap.

The chapter begins with a broader comparison of general financial market structures in these countries and then turns to the specific details of bond markets in each. Next follows a survey of the current literature on bond market development focusing on the benefits, development principles and problems involved in the processes of bond market development in reform economies. Special attention is given to the roles played by government and banks. The differences between the two regions and their impact on bond market development in each are explored. Specifically, with the fall of the Iron Curtain in 1989, 'transformation' and 'strengthening of market forces' became key goals. As command structures were liberalized and privatized, financial markets had to be created from scratch in each emerging postsocialist economy oriented towards international bond and currency markets. For countries preparing for European Union (EU) accession, bond markets play a particularly pivotal role not only in providing a solid financial base, but also as a proof of financial market stability to satisfy the criteria for integration into the European economy and possible entry into Economic and Monetary Union (EMU). In emerging Asian economies, bond markets were necessary to create the conditions for regional economic stability, particularly once the lessons of the Southeast Asia financial crisis in 1997–1998 demonstrated the importance of developed bond markets in assisting in economic recovery in the most impacted countries.[2] We argue that a common regional 'bond space' can play an important role in economic integration in both regions.

Financial market structures

The countries in these two regions share some similarities with one another, the most obvious of which is their several decades of experience with state-led economic development and more recent experiments with liberalization. Though the Asian countries have colonial legacies, all six countries have experienced periods of nationalization and more recently privatization with economic liberalization. Both CEE and the Southeast Asian countries were also hit by financial and banking crises in the 1990s. In terms of capitalization and their size relative to GDP, Asian financial markets, particularly Malaysia but also Thailand, are much larger than Central and Eastern European markets (Tables 5.1 and 5.2). While Poland's financial markets have been more heavily capitalized in absolute terms than those of Hungary or the Czech Republic, the size relative to GDP is smaller. Malaysia and Thailand have also experienced stronger development of their credit and equity markets, and these have played particularly important roles relative to other financial institutions, especially in Indonesia. CEE countries show similar patterns of development, with a slight advantage of bond market capitalization over credit markets, but their equity markets are much less developed. What is the significance of these differences and how can they be explained?

Though their economic development paths are quite diverse, in both regions the role and timing of privatization and the lifting of entry barriers have had a substantial impact on their current development. These variations in government actions have led to different financial market structures and dynamics, for example by attracting different types of investors. In the case of Hungary, the chosen method of privatization was to attract foreign investment and expertise through auction. Massive foreign bank FDI and bank recapitalization enabled the banks to provide fresh loans, but may also have 'crowded out' capital market development and led to lower rates of equity and debt security financing.[3] By contrast, the financial sector in Poland is characterized by higher non-performing loans (accounting for

Table 5.1 Financial intermediation for Asia-3 and CEE-3 (2003)

	ASIA-3[1]		CEE-3[2]		USA	EU-15
	in mn euro	in % of GDP	in mn euro	in % of GDP	in % of GDP	in % of GDP
Domestic shares[3]	264.962	63	64.426	19	116	67
Domestic bonds[4]	176.519	42	160.098	48	146	88
Domestic credit	365.292	87	143.345	43	80	111
Total financial intermediation[5]	806.772	192	367.868	111	343	266
Bank assets[6]	420.583	100	204.115	61	85	211
International bonds	26.603	6	21.774	7	25	51

[1] Indonesia, Malaysia, Thailand.
[2] Poland, Czech Republic, Hungary.
[3] stock market capitalization.
[4] bonds outstanding.
[5] domestic intermediation.
[6] domestic and foreign assets.

Sources: Bank for International Settlements, 2004, Securities Statistics, tables 14A, 14B, 16A and 16B, http://www.bis.org/statistics/secstats.htm; European Central Bank, 2003a, Bond markets and long-term interest rates in European Union Accession Countries, 2003 edition, 6 October, www.ecb.int/pub/pdf/other/bondmarketacc2003en.pdf; European Central Bank, 2003b, Developments in the debt financing of the euro area private sector, *ECB Monthly Bulletin*, November: 47–57, www.ecb.int/pub/pdf/mobu/mb200311en.pdf; Federation Internationale Des Bourses De Valeurs, 2004, 'Time Series 1990–2003 of Market Capitalization of shares of domestic companies', World Federation of Exchanges, 22 June 2004; International Financial Statistics, 2004, *International Financial Statistics*, Washington DC: International Monetary Fund; G. Jiang and R. McCauley, 'Asian local currency bond markets', *BIS Quarterly Review*, June (2004) 67–79.

about 9 per cent of total loans compared with 3 per cent in Hungary and the Czech Republic)[4] and a lower foreign share in banking assets (about 70 per cent in Poland compared with over 85 per cent in Hungary and the Czech Republic).[5] In all three CEE countries, company reliance on FDI is stronger than in the Asia-3 (Table 5.3). Retained earnings and funds from the parent company (e.g. intercompany loans) also play a role. In Asia, capital markets began to develop in the 1980s and 1990s focused on equity via initial public offerings (IPO) and secondary trading on local markets. As a result, local investors in these countries tend to focus on equity markets and are more familiar with them.[6]

Bond markets and corporate finance

In terms of corporate capital structure, all of these countries exhibit imbalances between the sources of credit, equity and debt security. Total financial

Table 5.2   Aggregate markets EUR mn in 2003

in mn euro (2003)	Indonesia	Malaysia	Thailand	Poland	Czech Rep.	Hungary
GDP	195.543	91.226	132.652	183.051	75.678	73.845
Domestic shares[1]	43.277	127.451	94.234	29.632	19.891	14.903
Domestic bonds[2]	53.399	78.147	44.972	69.462	45.146	45.490
Domestic credit	93.084	134.540	137.667	63.789	38.652	40.904
Total financial intermediation[3]	189.761	340.138	276.873	162.883	103.689	101.296
Bank assets[4]	102.394	160.347	157.843	88.712	68.398	47.004
Internat. bonds	2.534	16.865	7.205	9.660	2.217	9.897

In per cent of GDP	Indonesia	Malaysia	Thailand	Poland	Czech Rep.	Hungary
Domestic shares	22%	140%	71%	16%	26%	20%
Domestic bonds	27%	86%	34%	38%	60%	62%
Domestic credit	48%	147%	104%	35%	51%	55%
Total financial intermediation*	97%	373%	209%	89%	137%	137%
Bank assets	52%	176%	119%	48%	90%	64%
Internat. bonds	1%	18%	5%	5%	3%	13%

[1] stock market capitalization.
[2] bonds outstanding.
[3] domestic intermediation.
[4] domestic and foreign bank assets.

Data sources: IFS, 2004, *International Financial Statistics*, Washington DC: International Monetary Fund; BIS, 2004, Securities Statistics, tables 14A, 14B, 16A and 16B, http://www.bis.org/statistics/ secstats.htm; FIBV, 2004, 'Time Series 1990–2003 of Market Capitalization of shares of domestic companies', World Federation of Exchanges, 22 June 2004; G. Jiang and R. McCauley, 'Asian local currency bond markets', *BIS Quarterly Review*, June (2004) 67–79; ECB, 2004d, *Bond markets and long-term interest rates in non-euro area Member States of the European Union and in accession countries*, 3rd edition, November 2004, http://www.ecb.int/stats/money/long/html/index.en.html.

intermediation in both Asia-3 and CEE-3 (measured as the sum of stock market capitalization, bonds outstanding and volume of domestic credit outstanding relative to GDP) is below the level of the US or the EU-15 (see Table 5.1). As most bond finance in both CEE-3 and Asia-3 is government-driven (with the notable exception of Malaysia; see Table 5.3), the private sector in both country groups relies heavily on bank-based intermediation. Bank finance has been important because it is an effective means for funding initial high growth, especially in environments with large information asymmetries. But this can be problematic in emerging markets because it exposes the system to greater risk and shock, and results in international fluctuations being transmitted primarily through their impact on domestic banks.[7] Both regions are moving towards a more diversified financial structure, including an increase in public listings.[8] Listing on an official exchange safeguards small investors and facilitates the flow of information about company practices and prices.[9] Developing bond markets is a step in this direction.

Though countries in both regions have diversified their financial structures, their private sectors remain over-reliant on bank lending (Tables 5.1 and 5.2). With the exception of Malaysia, the ratios of both stock market capitalization to GDP and of (mostly government) bonds outstanding relative to GDP are fairly low.[10] In the Central Eastern European region, Hungary and the Czech Republic have higher levels of bond issuance relative to GDP (about 60 per cent), followed by Poland (about 40 per cent of GDP;[11] Table 5.2). In the Asian region, Malaysia has experienced the most marked growth, and is considered to be one of the more highly developed in the region with 86 per cent of GDP.[12] Thailand (34 per cent) and Indonesia (27 per cent) remain fairly underdeveloped and bank-credit-dependent (see Table 5.2). By comparison, the US, Japan and the EU-15 had debt market capitalization to GDP ratios of 146 per cent, 157 per cent and 88 per cent, respectively (Table 5.1).[13] In total financial intermediation, aggregate bond markets show similar patterns in the two regions of Asia-3 and CEE-3, with Malaysia having the most developed bond market. A similar picture emerges in sectoral bond markets (Table 5.3). In Indonesia, Poland and Hungary, government bonds dominate, with differing mixes of financial and corporate issues. In the Czech Republic, financial sector bonds are greater than the governmental share as Czech banks had to strongly tap the capital market after privatization. In Malaysia and Thailand there are greater non-governmental bond shares, though there is a different balance between financial sector and corporate non-financial issues. On the supply side, Malaysia stands out with high levels of corporate bonds (Table 5.3) and international bonds (Table 5.5) (Figure 5.1). On the demand side, Malaysia also stands out as having gross domestic savings (Table 5.4) and assets held by institutional investors (Table 5.7) of about twice the average of the other countries. As we will see, the fact that Malaysia, in particular, had a more developed bond market was important in its ability to respond to financial market turbulence in the late 1990s.

Lessons from the Asian financial crisis

The 1997–1998 Asian turbulence demonstrated the risk of unbalanced financial structures. The crisis was largely attributed to financial panic exacerbated by the capital structure of each country in which there was a maturity mismatch of assets and liabilities. Asia's aggregate long-term debt share was low, ranking below much of emerging Europe and Latin America and reflecting the low share of bond finance by the private sector (which normally is long-term).[14] Short-term (mostly foreign) liabilities were greater than short-term assets. Corporations relied heavily on short-term bank credit with maturities below one year to finance long-term

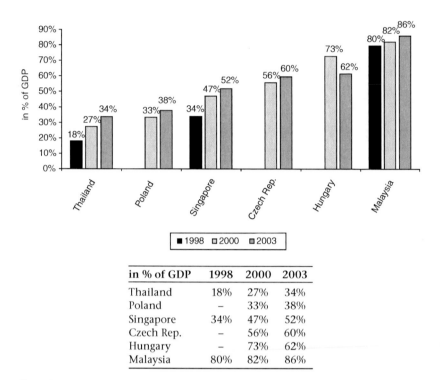

Figure 5.1   Development of bonds outstanding in Asia-3 and CEE-3

in % of GDP	1998	2000	2003
Thailand	18%	27%	34%
Poland	–	33%	38%
Singapore	34%	47%	52%
Czech Rep.	–	56%	60%
Hungary	–	73%	62%
Malaysia	80%	82%	86%

Data sources: BIS, 2004, Securities Statistics, tables 14A, 14B, 16A and 16B, http://www.bis.org/statistics/secstats.htm; ECB, 2004d, *Bond markets and long-term interest rates in non-euro area Member States of the European Union and in accession countries*, 3rd edition, November 2004, http://www.ecb.int/stats/money/long/html/index.en.html; IFS, 2004, *International Financial Statistics*, Washington DC: International Monetary Fund; P. Haiss and S. Marin, 'Options for Developing Bond Markets – Lessons from Asia for Central and Eastern Europe', *EuropaInstitut Working Paper* 63, January (2005), http://www.wu-wien.ac.at/europainstitut/forschung/wp63 (7 December 2006).

investment projects with assumed payback periods of 5–10 years. Though these were seen to be profitable in the future, they were costly to liquidate in the short term.[15] As long as creditors remained confident, this was not a problem. But any changes in the macroeconomic outlook or other factor might lead creditors to panic. The system was further hit with a currency mismatch in that there was too great a foreign exchange risk.[16] Panic became compounded in a system so reliant on short-term and foreign credit. The crisis essentially was self-fulfilling in that, when expectations changed from growth towards fears that companies might not be able to honour their debts, fewer loans were rolled over and less fresh money was made available, further reinforcing those same fears. The crises were characterized by massive attempts from all sides to liquidate claims. This in turn pressured banks (already engaged in risky practices) and ultimately the central bank and government. The illiquidity of these emerging markets has also been credited with some of the blame for panic and its results.[17]

Because the financial system was so dominated by bank lending, borrowers had no alternatives sources of borrowing to turn to. In more diversified financial markets, borrowers can chose between bank credit and bond issuance, among others, and the capital markets can complement bank lending and vice versa. Especially for long-term investment, bond finance plays a major role in more diversified financial markets. Developed bond markets are thus crucial for reducing and preventing this systemic risk. They are 'probably the most stable type of borrowing that a country of corporation can engage in'.[18] Unfortunately, this is also the source of investment capital that is least prevalent in emerging markets, because, for example, a domestic institutional investor base is absent and companies lack transparency and have poor credit ratings, and because public policy had previously prioritized stock market development and bank finance. As a result, it becomes even more important to consider the benefits and limitations of bond market development.

Similarities in bond market benefits

The aims of bond market development can be grouped into four types: (1) risk-management, in which the features and benefits of the bond market are focused on as preventive, mitigating causes of financial crisis; (2) economic benefits that a well-developed bond market brings; (3) social effects brought by bond markets as solid financial instruments; and (4) economic integration generated by the creation of a common 'bond space'.

Risk management and signal effects

The primary benefit derived from well-established domestic bond markets is in the enhancement of risk management. Publicly visible bond interest rates provide a signal to the market for risk assessment, pricing of debt and a measure of stability in expectations and projections. This is particularly vital as one looks to long-term financing. Bond markets encourage longer-term planning horizons, allowing companies to free themselves from the risk associated with short-term bank loans for financing necessary long-term investment. It is not only that bond markets are a nice long-term alternative, but also that they are a necessary tool for prudently balancing the maturity mismatch associated with bank loans.

This relates to the 'double mismatch' of currency and maturity that is generally cited as the major cause of the 1997–1998 Asian financial crisis.[19] Overreliance on bank loans and capital inflows forced into short-term obligations increased vulnerability and exacerbated the crisis.[20] In developing economies, the maturity mismatch faced by banks often tends to be systemic, because the information asymmetry between lenders and borrowers causes banks to use short-term credit as a means of limiting opportunistic borrowers.[21] Thus, despite the obvious problems associated with bank credit, short-term bank lending continues.[22] The effects of bonds on the maturity mismatch problem are contested, although the perspective – firm-level/microeconomic versus aggregate economy/macroeconomic – seems to play an important role. While bond issuance does extend the debt maturity structure of firms looking for long-term finance, at the aggregate level there is no major difference in debt maturity between bank and market-driven financial instruments.[23] In the absence of (long-term) bond markets, banks take on that role, further delimiting the options available to borrowers. For the economy as a whole, bonds can increase financing options and help stabilize the economy by mitigating the propensity of bank-dependent lending to lead to crisis. In his study on risk management and bonds, Pettis identifies this 'elegant' feature of fixed rate bonds:

> An automatic stabilization mechanism comes into play here, because as things get worse on the asset side, the liability side shrinks enough to reduce or even eliminate the debt burden. This is a radical and elegant concept: fixed rate local currency bond markets act automatically to stabilise markets both when times are good … and, most important, when times are bad. Borrowing in dollars or in short-term local currency does the exact opposite.[24]

This mechanism is of particular importance since the economies of both Asia and CEEC have what Pettis calls an 'inverted capital structure'.[25] Such an inverted capital structure is (foreign-denominated) credit-heavy, meaning firms are more prone to invest more when things are looking good, increasing their liabilities, and thereby intensifying any kind of shock later. In this context, bond markets can curb overinvestment and also ameliorate underinvestment. Because overall volatility is lower, a more bond-financed system will tend not to overinvest, and will thereby potentially avoid a negative scenario later. Thus, bonds not only allow corporations to diversify their capital structure and be less reliant on bank credit, but also help stabilize the firm's long-term financial situation itself.

As for the currency mismatch, because debt securities are denominated in local currency, foreign exchange risk is circumvented. Firms avoid overreliance on foreign credit and can hedge the foreign exchange risk. If bond issuance becomes a viable option, then firms will be less tempted to take up cheap foreign loans during a financial upswing, and thereby avoid more painful debts should the economy suffer any negative external or internal changes. It is important that bond issuance becomes an option, since the temptation is particularly great in these economies to take out foreign-denominated debt when domestic interest rates are comparatively higher.[26]

Moreover, with regards to monetary issues, developed and liquid (government) bond markets give the government an additional tool in monetary policy. Other government tools, such as raising the real interest rate, would also have more effect during a crisis when foreign-denominated debt decreases in the economy.[27]

Bonds as complementary source of capital

When corporate financial structures are diversified and thereby deepened through the introduction of a domestic bond market, crisis in one sector of the financial system will hopefully be mitigated.[28] For the CEE countries this is particularly important given the volatility of lending. During the crises in the 1990s, between 1995 and 1997, CEEC foreign bank deposits fell by USD19 billion.[29] Domestic bond markets also counteract the possibly distorting effects on capital cost of significant movements of capital in and out of a country, which in turn affects long-term development.[30] With foreign entry, banking is becoming increasingly competitive, driving down the cost of bank services and making bond issuance less attractive. High FDI and the resulting foreign ownership of large corporations favour intercompany funding and reduce their need to tap into the local bond market. In this sense, FDI may hamper the development of domestic corporate bond markets by reducing the number of possible issuers.

The more constructive growth and health-related benefits of bond markets have yet to be tapped into and may be more gradual than risk management, because they often concern structural issues; local bond markets support the necessary elements of sound economic growth, such as information disclosure and legal framework development. Bond markets prove highly constructive in part because they are much more demanding and have higher requirements of participants than, say, equity markets, and consequently often develop behind equity markets.[31]

More importantly, the establishment of a bond market leads to a more complete market interest rate by accurately reflecting the opportunity costs of funds at each date of maturity.[32] This should lead to more efficient investment and financing decisions, helping investors to better understand where and at what rate they should be investing.[33] In this way, the interest rates in the economy become market-driven, with the government bond setting the risk-free interest rate at short, medium, and, significantly, long-term maturity. Herring and Chatusripitak argue that while the equity market 'may flourish in the absence of the bond market, it may not be very efficient in the sense of aligning prices with fundamental economic values'.[34] A missing bond yield curve[35] also deprives the economy of 'a crucial source of information that helps coordinate decentralised decisions throughout the economy'.[36] Derivative markets are largely contingent on the development of a market-driven bond market, further aiding firms in hedging their risks. In this respect, the lack of a functioning efficient bond market means the lack of other functioning hedging tools. These missing tools have an impact.

Micro and macro aspects of bond finance

Since bond markets increase financing options as well as competition among banks, they have the effect of lowering the cost of loans that ought also to reduce the cost of capital.[37] Moreover, Wagner and Iakova argue, raising capital locally in bonds or equity might become more attractive, and this may further result in 'falling inflation, lower interest rates and improved legislation'.[38] This should be a principle of increasing the total capital pie, not just making credit cheaper. CEE countries, in particular, should see an increasingly stable macroeconomic situation as they are more fully integrated into the EU and by EMU candidacy. The amount of funds available should increase as capital account liberalization progresses and raising capital locally may become more attractive,[39] processes that will be further enhanced by the adoption of increasing information and communication technology.[40]

Bond issuance can also contribute to GDP growth. Besides providing financial funds directly for investment, bond issuance also provides important signals to the market.[41] That is, bond pricing is important for reliable market assessments and thus indirectly for investment and GDP growth. Szylagyi, Batten and Fetherston have argued that with a bond market the checking and screening of risk will occur faster, since the market then prices information into its daily trading activities.[42] This argument relies on functioning crediting agencies, readily available and high-quality information on firms, lowered information asymmetry and experienced investors. All of these ingredients of good corporate governance are only now emerging in Asia-3 and CEE-3.

Since bonds spread risk over a large number of primary investors, bond markets provide better risk pooling and their underdevelopment 'limits risk-pooling and risk-sharing opportunities for both households and firms'.[43] This is a significant problem for banks, since they must assume considerable risk in the mismatch between liquid short-term assets and illiquid long-term assets, a risk they cannot pass on to depositors.[44] Through bond markets, disintermediation occurs, savers and borrowers are matched directly and the distribution of risk changes as a result.[45]

The argument has also been made that more effective capital markets, and thus by implication bond markets, should increase funding especially for smaller companies as well as increasing the overall capital pool. Because movements on the bond market are more transparent, the health of the bond market might also be a better indicator of overall financial health and growth sustainability than bank credit. Thus, the deepening of capital markets would have 'far-reaching positive implications for development resource mobilization'.[46] However, given the experiences of Asian small and medium-sized enterprises (SMEs) and their continued reliance on bank credit, the actual benefits to SMEs are uncertain. This can be attributed to more idiosyncratic credit information on these firms, making the non-negotiable, standardized and inflexible terms of bond contracts less attractive.[47] In the light of these factors, venture capital might be the best financing option for smaller, often riskier, firms; venture capital would be better at evaluating such risks well and would bring more than just capital to the table, which is vital for the success of a small and medium enterprise sector. However, venture capital development requires an exit option, and this again links up to equity and bond markets. Bond markets do have an indirect benefit for small firms, because small firms can pick up the bank credit made available when larger firms turn to bond markets for financing.[48]

With regard to the maturity mismatch problem, which arises when funds raised via short-term borrowing are invested into long-term projects, bond markets can protect the economy from any bias towards long-term projects.[49] If bond markets deny long-term financing to specific firms, then projects that are not in line with market expectations may be avoided.[50] In terms of sheer volume, bond markets offer strong firms the ability to raise the large volume of financing they may need. As Harwood points out: 'Banks often cannot provide the size or structure of financing needed ... banks are increasingly constrained from financing longer-term, large-scale projects because they are trying to improve the quality of their operations'.[51] Also, as opposed to equity, the issuance of bonds is not as costly and does not dilute ownership. In this respect, a healthy bond market increases the potential and sustainability of local financing and local firms.

Corporate governance

Institution-building can also be an indirect benefit of bond market development. Bond issuance can prompt better governance and transparency on the part of firms, because investors demand to know about a firm's reputation and information about it before buying corporate bonds. Weaknesses in corporate governance are exposed as the development of bond markets raises transparency and visibility of financing decisions. With rising importance of bond markets, the impetus to implement good governance necessarily increases because otherwise institutional and private investors will flee the market and bond issues will not find adequate demand. Both Asia and Central Europe need better governance, particularly with regard to information disclosure and in ensuring that firms that issue bonds comply with high international standards.[52] The issue of information provision and credit ratings is vital, because investors run the same risks of moral hazard and asymmetric information in buying bonds that banks run in lending, except that the risk is not so heavily pooled in the bond market.[53]

While bond market development is of general importance for emerging market economies, bond markets are not without their drawbacks. Though possible benefits are widespread, they are often dependent on the depth and the activeness of the primary and the secondary market. Moreover, establishing a functional bond market with an active secondary market is extremely difficult. Bond market development is something of a chicken and egg problem. On the one hand, bonds help foster certain market developments and institutions. On the other hand, bond markets demand that these institutions and experiences already be in place. This is further complicated by the dynamic environments that emerging economies face in an increasingly complex and also interwoven global business environment.

Bond market structure and demand

Bond markets are more complicated and demanding than other financing options. This complexity is obvious in Harwood's comprehensive model of bond markets.[54] Harwood examines the components of a solid and functioning bond market through a three-dimensioned approach: inside, across and around. Whereas all financing options are affected by these factors, bond markets are particularly sensitive: 'But in economies that lack the infrastructure to support a bond market, investors are likely to have considerable doubt about what past earnings have been and what current earnings are, much less what expected future earnings will be'.[55] Because bonds are based on the premise that the bond will continue to pay interest until maturity, reliability and predictable future prospects are particularly important. Yoshitomi and Shirai further argue that there are three factors that determine the mix of liabilities that firms choose: '(1) the extent of severity of information asymmetry between ultimate creditors and ultimate borrowers; (2) the stage of economic development; and (3) the degree of sophistication with respect to the informational, legal and judiciary infrastructures.'[56]

The role of the public sector

One of the primary players in bond market development is the government. Governments can be instrumental in developing a domestic bond market as 'issuer, regulator, promoter and catalyst', though clearly financial structure cannot be seen as a product of solely legal tradition.[57] Governments must tread a fine line because their political constitution can affect investment and financial structure, while government involvement in the market may also be distorting. Most obviously, governments need to create a macroeconomic environment that is stable enough for a bond market to develop and allow firms and investors to make long-term plans. Governments are also responsible for the health of the market through regulation and the establishment of a monetary transmission mechanism. Regulations must also be adequate and stringent enough to foster confidence in an emerging market. For instance, CEE countries have higher listing standards; companies must publish their financial information according to International Financial Reporting Standards (IRFS), making bond issuance more expensive for firms.[58] Consequently, only select firms, often the largest, find bonds a cost-effective form of finance.[59] Middle-range companies often tend to list on the free unregulated market, which is an alternative but only an intermediate step towards the formation of strong public markets.[60] Nevertheless, even smaller firms will benefit from their larger clients having a broader funding base and from the general emphasis on transparency, the availability of reliable financial signals and improved corporate governance that mature bond markets bring about.

Government bond issuance can be seen as a means of jump-starting a domestic bond market, and should be seen as the first focus of domestic bond market development. Government issuance dominates the bond markets in most of Asia-3 and CEE-3 in a way similar to Japan (Table 5.3). Government bond issuance plays a vital role in creating volume and encouraging people to invest in bonds through confidence building, and government bonds function as a yield curve for the market. The government bond market, if sizable and efficient, can be used as 'benchmark' issues to form a term structure of risk-free interest.[61] To achieve this, a healthy and efficient primary market for government securities, and then an active secondary market for government bonds, needs to be established. Without active secondary market trading, the yield curve is 'much less reliable as a risk-pricing vehicle'.[62] At the same time, given the limited investor pool, the government must be careful not to issue bonds in such a way that they crowd out private bond issuance.[63] This is particularly important considering that corporate (non-sovereign) bonds lack the 'marketability' of sovereign issue.[64]

Investors and bond markets

The most significant limiting factor of a bond market is generally seen to be a narrow investor base, which can be attributed to 'restricted saving schemes, undeveloped mutual funds, over-regulation of the asset management industry and a limited role for insurance companies and pension funds'.[65] The broader the investment base, the better the market, since then there is a greater diversity in interest and maturity needs, as well as more available capital. In contrast to Asia, the CEE countries face a much lower rate of savings. This means there are less funds available, even if individuals were to invest what they save (see Table 5.4 for details).[66] Investors need to be educated as well, since many prefer equity to bonds because the yields on equities are perceived to be unlimited. Investor culture needs to be changed

Table 5.3 Size and sectoral makeup of domestic bond markets in 2003

Country	Total domestic		Government		Financial Institutions		Corporate (Non-fin.)		Sectoral makeup		
	in mn euro	in % of GDP	in mn euro	in % of GDP	in mn euro	in % of GDP	in mn euro	in % of GDP	Gov.	Fin.	Corp.
Indonesia	53.399	28%	51.492	26%	NA	–	1.907	1%	96%	–	4%
Malaysia	78.147	86%	31.987	35%	10.610	12%	35.550	39%	41%	14%	45%
Thailand	44.972	34%	24.307	18%	13.143	10%	7.522	6%	54%	29%	17%
Poland	69.462	38%	58.868	32%	4.515	2%	6.079	3%	85%	6%	9%
Czech Rep.	45.146	60%	17.867	24%	24.384	31%	2.896	4%	40%	54%	6%
Hungary	45.490	62%	36.032	49%	8.826	13%	0.632	1%	79%	19%	1%
USA	14,196.912	146%	3,976.247	41%	8,242.914	85%	1,977.751	20%	28%	58%	14%
Japan	6,448.931	157%	4,869.438	118%	969.834	24%	609.660	15%	76%	15%	9%
EU-15	8,213.064	88%	4,455.424	48%	2,772.367	30%	985.273	11%	54%	34%	12%

Data sources: IFS, 2004, International Financial Statistics, Washington DC: International Monetary Fund; BIS, 2004, Securities Statistics, tables 14A, 14B, 16A and 16B, http://www.bis.org/statistics/secstats.htm; ECB, 2004d, Bond markets and long-term interest rates in non-euro area Member States of the European Union and in accession countries, 3rd edition, November 2004, http://www.ecb.int/stats/money/long/html/index.en.html; G. Jiang and R. McCauley, 'Asian local currency bond markets', BIS Quarterly Review, June, 2004 67–79; FIBV, 2004, 'Time Series 1990–2003 of Market Capitalization of shares of domestic companies', World Federation of Exchanges, 22 June 2004.

Table 5.4   Gross domestic savings as percentage of GDP

in per cent of GDP	1997	1998	1999	2000	average 1997–2000
Indonesia	31.5%	26.5%	19.5%	25.1%	25.7%
Malaysia	44.0%	48.7%	47.4%	47.1%	46.8%
Thailand	33.6%	36.2%	32.9%	31.0%	33.4%
Poland	20.3%	21.0%	20.0%	19.6%	20.2%
Czech Rep.	26.6%	28.7%	26.5%	26.0%	26.9%
Hungary	27.7%	27.6%	26.0%	26.5%	27.0%

Sources: I. Dalla, *Harmonization of Bond Market rules and Regulations in Selected APEC Economies* (Manila: Asia Development Bank, 2003); M. Schrooten and S. Stephan, *Private Savings in Eastern European EU-Accession Countries: Evidence From a Dynamic Panel Data Model*, DIW Discussion Paper 372 (September 2003), http://www.diw.de/deutsch/produkte/publikationen/diskussionspapiere/docs/papers/dp372.pdf.

to understand the value and use of bonds. In increasing the investor base, the government again can play a large role by deregulating insurance and pension funds. Bond investment will increase as private pension is encouraged and grows, and as investors seek out better interest rate and maturity match-ups. The government should create an environment in which bond markets are permitted to grow without creating market distortions by favouring bond investment.

It might seem that the stress here is to wean these economies off bank credit. However, to say that the role of banks in these countries should be reduced would be an oversimplification. Granted, if banks are the central means of capital allocation, then the balance between bank lending and bonds would need to be adjusted particularly because injecting central bank liquidity to address bank crisis could actually prove counterproductive and exaggerate a credit crunch.[67] A spare tyre simile was once applied to describe the bond market–bank relationship, with the bond market being the spare, but the relationship is actually a much more a symbiotic one than this implies.[68] Bond markets and banks are typically positively correlated,[69] and banks are actually 'the most important issuers, holders, dealers, advisers, underwriters, guarantors, trustees, custodians and registrars in this market'.[70] There is some fear that bond markets will take all the best business, leaving banks with the lemons,[71] but large firms are unlikely to terminate their relationships with banks, and it is more likely that the nature of the relationship simply changes. If long-term bond issuance leads to a better overall firm position, then the bank loans that are taken out by a firm typically will be of higher quality.[72] It is possible that firms will imprudently issue bonds, making the scenario potentially worse for banks, but this is less likely given the existing obstacles to issuing bonds.

The quest for international bonds

Even if a healthy economic and regulatory environment, and all the players, were in place, a key question is: how far can domestic markets become viable alternatives to international bonds?[73] In spite of all the focus and efforts to develop a bond market, not every country will be able to develop a secondary bond market. This impacts the potency of bond markets and, therefore, their benefits. The question is whether the size of the market determines the liquidity of the bond market.[74] Bonds often become a captive market as institutional investors and banks buy and hold the bonds for security. But the danger is that they then discourage other investors and hence the development of a secondary market.[75] Domestic issuance may also be hindered by 'cream skimming', when the strongest best domestic companies go to international bond markets.[76] In response, some suggest that the use of open-market operations can encourage more secondary market activity.[77] Thus, though both regions stand to gain a lot from primary and secondary bond market development, they all face challenges of 'culture and cash-flow'. Bond market development cannot be a top-down affair, and participation scars must be carefully avoided.[78]

Bond strategy should follow market structure: like is not alike

All of these needs, policy recommendations and projected benefits may appear to be overwhelmingly similar among CEE and Asian countries, but in reality they indicate similarities in weakness, need and diversity of experience. Paradoxically, the generality of policy recommendations is

Table 5.5   Domestic and international bond markets in 2003

Country	Total domestic		Internat'l bonds	
	in mn euro	in % of GDP	in mn euro	in % of GDP
Indonesia	53.399	28	2.534	1
Malaysia	78.147	86	16.865	18
Thailand	44.972	34	7.205	5
Poland	69.462	38	9.660	5
Czech Rep.	45.146	60	2.217	3
Hungary	45.490	62	9.897	13
USA	14,196.912	146	2,459.937	25
Japan	6,448.931	157	95.645	2
EU-15	8,213.064	88	4,751.306	51

Data sources: IFS, 2004, *International Financial Statistics*, Washington DC: International Monetary Fund; BIS, 2004, Securities Statistics, tables 14A, 14B, 16A and 16B, http://www.bis.org/statistics/secstats.htm; ECB, 2004d, *Bond markets and long-term interest rates in non-euro area Member States of the European Union and in accession countries*, 3rd edition, November 2004, http://www.ecb.int/stats/money/long/html/index.en.html; FIBV, 2004, 'Time Series 1990–2003 of Market Capitalization of shares of domestic companies', World Federation of Exchanges, 22 June 2004.

accompanied by actual situations in which markets develop with their own peculiarities. It is possible that such market development really is general, in which case we would need to ask if everyone should look to develop the same bond market and capital structure.

There are, however, minor and major differences between the countries of CEE and Southeast Asia (see Table 5.6). In contrast to Asian economies still wary of the 1997–98 crisis, there has not been a marked increase in international bond issuance in most of the CEE.[79] This is not necessarily a bad thing, since issuance of bonds on international bond markets is similar to foreign credit. The fast growth of the corporate sector and the need for improved transparency, disclosure and infrastructure are clearly countervailing forces in this respect. Whether CEEC markets should look to international bond issuance, as the Asian countries have done, is questionable, since the Asian experience suggests some substitutability between intermediated finance with international bond issuance, but with primarily sovereign, and not private, bonds. Moreover, the increase in international bond issues has not been accompanied by adequate reductions in levels of international bank lending.[80]

Another major difference lies in the heavy inflow of foreign direct investment (FDI) into the CEE economies prior to and around EU membership and the high level of intercompany finance provided by foreign owners of CEE companies. Thus large CEE corporations, many of them foreign-owned, see no need to turn to bond financing, given that intercompany loans or loans from (again, majority foreign-held) local banks fighting for market share are readily available. Foreign bank ownership and FDI may to a certain extent 'crowd out' domestic bond market finance and replace it for the time being.

The primary difference that CEE countries face is the existence of a regional monetary union. The Czech Republic, Hungary and Poland all joined the European Union in 2004 with their currencies tied to the Euro

Table 5.6 FDI inward stock vs. outstanding financial and corporate bonds

in mn euro	FDI 1998	FDI 1999	FDI 2000	FDI 2001	FDI 2002	Financial and corporate bonds 2002
Indonesia	58.614	6.489	65.167	65.082	53.244	1.907
Malaysia	38.584	48.735	56.687	60.480	53.881	47.964
Thailand	19.244	25.484	26.295	33.085	28.822	17.546
Poland	19.247	25.956	36.783	46.557	43.053	12.185
Czech Rep.	12.308	17.472	23.261	30.741	36.664	27.558
Hungary	15.854	19.211	21.283	26.736	23.282	6.418

Sources: BIS, 2004, Securities Statistics, tables 14A, 14B, 16A and 16B, http://www.bis.org/statistics/secstats.htm; ECB, 2003a, Bond markets and long-term interest rates in European Union Accession Countries, 2003 edition, 6 October, www.ecb.int/pub/pdf/other/bondmarketacc2003 en.pdf; G. Jiang and R. McCauley, 'Asian local currency bond markets', *BIS Quarterly Review*, June (2004) 67–79; UNCTAD, 2004, FDI database, United Nations Conference on Trade and Development, http://stats.unctad.org/fdi/.

already in one way or another, and entry into European Economic and Monetary Union (EMU) is pending. This is the one impetus that the CEE countries indisputably have that the Asian countries do not. Thus, one of their primary economic goals at this time is fully-fledged 'return to Europe', EU convergence and EMU entry. Asia, on the other hand, has discussed a common Asian market and even currency, but has yet to realize one. It is possible that the adoption of the Euro will also lead to the importation, in some sense, of the Euro's financial markets and exchanges. These already well-developed debt markets would be able to address financial needs, though they would not be a perfect substitute for domestic bond markets at present.[81] By directing efforts towards utilizing the Euro-denominated bond market and by beginning to prepare for EMU entry and the introduction of the Euro as common currency, these countries could take early advantage of the fast-growing and large Euro-bond region. The Euro-bond shows great potential, growing to outpace the Euro equity market.[82] The question for the CEE countries is then whether it makes sense for each country to try to build a domestic bond market. Building all the components necessary for a well-developed bond market is costly and time-consuming, and consequently many small emerging markets are caught in a 'vicious circle of low liquidity and underdeveloped markets'.[83] And so there is discussion about regional markets and cooperation, although the Central European countries have not made any moves towards a CEE regional bond market.

Do the costs of a domestic bond market then outweigh the benefits, particularly since when EMU entry is gained these domestic markets will probably struggle to thrive, if they continue at all? The primary question seems to be when these countries will actually enter EMU. Because they are currently in something of a state of limbo, being in the EU but not in EMU, it is difficult to argue for or against a dedicated effort for domestic bond development. EMU entry seems to be 'back-loaded'.[84] On the one hand, a solid government bond market would furnish the government with additional tools for monetary policy, which is desirable in light of the Maastricht criteria demands.[85] These countries might do well to prime their economies for the current trend towards a more market-driven financial system, particularly because of their greater need for institutional deepening, and addressing 'residual legacies of the past', while bolstering a more competitive environment.[86] A domestic bond market would ameliorate all these areas. Wagner and Iakova also argue that, with EU accession and restructuring, capital inflow and outflow volatility will increase, making sound domestic financial structures vital to buffer such fluctuations.[87] Bonds might also provide an alternative channel to credit for foreign capital, which would be beneficial given that when capital is abundant bad credit decisions are often made.[88]

However, these countries already face a plethora of development demands on top of the steep requirements imposed by the Maastricht criteria as prerequisite to join the EMU. For instance, the issuance of sovereign bonds would be reined in by the need to keep government debt down, making it potentially difficult to develop a deep and active government bond market. The infrastructure needed for a liquid bond market is also costly and an added concern for the government. Their efforts might be better spent elsewhere, as their small size parallels developed countries without bond markets, indicating it may be doubly difficult for these countries to develop liquid markets in the first place. Regional efforts, as in Asia, may also be more economical in developing bond markets in CEE compared with separate country efforts which individually lack the critical mass.

Conclusion

In all the technical and financial information it is easy to lose sight of the actual effect of financial systems, which is on real people. Many of the drivers of bond market development, for example institutional investors such as pension funds, are closely linked to the saver who theoretically will be putting his money into domestic stocks as well. In light of these concerns, the dynamics of developing domestic bond markets changes again. Governments would do well to take advantage of the dual need to strengthen the domestic financial situation and to reform pension systems, as well as developing even rudimentary bond markets. Insurance and pensions are creating institutional investors with needs that match bonds – long-term, local currency liabilities, and with the option of fixed rates.[89] Among the countries we survey from emerging Europe (Poland, the Czech Republic and Hungary; CEE-3) and from emerging Asia (Indonesia, Malaysia and Thailand; Asia-3), Malaysia stands out with a much more developed bond market in terms of volume (aggregate bonds outstanding relative to GDP) and with regard to the sectoral mix (sizable corporate non-financial segment). We attribute this to a comparatively strong domestic institutional investor base (Table 5.7). Demand-side efforts towards bond market development should thus focus on the creation of a domestic investor base (particularly through pension fund reform) or on providing access for foreign institutional investors.

Without a functioning bond market, policyholders might be forced to pay higher premiums to offset the increased risks and management issues that funds face.[90] And, as the macroeconomic environment stabilizes, investors will be more willing to lock into fixed rates.[91] Bond market development seems vital in this respect, as there just is no real alternative offered outside a domestic bond market to address these needs. CEE governments should

Table 5.7   Assets held by institutional investors in per cent of GDP (2000)

in percent of GDP	Investment / Mutual Funds	Pension Funds	Insurance Companies	Total
Indonesia	0	2%	0	3%
Malaysia	6%	26%	1%	33%
Thailand	5%	5%	1%	10%
Poland	8%	2%	5%	15%
Czech Rep.	8%	2%	2%	12%
Hungary	12%	4%	3%	19%

Sources: I. Dalla, *Harmonization of Bond Market Rules and Regulations in Selected APEC Economies* (Asia Development Bank, 2003); S. Claessens, S. Djankov and D. Klingebiel, *Stock Markets in Transition Economies*, Financial Sector Discussion Paper No. 5 (World Bank, September 2000).

also pursue bond market development to support corporate governance and transparency, the creation of a more sophisticated investor base and market infrastructure.

The CEE-3 joined the European Union in 2004, and joining European Economic and Monetary Union (EMU) is planned as the next step for further economic integration. Once these countries (and other countries with the same option) enter the Euro-system, their bond markets will benefit greatly because their bond markets will be integrated into the large and liquid Euro-denominated bond market. Given the small economic size of some of the CEE markets, it may not make sense economically to develop their domestic bond markets on a stand-alone basis because they hardly can reach a critical mass individually. Regional linkups that follow existing ties from integration with neighbouring markets (such as trade, FDI, bank investment) or fast linking into the Euro-zone may make more sense.[92] Following the Southeast Asian way of creating regional bond funds might also help CEE in developing their bond market.

Why should these emerging economies work on their bond market at all? In reviewing the literature we find evidence that bond markets can support economic growth; that they are necessary for the proper functioning of financial markets via providing pricing signals; and that the absence of a well-developed bond market makes the non-financial sector more dependent on banks, as was observed in the 1997–1998 Asian financial crises. Optimistically, in either case, financial systems adapt to their situation, with greater macroeconomic stability, which is what EU integration aims to bring.[93] From the various efforts under way, it appears that regional models like the Asian bond fund and the path towards EMU can accelerate the development of the respective bond markets by improving regulation and supervision and by adherence to internationally recognized accounting standards. Given the mechanism of EMU entry which, like other mechanisms, relies on long-term interest rates derived from well-established bond markets, the Central European countries are probably better off focusing on EMU entry and only then developing their bond markets further. They should make domestic bond market development (or at least its rudimentary players and infrastructure) a part of that EMU strategy where market size allows for this, and focus on the fundamentals on which bond market development depends. Common logics, rules and practices in these regional bond markets are important vehicles fostering regional economic integration. Both the CEE and the Asian economies could achieve more by working with each other in developing bond markets than by acting alone. With an increasingly regional – if not global – focus among both issuers and investors, integrated bond markets create interdependencies, add breadth to financial resources and can forge transnational regional economic structure and practices.[94]

Notes

*Peter R. Haiss (peter.haiss@wu-wien.ac.at) is a lecturer at the EuropaInstitut, Vienna University of Economics and Business Administration, and is also with the Corporate Finance and Public Sector Department of Bank Austria, Vienna, Austria, member of UniCredit Group. Natalie Chou (ngchou@sas.upenn.edu) participated as a graduate student at the University of Pennsylvania during her visit to the Institute of European Studies, Vienna, Austria. The opinions expressed are the authors' personal views and not necessarily those of the institutions the authors are affiliated with. The authors are indebted to John Pickles and Robert Jenkins for comments, to Stefan Marin for assistance in data retrieval and editing and to the Jubiläumsfonds of the Oesterreichische Nationalbank (project No. 8868) for support granted.

1 IMF, 'Development of Corporate Bond Markets in Emerging Market Countries', chapter 4 in IMF, ed., *Global Financial Stability Report – Sept. 2005*, http://www. imf.org/External/Pubs/FT/GFSR/2005/02/pdf/chp4.pdf (7 December 2006); D. Mihaljek, M. Scatigna and A. Villar, 'Recent Trends in Bond Markets', *BIS Paper* No. 11, June (2002) 13–41, http://www.bis.org/publ/bispap11.htm (7 December 2006) 18.

2 R. Herring and N. Chatusripitak, *The Case of the Missing Market: The Bond Market and What It Matters for Financial Development* (Philadelphia: Wharton Financial Institutions Center, 2000).

3 Hungary's earlier opening to international standards also explains the relatively higher share of international bond issuance (Table 5). G. Sándor, 'Developments in the Hungarian Debt Markets', *BIS Paper* No. 11, June (2002) 115–117, http://www.bis.org/publ/bispap11.htm (7 December 2006).

4 EBRD, *Transition Report 2007* (London: European Bank for Reconstruction and Development, 2007). Polish banks managed to reduce the level of non-performing loans from 25 per cent in 2003 to roughly 9 per cent in 2006.

5 The higher risk inherent in the Polish banks may also explain the lower savings rate in Poland (Table 4), with repercussions on institutional investors' demand for investment into bonds.

6 S. Cheung and B. Chan, 'Bond markets in the Pacific Rim: Development Market Structure and Relevant Issues in Fixed-Income Securities Markets', *Asia Pacific Development Journal*, 9(1) (2002) 1–21, www.unescap.org/drpad/publication/journal_9_1/stephen.pdf (7 December 2006) 8.

7 D. Dwor-Frecaut, M. Hallward-Driemeier and F. Colaco, 'Corporate Credit Needs and Governance, Corporate Credit Needs and Governance', a paper presented at the Conference on Asian Corporate Recovery: Corporate Governance, Government Policy (Bangkok: The World Bank, Bangkok, 31 March–2 April 1999) 14.

8 N. Wagner and D. Iakova, 'Financial Sector Evolution in the Central European Economies: Challenges in Supporting Macroeconomic Stability and Sustainable Growth', *IMF Working Papers* No.01/141 (2001), http://www.imf.org/external/pubs/ft/wp/2001/wp01141.pdf (7 December 2006); for south-eastern Europe, see G. Fink., P. Haiss and M. von Varendorff, Serbia's Banking Sector Reform: Implications for Economic Growth and Financial Development, *Southeast European and Black Sea Studies*, 7(4) (2007) 609–636.

9 IOSCO, 'Development of Corporate Bond Markets in Emerging Market Countries', May 2002, http://www.iosco.org/library/pubdocs/pdf/IOSCOPD127.pdf (7 December 2006) 54.

10 Asian Development Bank (ADB), *Development of Domestic Bond Markets: Compendium of Best Practices* (2004), http://www.adb.org/Projects/Apec/DBM/practices.asp (7 December 2006).

11 J. Köke and M. Schröder, 'Prospects of Capital Markets in Central and Eastern Europe', *ZEW Discussion Paper* 02–57 (2003), http://www.zew.de (7 December 2006).

12 ADB, 2004.

13 IFS, *International Financial Statistics* (Washington DC: International Monetary Fund, 2004), http://www.imfstatistics.org (7 December 2006).

14 S. Claessens, S. Djankov and L. Lang, *Corporate Growth, Financing, and Risks in the Decade before East Asia's Financial Crisis* (Washington DC: The World Bank, 1998) 11.

15 R. Chang, 'Understanding recent crises in emerging markets', *Economic Review* 84(2) (Federal Reserve Bank of Atlanta: ABI/INFORM Global, 1999) 2.

16 J. Batten and Y.H. Kim, 'Expanding Long-term Financing Through Bond Market Development: A Post-Crisis Policy Task', in Y. H. Kim, ed., *Government Bond Market Development in Asia* (Manila: Asian Development Bank 2001), http://www.adb.org/Documents/Conference/Govt_Bond_Market/default.asp (7 December 2006) 6.

17 Chang, 1999, 12.

18 A. Harwood, *Building Local Bond Markets: An Asian Perspective* (Washington DC: International Finance Corporation (IFC), 2000) 58.

19 M. Yoshitomi and S. Shirai, 'Designing a Financial Market Structure in Post-Crisis Asia', 27 March (2001), http://www.adbi.org/publications (7 December 2006)

20 P. Turner, 'Bond Markets in Emerging Economies: An overview of policy issues', *BIS Paper* No. 11, June (2002), http://www.bis.org/publ/bispap11.htm (7 December 2006) 3.

21 IOSCO, 2002, 4.

22 M. Goldstein and P. Turner, 'Banking Crisis in Emerging Economies: Origins and Policy Options', *BIS Economic Papers* No. 46 (1996) http://www.bis.org/publ/bispapers.htm (7 December 2006).

23 G. Jiang, N. Tank and E. Law, 'The Costs and Benefits of Developing Debt Markets: Hong Kong's Experience', *BIS Paper* No. 11, June (2002), http://www.bis.org/publ/bispap11.htm (7 December 2006) 112.

24 M. Pettis, 'The Risk Management Benefits of Bonds', in A. Harwood, ed., *Building Local Bond Markets: An Asian Perspective* (Washington DC: IFC, 2000), 56.

25 ibid.

26 M. Goldstein and P. Turner, 'Banking Crisis in Emerging Economies: Origins and Policy Options', *BIS Economic Papers* No. 46 (1996) http://www.bis.org/publ/bispapers.htm (7 December 2006) 15.

27 ibid., 16.

28 M. Plummer and R. Click, 'Bond Market Development and Integration in ASEAN', *International Journal of Finance and Economics*, 10(2) (2005) 133–142; J. Batten and Y.H. Kim, 'Expanding Long-term Financing Through Bond Market Development: A Post-Crisis Policy Task', in Asian Development Bank, eds, *Government Bond Market Development in Asia* (2001), http://www.adb.org/Documents/Conference/Govt_Bond_Market/default.asp (7 December 2006) 7.

29 P. Szilagyi, J. Batten and T. Fetherston, 'Disintermediation and the Development of Bond Markets in Emerging Europe', *International Journal of the Economics of Business* 10(1) (2003) 69.

30 S. Cheung and B. Chan, 'Bond markets in the Pacific Rim: Development Market Structure and Relevant Issues in Fixed-Income Securities Markets', *Asia Pacific Development Journal* 9(1) (2002), www.unescap.org/drpad/publication/journal_9_1/stephen.pdf (7 December 2006) 1. Even though the banking sector has liberalized and allowed the entry of foreign banks from mature market economies, which presumably make fewer bad loans due to their superior risk-management skills, this is not an automatic guarantee that banking risk or default will be lower. Recent experiences in Latin America have proven that foreign banks are not necessarily more reliable or obligated to stay within the market in the event of a downturn; IMF, 'Development of Corporate Bond Markets in Emerging Market Countries', chapter 4 in IMF, ed., *Global Financial Stability Report – Sept. 2005*, http://www.imf.org/External/Pubs/FT/GFSR/2005/02/pdf/chp4.pdf (7 December 2006). For a broader discussion of the impact of foreign banks, see M. Eller, P. Haiss and K. Steiner, 'Foreign direct investment in the financial sector and economic growth in Central and Eastern Europe: The crucial role of the efficiency channel', *Emerging Markets Review* 7(4) (2006) 300–319.

31 A. Harwood, *Building Local Bond Markets: An Asian Perspective* (Washington DC: International Finance Corporation (IFC), 2000) 4.

32 R. Herring and N. Chatusripitak, *The Case of the Missing Market: The Bond Market and What It Matters for Financial Development* (Philadelphia: Wharton Financial Institutions Center, 2000) 30.

33 P. Turner, 'Bond Markets in Emerging Economies: An overview of policy issues', *BIS Paper* No. 11, June (2002), http://www.bis.org/publ/bispap11.htm (7 December 2006) 2.

34 Herring and Chatusripitak, 2000, 33.

35 A yield curve provides the term structure of interest rates and depicts the relation between the cost of borrowing (i.e., interest rate) and the tenure (i.e., time to maturity) of the debt for a given borrower in a given currency. Yield curves are important to understand conditions in financial markets. Government bond

yield curves provide major signals on financing conditions to financial markets and for bond issuance by the private sector.

36   Herring and Chatusripitak, 2002, 23.

37   IOSCO 'Development of Corporate Bond markets…', 2002.

38   Wagner and Iakova, 2001, 10.

39   Turner, 2002, 3; Herring and Chatusripitak, 2000.

40   Wagner and Iakova, 2001, 10.

41   G. Fink, P. Haiss and H. Kirchner, 'Die Finanzierung über Anleihenemissionen und Zusammenhänge zum Wirtschaftswachstum' [Financing by issuing bonds and the relationship to economic growth], *Kredit und Kapital* 38(3) (2005) 351–375; G. Fink, P. Haiss, and S. Hristoforova, 'Bond Markets and Economic Growth', *EuropaInstitut Working Paper* 49, April 2003, http://www.wu-wien.ac.at/europainstitut/forschung/nexus (1 August 2008).

42   Szylagyi, Batten and Fetherston, 2003, 80.

43   Herring and Chatusripitak, 2000, 23.

44   IOSCO, 2002, 5.

45   M. Yoshitomi and S. Shirai, 'Designing a Financial Market Structure in Post-Crisis Asia', 27 March (2001), http://www.adbi.org/publications (7 December 2006). Disintermediation is the removal of financial intermediaries (i.e., banks) in the monetary supply chain. Instead of going through banks as middle-men, companies tap the capital market directly via bond issuance. This is significant because bonds do not involve a maturity transformation, since investors are fully aware of the yield and time horizon of the debt security, whereas bank loans necessarily involve a maturity transformation via banks.

46   Szilagyi, Batten and Fetherston, 2003, 80.

47   IOSCO, 2002, 3.

48   D. Mihaljek, M. Scatigna and A. Villar, 'Recent Trends in Bond Markets', *BIS Paper* No. 11, June (2002), http://www.bis.org/publ/bispap11.htm (7 December 2006) 23.

49   P. Turner, 'Bond Markets in Emerging Economies: An overview of policy issues', *BIS Paper* No. 11, June (2002), http://www.bis.org/publ/bispap11.htm (7 December 2006) 2.

50   IOSCO, 2002, 4.

51   Harwood, 2000, 4.

52   J. Köke and M. Schröder, 'Prospects of Capital Markets in Central and Eastern Europe', *ZEW Discussion Paper* 02–57 (2003), http://www.zew.de (7 December 2006) 11.

53   Wagner and Iakova, 2001, 13.

54   Harwood, 2000, 8.

55   Herring and Chatusripitak, 2000, 33.

56   Yoshitomi and Shirai, 2001, 58.

57   Yoshitomi and Shirai, 2001, 7; IOSCO, 2002, 16.

58   J. Batten and Y.H. Kim, 'Expanding Long-term Financing Through Bond Market Development: A Post-Crisis Policy Task', in Asian Development Bank, eds, *Government Bond Market Development in Asia* (2001), http://www.adb.org/Documents/Conference/Govt_Bond_Market/default.asp (7 December 2006) 11.

59   Iakova and Wagner, 2001, 10.

60   Batten and Kim, 2001, 11.

61 IOSCO, 2002, 16.
62 M. Plummer and R. Click, 'Bond Market Development and Integration in ASEAN', *International Journal of Finance and Economics*, 10(2) (2005) 133–142.
63 Szilagyi, Batten and Fetherston, 2003, 67.
64 Szilagyi, Batten and Fetherston, 2003, 76.
65 Szilagyi, Batten and Fetherston, 2003, 79.
66 Köke and Schröder, 2003.
67 Wagner and Iakova, 2001, 24.
68 Hawkins, 2002, 43.
69 Jiang, Tang and Law, 2002.
70 Hawkins, 2002, 42.
71 Turner, 2002, 8; Hawkins, 2002, 45.
72 Hawkins, 2002, 45.
73 Turner, 2002, 3.
74 M.S. Mohanty, 'Improving Liquidity in Government Bond Markets', *BIS Paper* No. 11, June (2002) 49–80, http://www.bis.org/publ/bispap11.htm (7 December 2006) 50.
75 Yoshitomi and Shirai, 2001.
76 J. Bonin and P. Wachtel, 'Financial sector development in transition economies: Lessons for the first decade', http://papers.ssrn.com/sol3/papers.cfm?abstract_id=1015704 (1 August 2008).
77 IOSCO, 2002, 48.
78 Harwood, 2000, 9.
79 Only Hungary opened early to foreign inflows and international standards.
80 Batten and Kim, 2001, 17.
81 Szilagyi, Batten and Fetherston, 2003, 80.
82 Bishop, 2001.
83 Mohanty, 2002, 52.
84 IMF, 'Global Financial Stability: Market Development and Issues', *World Economic and Financial Surveys* (IMF, September 2003) 55.
85 EU members wishing to join EMU need to master the Maastricht criteria first. These criteria relate to price stability, the government budgetary position, participation in the exchange rate mechanism and convergence of long-term interest rates. The latter is a financial market stability measure based upon 10-year government bonds. See the article by A. Zachorowska-Mazurkiewicz in this volume for details on the Maastricht criteria and EMU.
86 Wagner and Iakova, 2001, 3.
87 Wagner and Iakova, 2001, 37.
88 Batten and Szilagyi, 2003, 96.
89 A. Jabre, 'A Strategic Priority for Emerging Markets', in A. Harwood, ed., *Building Local Bond Markets: An Asian Perspective* (Washington DC: IFC, 2000) 39–42; Harwood, 2000, 40.
90 IOSCO, 2002, 5.
91 Harwood, 2000, 5.
92 P. Haiss and S. Marin, 'Options for Developing Bond Markets – Lessons from Asia for Central and Eastern Europe', *EuropaInstitut Working Paper* 63, January (2005) http://www.wu-wien.ac.at/europainstitut/forschung/wp63 (1 August 2008).

93   M. Goldstein and P. Turner, 'Banking Crisis in Emerging Economies: Origins and Policy Options', *BIS Economic Papers* No. 46 (1996) http://www.bis.org/publ/bispapers.htm (7 December 2006) 34.

94   C. Pazarbasioglu, 'IMF Helps Develop Local Bond Markets', *IMF Survey Magazine* January 2 (2008), http://www.imf.org/external/pubs/ft/survey/so/2008/pol1012a.htm (3 January 2008).

6
System Transformation and Industrial Policy in Poland's Coal Industry

Ksymena Rosiek

Introduction

When the process of political and economic transformation began in Poland, intensive industrialization over many years had resulted in the development of heavy chemical and armaments industries, while environmental protection had been neglected. System transformation in the 1990s was predicated on commitments to the market as the main agent of reform, and, as a consequence, the role of state was under-theorized. In practice, the ownership structure of industry, market instability and the high social costs of reforms quickly generated a need for new state policies for industry. These were especially aimed at adjusting production to demand and increasing the competitiveness of enterprises. The process of accession to the European Union has had a huge impact on these changes.

The main goal of this chapter is to analyse changes in Polish industrial policy and in Polish industry over the past 15 years with particular emphasis on the hard coal industry and the costs of its transformation. The chapter concludes with an assessment of Poland's ability to meet the new challenges related to the fulfilment of the goals of the Lisbon Strategy. The document, subsequently referred to as 'The Lisbon Strategy', is the result of a European Council meeting of Europe's heads of state and governments in Lisbon in March 2000.[1] They declared their intention to make the European Union (EU) 'the most competitive and dynamic knowledge-based economy in the world, capable of sustainable economic growth with more and better jobs and greater social cohesion'.[2] To achieve this goal by 2010 they adopted what is now called the Lisbon Strategy of economic and structural reforms.[3] But, while initial results of the Strategy have been disappointing,[4] the strategy itself has recently been 'refreshed' in ways that have led to changes in both cohesion policy and the Lisbon Strategy implementation.[5]

Industrial policy in Poland

Industrial policy is a component of the state's social and economic development strategy. It focuses on industry transformation problems and uses economic, legal, and other instruments to encourage the development of what is hoped will be a rational structure of products responsive to market conditions.[6] A strategic objective of industrial policy is to raise enterprise efficiency, competitiveness and innovation. Given its history of state planning and ownership of enterprises, the term 'industrial policy' has a wider meaning in Poland than in the European Union.

The main goals of industrial policy in the EU and in Poland are similar, but the detailed objectives in Polish industrial policy have been defined more directly and embrace wider areas. The main goals of the EU industrial policy are:

1. supporting the scientific-technological development-influenced competitiveness of European Community goods;
2. supporting strategic industries, such as those based on modern technologies that are important for country's defence and prestige (IT, biotechnologies, electric and telecommunication, space research and development, air industry);
3. restructuring of traditional industries (mining, steel sector, electricity sector);
4. stimulating and restructuring industry in underdeveloped regions, particularly where industrial production has been declining and structural unemployment and environmental problems have been increasing.

The characteristic features of Polish industrial policy, and the resulting legacies with which adaptation to the Lisbon Strategy has to deal, are:

- Direct guidelines for industrial development were part of a coordinated strategic planning process dedicated to specific industries and their role in that sector.
- Industries were financed directly by the state.
- Rules relating to competitiveness and the common market were set down by state agencies.
- The sources and methods for structural change were defined.
- Technical policies and aid were similarly set out by the state.
- Export-oriented policies, along with timetables and institutions responsible for putting them into effect, were developed.

The most important difference between the EU and Polish approaches to industrial policy is that the EU, in parallel with the WTO, requires a horizontal approach to economic policy in which policy instruments are dedicated not to particular sectors but to supporting R&D, environmental protection, small and medium enterprises, etc. By contrast, in Poland sectoral planning prevailed. During the process of negotiating Polish membership, these differences had to be addressed. Polish policies are being redirected from sectoral to more horizontally organized policies and, at the same time, EU industrial policy has also been modified to focus even more on competitiveness and innovation, with the explicit goal of developing a responsive industrial policy that provides: 'the right framework conditions for enterprise development and innovation in order to make the EU an attractive place for industrial investment and job creation'.[7]

There are some important guidelines for EU industrial policy. Some of them are focused on the improvement of the European infrastructure and business environment in industry. In accordance with Communication 2005,[8] industrial policy seeks to create an adequate framework for the development and innovation of enterprises to make the EU an attractive place to invest and create jobs in industry. It is characterized by a strong stress on horizontal issues (that is, issues common to all industrial sectors), such as regulatory and administrative reform, enterprise investment support, innovativeness, research and development, and educating the public in the Member States to improve the quality of human capital. It also covers environmental and employment policies, particularly in its policy for sustainable economic development. In 2007, the European Commission began a review of the effects of these horizontal and sectoral initiatives.[9]

One of the most important challenges in the Polish economic transformation was the huge heavy industry sector. The collapse of several industrial sectors and increasing unemployment and costs led to social and institutional resistance to the reforms and a resurgence of interest in framing a new industrial policy and a new role for the state. Some authorities claimed that industrial issues should be left to the market, while for others implementation of the new industrial policies was not a priority because other rules and policies (such as those dealing with environmental protection, competitiveness and anti-monopoly activities) would remove the need for sectoral policies. These views were reflected in a popular saying of Tadeusz Syryjczyk, the Minister of Industry in the first Solidarity government, that 'the lack of industrial policy is industrial policy itself'.[10] The introduction of reforms in 1990–1992 in what was later referred to as '*the Balcerowicz Plan*' contained no direct programme of industrial policy.

The first phase of system transformation was aimed at stabilizing the macroeconomic situation in 1990–1992. The economic challenges faced by the new government necessitated immediate action: demand for industrial goods decreased, overproduction continued,[11] consumer goods were in short supply, inflation rose precipitously, enterprise bankruptcy increased and several heavy industry sectors collapsed. To stabilize the situation, monetary policy and 'shock therapy' were deployed to effect a rapid transition from a planned to a market economy.[12] The plan contained two parts: the stabilization programme and the system changes. Stabilization was to be achieved by reducing budget expenditures, cutting subsidies for goods and services, introducing market prices, salaries and interest rates and allowing unrestricted currency exchange. The plan did recommended that controls on energy and fuel prices be retained during the period of transition. System changes involved liberalizing property rights and private ownership, new legislation on private firm creation,[13] removal of state intervention in real estate transactions, the introduction of a clear tax system and full privatization of state property.

Inflation was lowered, domestic convertibility of currencies was introduced and the market was stabilized. But industrial output declined and foreign goods imports rose rapidly. The situation was exacerbated by the dissolution in 1991 of the Council of Mutual Economic Assistance (CMEA). Deep recession followed and this in turn stimulated policymakers and social movements to begin to press for a new industrial policy. The first guidelines were defined in 1992 and *'Polish Industrial Policy'* for 1993–1995 was accepted by the Council of Ministers in 1993. Rules and directions governing industrial strategies (independent of their ownership forms) were systematized, including the restructuring of enterprises, the development of small and middle-sized enterprises, environmental protection, energy and fuel saving, labour market reform and technical investment strategies. Fuel, energy and munitions sectors received particular attention. Special emphasis was also placed on restructuring in regions where declining industries were concentrated (particularly in coal mining and steel regions) and in developing technical infrastructure.[14] The economy rebounded slowly in 1994 and in June 1994 the then Minister of Finance presented an integrated pro-developmental programme of economic growth for the years 1994–1997 – *'The Strategy for Poland'*. This focused on three important goals: rapid economic growth, system stabilization and the improvement of living standards. The Strategy consisted of ten programmes: introducing partnership relations in work and salary negotiations, welfare system reform, employment creation, rural development, investment in human capital, changes in state ownership and returning to private ownership in some sectors, financial strategy, finance sector reform, the reduction of the grey economy and increasing international competitiveness.[15]

'Directions of Industrial Policy for the Years 1999–2002' (accepted in 1998) focused even more on the growth of international competitiveness measured by the ability of enterprises to compete in international markets, placing specific emphasis on quality and technical needs. Factors influencing the implementation of these objectives were defined as:

- changes in the structure of indirect growth factors such as direct investment, new technologies, and investment in human capital;

- changes in the production structure, growth in the share of goods with a high manufacturing level, and gross value added;
- changes in the ownership structure, with the particular goal of increasing the role of the private sector;
- development of small and medium enterprises.

These objectives were to be realized by programmes to support entrepreneurship and compliance with the EU regulations. These included rules governing the granting and monitoring of state aid, rules for running a business, protection of competition and protection of intangible and industrial property. Government intervention was allowed only in declining and sensitive markets and only to promote limited goods.[16] After 1996, various programmes for restructuring the coal, steel and armaments industries and programmes to protect small and middle-sized enterprise were implemented. Not all goals were fulfilled and programmes had to be modified and adapted as conditions changed.

In the strategic document *'Poland 2025'* (accepted in 2000) a long-term strategy of sustainable development was defined. The most important goals were again to increase the competitiveness and innovative aspects of the economy.[17] Following the model of EU policy, the goal for the Polish economy was for it to become a knowledge-based and sustainable economy. This was to be achieved by the modernization of the economy and the creation of specific models of social consumption. Particular emphasis was put on the restructuring of traditional branches of industry, which should lead to a decline of the share of heavy industry in gross value added, its modernization and overall decline in environmental degradation.

The most important recent strategic document defining the direction and objectives of economic development is the *'National Development Plan 2004–2006'*. The strategic objective of the national development plan is to develop a competitive economy based on knowledge and entrepreneurship, characterized by long-term harmonized development, employment growth and the improvement of social, economic and spatial cohesion with the European Union at regional and national levels.[18] The next *'National Development Plan 2007–2013'* is currently being prepared. The process of integration with the EU and access to its structures, especially regulations connected with state aid and environmental protection, have had a huge impact on the process of industrial restructuring and feature prominently in the new version of this document – *'Poland- National Strategic Reference Framework 2007–2013 in Support of Growth and Jobs – National Cohesion Policy.'*[19]

The main goals of the economic policy in the years 1990–1993 were, therefore, to stabilize the economy and implement free-market rules. Between 1994 and 2002, development processes in Poland were distinctly modified and priorities and goals were transformed. In the years 1994–1997, the main goals were to promote structural change and higher levels of economic growth. The main characteristic of this period was the acceleration of economic growth, achieved mainly through high levels of domestic consumption and new investment, but dependent on increased imports. One consequence was an adverse balance of trade. As result of the government decision in 1997 to cool the economy[20] and the financial crisis in Russia, the Polish economy slowed. From 1998–2001, GDP grew more slowly as levels of investment and consumption demand declined. The number of employees decreased, unemployment rose, disposable income decreased and the situation in public finance worsened. Imports declined while imports remained high. As a result, in 2002–2004 the main priority of Polish economic policy was to accelerate the economic growth, although GDP growth of 5.4 per cent in 2004 did not have any immediate significant impact on the number of people hired and unemployment remained high.

Industrial change in Poland between 1990 and 2004

Between 1989 and 1991 industrial output and GDP declined sharply. The index of industrial production fell by 25 per cent between 1989 and 1990, and in the next year by a further ten per cent. In 1992 industrial sales[21] increased by about three per cent, but even though industrial sales rose by about ten per cent between 1992 and 1993 they were still about 26.3 per cent lower than in 1989 (Table 6.1; Figure 6.1).

Initial growth in 1992 was followed by an acceleration of growth rates between 1993 and 1997, when industrial sales indices in particular rose dramatically (Figure 6.2). In 1998 growth slowed as a result of government policies to 'cool the economy', and resumed again in 2003–2006. While growth indices were low in 2005 and 2006, these occurred from a much larger base figure than the very high growth rates in the previous year. Still, with growth reaching 6.1 per cent in 2006, one of the biggest challenges for the government is to sustain such levels of dynamic growth in the coming years.

Between 1999 and 2002 structural change and privatization resulted in industrial employment declining by from one to seven per cent. While in 1990 almost 37 per cent of employed people worked in industry, this had declined to about 23 per cent by 2003 and industrial productivity had risen by about 12 per cent per year (Table 6.3). The result was a strengthening of the position of the private sector in industry and an increased role for manufacturing in the structure of production as the economy was rapidly integrated into broader EU production networks. Industrial sales rose by 145 per cent between 1990 and 2006, with particularly strong growth of between 8.5 and 12 per cent per year between 1994 and 1997 and 12.6 and 11.3 per cent per year between 2004 and 2006.

Table 6.1 The importance of industry in National Economy in Poland

Specification	1990	1995	2000	2001	2002	2003	2004	2005	2006
Gross output (constant prices, 1990 = 100)	100.0	113.8	154.0	156.0	157.6	163.6	174.9	181.7	196.4
Gross domestic product (constant prices, 1990 = 100)	100.0	111.4	145.0	146.7	148.8	154.6	162.8	168.7	179.2
Industry participation in creating (%)	44.9	29.7	24.0	22.5	22.4	23.7	25.1	24.6	24.8
GDP Indices (constant prices, previous year = 100)	–	–	104.30	101.20	101.4	103.9	105.3	103.6	106.1
Industrial sales (constant prices, 1990 = 100)	100.0	123.7	171.0	172.0	173.9	188.0	210.3	219.8	244.6
Indices of industrial output (constant prices, previous year = 100)	–	–	106.7	100.6	101.1	108.3	112.6	103.7	111.3
Investment outlays (constant prices, 1990 = 100)	100.0	133.4	170.1	163.0	150.0	159.5	174.7	211.4	249.2
Investment outlays (constant prices, previous year = 100)	–	–	101.4	90.5	90.0	100.6	106.5	107.7	117.9
Employees in industry (% employed persons)	36.8	25.5	21.5	20.8	23.1	22.9	23.04	23.1	22.8

2006 preliminary data.

Sources: Statistical yearbook of industry, 1991 (Warsaw: Central Statistical Office (CSO), 2004) pp. 38–65; Statistical yearbook of the Republic of Poland 2006 (Warsaw: CSO, 2006) p. 673; Statistical yearbook of the Republic of Poland 1991 (Warsaw: CSO, 1991) p. 118; Statistical yearbook of the Republic of Poland 1996 (Warsaw: CSO, 1996) p. 531; Poland 2004, Report (Warsaw: Industry, Ministry of Economy and Labour, 2004) p. 5; Concise statistical yearbook of the Republic of Poland 2007 (Warsaw: CSO, 2007) pp. 461–466 and 448; POLAND, macroeconomic performance in figures 1995–2006 (Warsaw: Ministry of Economy, Analyses and Forecasting Department, September 2007); Statistical yearbook of the Republic of Poland 2007 (Warsaw: CSO, 2007) pp. 54–55.

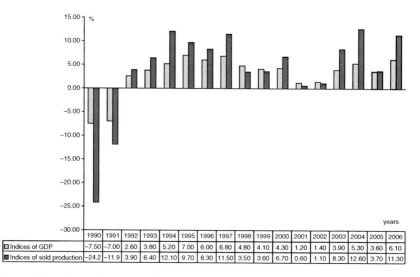

Figure 6.1   Indices of GDP and industrial sales in Poland between 1990 and 2004 (constant prices, previous year = 100)

Sources: Statistical yearbook of industry, 1991 (Warsaw: CSO, 1991) p. 114; *Statistical yearbook of the Republic of Poland 1994* (Warsaw: CSO, 1994) p. 310; *Statistical yearbook of industry 2001* (Warsaw: CSO, 2001) pp. 194, 368; *Statistical yearbook of industry 2004* (Warsaw: CSO, 2004) pp. 36, 114, 238; *Statistical yearbook of the Republic of Poland 2004* (Warsaw: Central Statistical Office, 2004) pp. 490, 671. *A study of Poland's economic performance in 2004* (Warsaw: Ministry of Economic Affairs and Labour, February 2005); *POLAND, macroeconomic performance in figures 1995–2006* (Warsaw: Ministry of Economy, Analyses and Forecasting Department, September 2007).

The structure of employment also underwent considerable changes, in 1990, almost 70 per cent of people employed in industry worked in the public sector, but by 2005 more than 80 per cent of those employed worked in the private sector. In 1990, 4,620,000 workers were employed in industry, but in 2004 there were only 2,890,000 workers, a decline of 38 per cent. The biggest changes were in manufacturing, where the relation between the public and private sectors was reversed (Table 6.3); 86 per cent of industrial production was in the public sector in 1990, but by 2006 84.2 per cent of industrial sales were created in the private sector.

Poland against a background of EU Countries

There are interesting differences in the growth patterns in Polish industry compared with those of other EU countries. In Poland, a growth slump occurred in 2001 (Table 6.4). Production remained at only 0.5–1.5 per cent in 2001–2002, while reaching 8.8 per cent in 2003, and more

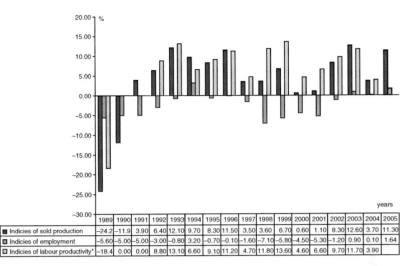

Figure 6.2 Indices of industrial sales, employment and labour productivity in Poland between 1990 and 2004 (constant prices, previous year = 100)

*Labour productivity in industry measured by industrial sales per employed person.

Source: ibid.

Table 6.2 Structure of employment in industry by ownership sectors (in %)

Specification	1990	1995	2000	2003	2004	2005
Public sector	68.8	49.5	26.0	20.4	18.27	17.2
Private sector	31.2	50.5	74.0	79.6	81.73	82.88
Total	100.0	100.0	100.0	100.0	100.0	100.0

Sources: *Statistical yearbook of the Republic of Poland 2000* (Warsaw: Central Statistical Office, 2000); *Statistical yearbook of the Republic of Poland 2004* (Warsaw: Central Statistical Office, 2004); *Statistical yearbook of the Republic of Poland 2005* (Warsaw: Central Statistical Office, 2005) p. 234; *Statistical yearbook of the Republic of Poland 2006* (Warsaw: Central Statistical Office, 2006) p. 237.

than 12 per cent in 2004 and 2006. In 2005 growth rates were lower (4.1 per cent) because of the 'statistical base effect' and the effect of EU accession. By contrast, in some EU-15 countries growth rates were low or even negative (Belgium, France, The Netherlands, the United Kingdom and Italy).

Compared with the ten New Member States, Poland has performed at about the average level. Estonia is an unquestionable economic leader. After a slump, it achieved production increases in 2000–2005 similar to Ireland's in 2000–2002. After a period of quick production growth in 1996–2002, Hungary's economy slowed, with the 2001–2002 slump having a particularly

Table 6.3   Industrial sales by sections and ownership sectors (in %)

Specification	1990	1995	2000	2001	2002	2003	2004	2005	2006
Total									
Public sector	82.6	51.3	28.0	24.7	23.7	21.9	19.1	17.5	15.6
Private sector	17.4	48.7	72.0	75.3	76.3	78.1	80.9	82.5	84.2
of which									
Mining and quarrying									
- Public sector	6.13	7.6	4.0	4.0	3.8	3.4	3.6	3.3	–
- Private sector	0.01	0.2	1.5	1.4	1.5	1.3	1.3	1.7	–
Manufacturing									–
- Public sector	76.50	34.1	15.0	10.0	8.7	8.2	7.6	6.5	–
- Private sector	17.36	48.3	70.0	72.8	73.4	75.3	77.4	78.0	–
Electricity, gas and water supply									–
- Public sector	–	9.6	9.2	10.7	11.2	10.3	7.9	7.7	–
- Private sector	–	0.2	0.5	1.1	1.4	1.5	2.2	2.8	–

Sources: Statistical yearbook of industry, 1991 (Warsaw: CSO, 1991) p. 114; *Statistical yearbook of the Republic of Poland 1994* (Warsaw: CSO, 1994) p. 310; *Statistical yearbook of industry 2001* (Warsaw: CSO, 2001) pp. 194, 368; *Statistical yearbook of industry 2003* (Warsaw: CSO, 2003) p. 66; *Statistical yearbook of industry 2004* (Warsaw: CSO, 2004) pp. 36, 114, 238; *Statistical yearbook of the Republic of Poland 2004* (Warsaw: CSO, 2004) pp. 490, 671; *A study of Poland's economic performance in 2004* (Warsaw: Ministry of Economic Affairs and Labour, February 2005); *Concise Statistical Yearbook of Poland, 2005* (CSO); *Statistical yearbook of industry 2005* (Warsaw: CSO, 2005) p. 110; *Concise Statistical Yearbook of Poland, 2007* (Warsaw: CSO, 2007) p. 341.

drastic impact on levels of production. Even so, growth was higher than in Poland. Taking 1996 as a base year, Ireland, Estonia and Hungary exhibited the highest levels of growth in industrial output; Latvia, Finland, Lithuania, Poland and Austria achieved 40–50 per cent growth levels. The United Kingdom, The Netherlands, and Italy had lower growth.[22]

The slump in industrial sales in Poland began in 1998. Several internal and external factors accounted for this. The internal factors (such as restrictive monetary policy and action leading to decreases in internal demand) had substantial impact on Polish industry in 1998–1999. Several external factors were also significant: slower growth in the world economy (particularly in Germany) and the crisis in Russia. While internal factors were more significant in shaping the Polish economy between 1989 and 1999, global economic conditions certainly had important effects on industry. One of the most important of these factors has been EU accession and participation in the common market. With all the adjustments that followed accession in

Table 6.4 Annual growth of industrial production (in constant prices) in selected EU countries and candidates in 1995 and 2000–2006

Specification	1995	2000	2001	2002	2003	2004	2005	2006
Austria	5.1	9.0	2.8	0.8	2.0	6.3	4.4	8.2
Belgium	6.5	5.4	−1.0	1.3	0.8	3.2	−0.4	5.1
Denmark	4.0	5.4	1.6	1.4	0.2	0.0	1.6	3.5
Finland	6.4	12.4	−0.2	2.2	1.2	5.0	0.3	8.1
France	1.9	4.1	1.3	−1.3	−0.3	2.4	0.2	1.0
Greece	1.8	7.2	−1.8	0.8	0.3	1.0	−0.8	0.5
Spain	4.9	4.4	−1.5	0.2	1.4	1.6	0.7	3.9
Netherlands	2.9	3.3	0.6	0.9	−1.4	2.5	−1.2	1.1
Ireland	20.5	15.4	10.0	7.2	4.7	20.5	8.1	5.1
Luxembourg	1.4	4.3	3.1	2.1	5.2	6.4	6.3	2.7
Germany	0.6	5.6	0.2	−0.1	0.4	3.0	3.4	5.8
Portugal	4.7	0.5	3.1	−0.5	−0.1	−2.6	0.4	2.7
Sweden	10.0	5.7	−1.1	−0.1	1.4	5.2	1.8	4.1
United Kingdom	1.8	1.9	−1.4	−0.2	−0.3	0.8	−1.8	0.1
Italy	5.9	4.2	−1.2	−1.3	−0.6	−0.3	−0.8	2.6
Estonia		14.6	8.9	8.2	10.9	10.5	11.0	7.3
Lithuania		5.3	15.9	7.5	11.3	10.9	7.1	7.3
Latvia		5.3	15.9	7.5	11.3	10.9	7.1	5.5
Poland	**10.3**	**7.5**	**0.4**	**1.4**	**8.8**	**12.7**	**4.1**	**12.2**
Czech Republic	8.7	5.3	6.6	1.9	5.5	9.6	6.7	9.9
Slovak Republic	8.3	8.3	6.9	6.4	5.1	3.9	3.9	9.9
Slovenia		6.2	2.9	2.4	1.4	5.5	3.3	6.9
Hungary	4.6	18.2	3.6	2.7	6.4	7.3	6.9	9.9
Bulgaria			2.2	4.6	13.8	17.3	6.7	5.9
Romania	9.4	7.1	8.3	4.4	3.1	5.3	2.0	7.1

Sources: POLAND in the World's and Europe's background in 1995–2006, (in figures) (Warsaw: Ministry of Economy, September 2007) pp. 17–18.

2004, trends were uneven and difficult to interpret, at least until 2007 when growth rates rose rapidly.

Growth in industrial output in Poland has been achieved mainly through productivity increases and improvements in management. In the EU-15 the main stimulus for such growth is innovation, but in Poland industrial expenditures on R&D decreased until 2003. Expenditures on innovation activity in industry were a little higher (production of technologically new and improved products and implementing new technological processes) including a wide range of scientific, technical, organizational, financial and commercial activities. Between 2001 and 2005 these expenditures rose by about 12 to 20 per cent per year, but questions remain about the uses to which spending is directed. About 60 per cent of expenditure is used to buy modern machines and technical equipment including transport vehicles, but only about ten per cent is spent on research and development (11.1 per cent in 2003, 7.5 in 2004, and 9.6 in 2005) and only a few per cent per year is invested in training and know-how (4.8 per cent in 2003 and 2.4 in 2005).[23]

Between 1995 and 2005, the growth in 'high technology products' grew slowly at about 4.5 per cent. Equally worrying has been the slow rate of decline in low technology in manufacturing, although between 2003 and 2004 this did drop significantly from 54.2 per cent to 38.6 per cent (Table 6.5).

The rate of innovation in enterprises is much lower in Poland than in the rest of the EU. One important indicator of companies' innovative activity is the share of industrial enterprises with agreements (contracts) of cooperation with other entities involved in innovative technologies; only 11.6 per cent of companies had such agreements between 1998 and 2000, but in the years 2003–2006 this ratio grew to 24.2% per cent.[24]

Levels of innovation can be measured in a variety of ways. For our present purposes we focus on the share of industrial output of new and modernized products in industrial output. This rose from 16.7% in 2000–2002 to 21.8% in 2002–2005.[25] However, institutional infrastructure to support innovation and technology transfer is not well developed.

The share of public sector production in high-technology products is 3.1 per cent, but it is 4.3 per cent in the private sector (6.3 per cent of which was in foreign-owned firms). Particularly interesting has been the decline in the rate of low technology in the public sector (dropping from 57.8 per cent to 47.8 per cent between 1995 and 2002) and in the private sector (from 59.4 per cent to 40.1 per cent, of which foreign ownership is 67.9–25.9 per cent).[26]

Most new-accession countries have a negative balance of international trade in high-technology products (excluding Estonia), and Poland has the highest negative balance. The rate of high-technology products in Polish exports remains small (2.2 per cent in 2002, and 3.2 in 2005) and the import

Table 6.5 Industrial sales in manufacturing by the level of technology in Poland between 1990 and 2003 (in %)

Specification	1995	2000	2001	2002	2003	2004	2005
Total	100	100	100	100	100	100	100
High technology	3.3	5.6	4.3	4.8	4.5	4.5	4.5
Medium–high technology	24.4	34.0	22.6	21.4	23.6	25.6	26.1
Medium–low technology	13.8	21.3	15.8	17.3	17.7	31.3	32.1
Low technology	58.5	39.1	57.3	56.5	54.2	38.6	37.3

Sources: Statistical yearbook of Industry 2004 (Warsaw: CSO, 2004) p. 393; *Statistical yearbook of Industry 2006* (Warsaw: CSO, 2006) pp. 433–435.

of high-technology products now accounts for ten per cent of total imports. By contrast, in the EU as a whole such high-technology products account for 17.8 per cent of total exports and 23 per cent of imports.[27]

Restructuring of the coal industry in Poland

The restructuring of heavy industry has been one of the biggest political and economic challenges facing Poland. Coal mining, steel, armaments and chemical industries have required very expensive reforms, while liberalization brought with it loss of employment, especially among low-wage manual workers and in regions with high levels of industrialization.

In Poland, hard coal accounts for 50 per cent of primary energy production and lignite for 13 per cent, compared with about 22 per cent worldwide and 12 per cent in the EU-15 (both types of coal) (Table 6.6).[28]

In 1990 there were 70 mines in Poland producing 148 million tonnes of hard coal employing approximately 450,000 people. At the beginning of the 1990s coal overproduction was estimated at 80 million tonnes, and overemployment[29] amounted to 250,000 workers. By 2003 coal production had declined to about 100 million tonnes from 40 mines and employment had dropped to 200,000 workers. By 2006 coal production had dropped to 61 million tonnes and employment to 182,000 people. This represented an employment decline of about 68 per cent compared with production declines of 36 per cent in the years 1990–2006.

Coal remains important in the Polish economy and Poland is still one of the biggest producers of hard coal in Europe, being higher than in any of the EU-15 countries (the United Kingdom 28 million tonnes, Germany

Table 6.6 Production of hard coal and lignite in Poland, and employment in mining and quarrying in 1980–2006

Specification	1980	1990	1995	2000	2001	2002	2003	2004	2005	2006
Hard coal production [m tonnes]	193	148	137	103	104	104	103	101	98	95
Lignite production [m tonnes]	37	68	64	60	60	58	61	61	62	61
Employment in mining and quarrying [in thousands]	412	563	357	223	217	209	200	189	185	182

Sources: Statistical Yearbook of the Republic of Poland 2004 (Warsaw: CSO, 2004) p. 30; *Concise Statistical Yearbook of Poland, 2005* (Warsaw: CSO, 2005) p. 333; *Concise Statistical Yearbook of Poland, 2007* (Warsaw: CSO, 2007) p. 348.

29 million tonnes, Spain 13 million tonnes, Czech Republic 14 million tonnes).[30]

The first postsocialist reforms for the industry (prepared in 1992) had as one of their goals the need to reduce coal production. The first programme for restructuring the hard coal industry was prepared in 1993, but by 1995 state energy safety was threatened by the reforms.[31] The next reform strategy was introduced in 1996 (*The Restructuring Programme for Polish Steel Industry*) and subsequently has been changed several times because of coal miners' protests. As a result, the aims of the reforms were only partially achieved. In fact, to ensure that pre-accession agreements were met, implementation of reforms had to be changed. Implementation of the 1996 programme was cancelled and a new programme for the years 1998–2002 was prepared: '*The reform of coal mining in Poland for years 1998–2002*' (accepted in 1998 by The Council of Ministers and modified in 1999). The most important difference in this programme was that its implementation was empowered by an act of law,[32] and consequently it blocked the ability of the government to make further modifications to the programme, particularly if coal miners were to exert pressure through striking (Table 6.7).

In fact, the reforms were modified and in April 2004 the report on *Restructuring of the hard coal mining sector during the period 2004–2006* and *Strategy for the period 2007–2010* was released.[33] To sustain state aid, the government had to prepare the *Plan of access to coal resources in 2004–2006* and the *Plan of closing coal mine in 2004–2007* listing all the mines that were to be closed and defining precisely the scale of subsidies to other mines (Table 6.8).[34]

Restructuring programmes in Poland have been extremely expensive, costing more than 24 billion PLN between 1999 and 2003 (Table 6.9. Figure 6.3). A particularly high level of state aid was provided in 2003, as accumulated government debt in coal companies was written off (Table 6.10. Figure 6.3), although by 2004 increasing prices on international coal markets resulted in four coal companies becoming profitable.

At the end of 2006, another stage of restructuring in the hard coal mining sector was completed.[35] *The Programme for restructuring the hard coal mining sector in the years 2004–2006 and strategy for 2007–2010* assumes two variants of the restructuring processes planned. First is *the target model*, which assumes capacity reduction by 14 million tonnes and employment reduction by 255,000 by the end of 2006. The second is *the alternative variant*, which assumes capacity reduction by 7.8 million tonnes and employment reduction by 19,500 by the end of 2006, but this latter depended on the demand for coal remaining high. In fact, between 2004 and 2006 the capacity in the hard coal mining sector was reduced by 6.6 million tonnes annually, i.e., 1.2 million tonnes less than expected in the alternative plan

Table 6.7 The aims and results of coal mining restructuring programmes in Poland between 1990 and 2002

Restructuring programmes	Main goals and objectives	Results*
Recommendations for restructuring programmes in the hard and light coal mining, gas industry, power generating industry and fuel industry, accepted in 1992, by The Council of Ministers	Legislation: none Governmental programme *The goals* - prepare the coal mines for free market - prepare plans for mine liquidation programme (18 mines should be closed by the end of 2000) - reduce subsidies - commercialize mines that are not to be liquidated (beginning in 1993) - eliminate monopoly in coal trade and export	*Liquidation of mines* - 3 mines were liquidated 7 coal mine corporations were created *Profitability* - net losses 1990–1992: 1,653.3 million PLN *Finance support* - subsidies and debt write-offs 1990–1992: 2,051 million PLN
The foundation of industrial policy accepted in 1993, by The Council of Ministers	Legislation: none Document status: Governmental programme	
Industrial policy implementation programme in the years 1993–1995, accepted in 1993	Implementation programme *The main aims* - make coal enterprises profitable - keep Polish coal prices competitive with world prices - strengthen capital reserves of the coal enterprises to facilitate investment and modernization *The objectives* - reduce coal production by between 123.6 and 128.6 million tonnes - reduce employment to 319,600 or even 288,500	*Achievements* - sector was still unprofitable (goal not achieved) - Polish coal was sold at a price lower than the costs of output (goal not achieved) - the main investments were realized by taking on increased liabilities (goal not achieved) *Decreasing coal production* - coal production 130.2 million tonnes (objective not reached) *Decreasing employment* - employment 319,600 million (objective was achieved)

Continued

Table 6.7   Continued

Restructuring programmes	Main goals and objectives	Results*
		Finance support - subsidies and debt write-offs in the year 1993: 354 million PLN *Profitability* - net loss in the sector in 1993: 1,500.7 million PLN
Industrial policy Implementation of the second part of the programme in the years 1994–1995, accepted in 1994, by The Council of Ministers	Implementation programme *The main aims* - achieve profitability of coal enterprises in the shortest possible period – achieve profitability in 1994 and maintain this through 1995 - maintain the competitiveness of the Polish coal in international markets - writ-off enterprise debt *The objectives* - reduce coal production to 135.3 million tonnes in 1994 and between 132.4 and 135.4 million tonnes in 1995 - reduce employment to 273,300 in 1994 and 252,800 in 1995	*Achievements* - enterprise liabilities grew, some companies achieved positive net financial result, but the effect was transitory (goal partly achieved) - Polish coal sold at a lower price than the cost of output (goal not achieved) - debt write-off (goal partly achieved) (level of liabilities = 8.1 billion PLN) *Decreasing coal production* - coal production 132.7 million tonnes in 1994 and 135.3 million tonnes in 1995 (objective achieved) *Decreasing employment* - employment 291,000 in 1994 and 274,900 in 1995 (objective not achieved) *Finance support* - subsidies and debt write-offs in 1994: 522 million PLN - subsidies and debt write-offs in 1995: 1,350 million PLN *Profitability* - net loss in the sector 1994–1995: 973.9 million PLN

Continued

Table 6.7 Continued

Restructuring programmes	Main goals and objectives	Results*
Coal mining, the state policy and sector policy for years 1996–2000, the programme of adapting the coal mining to the market economy and international competitiveness, accepted in 1996 by The Council of Ministers	Legislation: none Governmental programme *The main aims* - adapt the coal mining to the market economy and international competitiveness *The main objectives* - improve sectoral-level financial results by reducing losses by the end of 1997, with profits to start from 1998 - growing liabilities to 9.8 billion PLN in 1997 and then reduce to 8.6 billion PLN in 2000 - reduce coal production to 130 million tonnes in 1996, 128 million tonnes in 1997, 126 million tonnes in 1998, 123 million tonnes in 1999, 120 million tonnes in 2000 - reduce employment from 329,000 to 242,000 - liquidate selected coal enterprises	*Achievement in years 1996–1998* - improving sector financial results (goal not achieved) (all coal enterprises had poor financial results and made losses) - liabilities reached 13.3 billion PLN in 1997 (goal not achieved) *Decreasing coal production* - coal production 136.2 million tonnes in 1996 and 137.1 million tonnes in 1997 (objective partly achieved) *Decreasing employment* - employment in the sector 243,300 in 1997 (objective partly achieved) *Finance support* - subsidies and debt write-offs in 1996: 554 million PLN - subsidies and debt write-offs in 1995: 1,586 million PLN *Profitability* - net loss in the sector 1996–1997: 4406.6 million PLN Programme implementation was ended because of lack of adequate effects
The reform of coal mining in Poland for years 1998–2002, accepted in 1998 by The Council of Ministers	Empowered by legislation Governmental programme, Implementation programme *The main aims* - prepare coal enterprises to be economically effective in free-market economy	*Achievement in years 1998–2002* - preparing coal enterprises to be economically effective in a market economy (objective not achieved)

Continued

Table 6.7   Continued

Restructuring programmes	Main goals and objectives	Results*
	- satisfy domestic demand for coal and maintain rational export levels, while fulfilling the environmental protection and competitiveness requirements of the EU	
	The main objectives - achieve positive financial results in the sector by 2000 and positive net financial results in the overall economy by 2001 - reduce coal production by 25.5 million tonnes between 1998 and 2002 - reduce employment by 105,000 (to approximately 138,400) - privatize two selected coal enterprises	
The modification of governmental programme 'The reform of coal mining in Poland for years 1998–2002', accepted in 1999 by The Council of Ministers	Implementation programme *The main objectives modification* - achieve positive financial results in the sector by 2001 and positive net financial results by 2002 - reduce coal production by 36.1 million tonnes between 1998 and 2002 - reduce employment by approximately 115,000 (to approximately 128,000) - prepare pre-privatization analyses	

*constant price.

Source: *The report: coalmining*, ['The New Industry'] (org. 'Nowy Przemysł') (2002) 12, pp. 25 and 26.

Table 6.8   The aims, objectives and tasks of coal mining restructuring programme in Poland for the periods 2004–2006 and 2007–2015

Programme	Aims and objectives
Restructuring of the hard coal mining sector during the period 2004–2006 and Strategy for the period 2007–2010	*Target status:* The following achievements are expected upon completion of the restructuring process: - Business entities will be economically sound; - Primary focus of mines and other entities of the industry will be able to meet the national demand for coal; - Exports by the industry entities will be economically sound; - Costs will match revenues; - Employment in the industry will match production capacity, itself matching market demand; - Entities of the sector will finance upgrade and capital expenditure projects with their own funds; - Mining entities will not benefit from any public assistance not allowed under international treaties; and - Mining entities will comply with the environment protection and work safety standards.
Empowered by legal act: the Law of 28 November, 2003 on hard coal mining sector restructuring	*Objectives:* Key restructuring objectives include the following: - Maintenance of the energy security of the country and cooperation in improving the standard of energy security of the European Union; - Maintenance by mining enterprises of sustainable profitability, economic effectiveness and competitive advantage on the uniform market of the EU; - Securing satisfactory level of financial liquidity and creditworthiness in order to ensure sustained operation and development of mining enterprises; - Balancing of funds so as to enable current payment of liabilities, in particular those due to public sector creditors; - Adjustment of production capacity to the local market demand and economically viable exports to the uniform EU market and elsewhere; - Adjustment of employment to the actual production needs, along with ensuring a greater productivity and efficiency; - Actions towards a rational cost structure; - Privatization of mining enterprises. *These objectives will be achieved through delivery of the following tasks:* - Cost reduction in all business segments; - Marketing policy that enables reduction of sale costs, direct customer contacts, an effective competition with imported coal, along with blocking settlements by netting, or other barter practices, which reduce revenues and cause pathology and irregularities;

Continued

Table 6.8   Continued

Programme	Aims and objectives
	- Reduction of production capacity to approximately 88 million tonnes in 2006, (target model); - Less drastic reduction of production capacity of mining enterprises as assumed in the alternative model to a level not higher than 4.8 TPY by the end of 2006, provided the bullish market continues and mining enterprises retain sustainable profitability; - Reduction of employment using protective, adaptation and activation measures referred to in the Law on Hard Coal Mining Sector Restructuring, to the level matching the actual requirements, between 2004 and 2006; - Streamlining the organizational structure of mining; - Introduction of innovative management practices and optimization of company organization structures, along with pursuing a rational employment policy; and - Maintenance of supplies to the uniform EU market and export levels to third countries at between 20 million and 17.5 million tonnes, assuming break-even operation of the given production unit or group of production units.
Strategy for the hard coal mining sector in Poland in 2007–2015	- to ensure energy security for Poland through satisfying the domestic demand for hard coal, - to involve the use of coal to produce liquid fuels and fuel gas, - to maintain the competitiveness of Polish hard coal in the conditions of free-market economy, - to obtain funds to finance investments by privatizing coal companies on the stock exchange.

Sources: Restructuring of the hard coal mining sector during the period 2004–2006 and *Strategy for the period 2007–2010* (Warsaw: Ministry of Economy, Labour and Social Policy. (2004) p. 21; *Poland 2007, Poland 2007, The Report – Economy* (Warsaw: Ministry of Economy (2007) p. 121.

(84.6%). Employment at the end of 2006 was 119,300, which was 2,300 lower than predicted.[36]

The fundamental objective of the restructuring programme was the achievement of viability and financial liquidity for mining enterprises. In 2006, hard coal mining remained profitable, but at lower levels than in 2005. The result was to drive down profitability and financial liquidity rates. As a result, in July 2007 the Council of Ministers adopted a new plan prepared by the Ministry of Economy – *Strategy for the hard coal mining*

Table 6.9 State aid in the mining sector in 1999–2004 (million PLN, current prices)

1999	2000	2001	2002	2003	2004
1,701.0	1,390.8	2,644.6	1,712.9	17,488.5	5,836.7

Source: Program polityki w zakresie pomocy publicznej na lata 2005–2010 [the Policy programme in the area of state aid for years 2005–2010] (Warsaw: Ministry of Economy, and Office of Competition and Consumer Protection, March 2005) p. 9.

Table 6.10 Planned state aid in the mining sector in 2005–2010 (million PLN, current prices)

2005	2006	2007	2008	2009	2010
1,591.5	1,167.9	268.2	254.2	240.2	223.1

Source: ibid

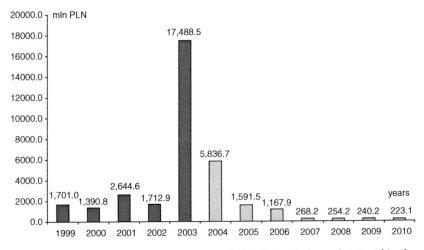

Figure 6.3 State aid in the mining sector in 1999–2004 and planned state aid in the mining sector in 2005–2010 (million PLN, current prices)

Source: ibid.

sector in Poland in 2007–2015. The goals adopted in the Strategy were as follows:

- ensure energy security by satisfying domestic demand for hard coal,
- use coal to produce liquid fuels and fuel gas,

- maintain the competitiveness of Polish hard coal,
- obtain investment funds by privatizing coal companies on the stock exchange,
- push along the reforms in consultation with social partners and with employee rights secured.

To achieve these goals, the Council of Ministers adopted the draft policy – *Act on the functioning of the hard coal mining sector in 2008–2015* – to permit the use of public financing to mitigate the consequences of earlier reforms and the *Information Document* on the *Report to the European Commission for 2006* to comply with Council regulations limiting state aid to mining enterprises.[37] The European Commission approved state aid for mines for 2004–2006, although the actual amount awarded was PLN 2.23 billion below the actual allocation. As a result, in February 2007 the Polish government requested and received an extension of aid for restructuring the hard coal mining sector until 2007.[38]

Conclusions

Polish industry changed radically after 1990, especially in the ownership structure and the scale and structure of production. While there have been unquestionable achievements, transformation costs have been high and have been borne differentially by society. Unemployment is high, social problems remain and a large proportion of the population depend on high levels of state aid. By 2004, state aid for industry supported declining industries and resulted in low levels of investment in R&D and it also hindered innovation. The turn to support for innovative sectors of industry has meant that production in the most problematic sectors has decreased and overemployment has been reduced. Ownership structures have changed, although privatization is not yet complete in some sectors and government influence continues in some larger companies despite their having been privatized.

Harmonization of laws and regulations with EU requirements has occurred for the most part and the process has been important in pushing the reform agenda. Because of strong social resistance and powerful trade unions, especially in heavy industries such as coal, reform programmes were often modified and goals compromised. As a result, EU accession processes were instrumental in forcing the government to focus on programme implementation and in giving it the political cover it needed to do so.

After 1989, Polish industrial policy shifted from one based on sectoral planning targeted to the restructuring of problem industries to horizontal policies in which the state no longer directly intervenes in market mechanisms, but is focused instead on policies that support market behaviour, competition, and competitiveness. These are particularly important insofar as they are able to contribute to the development of new sectors such as biotechnology, nanotechnology, robotics or satellite technologies.[39] These policies and expenditures will be necessary if Poland wants to fulfil the accession requirements and goals of the Lisbon Strategy.

In many ways, Polish coal mining is now at a turning point. Up to the end of 2006, the main objectives of industrial policy were to reduce production and employment, while EU Accession demands changed the role of state aid; debts were written off and mines began to operate without state aid or intervention from the EU. Starting from 2007, stress has been placed on the need to increase competitiveness and innovate in production, and – with increasing oil prices – to ensure national energy supplies. In 2008, rising energy costs have resulted in increased coal prices and consumption. As the leading producer of coal in the European common market, and with increasing public and governmental interest in coal as a crucial factor in the generation of greenhouse gases, climate change and emerging trading and off-set markets, Poland is becoming a more important player in European energy policy. One further effect of the reforms has been the aging of the workforce and the difficulty of recruiting younger miners. About 70 per cent of coal miners have been working for 16 to 25 years, most will retire by 2015, and, with vocational schools for mining being largely closed down early on, there is now a growing concern for human resource development and staff replacement (a concern targeted in the *Strategy for the hard coal mining sector in Poland in 2007–2015*). Strategic planning is now focused on ways of introducing new technologies, deepening models of research and implementing co-financing from national and international sources to support the production of liquid fuels and fuel gas from coal. Structural unemployment continues to generate huge social costs and will require much more thoroughgoing regional economic diversification, especially in those former industrial regions that are now the most depressed. The uneven effects of privatization, low expenditure on R&D and the lack of connection between research and business remain serious challenges that require continued large subventions from state aid, particularly in an industry that remains the biggest recipient of state aid.

Notes

1 The European Council brings together the heads of state or government of the European Union and the President of the Commission. It defines the general political guidelines of the European Union. The decisions taken at the European Council meetings are a major impetus in defining the general political guidelines of the European Union.
2 'Presidency Conclusions', Lisbon European Council, 23 and 24 March 2000, Press Release Library, European Commission.

3   The Lisbon Strategy can be usefully broken down into eight distinct dimensions, considered to be critical for national competitiveness: (1) creating an information society for all; (2) developing a European area for innovation, research and development; (3) liberalization: completing the single market and state aid and competition policy; (4) building network industries in telecommunications and in utilities and transportation; (5) creating efficient and integrated financial services; (6) improving the enterprise environment; for business start-ups, in the regulatory framework; (7) increasing social inclusion: returning people to the workforce, upgrading skills and modernizing social protection; (8) enhancing sustainable development. 'Presidency Conclusions', Lisbon European Council, 23 and 24 March 2000, Press Release Library, European Commission.

4   *Facing the challenge: The Lisbon strategy for growth and Employment*, Report from the High Level Group chaired by Wim Kok, November 2004, and 'The Lisbon strategy review 2004: an assessment of policies and reforms in Europe' (World Economic Forum, 2004).

5   *Working together for growth and jobs: A new start for the Lisbon Strategy*, Commission of the European Communities (COM (2005)) 24 final.

6   *Industrial Policy – Plan of execution for years 1993–1995* (Warsaw: Ministry of Industry and Commerce, 1993) p. 1 and P. Ikonowicz, 'Polityka przemysłowa kraju wysoko rozwiniętego' ['Industrial policy of developed countries'], *Ekonomista*, 2–3 (1994) 255.

7   Communication from the Commission, *Implementing the Community Lisbon Programme: A policy framework to strengthen EU manufacturing – towards a more integrated approach for industrial policy* (COM (2005)) 474 final; compare with: *Commission Communication: Industrial Policy in an Open and Competitive Environment: Guidelines for a Community Approach* (COM (1990)) 556 final; Communication from the Commission to the Council, the European Parliament, the Economic and Social Committee and the Committee of the Regions, *Industrial Policy in an Enlarged Europe* (COM (2002)) 714 final.

8   *Industrial Policy for an Enlarged Europe* (COM (2002)) 714; *Fostering structural change: an industrial policy for an enlarged Europe* (COM (2004)) 274; *Implementing the Community Lisbon Programme: A policy framework to strengthen EU manufacturing – towards a more integrated approach for industrial policy* (COM (2005)) 474.

9   *Poland 2007, The Report – Economy* (Warsaw: Ministry of Economy, 2007) p. 41.

10   K Górka, 'The development of industrial policy in Poland, Krakow University of Economics' (unpublished manuscript).

11   I use the terms 'overproduction' here to refer to the situation when the level of production is set by government and does not respond to demand.

12   B. Winiarski, *Polityka gospodarcza* ['Economy Policy'], (Warsaw: Wydawnictwo naukowe PWN, 2001).

13   The 1988 act enabled the creation of small private companies in limited areas.

14   B. Winiarski, *Polityka gospodarcza* ['Economy Policy'] (Warsaw: Wydawnictwo naukowe PWN, 2001] pp. 298–316.

15   B. Winiarski, *Polityka gospodarcza* ['Economy Policy'] (Warsaw: Wydawnictwo naukowe PWN, 2001] pp. 262–273.

16   B. Winiarski, *Polityka gospodarcza* ['Economy Policy'] (Warsaw: Wydawnictwo naukowe PWN, 2001) pp. 262–273.

17 *Polska 2025, długookresowa strategia trwałego i zrównoważonego rozwoju* [Polska 2025 – The Long-Term Strategy of Sustainable Development] (Warsaw: Council of Ministers, 2000) p. 16.

18 *Narodowy Plan Rozwoju 2004–2006* [Poland National Development Plan 2004–2006] (Warsaw: Council of Ministers, 2000) p. 63.

19 *Poland – National Strategic Reference Framework 2007–2013 in support of growth and jobs*, Initial Draft (adopted by the Council of Ministers on 14 February 2006).

20 'Cooling of the economy' was a political decision. The process involved diminishing the level of domestic demand by the strict control of money supply. The government tried to reduce the budget deficit significantly and the National Bank together with the Monetary Policy Council introduced very restrictive monetary policy, to limit consumption credit.

21 Industrial sales include the value of finished products sold, semi-finished products, parts of own production, the value of paid work and services rendered, including both industrial and non-industrial, lump sum agent fees in the case of concluding an agreement on commission terms and full agent fees in the case of concluding an agency agreement, the value of products in the form of settlements in kind as well as products designated for increasing the value of own fixed assets.

22 *Poland 2004, Industry Report* (Warsaw: Ministry of Economy and Labour, 2004) pp. 28–31.

23 *Statistical yearbook of the Republic of Poland 2004* (Warsaw: Central Statistical Office, 2004) pp. 376–379; *Poland 2007, The Report – Economy* (Warsaw: Ministry of Economy, 2007) p. 198.

24 *Poland 2007, The Report – Economy* (Warsaw: Ministry of Economy, 2007) p. 200.

25 *Poland 2007, The Report – Economy* (Warsaw: Ministry of Economy, 2007) p.200.

26 The higher level of medium–high technology and high technology production in 2000 and 2001 was caused among other things by relatively lower growth of industrial sales.

27 *Poland 2007, The Report – Economy* (Warsaw: Ministry of Economy, 2007) p. 201.

28 Data from 2001.

29 Overemployment refers to the policy that resulted from government efforts to ensure work for all citizens, in which state enterprises employed more people than necessary. This situation is called 'overemployment or 'employment excess'.

30 *The role of Polish Hard Coal in the European Union, Strategy for the hard coal mining sector in Poland in 2007–2015*, Council of Ministers, July 2007, p. 4.

31 While the government was preparing the new laws to liberalize the energy sector, coal prices remained controlled and reforms in the coal industry were limited. The results threatened energy supplies.

32 DZ.U. 1998, nr 162 poz. 1112, *Official Journal*, 162 (1998) item no. 1112.

33 Council Regulation (EC) No 1407/2002 of 23 July 2002 on State aid to the coal industry; *Official Journal* L 205, 02/08/2002 pp. 0001–0008.

34 ACT on hard coal mining sector restructuring DZ.U. 2003, nr 210poz. 2037; *Official Journal* 210 (2003) item no. 2037.

35 The programming basis for this stage was provided by *the Programme for restructuring the hard coal mining sector in the years 2004–2006 and strategy for 2007–2010*, adopted by the Council of Ministers on 27 April 2004. The legal basis for the

restructuring processes was the Act of 28 November 2003 *on hard coal mining restructuring in 2003–2006* and its implementing provisions.

36   *Poland 2007 The Report – Economy* (Warsaw: Ministry of Economy, 2007) p. 121.
37   *Poland 2007, The Report – Economy* (Warsaw: Ministry of Economy, 2007) p. 121.
38   *Poland 2007, The Report – Economy* (Warsaw: Ministry of Economy, 2007) p. 121.
39   *Poland 2007, The Report – Economy* (Warsaw: Ministry of Economy, 2007) p. 42.

7
A New Role for Banks in Poland

Elżbieta Mirecka

Introduction

The banking sector in Poland is modern, relatively safe and meets the high standards of the major financial centres of the world with which it cooperates. It is also an integral part of the European System of Central Banks with banking strategies, products and customer relations that are comparable with world standards. The system developed in a relatively short period after 1989. At the heart of these changes was the adaptation of the banking institutions and customers to new market conditions and to the new standards of service and care they demanded. In the process, new relationships between banks and customers emerged.

Stages of building a new Polish banking system

The creation of the contemporary banking system occurred in three stages and these, in turn, shaped the broader processes of economic reform after 1989.

The post-war banking system: 1945 to 1982

The post-World War II rebuilding of the Polish economy necessitated the creation almost from scratch of a new and efficient banking system. Rebuilding began formally on 10 January 1945 with the establishment of the National Bank of Poland (NBP). Pre-war commercial banks were liquidated and replaced by a few new large state banks, as well as three other state banks and a network of cooperative banks that were set up to provide services to enterprises and other places of work. Besides the provision of efficient centralized banking services, the goal of the new banking system was to control and direct the national economy.[1] In practice, a division of competences emerged between a few key banks; NBP took over credit operations for enterprises, *Bank Inwestycyjny* took care of financing investments, *Bank Handlowy w Warszawie S.A.* dealt with foreign transactions and *Państwowy Bank Rolny* was responsible for providing services for agricultural farms, and *Powszechna Kasa Oszczędności* and *Bank Pekao S.A.* provided services for individual customers.

This system operated until the end of the 1960s, when *Bank Inwestycyjny* was liquidated and its responsibilities were divided between NBP, *Powszechna Kasa Oszczędności* and *Bank Handlowy*. Nonetheless, the idea of a *monobank* remained a central goal of banking policy, especially when *Powszechna Kasa Oszczędności* was incorporated into the structure of NBP, which continued to strengthen its position as a centre of clearing transactions. The deepening social crisis after the 1960s further encouraged banking reform, particularly as economic conditions changed, with the result that banks were increasingly seen to have an even more active role in shaping the national economy.

Bank reform: 1982 to 1989

In 1982, the new Banking Act and the Statutes of NBP[2] regulated the banking system's relations with the Ministry of Finance, ensuring that the banks would be cooperative in shaping national economic policy. Bank–enterprise relations became more like a partnership and the newly appointed Council of Banks was charged with coordinating the implementation of a uniform monetary and credit policy for all banks.

In 1983, the rules governing bank loans to enterprises were changed, allowing banks to reject credit requests. The following year rules governing credit were clarified. Banks were given clearer guidance on how they should deal with non-payment of credits by enterprises, and interest rates were introduced for the first time since the War. These reforms were limited in their effects and failed to change some of the long-held assumptions and practices about soft-budget constraints in enterprises. While the uniformity of the banking system and the leading role of the central bank had been established and the Act had allowed banks to be created with different ownership structures and focused on particular kinds of specialization, enterprises continued to depend on bank credits and banks lacked any practical power to discipline their borrowing. Pressure for banking reform grew focused on decentralization of the banking system, reform of the system of the *monobank* and the creation of a central bank with specialized functions. It was even suggested that a two-level model be introduced to boost competition among banks.

Banking liberalization after 1989

With system transformation after 1989, the Polish banking system fundamentally changed. The Banking Act liberalized banking in a variety of ways. The central role of the NBP in shaping financial policy was increased, rules governing economic clearing in commercial banks were introduced, the territorial and sectoral structure of banking services was abolished and independent initiatives and entrepreneurship across the banking system were encouraged.[3] The new banking act also allowed banks to have varied ownership structure and to provide different kinds of services.

The result was a rapid growth in the number of banks, first controlled by Polish capital but quickly thereafter by foreign capital, and a lack of parallel controls over bank licensing, which created major problems in the sector. The amendment to the Banking Act from 1992[4] sought to redress some of these problems and provided more detailed requirements governing bank formation. The more restrictive policies resulted in a slow-down in the rate of new bank creation. This process was deepened even further by the National Bank of Poland Act, enacted in 1997, further regulating the creation and organizing of new banks, branch banks and offices of foreign banks in Poland.[5]

Ownership changes, restructuring and consolidation

The pre-1989 banking system was entirely different from that which emerged after 1989. Prior to 1989, legal regulations were lacking, the National Bank of Poland served some of the functions of a central bank and some of a commercial bank, and the other banks which existed[6] were not competitive with NBP, but fulfilled specific functions regarding the operation of enterprises in the economy.

The rebuilding of the system after 1989 had mixed results. State banks were privatized, nine new private banks were opened focusing their activities on deposit and credit services, and the number of commercial banks with mixed capital grew rapidly. However, bank liberalization was accompanied by liquidation, bankruptcy and consolidation, while the majority stake of foreign capital in joint-stock companies and the number and significance of branch offices of foreign banks grew. In 1993–1994, more restrictive licensing policies were introduced and these slowed the speed of bank creation. Soon thereafter new bank creation was halted entirely for fear of competition from foreign banks with the economically weak Polish banks.

Between 1995 and 1998 nine new foreign banks were established and foreign capital took control of seven banks that needed additional capital. The poor performance of Polish banks was driven largely by a lack of capital, a situation created in part by the capitalization requirement for new banks of ECU five million, an amount that Polish banks generally found impossible to meet.

In 1999, restrictions on foreign banks opening branches were cancelled. The number of foreign-owned banks increased, the number of domestically owned banks decreased and the relative importance of state assets declined as private assets increased (Table 7.1).

Table 7.1   Commercial banks by capital ownership structure

Banks	1993	1995	1997	1999	2001	2005	2006	2007
Banks with the majority of state capital	29	27	15	7	7	4	4	4
Banks with the majority of private capital, including:	58	54	68	70	65	51	54	47
- majority of Polish capital	48	36	39	31	17	7	11	11
- majority of foreign capital	10	18	29	39	48	44	43	40
Total	87	81	83	77	72	55	58	51

Sources: on the basis of: *System bankowy w Polsce w latach dziewięćdziesiątyc* [The Bank System in Poland in the 1990s] (Warszawa: NBP, 2001) p. 57; *Sytuacja finansowa banków w I półroczu 2005 – Synteza* [The Financial Situation of Banks in the First Six Months of 2005 – Synthesis] (Warszawa: NBP, 2005) pp. 23–24; *Sytuacja finansowa banków w 2007 – Synteza* [The Financial Situation of Banks in 2007 – Synthesis] (Warszawa: NBP, 2007) pp. 24–28.

After 1996 the process of consolidation intensified as bank mergers and market strengthening increased. The credibility of banks among their customers increased as external firm audits became the norm for enterprise loans and as staff skills and competencies expanded, particularly in assessing the financial standing of borrowers. Consolidation has continued, particularly since 2001, to the extent that the nine biggest banks now hold 70 per cent of total bank assets. Foreign investment in the sector has also continued to increase; 27 banks are controlled by Polish capital, 44 banks are controlled by foreign capital.[7] The most important investors in Polish commercial banks are German (*c.* 15 per cent), American (*c.* 12 per cent), Dutch (*c.* 8 per cent), Irish (*c.* 6 per cent) and French (*c.* 5 per cent).[8] Bank assets controlled by foreign capital now account for about 80 per cent of total bank assets, while older, less efficient and undercapitalized domestic banks have continued to struggle and many have gone into liquidation. The banking system now has a clear structure, with the central bank (NBP) serving the functions typically assumed by central banks, while commercial banks operate on a for-profit basis and make their investment decisions independently of their owners or shareholders.

Poland's accession to the European Union (EU) on 1 May 2004 further marked the formal adaptation of the Polish system to the Union's standards (Directive 2000/12/EC). Indeed, the banking sector was among the best prepared to meet the requirements of the EU, particularly in regard to the conditions to be met for opening a bank abroad, rules for the use of electronic payment instruments, rules governing capital flow and payments between Poland and the EU, and money laundering and terrorism financing prevention measures.

Current structure of banking sector

The stabilization and Accession trends have continued since 2004. Domestic banks remain important, with 51 currently conducting business in Polish financial markets (Table 7.2).

Despite the continued strength of domestic banks, 40 foreign-controlled banks dominate the industry, accounting for 80 per cent of all banks in the system. Among the Polish-controlled banks (20 per cent of all banks) those with a majority of private capital dominate. Only one state bank remains (*Bank Gospodarstwa Krajowego*), although 592 cooperative banks are still operating.

This structure of banking and its asymmetrical nature are further illustrated by the different outlooks on foreign-owned and domestically owned banks towards transborder banking. Following Polish accession into the EU, 87 foreign credit institutions expressed their willingness to operate in Poland, but only four domestic banks expressed interest in conducting transborder operations.

The changing structure of bank ownership has significantly improved banking services and access to credit for Polish investors. At the same time, the banks have been able to strengthen their financial position. Currently shares of 14 domestic banks and one Austrian bank are listed on GPW (Warsaw Stock Exchange) and investors from 17 countries are operating in the Polish banking system. The main foreign investors are now German

Table 7.2 Banks in Poland (2005 and 2007)

Banks	2005	2007
I. Domestic banks controlled by Polish capital, including:	11	11
1.1. Banks with the majority of state capital, including:	4	4
1.1.1. State banks	1	1
1.2. Banks with the majority of private capital	7	7
II. Domestic banks controlled by foreign investors, including:	44	40
2.1. Joint-stock companies with 100% foreign capital	24	19
2.2. Joint-stock companies with majority foreign capital	15	16
2.3. Joint-stock companies indirectly controlled by foreign investors	5	5

Sources: Own study on the basis of: *Sytuacja finansowa banków w I półroczu 2005 – Synteza* (Warszawa: NBP, 2005) pp. 22–23; *Sytuacja finansowa banków w 2007 – Synteza* (Warszawa: NBP, 2007) pp. 24–28.

(19.52 per cent), Belgian (16.82 per cent), American (13.91 per cent), Dutch (8.29 per cent), and Irish (7.04 per cent). Investors from European Union member states (excluding Poland) now account for 58.9 per cent of all capital invested.[9]

The degree of asset concentration remains high, with assets of the largest ten banks accounting for 70.5 per cent of total banking assets. However, the level of concentration (measured with the use of Concentration Ratio and Herfindahl–Hirschman index) has decreased as a result of slower growth of assets of huge commercial banks compared with an increase of assets in the whole sector. In part this has been driven by the dynamic growth of e-banking. Regardless of the size of a bank, the use of the internet to provide services has become standard. The number of banks in Poland has also grown and this is likely to continue because the banking market is not yet fully saturated and the number of customers per branch office remains higher than in banks in the rest of the European Union.

Bank image

With the deepening of financial structures and services in the banking industry, competition among banks has grown. In turn this has resulted in the growth of interest among customers not only in banking products but also in the banks themselves. The image of a bank has thus become an important element in the strategy of the banks. The creation of an image for a bank is a complicated process and increasingly has direct consequences for its competitiveness. The consequences for banks that continue to offer poor service and high interest rates can be serious. Once a bank is perceived as an institution that seeks unilateral benefits without offering customers the services they want, credibility suffers and customers are lost to competitors in the same market.

The external and internal environments in which a bank operates also have important effects on competitiveness (Table 7.3).

The key factors shaping the external environment are political, legal and economic in nature, and are in turn shaped by changing technological, economic and sociocultural shifts. Unlike the former state banking system, banks in a competitive environment have very limited abilities to shape these external factors. By contrast, the internal environment of a bank does depend to a large extent on a given bank. Capital resources, human capital, organizational structure, selected strategies of action and the model of the customer on which bank practices are built are all matters for individual banks. The effectiveness of bank philosophy is tested in an increasingly volatile market by the assessment of its customers, and not surprisingly banks are increasingly turning to external and internal consultant

Table 7.3 Bank environment

External	Internal
• Political and legal surroundings (international, domestic and EU legal regulations) • Economic surroundings (changes in demand, supply, competition, economic situation) • Technological surroundings (telecommunications and IT devices) • Sociocultural surroundings (civilizational changes, level of education)	• Capital resources (own and foreign capital) • Human capital (level of education of executive staff) • Flexible organizational structure (efficiency of adaptation to market changes) • Competitive edge (selection of the best method of strengthening its position) • Building a customer model for the needs of the bank (learning about the customers and taking care of them, cooperation with the customer)

Source: Author's data.

services to evaluate the effectiveness of day-to-day operations, services and marketing strategies.[10]

The bank is a trustee for its deposit holders. The customers entrust the bank with their capital and interest. The safety of assets and the degree of trust in the banking institution are fundamental. However, the increasing competition for customers is beginning to generate a conflict of interest as banks try to guarantee the security of the deposits while generating the highest possible profits from credits and investment operations. As with banking elsewhere, one result has been the further adoption of technology to reduce costs and facilitate wider capacities and product offerings. However, one indirect consequence has been a growing concern over the confidentiality of information.

As a result, pressures have been increasing for greater protections for consumers and for a clearer understanding and legal protections of their rights. So-called good banking practices aim to instil honesty, diligence, reliability and decency in customer service and are linked with better information handling systems to improve the public perception of respect for the customer. Banks are increasingly legally obligated to provide equal and partner-like treatment of the customers, not to use their expertise to the detriment of customers, and to inform customers of the kinds and conditions of the services provided and of the risk connected with them. To facilitate these legal requirements, bank personnel are increasingly trained to be courteous and tactful, to provide reliable information in a way that is understandable to customers and to explain precisely to the customer the essence of the services provided.[11]

These practices are aimed at creating an image of a 'partnership bank'. While such practices are enshrined in law in many EU countries, particularly through consumer rights legislation, such 'partnership bank' practices have yet to emerge in Polish customer relations. Instead of providing diverse products and good customer service to individual customers, many banks continue to offer standardized products and operate on a model of a mass retail customer. With limited customer knowledge and experience of bank services, these banks take advantage of their position; they make it impossible to compare the prices for the same services in different banks, and they continue to require time-consuming and at times incomprehensible rules and requirements. The current situation is particularly difficult because, while legislation requires banks to execute short agreements with their customers, the actual rights and obligations of the bank and customer are set out in the rules of the bank, not the contract. Standard international practices protecting customers against signing unfair or unwanted contracts, and their rights to change or cancel the contract after a limited period for reflection, are lacking. Instead, Polish banks tend to see the filling in a form and signing an application as completing an agreement, and the customer is unable to review and consider the information contained in the application. Some banks also conceal information and provide half-truths about customer accounts and loans, while also charging higher fees for a bank account than are typical in other countries of the EU. It is, for example, common practice to charge high commission fees on most banking activities, while also providing only late notification of changes of the level of fees and commission.

Customers are protected by law or through the Arbitration Court at the Polish Bank Association and through the Consumer Bank Arbitration, but these protections do not yet translate into standard banking practice. Analysis of decisions of the Consumer Bank Arbitration over the past few years indicates that the average of value of a dispute is PLN 3,128. In 2006, 755 decisions were issued, 215 (28 per cent) of which were favourable to the bank and 120 (16 per cent) to the customer, and 420 (56 per cent) disputes were dismissed.[12] While the impunity of banks is being challenged in these arbitrations, the small percentage of cases with a positive outcome for the customer should be a source of concern.

As banks fight for customers, those with limited knowledge of economics and banking practice can experience real difficulties in choosing a bank and a product. Banking practices are often complex and deliberately confusing. One common practice makes the bank look like a farmer's market. This practice involves the application of the '2-in-1 formula' and combines basic banking products with occasional promotions or discounts in the form of material prizes for the customer (such as pens, cars and vacations). Banks also practice a kind of customer entrapment, offering customers a credit card just before the end of repayment of one line of bank credit and thus prolonging the connection of the customer to the bank. In these ways and others, Polish banks are 'two-faced'. On the one hand, they are positive, helpful and open to the customer. On the other hand, they are uncompromising and profit-oriented when they are trying to 'catch the customer'. Caught in this penumbra, banks and customers continue to struggle to shape banking practices that meet both the imperatives of EU and state regulations and the many opportunities offered by the specific circumstances of the Polish transitional economy.

Conclusion

The condition of Polish banking is the result of the historic development and transformation of the banking, financial and credit systems, as well as the broader structural transformations that have occurred in the economy. Most specifically, the contemporary process of bank transformation has been conditioned by broader processes of privatization and consolidation. Beyond this imperative, the specific origin of this process was the transformation of the state socialist *monobank* into a two-level banking system. Poorly developed capital markets also encouraged the penetration of foreign capital in the process of creating a modern banking system, while the requirements of the European Union were crucial in shaping the development of the banking system.

Fundamentally, banks are independent businesses dependent on their ability to generate profits. The current conjuncture is one in which the articulation of formerly state-owned and centralized banking systems are transformed into customer-oriented competitive banking systems, but in conditions in which customer service runs headlong into the profit motive and efforts to regulate the excessive exuberance of the banking system. The future of a commercialized banking system in Poland reflects so many of the challenges and new articulations of an increasingly globalized national economy. It remains an open question whether a fully liberalized banking system can emerge that addresses the social and regional patterns of lending and saving of the new Polish economy.

Notes

1 W.L. Jaworski, *Współczesny bank* (Warszawa: Poltext, 1999) p. 37.
2 'The Banking Act', *Journal of Laws*, 7 (1982) item 56.
3 'The Banking Act', *Journal of Laws* 4 (1989) item 21; 'The National Bank of Poland Act', *Journal of Laws* 4 (1989), item 22.
4 'Amendment to the Banking Act', *Journal of Laws* 72 (1992), item 359.

5   'The Banking Act', *Journal of Laws* 140 (1997), item 939; 'The National Bank of Poland Act', *Journal of Laws* 140 (1997), item 938.

6   'Amendment to the Banking Act', *Journal of Laws* 72 (1992), item 359.

7   *Bankowość wobec procesów globalizacji* (Gdańsk – Jurata: Uniwersytet Gdański, Gdańska Akademia Bankowa, 2003) p. 85.

8   *System bankowy w Polsce w latach dziewięćdziesiątyc* (Warszawa: NBP, 2001) p. 58.

9   *Sytuacja finansowa banków w I półroczu 2005 – Synteza* (Warszawa: NBP, 2005) pp. 31–33.

10   M. Grzegorczyk, *Marketing bankowy* (Bydgoszcz – Łódń: Oficyna Wydawnicza Branta, 2004) p. 81.

11   *Biuletyn Bankowy,* 10 (2003).

12   *Gazeta Prawna* (18.03.2003).

8
Economic Transformation, European Integration and the Situation of Women in Polish Labour Markets

Anna Zachorowska-Mazurkiewicz[1]

Introduction

As one type of social relation, economic relations are defined by institutions in which people act or are constrained from acting by the social norms and expectations that structure institutional life. Institutions are understood here not only as frameworks, such as those provided by law, but also as repeated actions, norms and behaviour. The situation of women in labour markets is particularly defined by such institutional expectations and practices, and, as Neale suggests, these practices are structured by social organizations, including traditions, costumes and legal solutions, that create solid behavioural patterns.[2] In this sense, institutions are not only boundaries, but they function to shape the very essence of social life.[3]

The influence of the state on society, as well as the national economy, shapes institutions which systematically and constantly regulate the behaviour of individuals and social groups in formal and informal ways.[4] Formal rules include constitutions, statutes, legal regulations and other exogenously created laws, and they define systems: political (such as the structure of hierarchy, decision-making power and rights of an individual), economic (such as property rights and contracts), and safety (such the judiciary, police and army).[5] Informal rules have their roots in experiences, traditional values, religion, customs, ethnicity and other factors that influence human subjective perception. They all are a part of culture and heritage that are passed on from one generation to another through education, knowledge and imitation.[6] Both types of institutions are characterized by their reluctance to change. Thus the economic life and behaviour of economic agents is defined not only by rationality but also by formal and informal institutions. We make decisions based not only on the idea of maximization of outcomes but also on expectations coming from our environment. People behave in the market in a way they are expected to, and this is evident in gender relations.

Since 1989, Poland has undergone significant social, political and economic institutional changes, which have had important impacts on the gendered nature of labour markets. This chapter first characterizes the main transformations in Poland's post-War political economy – the command economy, system transformation, and integration with European structures – before turning to the changing situation of women in the labour market. Specifically, the chapter focuses on changes in the gendered nature of labour force participation, employment (glass ceiling), earning ratios and unemployment.

The command economy in Poland

Centrally planned economies were characterized by permanent shortages in which a demand surplus, caused by price controls, was typical for all markets, including the labour market. Wage controls resulted in low wages and salaries and poor working conditions, but there was no unemployment (at least not officially).[7]

Employment opportunities for which women had to struggle in other countries appeared in Poland after 1945 with little direct initiative from a women's rights movement. Socialist ideology labour demands in industry and low wages made it necessary for women to work to supplement family incomes with waged work. Women were thus pressured to enter the labour market by broader social forces and by the needs of the family,[8] tendencies exacerbated by increased access to education, migration from rural to urban areas, new laws that protected working women, and the development of day care centres and other institutions that helped to reconcile professional duties with family responsibilities. There is no doubt that a centrally planned economy needed women, while some domains fell entirely under women's control (i.e., kindergartens and primary schooling, the textile industry, and basic healthcare).[9]

During post-World War II reconstruction, labour shortages and the official concept of gender equality led to the abolition of work divisions in professional jobs, but not in household duties. Mass participation of women in the labour market thus led to a double burden for women and the creation and promotion of new models of women as workers and homemakers. In this way, the Polish language was enriched by the feminization of such words as 'coal miner', 'founder' or 'bricklayer', used to refer to women whose jobs were hard and physical but had until that time been reserved only for men. State-sponsored propaganda with pictures of a woman in a tractor, or a woman as a bricklayer in Warsaw, who at the same time was a person responsible for taking care of a family with at least three children, was widely promoted. The new model of a woman was one who, besides fulfilling the demands of her professional job, runs the family and is responsible for bringing up children and taking care of the elderly and sick.[10]

The high participation rates of women in the labour market were interpreted quite differently during this period. Some were concerned that the long-term social effects on families might be negative, bearing differentially higher costs than benefits from women's economic activity.[11] One consequence after reconstruction was that women were gradually withdrawn from traditional male jobs as regulations concerning the protection of working women were introduced. For instance, a list of jobs prohibited for women was created as well as other regulations.[12] The list included work under dangerous conditions such as jobs underground, and, as a result, it caused withdrawal of women from coal mines.[13] Concern for women's reproductive rights was used to justify expanded limitations on labour market mobility with new restrictions on the ability of women to enter certain professions. In addition, educational leave and sick days entitled women to take extended leave to take care of children, in turn resulting in a widely and officially accepted fact that women were the only ones who should care for the family.[14] In effect, women under socialism were treated as a flexible labour pool whose labour could be mobilized or discarded with changes in economic conditions.[15]

Labour participation rates for both genders in former communist countries were high – 85.3 per cent for males and 68.1 per cent for females in 1989.[16] Such high participation rates were the outcome of a system under which it was considered to be a duty of citizens to engage in productive labour to support rapid industrialization.[17] Despite these participation rates and social duties, prior to 1989 the Polish labour market was not exempt from 'glass ceilings', feminized work sectors or differential wage levels. According to Domański, in 1988 for every female manager with at least ten employees there were 2.6 male ones.[18] In 1983, women held 35.6 per cent of all managerial positions. Female managers made up the majority in the field of healthcare and social protection (70 per cent), education (63 per cent), trade and other services (61 per cent), and financial–insurance activities (66 per cent). Yet in industry only 12 per cent of managers were women and only 16.1 per cent in the universities.[19] In 1987, 75.3 per cent of urban women were employed in feminized sectors (in which more than 50 per cent of all employees were women).[20] Women also earned less for their work than men did. There was no official policy that differentiated wages of men and women, with actual earnings depending on the employee's position, not on gender. However, family income studies show that women in Poland actually earned 30 per cent less than men, despite legal equality and official antidiscrimination ideology.[21]

The myth of equal rights for men and women was prevalent under communism. Supporters cited the high proportion of employed women, the absence of legal discrimination, relatively large presence of women in Parliament as compared with the West,[22] and the principle of equal rights guaranteed by the Constitution. It is only today that this long-held belief is being re-examined.[23]

Period of system transformation

The centrally planned economy had three consequences for labour markets. First, the uncontrolled demand for labour resulted in inefficiencies in labour allocation throughout the economy. The privatization process revealed the fact that there were too many people employed in enterprises and other institutions, leading quickly to mass reductions of employment after 1989.[24] As a result, there was growing unemployment and frustration among the unemployed. Second, among people searching for employment many were not prepared to operate in competitive labour markets, responding to changes passively, refusing government programmes for retraining, remaining resistant to job change and being wary of seeking new skills or qualifications. Third, while some social benefits such as extended maternity and educational (parental[25]) leaves were viewed positively under the former regime, they paradoxically came to be seen by some as potential traps to extended labour market participation and professional advancement, disadvantaging some groups of women interested in extended participation in the labour market.[26]

Thus, the behaviour and attitudes of women during the period of economic and political transformation between 1989 and 1997 (when EU accession issues became more important) were shaped by a combination of elements from the former system and elements that appeared as a consequence of system transformation. Dorota Szkodny-Ciołek in her paper 'Wpływ restrukturyzacji na decyzje kobiet w życiu zawodowym' [The influence of restructuring on women's decision-making process in a professional life][27] summarizes the most important elements influencing the situation of women in the labour market (Table 8.1).

At the beginning of this period of transformation, labour market participation rates dropped significantly for both sexes, but especially for women. In 1992, female participation rates were 53.7 per cent, 53.1 per cent in 1994, and 51.1 per cent in 1995.[28] The deactivation of active employees in Poland was connected first and foremost with economic decline; difficulties in finding work (long-term unemployment and the discouraged worker effect), and structural changes in the labour market, as well as taking up work in a shadow economy. However, in the implementation of labour market practices during the 1990s the effects of transformation had differentially negative impacts on women.[29]

At the same time, the feminization of professions increased. In 1992, 82 per cent[30] of all urban women employees worked in the feminized sectors

Table 8.1   Elements shaping the situation of women in transforming labour market

Before 1989	After 1989
- traditional gendered division of work, in which women are responsible for most housework; - traditional picture of women as the ones who devote themselves to family and children, taking care of the well-being of every member of a family; - gender segregation in labour market, in which women work in 'less important' industries and sectors, in positions with low prestige and fewer possibilities for promotion, resulting in few women in managerial positions; - legal regulations that define women as mothers, regulations that are often perceived as advantages for working women, but are in fact obstacles for them; - retirement regulations that require women to retire earlier than men, with negative financial and psychological consequences; - perception of women as less efficient employees, as the ones whom you cannot count on, especially if they are mothers; - the absence of women's agency in protecting their own rights, whereby some women believe that it is a duty of the state to take care of women's issues, not their own.	- mass unemployment; - new methods of recruitment, in which women are openly discriminated against; - promotion of a traditional model of family, in which women should take care of home and family, not their own professional career (women's work is accepted only if they are forced to do it because of the difficult economic situation of the family); - liquidation or limitation of the state obligations and help towards women employees; - lack of serious discussion about the situation of women among decision-makers.

Sources: Based on D. Szkodny-Ciołek, 'Wpływ restrukturyzacji na decyzje kobiet w życiu zawodowym' [The influence of restructuring on women's decision-making process in a professional life] in K. Faliszek, E.M. Petras, K. Wódz, eds, *Kobiety wobec przemian okresu transformacji* [Women in the Period of Transformation] (Katowice: Śląsk, 1997).

of health and social care (80.3 per cent of employees were women), education (78.2 per cent), hotels and restaurants (68.3 per cent).[31] The wage gap between male and female employees actually began to shrink during the transformation period, but it did not disappear. In 1996, women overall earned 79.2 per cent of a man's income (Table 8.2). The biggest gap in earnings appears in the case of physical labourers and the smallest gap in office and service workers. Education does not necessarily prevent economic discrimination because jobs like managers and specialists are characterized by a wide gap between the wages of men and women.

Table 8.2   Monthly earnings by professions in 1996

Activity	Women's earnings as a percentage of men's in 1996
Generally	79.2
Managers and CEOs	75.5
Specialists	73.7
Technicians and other middle personnel	73.4
Office workers	93.8
Service workers	88.2
Industry and craft workers	65.1

Source: *Rocznik statystyczny* [Statistical Yearbook] (Warszawa: GUS, 1997).

Table 8.3   Unemployment according to gender and length in 1992 and 1996

The length of unemployment	The number of unemployed women for 100 unemployed men	
	1992	1996
Overall	114	140
1 month and less	69	64
1–3 months	85	83
3–6 months	111	131
6–12 months	104	145
24 months and more	139	254

Sources: J. Unlot, 'Wyniki badań nad bezrobociem kobiet' [The Consequences of Female Unemployment] in R. Horodeński, ed., *Gospodarka zasobami pracy* [The Economics of Labour Markets] (Białystok: Wydawnictwo Wyższej Szkoły Ekonomicznej [Bialystok Publishing House of Higher Economic Schools], 1998) p. 138.

Compared with the previous period, a new and rather disturbing characteristic of the labour market appeared – unemployment. According to unemployment statistics in September 1993, the unemployment rate for men was 13.5 per cent, while it was 17.6 per cent for women.[32] More than 60 per cent of unemployed women were under the age of 34, and, additionally, 25 per cent were between 35 and 44. The period of unemployment seemed to be gendered as well (Table 8.3), a condition that cannot be connected to the lack of education, since in both rural and urban areas women had higher levels of education.

Polish accession to the EU structures

In 1994, Poland began preparations for accession to the European Union and became a Member State on 1 May 2004. Prior to accession, Poland had to adjust its laws and institutions to match the EU requirements in all areas covered by European law. In certain cases this required significant changes in Polish laws, while in other cases there were only minor adjustments. One of the areas where a significant effort had to be made related to the laws on equality between men and women. Figure 8.1 summarizes some important primary and secondary European laws shaping the equal position of men and women in the labour market.

The adjustment of Polish law to *acquis communautaire* was made mostly by the revision of the Labour Law, the Employment and Unemployment Counteraction Act and the Government Recommendation from 28 May 1996 on Parental Leave and Benefits. Examples of changes made in order to fully adjust Polish legislation to the Union's directives were as follows:

- introduction of the definition of the comparable worth of work;
- creation of a universal system of valuing work to allow comparisons among occupations;
- making the application of the right to equal pay easier to use in court;
- change in Polish Labour Law that would make cases on discrimination cases of Labour Law;
- introduction of detailed sanctions for discrimination practices that would be specific for the Labour Law;
- establishing protection against dissolving work agreements with people who are launching appeals under antidiscrimination laws.

Treaties:
  − Article 119 of the treaty establishing the European Community
  − Article 141 of Amsterdam Treaty

Directives:
75/117 − 'The Equal Pay Directive'
76/207 − 'The Equal Treatment Directive'
79/7   − The Directive on the progressive implementation of the principle of equal treatment for men and women in matters of social security
86/378 − The Directive on the implementation of the principle of equal treatment for men and women in occupational social security schemes
86/613 − The Directive on the protection of women during pregnancy
92/85   − Health and Safety of Pregnant Workers Directive
97/80   − The Directive on the burden of proof in cases of discrimination based on sex
97/81   − The Part Time Workers Directive

Figure 8.1 European law defining the institutional position of women in the labour market

In Polish legislation there were no paragraphs that created or allowed any formal discrimination against women. In spite of this, Polish Labour Law had to be carefully amended to adjust to various European requirements. To do this, discrimination practices towards candidates applying for positions, promotion or training were made illegal. Further amendments were introduced to address conditions of work, unequal treatment in the courts and changes to the rules determining whether the employer or employee has to prove discrimination or the lack thereof.

Additionally the position of the Governmental Plenipotentiary for Equal Status of Men and Women was created in 2001. The creation of this institution was promoted by the European Union and its standards, which Poland had to adopt in order to become a member of the EU. Its main task was focused on an analysis and assessment of the current situation of men and women in the country, and initiating and coordinating activities aimed at the assurance of the equal status of men and women in all areas of social life. Thanks to the efforts of the Governmental Plenipotentiary for Equal Status of Men and Women, Poland took part in European Programmes dealing with gender issues, such as the Equal Community Initiative.[33] It also produced a web page to serve as a platform for information exchange for public administration institutions and NGOs dealing with the status of men and women in society. Despite its accomplishments, the Plenipotentiary was dissolved following the parliamentary elections in 2005.

Poland has now adopted all the changes in its legal system required by accession, although implementation in certain areas remains an issue in Brussels. However, it is worth stressing that there are still issues that have to be solved. The most urgent of these is that women are not aware of the legal protections afforded them by EU law and they lack information and access to information on these matters. Moreover, the legal procedures based on the new laws have yet to be developed. Without information and procedures for implementation, the new legislation remains ineffective. It is only in the past three years that cases based on the new legal framework are finding their way into Polish courts, a development pushed largely by the active involvement of NGOs.

These adjustments have changed the situation of women in the labour market. Between 1997 and 2003 employment rates for both men and women continued to decline (Table 8.4). Notably, the decline in participation rates is larger for men than for women, but this has not led to a growth in importance of women's work, with participation rates for women in 2003 remaining at 47.9 per cent.

One area of particular current interest among researchers is the gendered division of work. The most feminized professional group are office workers, with 235 women for every 100 men in 2003; the least feminized are machinery

Table 8.4 Employment rate by gender in Poland

Years	Women	Men
1997	50.0	65.5
1998	50.0	64.9
1999	49.7	64.3
2000	49.2	64.3
2001	48.8	63.4
2002	48.0	62.6
2003	47.9	62.4

Source: *Aktywność ekonomiczna ludności Polski. Informacje i opracowania statystyczne* [The Economic Activity of the Polish Population: Information and Statistics] (Warszawa: GUS, 2004).

Table 8.5 Unemployment by education and gender (2003)

	University degree	University education without diploma	High school graduation	Vocational school education	Primary education
Women	8.0	17.0	24.3	28.0	25.5
Men	7.4	16.1	20.3	21.2	26.3

Source: *Kobiety i mężczyźni na rynku pracy* [Women in the Labour Force], http://www.stat.gov.pl/gus/45_1532_PLK.HTML.htm (1 August 2008).

operators and mechanics, of whom for every 100 men only 15 are women. Other feminized sectors include health and social work (412 women for 100 men), education (337 women for 100 men) and financial services (243 women for 100 men).[34]

Moreover, as Socha and Sztanderska point out, women's unemployment rate is 26.3 per cent higher than the men's rate, a figure that rises to 49.6 per cent when long-term unemployment rates are taken into account. These differences have grown systematically throughout the 1990s and the early years of the 2000s. The period of unemployment for men has been getting shorter while for women it has been getting longer.[35] In spite of the fact that many women have better education, their unemployment rates remain higher (Table 8.5), suggesting that gender itself is the main factor differentiating patterns of employment and unemployment.

These gender differences are reflected in the wage gap between women's and men's wages. On the one hand, it is caused by structural factors – fewer

Table 8.6   Monthly earnings by profession in 1996 and 2002

	Women's earnings as a percentage of men's in 1996	Women's earnings as a percentage of men's in 2002
Generally	79.2	83.0
Managers and CEOs	75.5	72.4
Specialists	73.7	74.6
Technicians and other middle personnel	73.4	72.7
Office workers	93.8	97.5
Service workers	88.2	86.2
Industry and craft workers	65.1	62.5

Sources: *Rocznik statystyczny* [Statistical Yearbook] (Warszawa: GUS 1997); *Kobiety i mężczyźni na rynku pracy* [Women in the Labour Force], GUS, http://www.stat.gov.pl/english/index.htm (1 August 2008).

women hold well-paid managerial positions. On the other hand, even at the same level of hierarchy, women sometimes earn less than men.[36]

The proportions of women's and men's earnings by professions are also highly unequal, with the average woman's wage in the 1990s remaining 20–25 per cent lower than a man's.[37] Between 1996 and 2002, there has been a small improvement in some professions, but in others the gap between women's and men's earnings is growing (Table 8.6).

Conclusions

The situation of women in the labour market is shaped by institutions, norms and practices. The most difficult obstacle to greater equality between men and women is the historically defined division of labour and the ways in which this gets reproduced under new circumstances. Many aspects of these historically defined positions of women in society and the economy remain surprisingly resistant to change. This institutional resistance has been sustained even as processes of economic harmonization and integration have gone forward. Recent legal regulations and their corresponding institutions have attempted to improve the situation of women in the labour market, although many of these also demonstrate substantial lags between legislation and everyday economic practice.

As in other reforming countries, in Poland there never was a clean break with the socialist past. Instead, the former system is still embedded in contemporary society. As a result, any understanding of gender relations in the contemporary Polish labour markets must be rooted in a labour history of the command economy period. Under central planning the state's commitment to and policies to foster women's equality were often symbolic. After

1989 the position of women in the economy became a target. Equality promoted by the former, socialist system[38] was rejected, and a traditional division of labour with a man as a breadwinner and a woman taking care of the family was pushed hard by certain parts of the society, government and Church. Polish accession to the European structures has rolled back these attacks and the corset of traditional attitudes that limits female access to labour markets is being loosened. Change is beginning to occur in job/ home segregation and there is a growing consensus encouraging women to enter professional fields. But, despite expanded EU support for common labour market rights and rules, comparable changes in access to some professions, promotion in them and the equalization of wage levels are slow. Most striking is that many women do not fight for equality. Since the mid-1990s there have been only a few attempts to enact any legislation on the equal status of men and women, and none has been successful. Even female members of Parliament resisted these efforts, choosing to interpret these efforts to create greater gender equality as a direct attack on traditional values.

EU accession may change this situation. Signs of change towards greater gender equality in Polish labour markets are emerging, mainly resulting from the adoption of European policies and programmes, and to the necessity of not only adopting EU regulations but using them. EU policies such as gender mainstreaming to promote equality between men and women in political life at all levels are likely to improve gender relations in the near future.[39] But, insofar as the situation of women in the labour market is defined by formal and informal institutions, stiffness and inelasticity in gender politics remain strong. The extent to which the European norms of gender equality will actually and substantially transform the actually existing informal institutions of Polish labour market remains an open question.[40]

Notes

1   I would like to thank John Pickles for helpful editorial comments. I am also grateful to Grzegorz Mazurkiewicz and John Fischer for their detailed comments on earlier drafts of this paper. I would also like to take this opportunity to thank again Ewa Okon-Horodynska and Lucyna Frackiewicz.
2   W.C. Neale, 'Institutions', in G.M. Hodgson, W.J. Samuels, M.R. Tool, eds, *The Elgar Companion to Institutional and Evolutionary Economics* (Hants: Edward Elgar, 1993) p. 402.
3   G.M. Hodgson, *Economics and Institutions: A Manifesto for a Modern Institutional Economics* (Oxford: Policy Press, 1993) p. 134.
4   J. Wilkin, *Jaki kapitalizm? Jaka Polska?* [Which Capitalism? Which Poland?] (Warszawa: PWN, 1999) p. 118.
5   T.J. Yeager, *Institutions, Transition Economies, and Economic Development* (Boulder, Colorado/Oxford: Westview Press, 1999), pp. 9–10.
6   S. Pejovich, *Economic Analysis of Institutions and Systems* (Dodrecht – Boston – London: Kluwer Academic Publisher, 1997) pp. 23–24.

7   B. Żylicz, *Wpływ procesu prywatyzacji na położenie kobiet: kobiety polskie w gospodarce okresu transformacji* [The Effects of Privatization on the Position of Women: Polish Women in the Economy During the Period of Transformation] (Warsaw: Centrum Praw Kobiet, 2000) p. 5. The type of unemployment that could be found in command economies was hidden unemployment. It was used as an instrument of oppression against oppositionists, for instance, Vaclav Havel could not find a job in public enterprises and had to work part-time in the early 1960s.

8   A. Titkow, 'Kobiety pod presją? Proces kształtowania się tożsamości' [Women Under Pressure: The Process of Changing Identity], in A. Titkow, H. Domański, eds, *Co to znaczy być kobieta w Polsce* [What it Means to be a Woman in Poland] (Warszawa, IFiS PAN, 1995) p. 29.

9   A. Kowalska, *Economic Activity of Women and Their Position on the Labour Market* (Warsaw: GUS, 1996) p. 5.

10 M. Sokołowska, 'Obraz kobiety w świadomości współczesnego społeczeństwa polskiego' [The Image of Women in contemporary Polish society], *Kultura i Społeczeństwo* [Culture and Society], 3 (1978) 272.

11 M. Okólski, 'Deformacja przejścia demograficznego w Polsce Ludowej' [Poland's Distorted Demographic Transition], *Studia Demograficzne* [Demographic Studies], 1 (1990) 3–20.

12 This list is still valid although its title was changed thanks to the motion carried by the Governmental Plenipotentiary for Equal Status of Men and Women from 'The list of jobs prohibited for women' into 'The list of jobs especially burdensome for women'.

13 Women working as coal miners were a subject of discussion in a special Commission established by the Polish United Workers' Party to examine conditions of women's work underground. During the discussion in the Commission moral as well as economic issues of such coeducation were raised. The conclusion was to withdraw female workers from coal mines.

14 S. Walczewska, *Damy, rycerze i feministki; kobiecy dyskurs emancypacyjny w Polsce* [Ladies, Knights and Feminists: Women's Discourses of Emancipation in Poland] (Kraków: Efka, 2000) p. 87.

15 K. Erturk, N. Cagatay, 'Macroeconomic Consequences of Cyclical and Secular Changes in Feminization: An Experiment at Gendered Macromodeling', *World Development*, 23(11) (1995) 1970–1971.

16 European Commission, Employment Observatory Central and Eastern Europe, 3 (Brussels: December 1992).

17 M. Ingham, H. Ingham, 'Gender and Labour Market Change: What Do the Official Statistics Show?' in M. Ingham, H. Ingham, H. Domański, eds, *Women on the Polish Labour Market* (Budapest: CEU Press, 2001) p. 42.

18 However, it is worth noting that six years before this ratio was 1: 3.3. H. Domański, *Zadowolony niewolnik idzie do pracy* [Satisfied Slave Goes to Work] (Warszawa: Wydawnictwo IFiS PAN, 1999) p. 62.

19 Z. Janowska, J. Martini-Fiwek, Z. Góral, 'Bezrobocie kobiet w Polsce' [Female unemployment in Poland], *Polityka Ekonomiczna i Społeczna* [Politics, Economics, and Society], vol. 18 (Warszawa: Fundacja im. Fridricha Eberta, 1992) 2.

20 K. Janicka, 'Kobiety i mężczyźni w strukturze społeczno-zawodowej: podobieństwa i różnice' [The structure of female and male employment in professional occupations: similarities and differences], in A. Titkow, H. Domański, eds, *Co to znaczy być kobieta w Polsce* [What it Means to be a Woman in Poland] (Warsaw: IFiS PAN, 1995) p. 95.

21 M. Fuszara, 'Women's legal rights in Poland and the process of transformation' in *Beyond Law; Stories of law and social change from Latin America and around the world* (Latin American Institute of Alternative Legal Services, 1993), pp. 41–42; B. Kołaczek, 'Sytuacja zawodowa i rodzinna kobiet poszukujących pracy' [The Situation of Professional and Family Women Seeking Work], *Studia i materiały* IPiSS [Studying and Materials], vol. 21 (Warsaw, 1991), p. 16.

22 The participation rate of women in the last parliament before 1989 was 20 per cent, thus almost twice as much as ten years later in 1998. But what should be borne in mind is that the parliament played a different role at that time. It was a subordinate organ to the communist party. In the party which was the place where most important political decisions were made, the participation rate of women was insignificant. There were also disproportions in the level of age and education of women and men in the Parliament that were most visible in the years 1980–1985. At that time 23 per cent of members of parliament were women – 60 per cent of whom were 26–30 years old and 30 per cent of whom had finished their education at the primary or middle school level. In comparison, the same age group among men was 2.2 per cent, and almost 60 per cent of men held a university diploma. Such a picture may lead to the conclusion that women were to play the role of an adornment in the parliament at that time (S. Walczewska, 65–66).

23 M. Fuszara, pp. 41–42.

24 For Stenning, the result of these adjustments is employment insecurity, increasing pressure on workers to undertake difficult tasks and to work longer hours, with a resulting erosion of family and social life. A. Stenning, 'Życie w przestrzeniach (post)socjalizmu: przypadek Nowej Huty', http://www.nowahuta.info/reports/NH%20report%20PL.pdf (18 December 2007), p. 3.

25 At that time only women were entitled to parental leave. Fathers could use it under very special circumstances.

26 B. Żylicz, pp. 5–6.

27 D. Szkodny-Ciołek, 'Wpływ restrukturyzacji na decyzje kobiet w życiu zawodowym' [The Impact of Restructuring Decisions on Women in the Workforce] in K. Faliszek, E.M. Petras, K. Wódz, eds, *Kobiety wobec przemian okresu transformacji* [The Changing Role of Women During the Period of Transformation] (Katowice: Śląsk, 1997), pp. 25–26.

28 For men the labour participation rate was 66.5 in 1995. *Aktywność ekonomiczna ludności Polski. Informacje i opracowania statystyczne* [The Economic Activity of the Polish Population] (Warszawa: GUS, 1994, 2000).

29 B. Żylicz, pp. 25–27. But see K. Ghodsee (2007) for an example from Bulgaria where female workers in the highly feminized state socialist tourist industry were greatly advantaged during the period of transformation.

30 K. Janicka, p. 95.

31 *Aktywność ekonomiczna ludności Polski. Informacje i opracowania statystyczne* [The Economic Activity of the Polish Population] (Warszawa: GUS, 1994).

32 I. Reszke, *Wobec bezrobocia: opinie, stereotypy* [Facing Unemployment: Opinions, Stereotypes] (Warszawa: Scholar, 1995), pp. 47–48.

33 The objective of the Equal Community Initiative is to test and promote – within international cooperation – new ways of combating all forms of discrimination and inequality on the labour market, affecting both the employed and job seekers. It is a programme financed by the European Social Funds.

34   *Aktywność ekonomiczna ludności Polski. Informacje i opracowania statystyczne* [The Economic Activity of the Polish Population] (Warszawa: GUS, 2004).
35   M. Socha, U. Sztanderska, *Strukturalne podstawy bezrobocia w Polsce* [Structural Unemployment in Poland] (Warszawa: PWN, 2000), p. 171.
36   M.A. Knothe, 'Kobieta i praca. Problemy polskiego rynku pracy dla kobiet w okresie przejścia do gospodarki rynkowej' [Women and Work: Problems of Polish Labour Markets For Women in the Transition to a Market Economy] in K. Faliszek, E.M. Petras, K. Wódz, eds, *Kobiety wobec przemian okresu transformacji* [The Changing Role of Women During the Period of Transformation] (Katowice: Śląsk, 1997) p. 18.
37   B. Żylicz, p. 14.
38   Even though it was, in the majority of cases, only on the level of ideology.
39   Gender mainstreaming is the integration of the gender perspective into every stage of policy processes – design, implementation, monitoring and evaluation – with a view to promoting equality between women and men. The main characteristic of gender mainstreaming strategy is the introduction of gender perspective to the obligations of each authority or institution, not limiting such efforts to groups of experts.
40   As it was expressed by Thorstein Veblen: 'The change is always in the last resort a change in habits of thought' in T. Veblen, 'Why is Economics Not an Evolutionary Science?', *The Quarterly Journal of Economics*. 12(4) July 1898, pp. 373–397.

9
Convergence Criteria in New European Union Member States: The Polish Experience

Katarzyna Żukrowska

Introduction

On 1 May 2004, ten new countries became members of the European Union (EU). Eight of these were former command and planned states whose economies had been liberalized in the 1990s and after were further restructured to meet the requirements of EU accession. Accession agreements concluded between postsocialist states and the European Community were of two types: the Europe Agreements which created free trade areas with the Community leading towards accession, while Agreements on Cooperation and Trade created associational agreements to foster cooperation evolving more gradually into membership. Since 1997, the Commission has monitored the performance of each candidate country in meeting the requirements set down in these agreements and provided strong criticism in areas where the national strategies and implementation programmes of candidate states were inadequate.[1] Convergence criteria were not requirements at that stage of accession, but candidates were obliged to fulfil the Copenhagen criteria concerning political and economic reforms.

The Copenhagen criteria required Candidate States to develop functioning representative democracies and the institutions necessary for a working market economy. Further approval was required for integration deepening (including participation in the Economic and Monetary Union (EMU) and political integration) and 'opt out' clauses that had been occasionally used by former members were restricted. Candidate States were obliged to reform their institutions, laws and procedures in ways which allowed them to be well prepared for competition on the EU market and to meet all the obligations of membership. By the time of their respective accession dates, each accession state had to have passed these tests either nominally or in reality and each now faces the challenge of preparation for further political and economic integration, particularly for participation in the EMU. Four former planned economies and two market economies that became EU members in 2004 started to stabilize their exchange rates in the ERM-2 (Exchange Rate Mechanism), preparing for the introduction of the euro, shortly after their accession.[2]

This chapter assesses the extent to which Poland is prepared to join the EMU, and compares these efforts with the results achieved by the remaining new Member States of the EU. The analysis has important implications for how we understand political and economic integration, particularly since many of the assumptions made in preparing strategies for East Central European economies for EU membership and now for participation in the EMU have been based on theories formulated for the integration into the EU of formerly closed protective economies and predicated on a division between developed industrial countries and developing industrializing economies. These strategies assumed that the transition economies needed a gradual opening of markets to competition and that state aid for incubation of businesses would be necessary for up to two years following accession, but only in the new Member States' economies that opened the markets to competition quickly and where protections and state supports for businesses were relatively small.[3]

Convergence criteria

Monetary policy within the EMU is decided at the level of the European Central Bank (ECB), while non-EMU members still determine their own interest rates in shaping monetary policy. Even those countries that have been in the ERM-2 for the past two years are still able to adjust exchange and interest rates to stay within the required + 15 per cent fluctuation margins. Once a currency enters the EMU this tool loses its power because at that point monetary policy is guided by the ECB, while fiscal policy remains the responsibility of the Member States. Because the convergence criteria are strongly dependent on each other, this division of responsibility between monetary and fiscal policies creates tension in the system.[4]

Fiscal policies alone are inadequate instruments for dealing with the conditions and needs of the current stage of development in postcommunist economies, particularly as these are increasingly shaped by the opening of the economy, geographical shifts in production, intensified competition and the development of new markets and new economies. Integration into the internal EU market was also important, driving the move to a common EMU.

Enlargement of the EU, first by eight East and Central European economies and subsequently by two more, has forced the old Member States to speed up their own processes of structural change and has created renewed pressure for changes in fiscal policies. However, policies that were applied to other European countries have proven to be poorly tailored to the needs of the new accession economies and some older Member States, leading as they have to growing public debt and budget deficits beyond the limits set by the EMU.

Prior to entering negotiations for EMU membership, the new Member States were able to shape their own economic policies and, as a result, countries prepared to meet the convergence criteria in different ways. These resulted in different rates of growth in individual economies as well as different elasticity of adjustments to both external and internal changes in the conditions of production. In dealing with these challenges in the short term, economic policymakers needed short-term control over interest rates. Even though some of these approaches have not been sustainable even in the medium term, there was an urgent need for these kinds of independent fiscal responses, given the very different scope and pace of liberalization in the national economies of the EMU Member States.

The current phase of political enlargement of the EU has coincided with the launching of the EMU. Together, these require deeper and more far-reaching structural changes in a shorter period of time than was the case for any of the old Member States. Central to these structural adjustments is the withdrawal of all subsidies that support the artificial competitiveness of producers and products,[5] specifically (1) the control of budget deficits by reducing subsidies, subventions and privileges whose costs are no longer borne by the state, and (2) control of state aid towards companies (Table 9.1).[6]

Although in absolute terms state aid is smaller in the new Member States than in old Member States, it is still relatively high in comparative and per capita terms (Table 9.2). The result has been a massive interregional shift of employment and production as West European businesses have expanded their production networks in the lower wage areas of Central and Eastern Europe.

Table 9.1   Public aid (agriculture with fisheries and forestry and transport excluded) in selected EU Member States

Contents	Unit	EU15	New MS	CZ	LT	PL	SK	D
Average state aid in year terms	Mln €	39,839	6,067	2,050	41	2,403	130	15,897
Average state aid as % of GDP	% GDP	0.43	1.38	2.73	0.29	1.26	0.49	0.64
Average state aid per capita	PPS (Standard)	105	160	409	26	127	57	150

Sources: *Report: State Aid Scoreboard – spring 2005 update* (COM (2005)) 145 final, Brussels, 20.04.2005. For Germany, own calculations based on information published at http://www.aztn.hr/twinning/eng/documents/State%20Aid%20Scoreboard%20Spring%202005.pdf.

Table 9.2   State aid in PPS in per capita terms

Contents	EU 15	CZ	LT	PL	SK	D
2000	98	386	27	90	62	155
2001	101	268	15	64	58	148
2002	106	588	35	46	52	134
2003	97	404	29	307	61	164

Source: Eurostat Yearbook 2004, http://www.aztn.hr/twinning/
eng/documents/State%20Aid%20Scoreboard%20Spring%20
2005.pdf.

Particularly in the case of Poland and the Czech Republic, state aid will have to be reduced in the near future if they are to fulfil the convergence criteria. Such changes are already underway in old Member States, although some countries such as Germany resist reducing their per capita levels of state aid. State aid in the EU Member States declined sharply from 67,995 billion euro in 2002 (peak year) for EU-15 to 58,697 billion euro in 2005, and respectively from 74,105 billion euro for EU-25 to 58,697 billion euro for EU-25.[7]

Convergence criteria were formulated in Protocol 2 of the Maastricht Treaty, dealing with fiscal and monetary controls.[8] Monetary criteria change according to the inflation and interest indicators of the best-performing countries. Fiscal criteria are fixed and relate to budget deficit and public debt. In the Maastricht Treaty the convergence criteria require:

- **Price stability**: the average inflation rate in the preceding year should not exceed the average increase in the three best-performing economies by more than 1.5 % points.
- **Interest rates**: the average long-term nominal interest rate should not be higher than 2% of that in the three best-performing economies.
- **Budget deficit**: the share of the current or planned GDP deficit should not exceed 3% points measured in market prices for the preceding year.
- **Public debt** as share of debt in GDP should not exceed 60%.

Joining the EMU requires that states either meet these convergence criteria or demonstrate that policies are in place to achieve specified macroeconomic goals. Moreover, at the beginning, when the first members of EMU were selected by the European Monetary Institute and before final approval by the European Commission, two additional requirements were imposed on some of them concerning the independence of the national central bank and stabilization of their currency's exchange rates for at least two years in a mechanism specially constructed for that purpose – the Exchange Rate Mechanism (ERM). In other words, all EMU candidates had to demonstrate the ability of their national central banks to be able to keep their currencies' exchange rates stable within the bands defined by the ERM for two years. The bands have been expanded gradually from + 1.5 per cent when first attempts to coordinate the exchange rates were undertaken, through + 2.5 per cent and + 15 per cent in 1997.

After long discussions among Member States and because of increasing difficulties faced by the biggest EU Member States in fulfilling their own fiscal criteria, the Stability and Growth Pact seems to have been loosened recently. The average budget deficit in the euro area is currently very close to the three per cent threshold, and France, Germany and Italy have each had difficulties in reaching the target.[9] Greece has also had similar difficulties, although the size of its economy does not have the same kind of impact on stabilization across the whole euro area. According to Buti and Giudice, there are two principles of fiscal policy that are necessary to maintaining fiscal discipline in the euro area. First, Member States must embrace numerical goals that link fiscal indicators such as expenditures, deficit and debt to growth. Second, each needs to adopt more rigorous procedural measures designed to maintain more disciplined fiscal policies.[10] Numerical goals are considered to be easy to introduce and control, provided good standards of fiscal accounting are maintained. However, fixed numerical rules can cause problems where their requirement of fixed discipline can lead to antigrowth fiscal policy in periods of economic slowdown.[11] Consequently, in practice, there are differences in the application of policies in individual EU Member States because the numerical goals allow individual states some room for manoeuvre as long as they continue to meet their overall goals on expenditures.

Strategies used by EMU members in their preparation to meet the convergence criteria

Attempts to meet the fiscal criteria of convergence have not been without their difficulties. The only country that had problems meeting the monetary criteria before the EMU was created was Greece. It joined the EMU late, but managed to do so in the last stage of the launching of the euro, in part apparently through the use of creative accounting. The other economies that had problems meeting the convergence criteria tended to face difficulties with the fiscal requirements, not with the monetary ones.

Where rising costs of production intensified competition on domestic producers and resulted in offshoring or relocation of investments to lower-cost regions, the result was often the provision of state supports for sensitive and threatened sectors. Costs increased as subsidies, donations and privileges were extended to struggling enterprises. These were financed either from a growing budget deficit (borrowing on the capital market) or from increased taxes, but a growing deficit impacted the money supply and demand on capital markets, pushing up interest rates, while increased taxes pushed up the costs of production, lowering the real competitiveness of producers. The result was that labour markets were affected by the crowding out and moving abroad of some businesses or the slowing down of the economy. Unemployment grew and this further constrained the budget.

To deal with these issues, the OECD not only plans to pursue further and deeper liberalization of capital flows among its members, but it also foresees a new approach to taxes. This is evidenced by preparation of a *Model Tax Convention on Income and Capital*, whose goal is to introduce common rules across Member State economies.[12] There has been some resistance to these policies of harmonization, particularly where well-organized and powerful business and industrial coalitions are able to lobby successfully for protective measures and rewards for companies that maintain their businesses at home. On the other hand, domestic tax reduction in Central and Eastern Europe also generates opposition from Western Europe, where it may be seen as a form of 'tax dumping', while New Member States continue to benefit from the transfer of EU funds derived from taxes from Western European countries.

The whole procedure shifted the structure of the economy and labour markets towards one more focused on higher value and service activities in the Old Member States. Where these resulted in increased flexibility, they also increased pressure on state budgets for the payment of unemployment benefits. In other cases, however, elasticity was achieved by implementing six different approaches to consolidate budgets: (1) expenditure-based consolidation; (2) revenue-based consolidation; (3) mixed strategy cutting the expenditures and increasing revenues; (4) creative accountancy; (5) freezing expenditures during economic acceleration; and (6) increasing expenditures by a lower rate than the rate of growth of revenues.

The experience of current EMU members in consolidation of their own budgets shows that there is no easy or single solution. Expenditure-based consolidation was applied in Austria, Finland, Ireland, The Netherlands and Spain. Finland still had a budget deficit of −3.2 per cent in 1986 although by 1997 the deficit was halved to −1.5 per cent. Finland again exceeded the budget deficit threshold in 2000 but since then the problem has not recurred. Austria in 1996 had an even higher budget deficit than Finland at −3.8 per cent, while in 1997 the deficit was reduced to −1.7 per cent. Spain's deficit in 1996 reached −4.9 per cent and in 1997 it was still −0.2 per cent above the threshold of −3.0 per cent. Even so, Spain was approved to join the EMU because of the positive tendencies in its fiscal policy, and had met the convergence requirements by 1998.

Revenue-based consolidation was applied in Belgium, Greece and Portugal. All three passed the criterion in 1998 but in 1997 Greece experienced a budget deficit of −4.0 per cent. Since then both Portugal and Greece have had budget deficit problems. Mixed policies were applied in France, Germany and Italy. All three have budget deficit problems today (Table 9.3).

Table 9.3 Budget balance as % of the GDP in EMU Member States in the years 1993–2007

Contents	1993	1994	1995	1996	1997	1998	1999	2000	2001	2002	2003	2004	2005	2006	2007[a]
Austria	-4.2	-4.8	-5.1	-3.8	-1.7	-2.3	-2.0	-1.5	0.1	-0.4	-1.4	-1.3	-2.0	-1.4	-0.8
Belgium	-7.3	-5.0	-4.3	-3.8	-2.0	-0.7	-0.5	0.1	0.5	0.0	0.2	-0.5	-0.5	0.4	-0.3
France	-6.7	-6.1	-7.0	-4.9	-3.2	-2.6	-1.8	-1.4	-1.5	-3.1	-4.1	-3.7	-3.0	-2.5	-2.5
Finland	-7.3	-5.7	-3.7	-3.2	-1.5	1.3	2.3	6.7	5.1	4.3	2.1	1.8	1.2	3.8	4.6
Germany	-3.1	-2.4	-3.3	-3.4	-2.7	-2.1	-1.1	-1.0	-2.7	-3.6	-3.4	-3.6	-3.5	-1.6	0.1
Greece	13.8	10.0	10.2	-7.4	-4.0	-2.5	-1.8	-2.0	-1.4	-1.5	-3.3	-3.2	-3.2	-2.5	-2.9
Ireland	-2.3	-1.7	-2.2	-0.2	0.7	2.1	2.3	4.4	1.1	-0.1	0.2	-0.8	-0.9	2.9	0.9
Italy	-9.4	-9.1	-7.6	-7.1	-2.7	-2.8	-1.9	-1.5	-2.6	-2.3	-2.5	-3.2	-4.4	-4.4	-2.3
Luxembourg	1.5	2.5	2.4	1.2	3.7	3.4	3.4	6.0	6.1	2.1	0.5	-1.2	-0.1	0.7	1.2
Netherlands	-3.1	-3.6	-4.2	-1.8	-1.1	-0.7	0.7	2.2	0.0	-1.6	-3.2	-3.6	-2.2	0.6	-0.4
Portugal	-6.1	-6.0	-4.6	-4.0	-2.6	-1.9	-2.0	-1.7	-4.2	-2.7	-2.9	-3.5	-3.5	-3.9	-3.0
Spain	-6.7	-6.1	-7.0	-4.9	-3.2	-2.6	-1.1	-0.4	0.0	-0.1	0.3	0.5	0.5	1.8	1.8
Average	-6.4	-5.5	-5.4	-4.1	-2.2	-1.4	-0.6	0.35	-0.1	-1.0	-1.6	-1.9	-2.0	-1.3	-0.3

[a] Economic Forecasts, Autumn 2007.

Source: Autumn Report 2007 (European Commission).

The average budget deficit for EMU participants started to grow after 2001 but it did not surpass the –3 per cent threshold, while between 1993 and 2001 budget deficits were generally falling. Between 2002 and 2005 average budget deficits of the EMU states increased, while since 2005 the deficits have fallen again. The three Old Member States who are not in the EMU also follow the convergence criteria in their budgetary policies. Great Britain's budget deficit in 2005 was –3.3 per cent, while in 2006 it was reduced to –2.7 per cent and in 2007 it was also below the 3 per cent threshold, reaching –2.8 per cent. In Denmark the budget in three last years was closed by a surplus which reached 4.6 per cent of the GDP in 2005, 4.6 per cent in 2006 and 4 per cent in 2007. Sweden's budget was closed by a deficit but it was lower than in the UK, reaching the following values: –1.5 per cent in 2005, –1.2 per cent in 2006 and –0.7 per cent in 2007.[13]

Convergence criteria in New Member States

Fulfilment of the budget deficit criterion is the biggest problem in New Member States, although not all countries encounter difficulties in meeting this requirement. The performance is mixed, as it has been in the Old Member States. In all ECE states public debt is under control and inflation has declined dramatically, largely because state debt was generally low in the first place. In states where state debt was very low it has remained low (such as in Latvia, where it reaches 16 per cent). In other states, such as the Czech Republic, debt levels have started to increase again. There are also some difficulties in meeting the interest rate criterion. Interest rates can have negative effects even as they stimulate certain desired behaviours, such as limiting certain types of consumption (such as import goods) while stimulating other types (construction, housing, and education). Relatively high interest rates crowd out companies from credit markets and tend to force them to seek partners abroad and press for the internationalization of their business. Low interest rates, usually considered to be a stimulus to economic growth, tend to create a short-term boom and they stimulate state borrowing, consumption, imports in the medium term, but result in the slowing down of the economy in the longer term.

Data on general budget balances (Table 9.4) suggest that there might be a problem with some hypotheses which have emerged in recent publications. Philip Cerny, for example, has argued for the concept of the 'competitive state', where the state fosters internal competition among industrial enterprises for access to lower-cost labour pools, a model that draws heavily on the experience of the reunification experience in Germany.[14] The concept may have some interesting applicability to the Chinese economy, but its applicability to other CEE economies would result in regional shifts of production driven largely by access to low-wages markets. The result would be the squeezing out of technical investments and efforts to upgrade the

Table 9.4 General budget balances in new Member States in 1997–2007

Contents	1997	1998	1999	2000	2001	2002	2003	2004	2005	2006	2007[a]
Bulgaria	5.3	1.7	0.4	–0.5	0.2	–0.1	0.0	2.3	2.0	3.2	3.0
Cyprus	–	–4.1	–4.3	–2.3	–2.2	–4.4	–6.5	–4.1	–2.4	–1.2	–10
Czech Rep.	–2.7	–4.5	–3.2	–3.3	–5.5	–6.7	–8.3	–3.0	–3.5	–2.9	–3.4
Estonia	2.0	–0.4	–4.0	–0.4	0.2	1.2	–0.5	1.8	1.9	3.6	3.0
Hungary	–6.8	–8.0	–5.3	–3.0	–4.1	–9.2	–5.5	–4.5	–7.8	–9.2	–6.4
Lithuania	–1.1	–3.1	–5.6	–2.7	–1.9	–1.2	–1.5	6.7	–0.5	–0.6	–0.9
Latvia	1.8	–0.7	–5.3	–2.7	–1.6	–2.7	–2.0	–0.8	–0.4	–0.3	0.9
Malta	–7.7	–9.9	–7.7	–6.2	–6.4	–5.5	–9.8	–4.9	–3.1	–2.5	–1.6
Poland	–4.3	–2.3	–1.5	–1.8	–3.9	–6.7	–6.9	–5.3	–4.3	–3.8	–2.7
Romania	–	–3.2	–4.5	–4.6	–3.3	–2.0	–1.5	–1.4	–1.4	–1.9	–2.7
Slovakia	–5.7	–4.7	–6.4	–12.8	–5.6	–7.2	–5.0	5.5	–2.8	–3.7	–2.7
Slovenia	–1.2	2.3	–2.2	–3.2	–2.5	–3.2	–1.5	–1.9	2.4	2.5	3.0

[a]Economic Forecast Autumn 2007 (European Commission).

Sources: Regular Progress Reports of the Commission, 2002; Transitional Report Update 2004, EBRD, London.

quality of the workforce in favour of what can only be temporarily low labour costs.

There also seems to be some misunderstanding about the convergence criteria themselves. While it has been argued that 'nominal convergence is embodied by the Maastricht criteria and the ERM II disciplines, which should help to induce and sustain stable economic growth after entry to the EMU', we have already seen that there is no automatic solution for convergence criteria fulfilment or for its impact on growth. Convergence criteria can be met with different methods and meeting them once does not give any guarantee that the same conditions will apply later. Meeting the criteria in the long run has to be achieved by budget consolidation. Otherwise the whole policy will be short-sighted and potentially explosive in the long run.

Stanislaw Gomulka has pointed out that fiscal policy is a weak link in the process.[15] In the ECE there have been large differences in the exchange-rate policies applied in specific countries (specifically in regard to the pegs used in different stages of the marketization of the exchange rate and the speed of introducing a floating exchange-rate regime). These have had an impact on the rates of growth, the direction of observed changes in the exchange-rate value (appreciation, depreciation), competitiveness, changes of the current account balance, and the degree of turbulence in financial markets. A by-product of poorly tailored monetary and fiscal policy has been a sharp slowdown in the rate of growth, a large deterioration in public finances and a sharp increase in unemployment rates.[16] This was the situation in the Czech Republic. By contrast, Poland achieved the best monetary and exchange-rate policy regime in the region, despite failing to adopt much needed structural reforms in public finances and labour market reform.[17]

According to Gomulka, the biggest risk for the ECE countries preparing for EMU membership is the possibility that foreign debt will balloon because of former high levels of borrowing and the current credit expansion in Western markets. But even these risks are not the same in all the ECE economies, with each economy facing quite different constraints and challenges (e.g., Poland, the Czech Republic and Hungary). In the Czech Republic and Hungary, the risk of a ballooning foreign debt is low. After the crisis of 1995, wages in Hungary in euro were adjusted downwards, while in the Czech Republic a long-lasting recession lowered imports. In Poland, private sector foreign debt is low, levelling out at 20 per cent of the GDP in 2001. Most of this debt is owned by foreign companies and short-term capital, both debt and portfolio investments, remains at a lower level than official reserves. A balance of payments crisis is not a real threat in Poland.[18]

Policies applied in the three states are different and they indicate that the risks are also different. This is true of past results and current policies. In the past Hungarian and Czech currencies experienced appreciation, while the Polish currency has only recently begun to appreciate. But this did not affect export expansion to the EU, despite the fact that appreciation occurred at the very time that Polish exports were confronted with increased competition in EU markets from third countries, which had been awarded lower import tariffs under GSP and GSP+ than had been the case for Poland before accession. The result has been a sharpening of competition in the EU markets towards which Polish exports are directed.[19] This change in competitive position has been further exacerbated by productivity increases, the diminishing product of marginal capital, technological transfer, FDI, innovation, elasticity of labour markets, salaries, prices, the degree of differentiation in the economy and aid transfers, among others. There are also some factors which have a counteracting effect on the tendency towards appreciation: current account deficits, exports of capital, external indebtedness, payments reducing external debts (interests and rates), etc.

Until 2003, most experts assumed that there would be currency appreciation in Poland and that the Balassa–Samuelson effect might create problems for convergence and an obstacle to economic development. This was assumed to be the case despite the fact that the analysis of the Balassa–Samuelson effect did not indicate this explicitly, since they also demonstrated that the effect had a different power in the ECE economies. In fact, most calculations indicate that the size of the Balassa–Samuelson effect falls within the margin of statistical error (Table 9.5).

Table 9.5 Estimation of the Balassa–Samuelson effect in ECE economies

| Economist | Size of the sample | | Size of the Balassa–Samuelson effect |
	Number of states and their characteristics	Period	
Pelksman (2000)	10 states from ECE	1997–1999	3.8
De Broek and Slok (2001)	10 states from ECE	1993–1999	1.4–2.0
Halpern and Wyplosz (2001)	8	1991–1999	3
Coricelli and Jazbec (2001)	19 states with trans-forming economies	1990–1998	0.7–1.2
Fischer (2002)	10 states of ECE	1990–1998	1.9–2.6
Egert (2002)	5 states of ECE	1991–2001	0.5–1.8
Aratibel, Rodriguez-Palenzuela, Thimann (2002)	10 states of ECE	1995–2001	Not meaningful
Begg (2003)	9	1991–1998	0.4–1.4

Source: *Measuring the Balassa–Samuelson effect for the countries of Central and Eastern Europe.* Banque de France Bulletin Digest no. 122, February 2004.

For economies with lower levels of development, economic growth can lead to appreciation and this, in turn, may stimulate speculation and act as an obstacle for more rapid development. In such conditions a common currency may act to reduce some of these negative consequences of economic growth.

Empirical studies have shown that appreciation should be differentiated from overvaluation. In most cases the currencies in transforming economies did not appreciate but were overvalued and likely to depreciate instead. If the ECE currencies were to enter the ERM-2 system, fixing the exchange rate at the overvalued levels, then their competitiveness would be reduced in real terms. Any such limitation of competitiveness would result in lower rates of economic growth and would prolong the period of real convergence and economic development.

In all the cases in Table 9.6, currencies are overvalued. This explains why people often see the common currency as one way to eliminate the negative effects of an overvalued currency. But it remains unclear whether a single level interest rate would be good for all, particularly for the New Member States whose economies are still undergoing major restructuring.

Before joining the EMU each future member must first stabilize its currency in the ERM-2. When an economy is competitive, currency stable and market relatively big, there are good arguments for staying out of ERM-2

Table 9.6   Nominal exchange rates in second quarter of 2001

Contents	Poland	Czech Republic	Slovakia	Hungary	Slovenia
Observed exchange rate (national currency/euro)	3.49	34.30	43.00	257.46	214.44
Overvaluation towards euro (%)	15	11	10	2	2
Nominal exchange rate of equilibrium (national currency/ euro)	4.12	38.39	47.54	263.90	217.94

Sources: E. Balazs, A. Lahreche-Revil, *Estimating the Fundamental Equilibrium Exchange Rate of Central and Eastern European Countries, The EMU Enlargement Perspective* (CEPII, June 2003) p. 31.

and joining the EMU later. Where such conditions do not exist it is beneficial to the future member to join the ERM-2 quickly in order to consolidate fiscal and monetary policies by tying them to the economies of other EMU members. In general, the idea is simple and effective one, but questions remain about the wisdom of bringing the weakest and most unstable economies most quickly into the EMU.

The approach is based on theories of turbulence (or crisis) in which change is brought about more quickly and easily in this enforced manner than by having to first establish a broader social consensus about the wisdom of entry. The strategy is particularly effective where many actors would otherwise have to arrive at consensus, and it relies on the assumption that in situations of deep crisis it is easier to agree over the need to do something new, while it might be very difficult to achieve majority support for any specific policy. In this case, the mobilization of crisis is carried out consciously to achieve specific goals. Such has been the case in devising the convergence criteria, in the decision to drop the Stability and Growth Pact, in waiving penalties on the larger economies that have had problems in fulfilling their membership criteria, in the inability to reach agreement on new budget plans for 2007–2013, in rejection of the Constitutional Treaty by some states (including France) and the postponement of consideration of the Constitution by other countries, and in the rapid entry into the ERM-2 of the new Member States.

The ERM-2 is based on central bank rates, defined vis-à-vis the euro, which is considered to be the core of the system. According to the ECB, the standard fluctuation band is relatively wide. The central bank rates and the standard fluctuation band are set by mutual agreement between the ministers of the euro area Member States, the ECB and the ministers and governors of the central banks of the non-euro area Member States that are participating in the new mechanism. This also involves the European Commission and is carried out in consultation with the Economic and Financial Committee. The representatives of central banks of states which are not participating in the ERM-2 do not have any voting rights. Intervention, if necessary, will be automatic. The ECB and central banks of the remaining participating states could suspend intervention if it was running counter to the main objective of the agreement, which is the stabilization of prices. There is also a require-ment that central bank rates will be adjusted in a timely fashion in order to prevent instability. All participants of the agreement will have right to reas-sess their primary lending rates.

Exchange-rate policy cooperation among the European Central Banks may also be further strengthened. One of the options here is to allow closer exchange-rate links between the euro and currencies stabilizing their exchange rates in the ERM-2. This can be done where such a solution would assist cooperating countries in reaching their convergence goals. In such cases, the procedure would depend on how such links were created. The procedure would be initiated by a non-euro area member state. According to the ECB 'the existence of such closer links, in particular if it implied nar-rower fluctuation bands, would be without prejudice to the interpretation of the exchange-rate criterion pursuant to Treaty Article (EC) 109j.'[20]

The ECB General Council is responsible for monitoring the work of the ERM-2 and serves as the coordinator of monetary and fiscal policy. It is also responsible for intervention and the financing mechanism. The relation-ship between the Member States of the euro area and states outside the EMU that stabilize their currencies in the ERM-2 is clearly defined.

Conclusions: when is EMU membership realistic?

Four New Member States (Estonia, Lithuania, Latvia and Slovenia) started earlier than the other new Member States to stabilize their currencies in the ERM-2 (Figure 9.1).

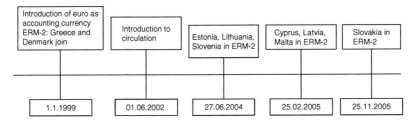

Figure 9.1 The ERM-2, currencies stabilized within the system and dates of membership

Source: European Commission *Report: State Aid Scoreboard – spring 2005 update* (COM (2005)) 145 final, Brussels, 20.04.2005. For Germany, own calculations based on information published at http://www.aztn.hr/twinning/eng/documents/State%20Aid%20Scoreboard%20Spring%20 2005.pdf.

Hungary started negotiations to join the ERM-2 in October 2005. Stabilization of currencies for entry takes two years. In 2006 Estonia and Slovenia were approved to join the EMU. Lithuania was supposed to remain longer in the ERM-2 because it failed to meet the inflation criteria. Cyprus, Latvia and Malta will stabilize their currencies' exchange rate for two years from February 2007. Others are preparing to fulfil the convergence criteria by meeting the budget deficit requirement.[21] All New Member States are also obliged, as a condition of membership, to participate in the deepening of their integration into EU structures. In this case, there is no opting out.

After this group enlargement of the EU is completed, membership in the EMU will be more gradual. But it does appear that all New Member States will join the EMU and they will do so as soon as they are ready, probably sometime between 2008 and 2010. However, to understand this process of enlargement in the EMU requires careful assessment of the ways in which particular instruments and requirements actually work in specific countries. Poland is illustrative of some of the challenges still facing economies as they prepare for membership; its preparation for entry into the EMU has been halting and, as a result, it currently would not pass the requirements formulated by the convergence criteria. While many criteria have been met or are close to being met (such as the criteria on interest rates), there remain particular problems with the budget deficit. In Poland, as well as in the Czech Republic and Hungary, budget deficits are being reduced, but largely by accelerated rates of growth, not by institutional reform. Moreover, Poland also continues to apply different monetary and fiscal policies. That these conditions may be sustained and still not prevent the gradual process of Polish accession to the EMU poses interesting questions about the future of this emerging common economic space.

Notes

1 The first evaluation occurred in Agenda 2000 and consecutive opinions were published in annual Regular Progress Reports on each future Member State. The last was published in 2003.

2 Denmark, Estonia, Cyprus, Latvia, Lithuania, Malta and Slovenia are members of the exchange rate mechanism (ERM-2) (www.ecb.int/bc/intro/html/map.en.html (11.11.2005). In October 2005, Hungary started official negotiations to join ERM-2. In December 2007 13 states are EMU members: Austria, Belgium, Finland, France, Germany, Greece, Holland, Ireland, Italy, Luxembourg, Portugal, Spain and Slovenia. Slovenia was able to pass all the requirements to join after stabilizing its currency in ERM-2. Monaco, San Marino and Vatican – being non-EU members – also use the euro as their currency. Additionally Andorra, Monte Negro and Kosovo have independently introduced the euro, which means they were not required to pass all the tests and requirements, including the two year period of stabilizing their currencies' exchange rates in ERM-2.

3 These patterns had been foreseen (e.g., in the Balassa–Samuelson effect) and were evident in economies which applied shock therapy, but the scale of the effects was smaller than expected, driven in part by the branch structure of the economy inherited after 1989, by differences in competitiveness and by other factors such as external indebtedness, the direction of capital flows and the sequencing of international relations. See K. Żukrowska, *Methods available to overcome the Balassa-Samuelson effect in a catching-up economy*, Economic Paper no. 40 (2006) pp. 201–208.

4 Nevertheless, the current evaluation of convergence criteria for 2006/2007 indicates that the budget deficits of most states have been reduced. This is the case in both Old and New Member States.

5 According to Article 87 TWA:
   Save as otherwise provided in this Treaty, and aid granted by a Member State or through Member State resources in any form whatsoever which distorts or threatens to distort competition by favoring undertakings or the production of certain undertakings or the production of certain goods shall, insofar as it affects trade between Member States, be incompatible with common market.

6 State Aid is regulated by treaty law in the EU, where generally state aid is forbidden. Certain exceptions to this rule are introduced in Art 87–89 of the Treaty of Amsterdam.

7 *State Aid in the European Union. Statistics in focus. Economy and Finance 125/2007. Completed 04.12.2007* (European Commission, 2007).

8 The version of convergence criteria formulated in the Amsterdam Treaty was slightly changed and loosened. The results have been to further slow down the rate of growth in economies which observed this loosening and have adjusted their policies accordingly.

9 In 2007, Germany has finally been able to reduce its budget deficit, meeting the threshold of −3 per cent. This was done thanks to reduction of financial responsibilities and restructuring and reducing expenditures. This was done in two ways: reforms of the pension system as well as reducing the financial support for co-financing of the transfers from the EU. The first means departing from the old 'pay-as-you-go' system. The second derives from the fact that, with enlargement and growing wealth in old Member States, some regions of the wealthier countries are no longer eligible to receive money from EU structural or cohesion funds. This in turn reduces obligations of the national budget to participate in supporting those regions.

10 M. Buti and G. Giudice, 'EMU's fiscal rules: What can and what Cannot Be Exported?' European Commission paper prepared for Conference on Rules-Based Macroeconomic Policies in Emerging Market Economies, 2002.

11 ibid.

12 *Model Tax Convention on Income and on Capital*, Condensed version, January (Paris: OECD, 2003).

13 Statistical Annex of European Union Economy. European Commission 2007. EC/FIN/REP 52309/2007, release 24 October 2007, pp. 178–179.

14 R. J. Leiteritz and L. Handrich, 'Post-Communist Transformation and Industrial Relations' in A. Hulsemeyer, *Globalization in the Twenty-First Century: Convergence or Divergence?* (Palgrave McMillan, 2003), pp. 68–82.

15 S. Gomulka, 'Policy challenges within the (enlarged) European Union: how can economic convergence be fostered?' in G. Tumpel-Gugerell and P. Mooslechner, eds, *Economic Convergence and Divergence in Europe: Growth and Regional*

Development in an Enlarged European Union (Cheltenham, Northampton: Edward Elgar, 2003), pp. 436–447.

16   ibid.
17   ibid.
18   ibid.
19   K. Żukrowska, 'Klasyfikacja modeli transformacji gospodarczej' ['Classification of models of transformation'] in K. Żukrowska and D. Sobczak, eds, *Rozszerzenie strefy eurona Wschód* [Eastern enlargement of Euro-zone] (Warszawa, 2004) pp. 13–32.
20   Cibs.tamu.edu/gaspar/HTML/EURO/HTML/00057/5/page38.htm (13.11.2005).
21   Fulfilment of convergence criteria is not a precondition for a state to enter the ERM-2. Criteria have to be fulfilled at the moment of withdrawal from ERM-2 and entrance to EMU.

10

Accession and Its Limits: The Need for Special Safeguard Clauses in Romania's Accession Treaty

Ştefania Panaitescu

Introduction

The transition of Central and Eastern European countries (CEECs) from a totalitarian communist system to Member States (MS) of one of the world's largest political and economic unions constitutes one of the major events of the 20th and early 21st centuries. All of the CEECs have demonstrated a strong desire for a 'return to Europe' and a willingness to reform almost all aspects of their societies. The costs of this transition have fallen heavily on both the countries themselves and on the European Union. This Chapter explores this transition through a case study of Romania, where these costs and barriers to reform have been particularly high.

The winter meeting of the European Council, held in Brussels in December 2004, had on its very busy agenda two important items. One referred to Romania: the Council was to decide whether to make official the concluding of its accession negotiations, based on the European Commission's positive *avis* regarding the completion of negotiations from the technical point of view.[1] The second one referred to the opening of Accession negotiations with Turkey in 2005. The Council gave a 'green light' to both, despite, in Romania's case, recent calls by both the Commission and the European Parliament for increased monitoring.[2] Moreover, both the Commission and the European parliament have repeatedly reiterated the need for further far-reaching reforms before Romania's accession could actually take place.[3] It was indeed poignant that 2004, the year that should have marked an ascendant trajectory for Romania, was, yet again, overcast with more criticism coming from the EU.[4]

The European Union was not satisfied with the state of reforms and preparations for Romanian accession, but it was willing to retain the calendar for accession. In order to conclude negotiations, however, the EU added several safeguard clauses to both Bulgaria and Romania's Accession Treaties, including *a one-year postponement clause*. The idea of including general safeguard clauses to the Accession Treaty was not completely new; previous Treaties did contain them, as did the 2004 Accession Treaty with the ten new Member States.[5] However, in addition to the general safeguard clause in Romania and Bulgaria's Treaties, several *special clauses* had been added, including the postponement clause allowing delay of accession for either state until 2008 should any of the special clauses be activated. Such postponement clauses had not previously been used by the EU against any other candidate state.

This chapter explores the exogenous and endogenous causes that led to the addition of the special safeguard clauses to Romania's accession treaty. It concludes that, although the activation of the clauses hung over the accession states like the sword of Damocles, the postponement clause functions as a safeguard for both the EU and Romania. Were Romania to have joined the EU before it was prepared to face the competition of the single market, its economy would have been negatively affected. Thus, the chapter also investigates the criteria and reforms that needed to be fulfilled and implemented for the accession target year of 2007 to be met.

The Luxembourg 5 + 1 Group and the Helsinki Group

The process of applying for EU membership involves several milestones: signature of a Europe Agreement concerning mostly economic ties with the EU (heavily asymmetric), then signature of an Association Agreement, thus obtaining the status of associate country, then actually filing the country's application dossier for membership and waiting for a Commission positive *avis* which only comes once it gets a mandate to this scope from the European Council. Once a positive *avis* is issued, the Council decides whether to invite the country to open negotiations. When negotiations commence, the country acquires the status of candidate country and works closely with the EU for the harmonization of its legislation with European legislation, the *acquis*, and strives to fulfil the Copenhagen accession criteria.[6]

The Central and Eastern European countries (CEECs) aspired to EC membership as soon as these former communist states obtained their freedom. All of them made public their intentions of joining the EC soon after 1990. Although diplomatic and trade agreements were established during the 1990s and CEECs were granted the status of associated countries by 1995, it would take another three years for a first group of CEECs to be invited to officially open negotiations.

The process of inviting countries to begin negotiations had two phases: the 1997 Luxembourg Summit launched the process which made Eastward Enlargement possible by inviting six countries (the so-called 5 + 1 Luxembourg group including the Czech Republic, Estonia, Hungary, Poland,

Slovenia and Cyprus), and the 1999 Helsinki Summit, which added a further six states to the number of candidate states (Bulgaria, Latvia, Lithuania, Romania, Slovakia and Malta).

Accession negotiations were opened by the European Council on 31 March 1998. This was the materialization of the Luxembourg decisions. The positive *avis* meant that the Commission considered these countries were complying with the Copenhagen criteria. Those countries less advanced in their process of restructuring were worried about the economic and political consequences of separating the applicant countries for the opening of negotiations, creating artificial and discriminatory frontiers, contrary to the continuity principle of the EU enlargement process.[7] Hence, in the months after the publication of the *avis*, a key policy element of the first Romanian centre-right government[8] was a concerted diplomatic effort towards the EU to ensure that differentiation and discrimination within the accession process would be kept to a minimum.

Thus, even though Romania was not formally invited to negotiate, differentiation had been minimized by the Luxembourg Summit's *Enhanced Pre-accession* strategy,[9] which was 'intended to enable all the applicant states eventually to become members', a strategy for which the Romanian centre-right government has lobbied. This would be established through the new *Accession Partnerships* with each CEEC applicant. In addition, Romania and the other CEECs not invited to open negotiations were promised a regular review of their progress in meeting the criteria for membership and that a positive review might lead to the opening of accession negotiations. A further new development was the establishment of an annual European Conference. As a result, when the EU enlargement process was launched on 30 March 1998, it was welcomed. Romania appeared to be part of the accession process and moving closer towards EU membership.

Participation in the European Conference in March 1998 and the signing of an *Accession Partnership* with the EU the following month confirmed Romania's involvement in the accession process. This was the result of continuous endeavour by Romania's first centre-right government in 50 years. Through intense diplomatic lobbying, it secured the country's participation in the accession process, which had been jeopardized by the previous Vacaroiu centre-left government.

In parallel with ensuring the country's position in the accession process, the centre-right government was struggling to implement long-overdue macroeconomic reforms needed to stabilize the economy and create an environment open to foreign direct investments and speed up the privatization process. The year 1998 was yet another test for the first centre-right government; it had to service the high foreign debt payments inherited from the previous left *nomenklatura* governments. These governments had left the country indebted and with less than 0.9 billion dollars in the National Bank's foreign reserves. The centre-right government successfully avoided the real danger of having to file for default and managed to set a healthier economic policy underwritten by a policy of rebuilding foreign reserves.

At the 1999 Winter Summit in Helsinki, Romania was invited together with Latvia, Lithuania, Bulgaria, Malta and Slovakia to start negotiations. These were formally opened on 10 February the following year. The government was rewarded abroad for its diplomatic efforts and its successes in domestic economic reforms, but at the cost of seriously eroding its popularity at home and serious losses in the following year's elections (Table 10.1).

In order to see why Romania was only invited in the Helsinki group of countries, and why the EU felt it necessary to add several safeguard clauses in its Accession Treaty and establish accompanying measures and a new monitoring and reporting system, it is necessary to look at the diplomatic and economic developments of 1990–1995 and the ways in which successive Romanian governments dragged their feet on implementing reforms.

Delays and obstacles

The Romanian centre-left governments of the early 1990s lacked the political will to operate strong economic and political reforms and, between 1990 and 1997, Romania pursued a form of hesitant diplomacy towards the EU. The neocommunist government and presidency set as their state priority for 1990 conclusion of a Treaty with the USSR at the very time that it was on the verge of collapse. By signing this Treaty, the neocommunist officials in Bucharest indicated their interest in being oriented more to the East than to the West. It was a costly diplomatic error and signalled that Romania was not really trying to join the European Union. At home it signalled to *nomenklatura* and former party structures that they would be able to resume their activities with impunity, after a period since the December 1989 Revolution when they had been unable to shape political and economic reforms.

This initial mistake would cost even more in terms of economic development, prolonging indefinitely the transition to a market economy. While other CEECs applied 'shock therapy' reforms, the centre-left Romanian governments of 1990–1996 resisted structural reforms, and instead adopted a stop-and-go approach. Almost no economic reforms were implemented until 1993. Galloping inflation with an incoherent macroeconomic policy and a corrupt privatization process characterized the next three years. Reforms were postponed as vested interests among the nomenclature resisted them.

In late 1996, Romania's first centre-right government in over 50 years of communist dictatorship inherited a disastrous economic situation. It managed to service the huge foreign debt which it had 'inherited' and avoided default with its international creditors in 1998. It implemented painful reforms that lead to macroeconomic stabilization and passed legislation

Table 10.1 A case study of the EU's model of accession negotiations – major landmarks of Romania's accession negotiations

---

1993
1 February – Romania signs the Europe Agreements.
May – the implementation of the commercial provisions within the European Agreement has been initiated, through an Interim Agreement.

1995
1 February – the European Agreement enters into force.
June – Romania officially applies for EU membership.

1997
The European Commission formally approves the Agenda 2000. It covers the Commission's opinion on Romania's membership application.

1998
March – the European Union officially launches the enlargement process.
November – first regular reports are issued by the European Commission (reports regarding progress registered by candidate countries in preparing for EU accession).

1999
June – Romania adopts the National Plan for EU Accession.
October – the European Commission releases the second Regular Reports on Romania's progress towards EU accession. December – the European Council in Helsinki decides to start accession negotiations with six candidate countries, including Romania.

2000
February – the accession negotiations with Romania officially begin, at the opening session of the Intergovernmental Conference.
March – Romania adopts its Mid Term Economic Strategy and presents it within the EU–Romania Council Association. During the Portuguese Presidency of the EU (the first semester) five negotiation chapters are opened: Small and Medium Sized Enterprises (Chapter 16), Science and research (Chapter 17), Education and Training (Chapter 18), External Relations (Chapter 26) and Common Security and External Policy (Chapter 27).
May – The Romanian government adopts the revised National Plan for EU Accession, as well as the Action Plan and the Macro-economy Framework, in addition to the Mid Term Economic Strategy.
24 October – During the French Presidency of the EU two negotiation chapters were opened: Statistics (Chapter 12), and Culture and audiovisual (Chapter 20).
8 November – the European Commission releases new Regular Reports on Romania's progress towards accession.
November – two new negotiation chapters were opened: Competition policy (Chapter 6) and Telecommunications and Information Technology (Chapter 19). By the end of the year only one negotiation chapter is provisionally closed: Statistics (16).

Continued

Table 10.1   Continued

December – during the European Council in Nice, EU Member States agreed on a new institutional formula for the European Union. The Treaty of Nice is a prerequisite for the admission of new Member States to the Union amid the candidate countries that are fully prepared by the end of year 2002, as it contains provisions on the distribution of power and on decision-making procedures in a Union with as many as 27 member countries.

2001

January – June: during the Swedish EU Presidency five new negotiation chapters were opened: Free movement of capital (Chapter 4), Company law (Chapter 5), Fisheries (Chapter 8), Transport policy (Chapter 9) and Customs union (Chapter 25). Only one negotiation chapter has been provisionally closed during this presidency.
13 November – the fourth issue of the Regular Reports was published.
November – the Commission revised the Accession Partnerships with Romania.
14–15 December – the European Council in Laeken, for the first time, nominates ten candidate countries to finish the accession negotiations by the end of year 2002, except Romania and Bulgaria.
July–December – during the Belgian EU Presidency, another three negotiation chapters were opened: Taxation (Chapter 10), Social policy and employment (Chapter 13) and Consumers and health protection (Chapter 23). Two chapters have been provisionally closed: Company law (Chapter 5), Consumers and health protection (Chapter 23).
December – the total number of the negotiation chapters provisionally closed by Romania is nine.

2002

January–June – during the Spanish Presidency of the EU nine negotiation chapters were opened: Free movement of goods (Chapter 1), Freedom of movement for persons (Chapter 2), Economic and Monetary Union (Chapter 11), Energy (Chapter 14), Regional policy and coordination of structural instruments (Chapter 21), Environment (Chapter 22), Justice and Home Affairs (Chapter 24), Financial control (Chapter 28) and Institutions (Chapter 30). Three negotiation chapters were provisionally closed: Economic and Monetary Union (Chapter 11), Social policy and employment (Chapter 13) and Institutions (Chapter 30).
9 October – the European Commission releases the fifth Regular Report.
13 November – the Commission adopts the 'Road maps' for both Romania and Bulgaria.
20 November – the European Parliament takes into consideration 1 January 2007 as target date for Romania's accession to the European Union.
12–13 December – the European Council in Copenhagen decides the accession of ten new member states and adopts the road maps for Romania and Bulgaria.

Continued

Table 10.1 Continued

July–December – during the Danish Presidency of the EU, the last four negotiation chapters were opened: Freedom to provide services (Chapter 3), Agriculture (Chapter 7), Industrial policy (Chapter 15) and Financial and budgetary provisions (Chapter 29). During this presidency, four negotiation chapters were provisionally closed: Industrial policy (Chapter 15), Telecommunications and Information Technology (Chapter 19), Culture and audiovisual policy (Chapter 20) and Customs union (Chapter 25).

2003
23 March – the European Commission releases the revised Accession Partnership with Romania.
January–June – during the Greek Presidency of the EU – three negotiation chapters were provisionally closed: Free movement of goods (Chapter 1), Free movement of capital (Chapter 4) and Taxation (Chapter 10).
5 November – a new Regular Report regarding the process registered by Romania in preparing for EU membership was released by the EC.
June–December – during the Italian EU Presidency – another three chapters were provisionally closed: Freedom of movement for persons (Chapter 2), Transport policy (Chapter 9), Financial and budgetary provisions (Chapter 29).
December – out of 30 negotiation chapters, 22 are provisionally closed.

2004
January–June – during the Irish EU Presidency – another three chapters were provisionally closed: Agriculture (Chapter 7), Energy (Chapter 14), Financial and budgetary provisions (Chapter 29). June 30 – by the end of the Irish EU Presidency 25 of 30 negotiation chapters have been provisionally closed.
17 December - the Brussels European Council decided the conclusion of the accession negotiations with Romania. Romania must continue reforms and the fulfilling of the commitments regarding the *acquis communautaire*, especially in the fields of Justice and Home Affairs, Competition and Environment. The European Union will continue the monitoring of the accession preparations and considers that Romania will be capable to assume membership obligations from 1 January 2007. Also, the European Council recommends the signing of the common accession Treaty for Romania and Bulgaria in April 2005, after the agreement of the European Parliament, and effective accession from 1 January 2007.

2005
13 April – the European Parliament has given the green light for the entry of Romania and Bulgaria into the EU. On the accession of Romania, MEPs voted by 497 in favour, 93 against and 71 abstentions.
25 April – during an official ceremony, taking place at the Neumunster Abbey in Luxembourg, the President of Romania, Traian Basescu, signed the Treaty of Accession to the European Union, together with the Prime Minister of Bulgaria, Simeon de Saxe-Coburg, and the 25 representatives of the EU member states.

Continued

Table 10.1   Continued

---

25 October – the European Commission publishes its first Comprehensive Monitoring Report (COM (2005)) 534 final, Brussels, 25, SEC (2005) 1354. The new Strategy and Action Plan 2005–2007 is well received; progress was evident but the need to implement both economic and judicial reform was still cited by the EC.

2006
16 May – the European Commission publishes its Progress Report on accompanying measures following Accession, Brussels, 27 June 2007 (COM (2007)) 378, identifying progress in dealing with some of the 11 red flags; the one referring to justice still remain.
17 October – the Council takes note of the Commission's Report on Romania's Progress on accompanying measures following Accession, and it appreciates that the Mechanism on Cooperation and Verification was working well and contributed to the results achieved until then.

2007
1 January – Romania and Bulgaria join the EU.
27 June – the European Commission publishes its Monitoring Report and acknowledges the progress made on the clear benchmarks set for the justice system; monitoring will continue until the next review in December.

2008
January – Commission publishes second Progress Report on accompanying measures following Accession.

---

that accelerated the privatization of the large loss-making state-owned enterprises. Macroeconomic indicators showed no signs of recovery until 2000, but to a large extent this too can be seen as a result of the desperate situation inherited after three centre-left governments and the ferocity with which the ex-communist *nomenklatura* stripped state-owned enterprises and banks prior to or during the dubious privatization process. The scandal over Romania's former foreign trade bank, BANCOREX, and the huge pyramid schemes of the period are both symptomatic of the legacies of the Iliescu and Vacaroiu regimes.

The first wave of privatization had two serious consequences. First, it led to a massive distribution of shares into the hands of an ill-informed and inexperienced population in conditions in which the institutions regulating share ownership were not in place. For example, it took five years to create the Romanian Stock Exchange. Second, legislation governing privatization left enough legal loopholes for the 'system people' to exploit the process through fraudulent privatizations, which in the mid-1990s almost equalled the actual number of privatizations occurring.

In late 1996, the newly elected centre-right government vouched it would improve the financial environment, making it more attractive for foreign direct investments by reducing the enormous fiscal burdens faced by foreign companies. Its first decision, by an Urgency Ordinance, was taken on the day it was invested into office; income tax was reduced to 16 per cent and the tax on profits was also cut from 25 per cent to 16 per cent.

The right-wing coalition governments lost popularity and were replaced in 2000 by a new centre-left government. An important element in their loss of support was the carefully fabricated rise and fall of the National Investment Fund, managed by *nomenklatura* led by O. S. Vantu. Despite positive economic growth, the new government soon returned to policies that led to the accumulation of arrears and state bailouts for companies under the political influence of cronies and party members. By the end of 2004, the economic situation was far from being a 'functioning market economy'. The EU granted this title to Romania purely on political grounds, as a gratification to a centre-left government willing to continue the tough reforms initiated by the previous government, albeit at a slower pace.

However, the involutions in the political, legal and social domains were worrying to analysts. Political figures dominated the legal system and the whole fabric of Romanian society and the judicial system had been infected by rampant corruption.

Indeed, corruption continues to be one of the major obstacles to reform and probably the strongest reason for the EU safeguard clauses. The perceived threat is that unless corrupt practices are uprooted from the Romanian way of life they will erode the fabric of the democratic state. Repeatedly, both the European Commission and the European Parliament called for real reforms of the legal system, asked for its independence from politics and insisted on greater transparency. In March and April 2005 the Director and all three Deputy Directors of the Directorate-General for Protection and Anti-Corruption (DGPA) were dismissed following the discovery of irregular activities. A new Director was appointed in April 2005. Considerably more openness and transparency was imposed on the DGPA. The Commission's 2005 Monitoring Report takes note of the fact that the fight against corruption was one of the new Government's highest priorities together with the preparations for EU accession, even describing corruption as a threat to national security. In January 2005 an international non-governmental organization was contracted to audit the results of the old National Anti-Corruption Strategy 2001–2004. This report was published in March and its recommendations were reflected in the new Strategy and Action Plan 2005–2007. But the report argues: 'Nevertheless, it is widely acknowledged that Romania's legislation already broadly complies with the relevant EU *acquis* and that what is urgently required is to implement the existing legislation more rigorously rather than proposing new laws. The Action Plan also focuses heavily on corruption within the judiciary, an institution that must have a central role in fighting corruption but in which integrity problems continue to be reported and which suffers from low public confidence.'[10]

Implementation of these reforms were fought fiercely by the system people and each of the changes that has occurred has taken longer than in any of the other CEECs. For example, access to documents of public interest has been granted through Law 544/2001, although this came well after similar legislation had been adopted by the other CEECs; Poland, Slovakia, the Czech Republic, etc. all adopted such legislation in 1997–1998. The problem of the freedom of the judicial system has also been one of the most pressing issues, and the 2004 centre-right coalition government of the Democrats and Liberals signalled its importance as one their priorities by the appointment of a notable member of civil society, Ms Monica Macovei, as Minister of Justice.

However, she was soon removed from office, falling victim to the same system forces that have sucessfully managed to delay legal reforms. It was for these reasons that the reform of the judiciary and the fight against corruption have been so closely monitored by the Cooperation and Verification Mechanism. Four clear benchmarks have been established to gauge implementation. The first Report of June 2007 suggested that: 'Romania has made progress in varying degrees in meeting the benchmarks set out in the Cooperation and Verification Mechanism. It is important to see these benchmarks as representing more than a checklist of individual actions that can be ticked off one by one. They are all interlinked. Progress on one has an impact on others.' Overall the tone is positive but the ten pages of analysis conclude that more rapid and substantial changes are needed. Thus, the progress report of 27 June 2007 concludes that 'progress in the judicial treatment of high-level corruption is insufficient. However, the Commission finds that it is too early to trigger or remove the threat of sanctions against the two countries.... While safeguard clauses are not being proposed by the Commission at this stage, we will remain vigilant. The further changes that are necessary require a long-term commitment', as Commission President José Manuel Barroso stated.[11]

Romania has also lagged behind in the adoption and implementation of the *acquis communautaire*. Such delays were also the result of the immense volume of work that had to be invested in drafting of *Position Papers* for the chapters and in translating the *acquis*. Arguably, the Ministry of European Integration with its complex structure was more able to face all the challenges involved in translating the 80,000 pages of *acquis*, making recommendations on legal harmonization and drafting Position Papers and annual National Plans. However, other CEECs did not have a Ministry for Integration per se, but instead they integrated Directorates in each Ministry and this appears to have been much more efficient. The need for institutional reform, for *europeanizing the whole system of public administration,* remains in a system still very much plagued by widespread corruption. However, the real task remains one of implementing legislative goals. In the first year after accession, Romania resists legislative reform and implementation, and there are concerns that this will prevent effective application of EU laws, policies and programmes.

Closing the gap with the New Member States

Romania's first-centre right government (from 1997 to 2000) made enormous efforts to close the growing gap with the other CEECs by implementing economic reforms. The difference between Romania and the other CEECs was most evident in macroeconomic indicators, in general living standards and in the degree to which implementation of the *acquis* was being pursued. According to Eurostat's statistics for 1999, Slovenia was the most developed country among the ten Central and East European candidate countries for accession to the EU, with 13,200 ECU per capita GDP in PPS (71 per cent of EU average 21,000 ECU). The Czech Republic had 12,400 ECU (59 per cent of EU average), Hungary 10,700 ECU (51 per cent of EU average), Romania 5,700 ECU (27 per cent of EU average) and Bulgaria was last with 4,389 ECU (representing 22 per cent of EU average).

The economy was the area where it was, and still is, most difficult to catch up with the rest of the CEECs. Unpopular measures of macrostabilization and financial discipline were implemented, but at great political cost to the centre-right government. Trade integration with the EU proceeded apace, promoted by the Europe Agreements of the early 1990s and by the newly upgraded Association Agreements, containing improved terms of trade for Romanian exports to EU countries.

The last *Regular Report Regarding [Romania's] Progress to Accession* (http://www.euractiv.ro/www/storage/analize/128.pdf) granted Romania the status of 'functioning market economy', but this was very far from reality. Indeed, Romania still does not fully comply with either of the two economic criteria of the Copenhagen Accession Criteria, as the wording of the 2005 EU document clarifies:

> Concerning the economic requirements for membership, Romania continues to comply with the criterion of being a functioning market economy. Vigorously implementing its structural reform programme should enable it to cope with competitive pressure and market forces within the Union. Romania has broadly maintained macroeconomic stability, even though the policy has widened macroeconomic imbalances. Furthermore, the legal and administrative business environment, including enforcement of decisions on bankruptcy, still requires improvement. (pp. 3–4)

The in-depth analysis of this Report is symptomatic, driving home the central argument of this paper:

> The implementation of the government's structural reform agenda continued, although the privatisation process slowed down, insufficient financial discipline persisted and the functioning of the judiciary remained an obstacle for an enabling business environment. The privatisation process continued, but at lower pace. For the companies in the portfolio of the privatisation agency (AVAS), the divestiture slowed down due to the difficulties of many of the remaining enterprises, the bounce back to state ownership of some enterprises for which privatisation contracts were previously signed, as well as the limited success in selling the state's minority stakes in enterprises. For the companies owned by various ministries, further privatisations were gradually advanced in the energy and banking sector, while little progress took place in the defence, transport and agricultural sectors. Some progress could be observed in further restructuring the energy, mining and transport sectors in preparation for speeding up the privatisation of some of the companies in these sectors, but large parts of the sectors continue to make losses and rely on direct subsidies and debt cancellations. Efforts to strengthen financial discipline were upheld, but results were mixed. (pp. 22–23)

The report continues:

> The divestitures also fall short of the target set in Romania's privatisation programme. The total number of companies in state ownership decreased from 1187 in mid-2004 to 1180 in mid-2005, of which close to 90% belonged to the AVAS. Out of 153 majority state-owned companies deemed fit for privatisation in June 2004, privatisation contracts were signed for 46 companies, while 34 companies undergo liquidation. In June 2005, AVAS' portfolio also included 544 companies considered unfit for privatisation, and it monitored close to 6500 companies in the process of reorganisation or bankruptcy. Companies continued to bounce back to state ownership due to unresolved disputes between government and investor over the privatisation contract, and problems were encountered in divesting such companies again. (p. 26)

The slow pace of economic, judicial, and public administration reform has marked the period after the signing of the Accession Treaty. The Country Report for 2006 warned of social and political involution, raising alarm signals regarding the liberty of the press, corruption and liberty of the justice system. Romania's new centre-right government, a minority government of the liberals with a very fragile majority in Parliament, clearly has its hands full and it will be an enormous challenge to close the gap that separates today's Romania from the rest of the new member states. Nonetheless, in January 2007 the EU confirmed the calendar and the roadmap regarding accession and Romania became a Member State.

Accession 2007: the politics of promise and delays

In early 2001, at a time when there were still many issues to be solved regarding the EU's expected Eastward Enlargement policies, the newly elected centre-left government advanced the year 2007 as its accession target. At the time, analysts were discussing the prospects of a two-wave enlargement: a first wave comprising the frontrunners (Slovenia, Estonia, the Czech Republic and possibly Hungary) and a second wave to include the rest of the candidates that were trailing behind in their accession negotiations. Poland fiercely opposed this arrangement, wanting to be included in the first wave. The big-bang enlargement was not even deemed plausible.

The EU did not respond in any way to the government's goal of 2007. Its silent approval, based on the argument that a self-set target might be an incentive for carrying out needed reforms in all areas – economic, legal and institutional – actually opened the door to the centre-left government's politics of *promise in Brussels and delay-at-home policy*. In the end, Brussels came to accept the self-set goal. However, starting with the 2002 Monitoring Report, the Commission and the European Parliament began more systematically to insist that the Nastase government deliver at home on the promises laid out in Brussels.

In fact, the government was using elaborate techniques to procrastinate over domestic reforms. The self-set goal technique was meant to serve abroad as a sign that serious intent and energy were being channelled towards completing reforms and accession negotiations. At home it was supposed to be a goal for which the population would be prepared to make yet more sacrifices, which it did.

However, the 2007 target did manage to polarize the government's energies in drawing up the documents necessary for negotiations: the Position Papers for each Chapter, the National Programmes for the Adoption of the *acquis* and the Medium Term Economic Strategies and Action Plans. Nevertheless, only part of the Action Plans and National Strategy documents were fully implemented. This is the real reason the special safeguard clauses made their way into Romania's Accession Treaty. This is also the biggest challenge facing Romania over the next two years. Adding to the pressure of meeting these major challenges, the newly elected government has to manage a fragile majority in Parliament and it faces anticipated elections with political and social instability looming.

Delays coming from the EU: the first wave of Eastward Enlargement

Following Enlargement in 2004 and 2007, the EU has needed time to accommodate the new Member States. Eastern Enlargement affects both the future of Central and Eastern Europe and what kind of European Union will eventually emerge. Some authors, including Merkel and Schmitter, have argued that the Eastward Enlargement constitutes a sharpening of the dilemma inside the EU as it is. The respective roles of national governments of the Member States and supranational European structures still have to be worked out.[12]

However, the uncertainties made completion of the eastward enlargement ever more important and the necessity for the special safeguard clauses even clearer. As the *Report on the Results of the Negotiations on the Accession of Bulgaria and Romania to the European Union,* prepared by the Commission's Departments in February 2005, put it: 'After closure of the accession negotiations in December 2004 and signing of the Accession Treaty in April 2005, Romania must live up to its accession commitments.'

Crystallization of the special safeguard clauses and their path into the Accession Treaty

It is interesting to look at how the inclusion of the special safeguard clauses crystallized in EU institutions and what the final wording was in the Accession Treaty with regard to Romania.

We have already seen that the centre-left government received several criticisms from the Commission for not implementing reforms and for its failure to address concrete issues brought to its attention during negotiations. In response, the government made promises and commitments at Summits and during accession negotiations, but later failed to fulfil them at home. The Commission responded by issuing a clear wording about what went wrong and where. A compromise emerged during the December 2004 Winter Summit with the agreement that only failure to move on particular issues would result in postponement of accession. This compromise made it possible to close the accession negotiations and advance according to the accession calendar. As the Commission reported:

> Transition towards accession may entail the use of **safeguard clauses** and include a **postponement clause**, should the necessary preparations and reforms not be in place on time. For cases of serious shortcomings, the accession treaty provides for three safeguard clauses as well as for a clause allowing the Union to postpone, upon the Commission's recommendation

before the entry into force of the Accession Treaty, Romania's accession by one year to January 2008 in very problematic cases. Such remedial measures should be invoked, as a last resort mechanism, in order to avoid very negative consequences upon accession.

By February 2005, the Commission had already drawn up its *Report on the Results of Accession Negotiations*, which was meant to be the core of the Accession Treaty. The Report presented the results chapter by chapter. In the case of many of the chapters, the report notes that the totality of the *acquis* would be taken over and implemented following accession (chapters 1, 8 / Fisheries, 12, 15, 16, 17, 18, and others). It also anticipated what the wording of the clauses would be in the actual Treaty: 'The Accession Treaty will feature four safeguard clauses: a general economic safeguard clause, a specific internal market safeguard clause, a specific JHA safeguard clause and a postponement clause.'[13]

The general economic safeguard clause covers any sector of the economy or economic situation of a given area, in both current and new Member States. The internal market safeguard clause covers all sectorial policies involving economic activities with cross-border effects. The JHA safeguard clause covers mutual recognition in the area of criminal law and civil matters. Both the internal market and the JHA safeguard clause may be applied *vis-à-vis* new member states only.

Safeguard measures may be implemented under these three clauses for a period of up to three years after accession, but they may remain in force beyond this period. However, any safeguard measure shall be maintained no longer than is strictly necessary and must be proportional in scope and duration.

A fourth safeguard clause was included in the Treaty, which allows the Council to decide, based on a Commission recommendation, that accession be postponed by one year

> where there is clear evidence that the state of preparations for adoption and implementation of the *acquis* is such that there is a serious risk of Bulgaria/Romania being manifestly unprepared to meet the requirements of membership by the envisaged date of accession in January 2007 in a number of important areas.[14]

The safeguard clauses: were they necessary?

Why were such clauses necessary? As we have seen, in Romania there were clear signs of involution in the three years prior to accession, especially in regard to the political and legal criteria for membership, the lack of independence in the legal system and the media, and the fight against corruption.

The new Enlargement Commissioner, Olli Rehn, stressed that the safeguard clause was not included in the accession treaty 'just for fun' and that it was 'a serious clause and, were Romania not able to achieve the European standards in time, then we would not hesitate to use this safeguard clause'. The Commission reviewed Romania's accession status in 2006 and continued to monitor the reforms in the justice system in the first part of 2007. Indeed, on 1 January 2007, the Commission established a **Cooperation and Verification Mechanism** to assess the commitments made by Bulgaria and Romania in the areas of judicial reform, measures to deal with corruption and organized crime. The Commission was asked to report on the accompanying measures on a regular basis. In the case of the Cooperation and Verification Mechanism, reports have been requested on a six-monthly basis, starting in June 2007. This measure was announced by José Manuel Barroso, President of the European Commission, in his speech to the European Parliament's plenary session in Strasbourg on 26 September 2006.[15]

These measures were aimed at leveraging change, as the Barroso document indicates:

> Bulgaria and Romania have found the right answer to our strict conditionality by addressing the areas we highlighted in May. In doing so, they have achieved considerable progress. However, today's report also outlines some areas where both countries need to achieve further progress by sustaining the current reform drive until accession and beyond.
>
> The Commission has fixed a number of measures to accompany the accession of Bulgaria and Romania. In particular, the Commission will set up a **mechanism for cooperation and verification of progress** in the areas of judicial reform, the fight against corruption, and organised crime. The mechanism contains specific benchmarks which have to be met.
>
> The Commission will report regularly to the Parliament and to the Council on the progress achieved. On that basis, the Commission may, if necessary, invoke the safeguard measure set out in the Accession Treaty.
>
> The Commission has further accompanying measures at its disposal, which ensure the proper functioning of the Union up to and beyond the accession of both countries.
>
> EU rules provide us with a comprehensive set of measures which allow us to combat potential risks in acceding and in current Member States.'

The EU was clearly concerned about the possibility that the Romanian government might not follow through on some of these measures, and its response was this unprecedented system of review and monitoring. Well into 2006, long-overdue reforms had still not been implemented, particularly in the judicial and public administration systems, in the country's ability to absorb European funds, and in its efforts to combat corruption by creating a National Agency for Integrity. Throughout the election campaign, the new centre-right government had professed its intention to implement the necessary reforms and continue the fight against corruption, and the commitment was further reinforced by the new Minister of European Integration, Ene Dinga, who, in an address to the European Academy in Berlin, argued that: 'We must keep the pace and continue the reforms, as there is still a lot to be done, and the time until accession is very short. Within the 20 months left until accession, we must intensify our internal preparations and work even harder [...]'.[16] Moreover, the EU also preserved its leverage since each of the 11 red flags included in the Accession Treaty may lead to the activation of the postponement clause (Table 10.2). The Commission's Comprehensive Monitoring Reports, its Progress Reports and Verification Mechanisms, as well as other instruments for assessing the progress in these sensitive areas, will signal whether the postponement clauses might be activated.

Table 10.2 The 11 red-flagged areas in the Accession Treaty

Competition
1. The effective control by the Competition Council of any potential State aid.
2. The strengthening, without delay, of Romania's state aid enforcement record.
3. The respect of Romania's commitment not to grant or pay any State aid to the steel mills covered by the National Restructuring Strategy from 1 January 2005 to 31 December 2008 and the respect of State aid amounts to be decided in the context of Protocol 2 of the Europe Agreement.
4. The allocation of adequate financial means and qualified human resources to the Competition Council.

Justice and Home Affairs
1. The implementation without further delay of the Schengen Action Plan.
2. Obtaining a high level of control and surveillance at the future external borders of the EU.
3. The development and the implementation of an updated and integrated Action Plan and Strategy for the reform of the judiciary.
4. The considerable acceleration of the fight against corruption and specifically against the high-level corruption by ensuring the strict application of the anti-corruption legislation and of the effective independence of the National Anti-Corruption Prosecutor's Office.
5. The conduct of an independent audit of the results and impact of the current National Anti-Corruption Strategy as well as the revision of the protracted criminal procedure by the end of 2005.
6. The adoption by March 2005 of a clear legal framework for the respective tasks of, and cooperation between, the gendarmerie and police.
7. The development and implementation of a coherent multi-annual strategy to fight organized crime.

The European Commission and the Romanian Ministry of Justice have agreed on clear benchmarks to assess progress during 2007. Monitoring reform in the judicial system continued through 2007, and in its 27 June 2007 Report the European Commission acknowledged that, while some progress had been made on the four benchmarks (reform the judicial system, establishing an integrity agency, tackling high-level corruption and fighting corruption within local government), several problems remained, particularly in dealing with the backlog of cases of high-level corruption and implementing the new Penal and Civil Codes. It felt that monitoring should continue and thus postponed the end of monitoring until December 2007 when another of its Reports is due.

In the meantime, continued political conflict between the offices of the Presidency and the Prime Minister has resulted in the removal of Ms Monica Macovei, the Minister of Justice, who pressed for reforms to ensure the independence of the judges and of the Constitutional Court. The so-called 'crisis between the Palaces', that is, between Cotroceni Palace, the seat of the Presidency, and Victoria Palace, the seat of the Prime Minister, continued well into 2007 with efforts to impeach the President. The EC followed these events closely. Few observers now expect monitoring of judicial reforms to end in December, especially if the impasse continues. However, the Commission did not consider that it was warranted to invoke the safeguard provisions of the Accession Treaty, despite this slow progress and the deep political crisis in which the country was thrown by the rift between former democratic and liberal coalition partners. The Commission continues to work in close partnership with Romania to support its efforts to meet the benchmarks under the Cooperation and Verification Mechanism. The Decision establishing the Cooperation and Verification Mechanism requires reports from the Commission every six months.

The Romanian case perhaps more than any other exemplifies the necessity of the safeguard clauses and illustrates well how, under sustained resistance, they have provided important tools for those who continue their efforts to reform what appears to be an intrinsically reform-resistant administrative and judicial system.

Notes

1   An *avis* is a Commission opinion related to an issue it has received as a special mandate from the Council to delve into and publish an informed document for the Council's use in its decision-making on that particular matter. The Madrid European Council in December 1995 called on the European Commission to submit an assessment of the candidate countries' applications for membership and to prepare a detailed analysis of what enlargement would mean for the EU. In July 1997, the Commission presented *AGENDA 2000*, a single framework in which the Commission outlined the broad perspective for the development of the EU and its policies beyond the turn of the century, addressed the challenge

of enlargement, the impact of enlargement on the EU as a whole and the future financial framework beyond 2000, taking into account the prospect of enlarged Union.

2   Parliamentary Report of Pierre Moscovici, Member of the European Parliament, the Socialist Group, *Rapporteur* for Romania.

3   Speech by Mr. Olli Rehn, Commissioner for Enlargement, 'Commission calls on the European Parliament to give its assent to Bulgaria's and Romania's accession to the EU', European Parliament Plenary Session, Strasbourg, 12 April 2005.

4   Council of the European Union, *Presidency Conclusions – Luxembourg European Council* (Brussels: Council of the European Union General Secretariat, December 1997) point 5.

5   Wolfgang Merkle, *Deepening and Widening? The Limits of European Integration*, in European Studies 2 (Hungarian Political Science Association and the Institute for Political Sciences of the Hungarian Academy of Science, 1996) p. 47; Philippe C. Schmitter 'Imagining the Future of the Euro-Polity With the Help of the New Concepts', in Attila Folsz, *Politics of European Integration* (Budapest: CEU, 2000) p. 148.

6   One of the landmarks of the Eastern enlargement process was the 1993 Copenhagen Summit when for the first time a set of criteria, the so-called five Accession or Copenhagen criteria, were established to be fulfilled by the states that desired to join the EU.

7   In S. Panaitescu, *An Assessment of Romania's Prospects of Accession to the European Union* (University of Oradea Publishing House, 2004) pp. 24–25. Enlargement is considered one of the most successful policies of the EU and its fundamental principle is that the door is open to European states which desire to join, provided that they fulfil the accession criteria.

8   In November 1996 Romania's first centre-right government came to power after 50 years of Communism. It was a coalition government of four parties establishing the Democratic Convention. Its most consequential party was the Romanian National Peasants' Party, and then followed the Liberal Party, the Democratic Party and lastly the Hungarian Alliance. Inheriting a disastrous economic situation and an ailing civil society, the coalition government did manage to implement reforms. It was the Democratic Convention that set Romania on its path to EU accession. In the European Commission's own terms: 'The current improvement in Romania, following the arrival in power of a new government, indicates that Romania is on its way to satisfy the political criteria.'

9   Council of the European Union, *Presidency Conclusions – Luxembourg European Council* (Brussels: Council of the European Union General Secretariat, December 1997) point 5.

10 The European Commission. Romania, 2005 Comprehensive Monitoring Report (COM (2005)) 534 final, Brussels, 25 October 2005, SEC (2005) 1354, pp. 12–13, available at http://www.guv.ro/engleza/presa/documente/200510/raport-monitorizare-2005.pdf

11 Report from the Commission to the European Parliament and the Council on Romania's Progress on accompanying measures following Accession, Brussels, 27 June 2007 (COM (2007)) 378, pp. 4, 10–20, available at http://ec.europa.eu/dgs/secretariat_general/cvm/docs/romania_report_en.pdf

12 Wolfgang Merkle, *Deepening and Widening? The Limits of European Integration* in European Studies 2 (Hungarian Political Science Association and the Institute

for Political Sciences of the Hungarian Academy of Science, 1996) p. 47; Philippe C. Schmitter, 'Imagining the Future of the Euro-Polity With the Help of the New Concepts'.

13 The safeguard clauses are enacted by the European Commission in cases of serious shortcomings or delays in the fulfilment of commitments by any new Member States before or after accession. For Romania and Bulgaria, a specific additional safeguard clause has been introduced, the postponement clause, which can lead to the postponement of the accession for either country by one year, until 2008. There is another special clause, applicable only to Romania, and confined to two of the 30 negotiated chapters, Justice and Home Affairs, and Competition. The clauses come in the Accession Treaty under Title IV, Other Provisions, Articles 36–39, while the Annex IX refers to the 11 precise red flags that Romania has to tackle and improve preparations in those particular areas. Four of them refer to Competition Policies (chapter 6 of the negotiations) and seven to Justice and Home Affairs (chapter 24); see annex for the red flags.

14 *Report on the Results of the Negotiations on the Accession of Bulgaria and Romania to the European Union*, Prepared by the Commission's Departments, February 2005, pp 24–25.

15 Speech of José Manuel Barroso, President of the European Commission, at the European Parliament, Strasbourg, 26 September 2006, available at http://www.roembus.org/EU/Romania%20will%20join%20the%20European%20Union%20in%202007.htm

16 *The signature of the Accession Treaty: a decisive step on the path towards the EU.* A speech given by Ene Dinga, Romanian Minister of European Integration, at the European Academy Berlin, 18 April 2005.

11

The Consequences of EU-Enlargement for Romanian Border Regions – Between Cooperation, Centralism and Customs Frontiers

Hans-Heinrich Rieser and Christoph Waack

Introduction

On 1 January 2007, Romania became a member of the EU. The realization of this political aim has far-reaching consequences for the country's border areas and for its neighbours Hungary, the Ukraine, Moldova, Bulgaria and Serbia (Table 11.1 and Figure 11.1).

The total length of Romania's land borders is 2,508 km and the changed situation along them reflects the country's peripheral geopolitical situation within the EU. The expansion of the EU to include Serbia will take at least another decade, and under current conditions the Ukraine and Moldova cannot expect entry into the EU in the long term. Romania's new internal and external EU borders will therefore have to fulfil a considerable range of functions in a European context for quite some time. The degree of openness of the borders for the movement of capital, goods and people will change in comparison to the diverse conditions along the current borders (Figure 11.1).

The internal EU borders will become more open for these types of transfer, while the external EU boundaries will generally become less open. There is a risk that, as new borders to the west (Hungary) and south (Bulgaria) are opened further, historically established regional connections may be lost. In contrast, regions along the new internal EU borders that have hitherto failed to develop strong linkages will be encouraged to develop cross-border cooperation. Regional cross-border cooperation will thus have to cope with different types of contact, depending on the type of border involved.

Table 11.1   Romania's borders after EU entry

Border section	Length of border (km)	Number of border-crossing points	Length of border by crossing points	Type of border after 2007
Romania – Hungary	442	6	73.7	Internal EU border
Romania – Ukraine	531	2	265.5	External EU border
Romania – Moldova	450	5	90	External EU border
Romania – Bulgaria	609	6	101.5	Internal EU border
Romania – Serbia	476	4	119	External EU border
Total	2,508	23	109	–

Internal EU border: 1,051 km (42%); External EU border: 1,457 km (58%)

Source: Ilieş, A. (2003).

Figure 11.1   Romania's borders after EU entry

Regional, national and European expectations of the forms that this cross-border cooperation might take will first have to be formulated in a process of 'border governance' and implemented through political and regulatory reform. The model of the so-called 'Euroregion' (starting with 'Euregio' in 1958) was developed after the Second World War between the Netherlands and Germany with the intention of institutionalizing cross-border cooperation. This model was based on a private association of local and/or regional public corporations and was transferred to the borders of transition countries after 1989. Today this institutional model for cross-border cooperation is by far the most usual one in Europe.

This chapter is primarily concerned with the potential of Romania and its neighbours for cooperation in these new Euroregions, EU funding potential along the internal borders in the context of cohesion policy from 2007 and the implementation of the New Neighbourhood Instrument (NNI) along Romania's external borders. This latter is becoming more important as the EU tightens its requirements that Romania (and other countries) control the new external EU border and prevent trafficking and smuggling along it, a point that was given remarkably high priority in the report of the European Parliament on Romania's application for EU membership on 1 April 2005.[1] Consideration is also given to the potential for the population of the border regions to develop and maintain cross-border contacts.

The differences between South-Eastern Europe and Western Europe with regard to state borders can be highlighted by a statistical comparison. In the EU-15, only 14 per cent of all borders were land borders; in South-Eastern Europe, however, they account for 59 per cent of all borders.[2] There is also only one border in the region where neither the course of the border nor the names of the adjoining states have changed in the twentieth century. This is the section of the border between Romania and Bulgaria along the Danube, some 420 km long. Many changes took place in the last decade of the twentieth century. Border changes (physical and functional) are not history in South-Eastern Europe but are part of modern life.

Countries like Romania with neighbours that are not part of the EU, and with whom there may be no common border arrangements, must have independent treaties and policies to regulate often contradictory development imperatives. On the one hand, they are legally bound by the EU to maintain strong monitoring against illegal immigration and trafficking. On the other hand, they must develop regional policies to support border area development. These individual treaties can often do more justice to conditions in the individual border regions than general regulations, such as those prescribed by the Schengen agreement, but they can also negatively affect cross-border contacts and the speed of movement of goods and workers across borders with combined economies. The congruence or disparity between national and regional needs can, as a result, be very significant, and is often made more sensitive in regions that have experienced sometimes violent political transformations in the past, including regional separation and the deportation of people. One result is that the behaviour and actions of both politicians and the population are directly touched by border issues; politicians must reach agreement with the neighbouring states on border issues (ranging from the delimitation of the border to issues involving the cross-border movement of capital, goods and people) while the local population, often dependent on cross-border economies and contacts, must cope with these regulations. In this context it makes sense to think of those living directly at the borders as in some important ways different from the population of the rest of the country.

In this chapter we present and analyse three case studies from the five different border areas in Romania with particular emphasis on their potential for cross-border cooperation under changing border regimes, the role of the central state on border regions and their effects on economic relations.

Examples of incipient regional cross-border cooperation at the borders of Romania

Euroregion Danube–Körös–Mureş–Tisza (DKMT)

The DKMT (Figure 11.2) is a little larger than Bavaria, with an area of just under 72,000 km². However, with 5.4 million inhabitants it has considerably less than half the population of the Bavarian Free State. The population density is 75 persons/km², about a third of that in Germany.

In political terms the DKMT consists of eight administrative units which belong to three states: the autonomous Serbian province of Vojvodina, the three south-eastern Hungarian districts (megyék) of Bács-Kiskun, Békés and Csongrád, as well as the four western Romanian districts (judeţe) of Arad, Hunedoara, Caraş-Severin and Timiş.

By the time of the 'revolution in Timişoara' just before Christmas 1989, early contacts and charitable cooperations between individuals, civil society organizations and regional administrative units were already in existence, crossing the formerly rigid borders. As a result, at this time serious consideration was given to some form of institutionalized border cooperation. As early as 1992 the cities of Timişoara and Szeged, as well as Arad and Békéscsaba, made the first official agreements, followed in 1994 by similar ones between the districts of Timiş and Csongrád as well as Arad and Békés and with the Vojvodina.

Figure 11.2   Euroregion Danube–Körös–Mureş–Tisza (DKMT)

Thus the DKMT developed from the bottom up out of regional administrative units and civil society organizations. Indeed, up to 1996 this took place in the context of resistance from the three central governments, which was particularly marked in Romania, and at a time when embargoes against former Yugoslavia were still in effect. On 31 May 1997 a first 'youth meeting' took place at the *'triplex confinium'*, the meeting point of the three borders, which were opened specially for the occasion. And on 21 November 1997 the district councils, the city corporations and the chambers of industry and commerce of the nine administrative units officially signed the 'Euroregion Danube–Körös–Mureş–Tisza' treaty. For six years after the signing of this treaty cross-border cooperation was developed and implemented. In 2003 the relevant authorities agreed to revise the agreements in favour of stricter and more effective organizational forms. A private limited company was founded to deal with everyday business and project management under the aegis of the DKMT association.

The history of its development, the multi-ethnic character of the region with up to 20 ethnic groups and the fact that the region for the most part had a shared history up to the end of the First World War explain why this Euroregion is highly effective compared with many others. Even the changed character of the borders after 1 May 2004 only impeded cooperation a little but did not bring it to a standstill. Most noticeably the relationship with the Serbian Vojvodina, which has no prospect of EU entry in the short term, has worsened, as the external EU border is now more of a barrier than was previously the case when it was merely a state border. Nevertheless, all three partners are attempting to overcome these difficulties as far as possible.

One important imperative is economic. As a result, both the chambers of industry and chambers of commerce of the administrative units involved play an active role in fostering cooperation. They not only mediate contacts, but now also run Euroregional trade fairs, which take place in rotation in the regional centres. Numerous limited cooperative cultural and research ventures have also come into being. Joint development of cross-border infrastructural projects has already borne fruit with the opening of a road connection between Szeged and Timişoara. Further projects are in the early planning stages. Shared environmental protection projects are also urgently needed, as catastrophic flooding throughout the region in early 2005 demonstrated. However, little cooperation has been achieved in this regard because the available funding is limited and not even sufficient for national projects. At the political level, the DKMT works on the European regional committees. It looks for ways of mitigating the effects of the external EU border and centralism, and presents commonly agreed projects to the three central governments.

A broad network of contacts and cooperative initiatives spanning many spheres of society has already developed, presenting a solid basis for deepening and expanding cooperation. Official acceptance of a common '*Strategy plan for cross-border regional development*' at the ninth youth meeting at the '*triplex confinium*' at the end of May 2005 opened up further fields of activity and starting points for cooperation.

Maramureş

History of the region

The historical region of Maramureş is bisected by the modern Romanian–Ukrainian state boundary along the river Tisza (Figure 11.3). The Romanian district of Maramureş (6,304 km²) adopted the old name, but only includes the southern part of the historical region (9,720 km²).

Figure 11.3 The Maramureş in the past and present

The regional name has been lost in the Ukrainian part where the majority population of Rusins (Ruthenians) introduced the name 'Karpatska Rus'.

The region of Maramureş belonged to the kingdom of Hungary from the eleventh century onwards, but was divided as a result of the First World War. Since then there has been a 62 km border along the Tisza and a further 100 km in the Maramureş Mountains (Munţii Maramureşului). The northern part was initially ceded to Czechoslovakia.

The historical Maramureş region was reunited between 1940 and 1944 under the Hungarian Horty regime. From September 1944 until April 1945 the entire Maramureş was briefly under Romanian rule, before the Soviet Union claimed the area north of the Tisza and integrated it into the Soviet Union. Since 1946 this region has been known as Transcarpathia (Zakarpatia).

The historical centre of Maramureş, Sighetu Marmaţiei on the south bank of the Tisza, lost its function. Cross-border contacts were no longer really possible, although respective ethnic minorities lived on both sides of the border. On the Ukrainian side these included ca. 35,000 Romanians in 2001 or 2.6 per cent of the population of Transcarpathia, while on the Romanian side there were ca. 34,000 Ukrainians or Ruthenians or 6.6 per cent of the population of the district of Maramure (Judeşul Maramureş). The Jewish population, which was quite large and particularly important for the economic development of the area in the nineteenth century, was removed through deportation and emigration.

Regulation of cross-border relations, travel and tourism

An essential precondition for cross-border relations is a transport infrastructure that allows direct contact. In order to improve conditions for cross-border visits, the so-called Izmail treaty was signed in 1996. Simplified procedures for crossing the border at regional crossing points applied initially to the residents of a 15 km strip along the border, and this was later extended to apply to the entire region. On 6 November 1996, a regular daily train service was initiated between Teresva and Sighet as well as a twice-weekly service between Sighet and Dilove. These are now used by about 50,000 persons annually on each side of the border. The fragile nature of this contact was symbolized by the severe flooding of the Tisza in 2000, when the railway bridge was undermined and service interrupted.

Traffic between Romania and the Ukraine, including regional cross-border movement, is currently regulated by an agreement completed on 19 December 2003, and ratified by the Romanian government on 12 February 2004. The old passenger passes for the population of the border region became invalid and were replaced by a new, general visa regulation. The population in the border region, however, is entitled to visas that are valid for several journeys per year. The agreement also regulates the establishment of three international border-crossing points in the Maramureş region, including the two rail crossing points (Câmpulung la Tisa – Teresva and Valea Vişeului – Dilove) as well as a road crossing point between Sighetu Marmaţiei and Solotvino. A bridge over the river Tisa has been completed since 2002, but the crossing point was only fully opened for a short period between January and August 2007. The bridge, a single-lane wood construction financed by EU funding, has already deteriorated and has now been closed by official order. The need for this border-crossing point was demonstrated by the huge number of people from both sides of the border waiting to cross the bridge when it was open. These long waiting lines mark the border as a special kind of micro-practice.

Euroregion

The historical Maramureş region now lies in the Euroregion Carpathians, founded in 1993, which is the largest cross-border cooperative association in Europe in terms of both area and population with an area of 161,000 km^2 and almost 16 million inhabitants from five states. Up to now, the varying conditions at the different borders within this mega-Euroregion have impeded specific plans for regional cooperation. The development of cross-border cooperation within the Euroregion Carpathians in the western section of the Ukrainian–Romanian border is currently under consideration. Four variants are possible (Figure 11.3):[3]

1. A Euroregion Maramureş, based on the historical region of Maramureş, whose centre would be Sighetu–Marmaţiei. This would not correspond to current administrative boundaries.
2. A Euroregion Maramureş-Transcarpathia would go beyond the historical region of Maramureş and take into account the current administrative boundaries of the Romanian Judeţ Maramureş and the Ukrainian region Transcarpathia.
3. A Euroregion Maramureş–Satu Mare–Transcarpathia, including the western Romanian district of Satu Mare, which also shares a boundary with the Ukraine to the north.
4. A trilateral Euroregion 'Upper Tisza', including the Hungarian district of Szabolcs-Szatmár-Bereg.

Discussion of the formation of a specific Euroregion in this area is not yet concluded. Romania's entry into the EU and the transformation of the Tisza in this area to an external EU border from 2007 increased the importance of greater cooperation and articulation of regional interests, particularly for the minorities living on the respective 'wrong' side of the border. The improvement of cross-border transport infrastructure is essential for future development in these economically disadvantaged peripheral locations. As demonstrated by the bridge between Sighet and Solotvino (completed three years ago but still not open for general traffic), the regional and European levels of government that encourage cross-border cooperation must be augmented by a readiness at a national level to work on shared projects. The changeover of power after the parliamentary elections in both countries in 2004 did result in some improvement in these efforts.

The Euroregions Giurgiu–Rousse and Danubius

The Romanian–Bulgarian border is 631 km in its entirety, and the river Danube forms 470 km of this. Up to now, in this section of the river there has been only one road and rail bridge that can be used as an international border crossing.[4] It was opened in 1954 between the twin cities of Giurgiu on the Romanian and Rousse on the Bulgarian side. Local traffic had historically been very limited and the bridge was intended mainly for international goods and passenger transport. There are no significant ethnic minorities of the neighbouring population on either side of the border and cross-border contacts have not been politically desired or encouraged.

This situation has been changing since 1989, but progress has been very slow and the process of founding a Euroregion is not yet complete. Relations between the two countries are marked by a mutual reserve at the national level, based on historical experience. The centralist state structure during the socialist phase also prevented cross-border contacts at the regional and local level. For the actors and the populations in the border regions as well as for the actors at national level, the political instrument of regional cross-border cooperation is a complete reversal of previous policy towards the border regions.

The trigger for contacts between the city administrations of Giurgiu and Rousse was serious environmental pollution by a chemical factory opened in Giurgiu in 1983. The unbearable conditions for the inhabitants of Rousse led to the creation of a bilateral expert group in 1987, which was at least able to achieve an end of chloride production, which was the main health threat. A cooperation agreement between the two cities was not signed until 2001, but this was a step towards the creation of a Euroregion Giurgiu–Rousse which could include the rural hinterland of Giurgiu and Rousse with 350,000 inhabitants.[5] Both cities have experienced considerable population decline since 1989 (6 per cent in Giurgiu and 13 per cent in Rousse between 1992 and 2002). Rousse, with better infrastructure including a free trade zone since 1998, has considerable potential for positive development. EU membership for both countries and the associated abolition of border controls provide added impetus for Rousse to pursue these linkages, particularly with its proximity to the Romanian capital Bucharest (ca. 60 km).

Willingness to cooperate has, however, been largely lacking among the political actors, particularly at local and regional levels. At the suggestion of the respective district councils (*consiliul judeţean*), the idea of a Euroregion Danubius was born in 2002, in addition to the model of a Euroregion Giurgiu–Rousse. In this Euroregion the districts of Giurgiu and Rousse together with the towns of Giurgiu and Rousse could join together into a unified Euroregion (Figure 11.4), with a population of more than 560,000.

One advantage of this Euroregion Danubius would be the much more even distribution of population than in the Euroregion Giurgiu–Rousse (53:47 and 30:70), by means of which discrimination against one side could be avoided. However, the choice of which model will be implemented will depend on political negotiation between the actors at the local and regional level. It is a significant new development that these processes are taking place at all.

The BRIE project (Bulgarian Romanian Interuniversity Europe Centre with twin headquarters in Giurgiu and Rousse), operating under the aegis of

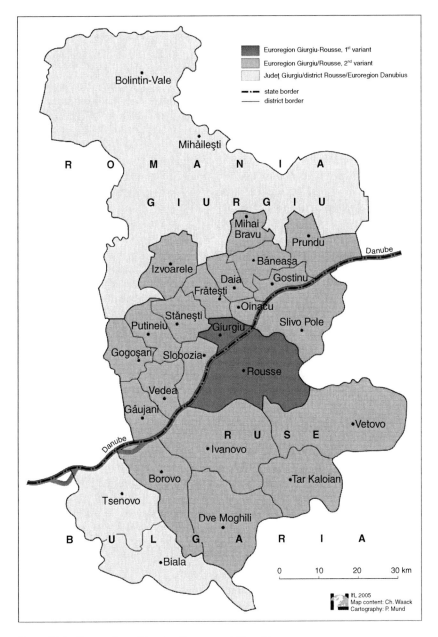

Figure 11.4 Euroregions Giurgiu–Rousse and Danubius

Source: Ilieş, A. (2004).

the German HRK (German Rectors' Conference), is a potentially significant contributor to the emerging dynamism in regional cross-border cooperation. It was initiated late in 2000 in the framework of the Stability Pact for South-Eastern Europe and is hosted by the Romanian Academy of Economic Sciences and the Bulgarian University of Rousse. The BRIE project sees itself as an 'engine of regional development' with the aim of enlivening university contacts between the two countries as well as 'the minds of the future elites of the region'.[6]

However, the project has faced major problems and resolution of these problems requires cooperation and participation from all administrative levels and the border and customs authorities. In particular, the absence of regular border traffic because of a high toll for the use of the bridge and other bureaucratic hurdles meant that a daily exchange of students and teachers across the border at first seemed impossible. The existing, highly bureaucratic and continually changing border regulations not only discouraged academic exchange, but also hindered contact among the broader population of the border region. The result has been that small traders, so-called shuttle-traders, are the main users of the bridge, travelling back and forth on the thrice daily train, heavily laden with goods as they take advantage of the varying price gap for foodstuffs and tobacco in Romania and Bulgaria.[7]

Similarities in views of the Romanian border region before EU membership

Staggered expansion, staggered border regulations

Before its western neighbour Hungary joined the EU in May 2004, with the associated shift of the external EU border to the Romanian–Hungarian border, the EU had already influenced the situation at the border and Romania's border region. Since the beginning of the pre-entry process the character of the borders had changed, as many measures (visa regulations, border controls, custom laws etc.) already had to be introduced before EU entry. Thus, the Schengen system was already in effect at the then future external EU border in Romania: e.g., through the introduction of passport and visa requirements for residents of Moldova in 2003 and of Serbia–Montenegro in summer 2004.

Romania's western border with Hungary remained an external EU border until 2007 and was therefore also an economic and Schengen border with a corresponding effect on capital, goods and passenger movement. However, with Romania's accession to the EU in 2007, special arrangements for the free movement of goods and passenger transport without visa obligations between Hungary and Romania were made. From the date of accession, this border has become an internal EU border, losing its controlling and dividing function. Integration in the Schengen area is closely associated with the implementation of the Schengen vested rights at the Romanian external borders of the EU. The only exception to this is the new internal EU border with Bulgaria, which also entered the EU in 2007. The northern and eastern Romanian borders will be permanent external EU borders with correspondingly restricted freedom of movement, which will not take national or regional interests into account, but can only be developed in accordance with the security requirements of all 27 EU states.

At the border to Moldova it was unavoidable that the slackening of restrictions in 1989 (visa- and passport-free passenger movement, etc.) would have to be reversed. This was the price that the Romanian government was willing to pay for EU membership, but to the disadvantage of the local population. In exchange for this the European Commission has indicated that this external EU border will not be a new dividing line, 'but [will be] the focus of more intensive co-operation'.[8] For this reason, Moldova received a total of 253 million euros from the EU between 1991 and 2003 in the framework of the TACIS programme. Since 1996, 17.4 million euros of this have been invested in programmes for the advancement of cross-border cooperation. A further ten million euros in the context of TACIS-CBC were provided for 2004 to 2006 and new neighbourhood instruments are planned for the period after accession.

The funds for cross-border cooperation are used not only to finance activities which support border regions in their economic and social development, environmental protection, health services and personal contacts, but also for measures against illegal immigration and illegal trading. The latter two aspects are major concerns on the part of the EU, but of less importance for the population in the border regions. In this context the word 'illegal' is contentious. It is in the nature of things that in a border milieu structures develop which are outside national laws. The strength of these structures is in direct relation to the degree of contrasts that develop on both sides of a border as a product of national conditions. Insofar as a border is not hermetically sealed, equalizing mechanisms will develop, which from a legal point of view could be described as smuggling or illegal trading. For the population in border regions with less well-developed infrastructure, such as in Romania, these activities play a not insignificant role in many people's earnings. Illegal immigration at a larger scale as part of the global migration of the poor to richer countries only becomes a problem for the population of border regions if there is an increase in associated criminal activity as a result of forced longer stays at the respective borders. As the population of Moldova is itself part of the migration phenomenon (some sources assume that 30 per cent of the workforce in Moldova will emigrate), the EU must take action which is not congruent with the interests of the population in the region.

The Romanian/Serbian border will also continue to be an external EU border for quite some time. If, as a result of the tendency towards introversion which is spreading in the EU after the rejection of the EU Constitution by France and The Netherlands, Serbia and Montenegro should not be granted the prospect of membership in the foreseeable future, this border could become a problematic dividing line facing an uncontrollable trouble spot in the middle of the EU. The initiation of EU talks with Serbia on a 'Stabilization and Association Agreement' in October 2005 should, however, ward off this danger.

Cooperation

Work has been carried out on cross-border cooperation in the Romanian border regions since 1990, and since 1996 it has increasingly been possible, but is still only moderately effective. There now exist Euroregions shared with almost all the neighbouring states. They cover almost the entire course of the border; only some sections along the Danube are not yet included (Table 11.2 and Figure 11.5).

These emerging Euroregions face other challenges. While intended to intensify cooperation following the example of the EU, the Euroregions differ considerably in size, age and especially efficiency. The examples of the

Table 11.2   Euroregions with Romanian participation

Euroregion	Year of foundation	Area (km²)	Inhab. (Mio.)	Countries of participation (without Romania)
Carpathia	1993	161,000	15.5	Poland, Slovakia, Ukraine, Hungary
Danube–Körös–Mureş–Tisza	1997	72,000	5.4	Serbia and Montenegro, Hungary
Lower Danube	1997/1998	53,500	3.9	Republic of Moldova, Ukraine
Upper Prut	2000	43,000	4.2	Republic of Moldova, Ukraine
Giurgiu–Russe	2001	2,800	0.3	Bulgaria
Danubius	2002	6,300	0.6	Bulgaria
Danube 21	2002	9,500	0.5	Serbia and Montenegro, Bulgaria
Siret–Prut–Dnjestr	2002	31,500	3.3	Republic of Moldova
Southern Danube	2002	1,600	0.2	Bulgaria
Bihor–Hajdu–Bihar	2002	13,700	1.1	Hungary
Danube–Dobrudscha	2002	24,200	1.7	Bulgaria

Source: Ilieş, A. (2004).

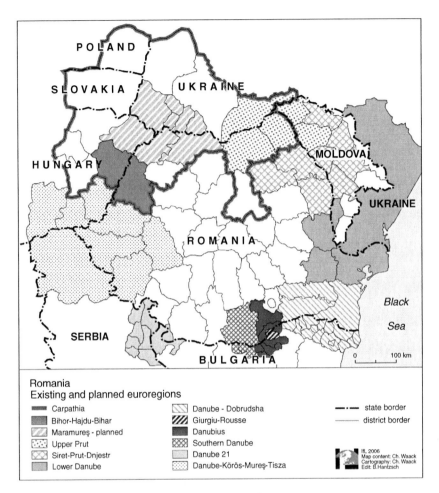

Figure 11.5 Existing and planned euroregions in Romania

Euroregion Danube–Körös–Mureş–Tisza and the Euroregion Carpathians are quite typical. Moreover, with the entry of Romania and Bulgaria into the EU in 2007 the majority of existing Euroregions now extend beyond the external border of the EU. Here they provide an opportunity; because they fall within the framework of the EU's NNI, they provide an institutional basis for measures that facilitate cooperation in spite of the limiting effects of the regulations for passenger traffic. The DKMT is an example of a functioning pilot project for cross-border cooperation especially in the context of the 'EU-entry-relay'.

Centralism

Decentralization is the basic precondition for the establishment of cross-border cooperation between the regions on both sides of the Romanian border. The fact that, until 1990, Romania and all of its neighbouring states were strongly hypercentralized is somewhat detrimental to this process (although Yugoslavia was a federal state, the constituent state of Serbia was strongly centralized). Accordingly there are still impediments to regionalization, decentralization and the introduction of the principle of subsidiarity that are of a practical nature (the absence of legal, financial or personnel means and expertise) and a psychological nature ('the state will look after things'). They are also important in the broader context of power politics. This is particularly disadvantageous for border regions as they have to work together beyond the central state line and on both sides of this line all decisions are and will be oriented towards the respective centre but not towards the neighbouring state.

Romania sees itself primarily in the position of border watchman. In an interview with the *Frankfurter Allgemeine Zeitung* on 6 July 2005, the Romanian President Băsescu said: 'We are under an obligation to pursue good neighbourhood policy, because this means security for all of Europe.' Thus at a national level, neighbourhood policy is understood primarily as security policy.

EU cohesion policy, which assigns a special role to cross-border cooperation, makes it easier for the regional level to argue against the central government, although the entire process is rather slow and has to work against tenacious opposition. The potential prospect of EU grants, however, means that regional institutions can expect certain openness to their concerns in the respective capital cities. Thus, for example, the Romanian government can no longer afford to remove individual district leaders because of participation in founding meetings for Euroregions, as was the case in 1993. This is a success that has already been achieved by the EU expansion process in its early stages.

Customs borders

In the course of the 'EU-entry-relay' a rapid transformation of the character of the various Romanian border sections has been taking place, especially on the western border. This was temporarily halted between May 2004 and January 2007, but has subsequently become more open to Hungary. Border regulations became stricter along the entire external EU border in 2007 in order to meet the demands of the Schengen Agreement.

Since 1996 the Romanian–Hungarian border has been undergoing systematic preparation for the more open situation following Romania's entry into the EU, although both sides continue to have reservations about this. This can be seen, for example, in the low intensity of cross-border cooperation at a regional level, although funding is available from the EU.

The Romanian–Bulgarian border is still not very well prepared for having an internal EU border, without a transitional period as is the case with Hungary. There are still long border sections along the Danube with no Euroregions or other forms of cooperation. There is often little mutual knowledge or familiarity or the will to acquire it. In this case well-funded regional rapprochement processes, cautiously advanced with the consent of the population, could have long-term positive effects.

Through the extension of the customs union to the New Member States (NMS) and the adoption of EU standards and regulations, Romania can benefit from trade with Hungary and Bulgaria. As regards trade with other neighbouring states, better trade opportunities with Romania could develop for the neighbouring states in particular, because:

- protectionist potential of the NMS is declining overall,
- common EU customs rates at 4.4 per cent are considerably lower than the previous average national customs rates of the NMS,
- the same standards and regulations are now in effect for exports from the neighbouring states as for exports from the EU-15. This brings cost advantages,
- the potential disadvantages arising from the expected decline in legal and illegal border trade and for some products will be considerably overcompensated by the effects listed above. Favourable visa regulations, and the ongoing creation of Euroregions will improve economic development or prevent decline in these regions.[9]

There are, however, the medium-term effects of Romanian EU membership on the customs borders with non-EU states. Firstly, the Ukraine is still not a member of the WTO, which makes trade relations more difficult. Secondly, it is well known how difficult it is to guide economic development in the framework of Euroregions towards regional economic prosperity. The circumstances under which Euroregions produce economic dynamism are due to regionally specific characteristics and cannot be implemented across the board as *best practice*. The model which has been successful in Western Europe has not yet been tried and tested in Eastern Europe. The search for short-term options in the relevant border regions is therefore not over.

Romania's border with Moldova and the Ukraine, i.e., the entire border of the country to the north and the east, is already characterized by increasing impermeability and stricter controls. From the point of view of the EU, Moldova is not in a position to implement WTO customs regulations adequately, although it is already a member of the WTO. More openness cannot be expected until regulated customs procedures in accordance with EU standards are established on the Moldovan side. The issue of Transnistria is also significant, as this officially unrecognized separate republic has its own customs laws.

The new governments in Romania and the Ukraine since the end of 2004 and early 2005 respectively have already made mutual advances to each, so that the future of cross-border cooperation can be viewed with some optimism. Because of decades of estrangement dating back to the end of the Second World War, it will take quite some time to develop more trusting cooperation at local and regional levels, but the European Commission's extension of tariff reduction through GSP status (the General System of Preferences) bodes well for cross-border industrial traffic.

On 17 May 2004, Romania signed a free trade agreement with Serbia and Montenegro. The first stage of the agreement, which will be fully implemented by 2008, came into effect on 1 July 2004.

Conclusion

The EU expansion process is transforming the situation at the Romanian border from a challenge to national policy to a European issue. The staggered nature of this development, in terms of both time and the character of individual sections of the border in their function as internal or external EU borders, influences the potential for cross-border relations with neighbouring countries in a special way. With regard to the external borders, regional and national interests are subordinate to European security considerations which limit free movement of persons. In contrast, at the internal EU borders new forms of cooperation are encouraged. The new situation at the borders does not, however, reflect historical relations or those cultivated by the inhabitants. The new borders created in the twentieth century and the political processes of integration and disintegration at the beginning of the twenty-first century overlie older social structures in the region as a whole. There is a danger that these could only survive or be filled with new life if this is politically opportune.

The new development of cross-border relations in South-Eastern Europe is therefore a special challenge for Europe of the regions. A contradictory aspect of the establishment of Euroregions in South-Eastern Europe is that, during the EU expansion process, little attention was given by the state to regional cross-border cooperation between two future EU member states and any impetus usually came from outside, as is the case with the BRIE project.

If the new model of cross-border cooperation is to be successful, it has to become firmly established in the minds of the population of the South-Eastern European states, particularly among the elite groups. Therefore this new model must be intensively promoted, just as national isolation was constructed and established in the past. This process of the new construction of regional models and their establishment will take some time, as has been learned from experience at the borders within the 'old' EU. The EU will be well advised to encourage and support projects in this process of regional cross-border integration, where the long-term advantages can be demonstrated by concrete examples. Similar to the European Single Market on a supranational level, cross-border micro-practices of everyday economies may generate profits at the regional level in the short-term. Probably the most important precondition for the development of cross-border cooperation is mutual trust. This can only grow with long-term, continuous support and encouragement. Euroregions thus act as instruments of European harmonization in two senses; as instruments of technical adjustment and regional integration.

Notes

1 The report cites a total of nine points where a particular effort must be made in Romania: (1) effective implementation of reforms in administration and justice; (2) the fight against corruption; (3) control of the future external borders; (4) freedom of the press; (5) strengthening of local and regional administration; (6) recognition and support of minorities; (7) implementation of legal provisions for the protection of children; (8) transparent application of new legal provisions for state subsidies; (9) further efforts in environmental protection. See European Parliament, Committee on foreign affairs, *Report on the application by Romania to become a member of the European Union, 1 April 2005*, http://www.europarl.europa.eu/ (16 April 2006).
2 I. Illés, 'Border and Cross-border Co-operation in the Countries of Central and South-Eastern Europe', *Südosteuropa Munich*, 51 (2002) 289.
3 A. Ilieş, *România. Euroregiuni* [Romania. Euroregions] (Oradea, 2004), pp. 186f.
4 A second road bridge between Calafat in Romania and Vidin in Bulgaria in the western border area is being constructed since 2004 after long and complicated planning. The construction of the new bridge is one of the priority projects in the stability pact for South-Eastern Europe.
5 A. Ilieş, *România. Euroregiuni* (Oradea, 2004), p. 129; see also R. Săgeată, 'The Role of the Double Settlements In the Euro-Regions Structure – A Case Study: The Romanian-Bulgarian Border Space in the Danube sector' in J. Wendt et al., eds, *Poland and Romania before Enlargement of European Union and NATO* (Warsaw: Carta Blanca, 2004), 125–131.
6 G. Duda, Das Projekt 'BRIE' und die Euroregion Rousse/Giurgiu [The project 'BRIE' and the Euroregion Rousse/Giurgiu] in B. Neuss et al., *Die MOE-Staaten vor dem EU-Beitritt – Chancen und Probleme aus politik- und regionalwissenschaftlicher Sicht* [The states in middle eastern Europe before EU-accession – Chances and problems in a political- and regional science view], Occasional papers of the European Centre for Federalism Research No. 27, Tübingen, 206–210, p. 210.
7 Railway traffic between Giurgiu and Rousse consists of only three international long-distance connections in each direction (D 461 Budapest – Thessaloniki and D 460 in the opposite direction; D 383 Moscow – Sofia and in the opposite direction; D 499 Bucharest – Istanbul and D 489 from Istanbul). The train journey itself only takes 25 minutes. There is no regional cross-border rail connection.

12

The Property Rights Hurdle: Reconciling EU and Russian Traditions*

Stefan Hedlund

Introduction

The fall of the Berlin Wall triggered expectations for regional integration that would fundamentally recast Europe as a whole. With the eastward expansion of the European Union, many of these expectations have at the very least come within reach, and theories on globalization have found at least some application and justification. Whatever we choose to believe about the prospects for a politically unified Europe to achieve successful integration on a more fundamental level, there will, however, remain one issue that trumps all others, namely what to do with Russia.

Ever since Brussels began its deliberations on a major eastward enlargement, the name of this game has been major confusion. If the purpose of expansion is indeed to be sold as that of a 'peace project', which has appeared to be the politically correct way to go, should not Russia then be included? Would not an enlargement that stops at Russia's borders effectively serve to draw new lines of division on the continent? And would this not produce the very opposite of enhanced peace and security?

While many balk at the suggestion of admitting Russia to the EU, there is another option available which holds that keeping an open door for possible future membership could serve as an effective external policy instrument. Much as the prospect of becoming members served to focus and support reform policy in Central Europe and in the Baltics, that very same purpose would be served in the Russian case. Or so, at least, it is claimed.

However laudable the latter ambition may seem, it also reflects a serious asymmetry in perceptions of the relation between Russia and the EU. On the Russian side, the whole point of the exercise is clearly linked to trade and investment. Hoping to achieve a much-needed reduction in dependence on hydrocarbons, Moscow's negotiators focus in any way possible on facilitating Russian non-energy exports to the EU. Meanwhile, Brussels appears bent on achieving an extreme makeover of the institutional matrix of the Russian Federation, ranging from improvement in corporate governance and the rule of law, to democratic institution building and respect for human rights.

Exactly how these two approaches may be reconciled is very far from clear, as is the role of 'peace' in continued negotiations. What is clear, however, is that if the two sides do not succeed in coming to some form of agreement on what they are and should be doing together, then we may expect to encounter further aggravation down the road of the kind that dominated the lead-up to the G8 meetings in June 2007.

Some seek to assume the problem out of existence, by presenting Russian membership in the EU as mutually beneficial: 'This co-development path is of *mutual interest*. For Russia it offers a way to diversify an economic system based mainly on exploitation of natural resources and permanently exposed to Dutch disease, and to organise a diversified competitive economy based on relevant investment.'[1] The specific benefit to the EU would lie in capitalizing on economic strengths through increased complementarities, and both sides would gain in increased security.

Others choose to point at matters that divide rather than unite. Commenting, for example, on the outcome of a trilateral German–French–Russian conference in June 2004, Alexander Rahr highlights what surely must be the real crux of the matter: 'Russia offers the EU a community based on interest, instead of values, economic pragmatism instead of civil dialogue, a modernization partnership instead of democratic partnership.'[2]

With such widely different goals and ambitions, the prospects for success are slim. Far worse, there is an obvious risk that a growing sense of mutual frustration may eventually lead to a serious deterioration in the relation as such: 'When one side talks about the rules of behaviour and the other thinks they are talking about trade, it is inevitable that misunderstandings and clashes will occur.'[3]

Given that the partnership between Moscow and Brussels began with these asymmetrical initial assumptions and a lack of agreement on what the final outcome was to be, it should not come as a surprise that negotiations have been fraught with ever-increasing difficulties. Following the Big Bang of EU enlargement in spring 2004, relation between the EU and Russia has tumbled to a post-Soviet low.

In one sense, this reflects a general deterioration in relations between Russia and the West, a deterioration that is due to what is generally perceived as 'democratic backsliding' under President Vladimir Putin. As one Russian commentator puts it, 'To all appearances, the West has stopped pretending it believes in Russian reforms.'[4] Europeans remain uneasy about the ongoing war in Chechnya, and this is causing an increasing number of commentators to argue that further discussion should be focused not on admission to the EU but on expelling Russia from the Council of Europe.

When Russia was admitted to the Council in 1996, Moscow agreed to adhere to the principles of respect for human rights that form the main rationale for membership. The commitment on Russian entry to the Council was made while the first war in Chechnya was still being prosecuted, and resulted in strong and vocal opposition. Today, such protesters would argue that their criticism has been vindicated. In a recent report, the Council's Commissioner for Human Rights, Alvaro Gil-Robles, called on Russia to do more to protect the freedom of the press, to deal with serious crimes in Chechnya, and to stem a rising tide of anti-Semitism and racist attacks.[5]

On the Russian side, there is also discontent, albeit for different reasons. On the one hand, it is both understandable and somehow healthy that an increasing number of Russians are becoming fed up with what they see – quite rightly – as a Western obsession with knowing what is best for Russia, and with offering unsolicited advice that has often proven to be purely self-serving.[6] On the other hand, what must be seen as perhaps equally understandable but far less healthy is the fact that an increasing number of Russians are also beginning to view the West as being bent on excluding and/or isolating Russia: 'The latest opinion polls show that a new fear is emerging among the Russian population that, more than 15 years after the fall of the Soviet Union and the Iron Curtain, a new wall is appearing between Russia and Europe.'[7]

In sum, the relationship between Russia and the EU has the makings of a problem that could have serious implications. The main ambition of this paper is to show that the root cause of this ongoing deterioration is found on a much deeper level than democratic backsliding, the war in Chechnya, or even Russian superpower hangover. What we are witnessing is a true clash of cultures, not in Huntington's sense of a pending clash between civilizations, but in the deeper sense of institutional incompatibility that produces different approaches to and understanding of the most basic of the rules of the game.

Because the policy of the EU is based on achieving a successful Russian transition to liberal democracy, and to a market economy that is rooted in the rule of law, the brunt of the burden of called-for adjustment falls on the Russian side. During most of the 1990s, accounts of whether or not real progress was being made diverged widely. Following the August 1998 crash on Russia's financial markets, there has, however, been a growing realization that obstacles are of a fundamental nature and will not be easily overcome. Speaking to a Washington audience in 1997, Alan Greenspan underscored what many economic advisors had apparently failed to realize, namely that 'much of what we took for granted in our free market system and assumed to be human nature was not nature at all, but culture'. The failure of Russian reform, in his view, had a very simple explanation: 'The essential infrastructure of the market is missing.'[8]

At the core of what Greenspan refers to as 'culture' are some of the most basic features of a functioning market economy, namely a willingness to honour contracts and respect property rights, and to accept the state as a legitimate and credible enforcer of rules. If such rule-obedience has been internalized, to the point of becoming an important norm guiding the behaviour of economic actors, then we may expect economic activity to be guided in a Smithian rather than a Hobbesian direction. If this is not the case, then the social sciences are at a loss suggesting what to do. Whether and how social norms may be influenced by deliberate policy remains something of a *terra incognita*.

While it is clear that relations between Moscow and Brussels will have to be formulated with such factors taken into account, it remains unclear what the more specific implications are. Should Euro-politicians remain insistent on a partnership that is founded on common values, and continue searching for ways in which Russia may be enticed to Westernize? Or should they simply accept that Russia will never graciously accept status as just another rank-and-file rule-obedient member of the EU, and conclude that special rules will have to apply?

The choice between these options goes to the very heart of what EU enlargement is all about. The challenge lies in coming to agreement on whether Russia really is both ready and able to implement the required institutional transformation. Beyond the need to abstain from political posturing and sloganeering, this calls for a serious assessment of the prospects for Russia to finally overcome what we have referred to in the title of this paper as the property rights hurdle. Given the heavy burden of Russian history, this must be seen as a task of real magnitude.

A fundamental line of division

In a more general sense, private property rights are a *sine qua non* not only for functioning market economy but also for democratic politics. If economic actors do not feel that they have secure rights to the fruits of their own labour, they can be expected to direct their efforts to redistributive rather than productive undertakings, and if political actors do not feel that they have a sphere of their own into which the state can penetrate only according to strict rules, then they will succumb to an unhealthy feeling of dependence that undermines any form of government commitment to accountability. However, to the extent that this really is a consensus opinion, it is a fairly recent one.

Up until the end of the Cold War, the sheer volume of work that went into writing and lecturing about alternative economic systems reflected an implicit belief that the command economy did represent an alternative to the market economy. Since, by definition, the command economy rests on a suppression of all rights to clearly defined property in the means of production, the implied understanding was that even non-market systems without enforceable rights to property could be viable.

As time wore on, the initial belief, held especially by enthusiasts on the left, that central planning was actually *superior* to the market[9] began to give way to more general disillusionment. In the Soviet Union, faith in the merits of central planning did go through something of a renaissance during the 1960s and early 1970s, when enthusiasm over the cybernetic revolution provided a temporary boost in confidence. Then it fizzled. Both Western and (tacitly) Soviet experts began professing belief in 'muddling through'.

Although the impression of Soviet economic performance was thus being cut down to size, most Western observers remained convinced that the command economy, with its emphasis on forced resource mobilization, did remain a viable economic system capable of at least staying within sight of the Western market economies. Warped statistics help reinforce such beliefs. Up until 1992, both Goskomstat and the CIA placed Soviet GDP at two-thirds the size of that of the United States. The implication was that the USSR was 'the world's second largest economy, with a first-tier per capita income just shy of the Western European mean, making Russia a military and consumer great power'.[10] But, for those who did believe in such numbers, it was difficult to then explain how reported Russian aggregate GDP only a year later could be on par not with the US but with Sweden, and that Russian GDP per capita was approaching third world standards. Perceptions of Soviet performance quite obviously had been far off the mark.

Given the copious amount of work that has been devoted by professional economists to writing about property rights, it is strange that the extreme nature of limitations on rights to property in the Soviet-type economies was taken so lightly. Even more striking is the fact that so few conclusions were drawn from János Kornai's widely acclaimed work about the political economy of communism, which placed a great deal of emphasis on the consequences of suppressing rights to private property. Kornai's argument is presented in evolutionary terms, where the taking of one step leads to another, then a third, etc. More specifically, what sets the chain of events in motion is the introduction of a monopoly on power, which leads to the suppression of private property, which in turn eliminates market exchange, which produces a distinct 'quantity drive', etc.[11]

The main point lies in the emphasis that is placed on the parallel introduction of a totalitarian ideology, which in a sense provided the system with a purpose and a will of its own. Without this system of norms imposed from above, the formal introduction of new rules regarding power and property relations would not have resulted in the very special case that was the socialist economic system. In order to drive the point home, Kornai referred to this combination of rules and norms as that of 'body and soul'.[12]

What makes this so relevant to our current concern is the fact that a suppression of property rights will impact economic performance not only directly, by altering economic strategies, but also indirectly, by causing collateral damage to other dimensions of the institutional matrix. The main victim on this list will be the ability of the state to act as an impartial third-party enforcer of the rules of the game. If this function is lost, or seriously degraded, it will have a substantial impact on the long-term performance of the economy.

We draw two important conclusions. The first is that if we do accept Kornai's main conclusion that the socialist economy forms *sui generis*, where the 'economics of shortage'[13] renders much of the traditional neoclassical approach inapplicable, then we have said something important about convergence, perhaps also about transition, and certainly about the issue of possible Russian membership in the EU; without successful institutional change, in the directions indicated above, the issue collapses.

Our second conclusion concerns the link between democracy and a market economy. Since it would be difficult to identify a democratic system that is not also a market economy, and since market economy without secure rights to property is a bird that just won't fly, it follows logically that there is indeed a link between the two. What does not follow quite as obviously is the problem of possible collateral damage that is reflected in Kornai's metaphor of 'body and soul'.

In order to disentangle this issue, we make a distinction between an undemocratic system that has a totalitarian bent, and one that is a more traditional autocracy. While both are similar in the sense of failing to guarantee the sanctity of property rights, they differ in the norms each supports. In the former case, norms have evolved to support and rationalize servitude and the absence of enforceable rights. In the latter, the autocrat preserves his power by force alone. If that force collapses, there will be no remaining obstacles to 'transition'. If, as we suggest, Russia falls into the former category, its attempt to undertake transition will be all the more complicated.

In the following, we shall argue that the real key to understanding *The Rise of the Western World*[14] rests in the introduction of secure rights to property combined with a state that is ready and able to act as a credible and legitimate enforcer of such rights. This not only points us in the direction of neo-institutional theory, which derives much of its rationale from studying the interplay between formal rules and informal norms.[15] More specifically, it also underscores the abovementioned role of the state as a guarantor of the rules of the game.

Mancur Olson, the great pioneer of theories on collective action, had already emphasized that the prospects for the rule of law to emerge as a result of *laissez faire* policies are slim indeed: 'So logic tells us that the collective good of law and order, like other collective goods, can never be obtained through voluntary collective action in really large groups.'[16] The implication is that the attempt by Russia's young reform economists to place the 'grabbing hand of the state' safely into the 'velvet glove of privatization' was seriously off the mark.[17] That the Russian economic reform programme could end in such failure was for Olson a result of a naïve belief in deregulation: 'Some enthusiasts for markets suppose that the only problem is that governments get in the way of the market and that private property is a natural and spontaneous creation.' This view he brands as 'unquestionably and drastically wrong'. The reason given goes to the very heart of the matters at hand: 'Though individuals may have possessions without government, the way a dog possesses a bone, there is no private property without government. Property is a socially protected claim on an asset – a bundle of rights enforceable in courts backed by the coercive power of government.'[18]

In this reading, the real roots of the Russian predicament lie in the absence in Russian tradition of a state that is ready, willing and able to shoulder the role of a legitimate guarantor of the rules of the game, and in the evolution of organizational responses and mental models that help economic actors exploit the opportunities for gain that are offered by such a weak state. Recalling what was said above about the need to make a distinction between traditional autocracies and those that have succeeded also in endogenizing norms that support autocracy, we thus argue that the institutional matrix that has been associated with Russian tradition has proven over time to be path-dependent and highly resistant to even the most ambitious of reforms.[19]

In order to capture the full complexity of these matters, we take the argument on property rights a step further, arguing that the right to private property forms part of a broader notion of rights that determines fundamental aspects of statehood, such as setting and enforcing the rules of the game. We refer not only to rights to property in the means of production, but to rights in the more general sense that is captured in the notion of *pacta sunt servanda*, that is, that rules are there to be obeyed by rulers and the ruled alike.

Under the rule of law, a wronged party will be confident in the right to get redress in a court of law, which is presided over by a magistrate who would not even consider selling verdicts to the highest bidder. Under the rule of men, there will be a constant need to engage in games of influence, which by necessity will be opaque and geared into maximizing the value of relations to those in positions of power. In the latter case, the state itself is dissolved into a maze of bonds of allegiance. Path dependence arises via investment in skills that are needed to play the influence games, and via the evolution of norms that support and rationalize such activity.

Thus defined, the institution of property rights also makes up the mainstay of the argument that views 'culture' as an important line of division. While there can be little if any doubt that the role of property has indeed served, over the centuries, to place Russia in a category of its own, this is far from the same as also arguing that it will have to remain this way. Indeed, both previous theories of convergence and current theories of transition are rooted in a belief that Russia's institutional matrix is amenable to change by deliberate action.

In Russian historiography, there have emerged two different schools on this matter. The first, to which we subscribe, is associated with Richard Pipes, and maintains that Russia evolved an institutional makeup that cannot be usefully compared to any other country.[20] The other school, following Martin Malia, holds that Russia is backward only in a relative sense. Due to a set of unfavourable initial conditions, the country got off to a slow start but then proceeded along the same track of development as the West. As the only real deviation from that track was the introduction of communism, it follows that the process of postsocialist transition would not be marred by problems with any deeper historical roots.[21]

The distinction between these two schools is of fundamental importance, and may be said to reflect a difference of opinion on whether Russia has succeeded over the centuries in modernizing with or without also Westernizing. It is one thing to note that the social and economic infrastructure has become increasingly similar to that of other European countries, and that formal rules may have come closer to those that characterize the West. It is something completely different to also argue that the games that are being played are played according to, rather in contravention of, those very rules, and that economic outcomes of similar policies may be realistically assumed to be similar in nature.

What Steven Rosefielde refers to as a 'countervision of Russia as a modernizing state heading toward its European home' may, to his mind, be conceptualized in what Samuel Huntington has referred to as the 'idea of the West'. The definition embraces the institutional matrix as a whole:

> For a nation to be classified as Western, its people must be rational, individualist utility seekers who possess or embrace consumer sovereign markets, democratic government, social justice, and pluralism responsive to the people's will – in other words something approximating either the American free enterprise or the European Union social democratic ideal.[22]

While this can surely never be more than an 'aspirational ideal', it remains the case that some nations group closer to this ideal than others. What is of particular relevance is that the 'social contract, the Golden Rule, the rule of law, and rationality foster fairness by eradicating market power, privilege, and discrimination'.[23] The real core of this argument, if viewed from an institutional perspective, must concern the degree to which the rule of law, and the associated belief in first principles such as *pacta sunt servanda*, has been internalized and may be seen as an essential part of a nation's system of values and norms.

Having identified these dimensions as the core elements of the institutional matrix of a successful market economy, we must be wary of being misled by casual observation of periods of high growth. It is surely the case both that the USSR did, for a time, achieve impressive rates of growth, and that the same can be said about certain periods under the Russian Empire. There is, however, nothing remarkable in this. Returning again to Olson, we may learn that 'from the time of Hammurabi if not of Sargon, and in China, Europe, and Mesopotamia as well as in the Middle East and South Asia, there have been innumerable periods of economic progress under strong autocrats'. Of far greater importance is the fact that 'many of the most remarkable periods of economic progress over the course of recorded history appear to have occurred in relatively non-autocratic, or somewhat democratic, jurisdictions that have soared ahead of the absolutist regimes around them'.[24]

Summing up the argument, we have here something of a litmus test for the long-term performance and perhaps even viability of an economic system. The point is that the quality indicator will rest more in the dimension of informal norms and mechanisms of enforcement than in the quality of formal rules that seek to guarantee the sanctity of property rights. It is in precisely this sense that the notion of 'culture' may serve to capture and define the line of division between high and low-performance economies.

The very simple fact that autocratic regimes can and do generate periods of economic growth must be viewed in the context of what type of means are being deployed in order to secure growth. To take a relevant example, Russian economic development under the Putin presidency has indeed been marked by impressive rates of growth. If we look beyond the ongoing controversy on whether this has been caused solely by devaluation and high oil prices, we may arrive at the real crux of the matter. Putin has placed much emphasis on the building of a strong state, and he has cashed in on high growth. Are the two causally connected, or simply coincidental?

One answer suggests that both Putin and Western believers in the new-found stability of Russian markets, in a sense, are barking up the wrong tree. A truly strong state will be one where institutions are sufficiently robust to function smoothly even in times of serious leadership malfunction, and a truly strong state will be one that offers sufficient guarantees for the sanctity of contracts and of private property for entrepreneurs and investors to feel good about undertaking long-term structural investment. On both counts, Putin's Russia surely must be viewed not as a success, but as a rather tragic farce.

Since our argument on whether Russia can or even should be integrated into Europe rests so heavily on the role of property in determining the quality of the institutional matrix as a whole, encompassing political, economic and legal systems, we turn again to the role of cultural tradition. We shall see that the respective paths of Russia and Europe began to diverge at a very early stage, and that since then there has been precious little in the way of sustainable convergence. While this does not predetermine that the two will remain forever apart, it does suggest that we must take a rather dim view of some of the more simplistic beliefs in rapid transition.

The roots of rights[25]

From antiquity onwards, Western cultural tradition has been marked by at times heated debates regarding the role of private property. At the heart of such debates lies the question of whether the right to property forms part of man's natural rights, or whether it is determined by convention. Morally, as well as politically, we may see root causes here for strong emotions to branch out in various directions.

Is the right to property a birthright, to be protected by the state, or is it perhaps the case, as the French nineteenth-century socialist Pierre-Joseph Proudhon used to argue, that property itself represents theft? If initial property rights in land are vested in those who take first possession, then what about the latecomers? And what are the moral consequences of the striving for material possessions? The questions are legion, and the answers to a large degree dependent on ideological outlook.

There is, however, one important dividing line that runs through all of these debates, namely that which sets ethical arguments apart from pragmatic arguments. In modern-day economic thinking it is exclusively the latter that matter. Economists have put a great deal of effort into theorizing around the technical aspects of property rights, but in so doing they have lost sight of the ethical dimension, i.e., they have lost sight of the notion of property rights as a social norm in the institutional matrix of a society.

In order to highlight the implications of this essentially ethnocentric bias in traditional neoclassical economic policy analysis, we shall begin by looking at the development of the normative Western tradition and then turn to compare with the Russian counterpart. The contrast will reveal a world of difference, which will help us understand why the relation between Russia and the EU is fraught with such complications.

The Western track

The real roots of what we know today as rights to property may be found in ancient Rome, where all those principles were formulated that still today are being taught in law schools all over the world. It was, for example, the implied notion of rights and of privileges that gave rise to the great trading cities of Western Europe. With Magdeburg in Saxony as one of the first examples, the old German expression *Stadtluft macht frei* reflected the fact that cities secured for themselves the rights to self-government, to administer their own justice and to be exempt from feudal obligations. This was the birth of a commercial urban middle class.[26]

In mid-seventeenth-century England, Thomas Hobbes presented a powerful case for the role of the state in protecting property rights. To him, property was determined by convention and was far from being a birthright. The main gist of his argument was that goods available in the natural state belonged to no one, and that the drive by men to acquire property was so strong that it risked leading to a 'war of all against all', where life becomes 'solitary, poor, nasty, brutish and short'. Motivated by self-preservation, individuals will abandon to a strong state the right to control their mutual relations. Here the state comes before society. The freedom of the individual is not a birthright, but something that is guaranteed by the state, and the same goes for property. As there can be no property without a strong state, it follows that the authority of the sovereign must be absolute.

With John Locke, we may find the opposite position, namely that property predates sovereignty. In his view of the world, the natural state is a happy one of freedom and equality. The reason for people to abandon these rights is, however, again linked to the rise of property, and the resulting greed and discord it generates. By giving up freedom and equality and accepting a state they may gain both material and personal security. In sharp contrast to Hobbes, though, Locke argues that the state stands and falls with its ability to uphold that security. In this view, under no conditions must the sovereign violate the rights to property. If the people feel that the King fails in his supreme responsibilities, they have the right to rebel.

For Adam Smith, it was 'not from the benevolence of the butcher, the brewer or the baker that we expect our dinner, but from their regard to their own interest'. If all producers strive to maximize their own gain, they will be led, as if by an 'invisible hand', to promote the interests of society. Smith thus placed emphasis on the *functions* rather than the morality of private property. Ever since, the logical conclusion that private markets should be liberated and interference by government limited to a minimum has been the creed of liberal economics and a standard component in undergraduate economics teaching. In the world of Adam Smith we have a communality of values and a respect for the rules of the game that make it possible for the invisible hand to operate. From the notion of self-regulating markets, it follows that the main task of the government must be non-interference in the market. This also becomes the guiding principle of economic liberalism: deregulation and a hands-off approach for the state.

Modern institutional theory, inspired by Douglass North, has added to our understanding of how the evolution of market-conforming rules and norms served to produce what we now know as a rules-based market economy. Here we find a strong emphasis on the role of the state in acting as a third-party enforcer, as a guarantor of the common rules and a credible upholder of enforcement mechanisms against those who seek private gain by breaking the rules.

The fundamental difference between Hobbes and Smith lies in the fact that in the intervening century the economy had come to be supported by such pervasive systems of norms – ranging from basic business ethics to trust in the role of the state – that the metaphor of the invisible hand could be used to illustrate a reality where the majority of all economic actors realized that abiding by the rules really *was* a common interest.

In the following two centuries, different states and different polities would find different ways of integrating that market economy into society, but the basic construction as such was finished already by the time Smith published his *magnum opus*. Since the norms of a rules-based society had been successfully integrated into the institutional matrix, the crucial role of the state in achieving and sustaining that integration could be assumed out of existence.

In contrast to this history of liberal democratic economies, the Russian tradition has been one in which the ability of the state to act as a credible and legitimate third-party enforcer of contracts was seriously degraded.

Russian tradition and the Soviet order

Following Max Weber, Richard Pipes defines old Russia as a 'patrimonial' state. Comparing Russia with the case of a primitive family that is run by a *paterfamilias*, he presents as the true hallmark of this type of state its complete fusion of sovereignty and property rights. This, moreover, he views as *sui generis*, as a regime in its own right, rather than a corruption of something else. Where a despot, for example, will violate the property rights of his subjects, a patrimonial ruler will not even acknowledge their existence.

The core conclusion is that

> under a patrimonial system there can be no clear distinction between state and society in so far as such a distinction postulates the right of persons other than the sovereign to exercise control over things and (where there is slavery) over persons. In a patrimonial state there exist no formal limitations on political authority, nor rule of law, nor individual liberties.[27]

Where Western feudalism was marked by a strong sense of mutual rights and obligations, Russian rulers followed the Mongol example of insisting on absolute obedience from below, with no accompanying sense of reciprocity. Pipes places particular emphasis on this contrast: 'This mutual obligation [in feudalism], formalised in the ceremony of commendation, was taken very seriously by the parties concerned and by society at large. Violation of its terms by either party nullified the contract. ... What do we find in Russia? Of vassalage, in its proper sense, nothing.'[28]

While Western feudalism went through a process of gradual strengthening of the rights of vassals and subjects, and eventually led to the end of feudalism, Russia went through a process of retrogression, where the power of the tsar was gradually strengthened, to the point where the system as a whole degenerated into complete submission of the whole population. By the early seventeenth century, as Robert Crummey puts it, 'the Russian nobility wore the harness of service like a well-trained horse'.[29] And so it would remain.

The overriding ambition by a series of Russian rulers to eradicate all sense of rights or contractual obligations was manifested above all in the process of removing private property in land, which was roughly completed in the sixteenth century. The next step was that of fixing the peasantry to the soil, a process that was accomplished in a series of laws on the capture of runaway serfs. With the Russian law code of 1649, the *Ulozhenie*, the patrimonial system was completed – and codified.

These observations point at some fundamental features of the role of law in Russian tradition. While in the Western case, law developed on contractual foundations, i.e., rules were made by the elected representatives of the people in order to regulate both relations amongst themselves and relations to their government, in Russia law has always been an instrument of power in the hands of the ruler. In the words of Thomas Owen, 'the various codes of laws issued from 1497 onward, indicated the vigour with which tsarist bureaucrats sought to regiment society by means of statutory compulsion and restriction. The law functioned as an administrative device, not as a set of rules to be obeyed by state officials.'[30]

From this development followed a virtual eradication of the very notion of rights, understood here in the broader sense indicated above. The ruler made laws that were pointed at the subjects and thus never acquired any form of legitimacy, as fair and generally accepted rules of the game. It would not be until in the reign of Catherine the Great that the Russian autocracy took the first steps on the road towards rights to property and due process, and then only for the nobility. The most important component of Catherine's reforms was her decision, in 1767, to call a legislative commission. The 'Instruction' (*nakaz*) that she provided for this commission drew heavily on Montesquieu's *L'Ésprit des Lois*, and for an emerging corps of young Russian jurists it would serve as a beacon of enlightenment. In 1785, the tsarina followed up by introducing a Charter of the Nobility, in which it was clearly stated that a 'noble will not be deprived of his property without due process of law'.[31]

Throughout the nineteenth century, the seeds that she had sown would begin to develop roots, and perhaps it was the case that Russia at the beginning of the twentieth century was on the verge of undergoing a truly fundamental transformation, in the direction of a rules-based system. No matter what we believe about this controversial proposition, when the Bolsheviks came to power all movement in the direction of a potential separation of power from property was abruptly halted. Masked behind talk of 'people's property' and 'socialist legality', the real core of Lenin's programme was that of a resurrection of the patrimonial and essentially rights-free system of old Muscovy. The party reserved for itself all power and full control over the country's productive assets. Up until 1991, the Soviet system would be marked by an absence of private property, market-based pricing and a role of the state as a guarantor of generally accepted rules.

Boris Yeltsin's rule would provide a great number of illustrations of the lingering power of this heritage, but nowhere would it be more prominent than in the question of power and property. Against the notion that there can be no property without government, which has been detailed above, Russia's reformers pitted their own neoliberal convictions of the needs for deregulation and a minimal state.

The fundamental problem that no one really seems to have been willing to recognize at the time was that Russia had still not reached the point in development where deregulation may be relied upon to free up constructive forces. There appears to have been instead a warped belief that rules-based market economy forms something of a societal default position, to which all societies will revert if they can only be sufficiently deregulated.

The risks that were involved in acting upon such beliefs had been understood long before the Soviet collapse. Already in 1952, Lord Lionel Robbins noted that 'The pursuit of self-interest unrestrained by suitable institutions, carries no guarantee of anything but chaos.'[32] In 1982, Douglass North noted very much the same: 'Indeed, a neoclassical world would be like a jungle and no society would be possible.'[33]

The consequences of launching a reform programme that failed to take such insights into account would be frightful.[34] It was not simply that asset-grabbing oligarchs would wreak serious havoc by devastating the country's industrial base and reducing a large part of the population to stark poverty. They would add further and perhaps even more serious long-term damage by creating a system of power that was geared into facilitating corruption, plunder and capital flight. Under this new form of predatory regime, stealing from the state was encouraged rather than prevented.

One of the most important keys to understanding the failure of building a rules-based system of market economy lies in a deeply rooted Russian pattern of rule-aversion, which over time acquired a strongly path-dependent nature.[35] Over the centuries, economic actors viewed tsarist legislation as weapons that were pointed at them, and consequently sought ways of evasion. In that endeavour, they invested in networks and human capital that was marked by increasing returns, and they evolved mental models rationalizing such behaviour.

Though the Bolsheviks did succeed in transforming the external *décor* of the system, its inner workings remained geared into operating highly personalized networks that were aimed at 'beating the system'. Given the predominance of such individually rational strategies, it was logical that in the eyes of its subjects the Russian state never did win much legitimacy for itself as a maker and guarantor of rules.

When the Bolsheviks came to power, they in turn immediately made it clear that a rules-based society was not on the agenda. In declaring the principle of 'socialist legality', they said that tsarist legislation would be applicable only so far as it did not contravene revolutionary morality. By thus placing their own interpretation of morality before the law, the Bolsheviks effectively voided all prospects for the Soviet state of becoming a legitimate rule-maker and a guarantor of contracts. (The traditional veneration of the Tsar as an icon, which was continued in the Soviet cult of Lenin, is something altogether different.)

The development of the Soviet system as a whole would be marked by this path-dependent triumph of rule-aversion and evasion. In such a system, as in old Russia, there can be no claiming of rights, only appeals for mercy. As the right to productive assets in particular can never be but conditional, the very notion of property again was rendered void of meaning. All efforts that had been made from Catherine the Great onwards to move in the direction of a rules-based society were thus eradicated. From an economic point of view, a notion such as 'people's property' has no content. What is owned by everyone is *de facto* owned by no one.

The main lubricant that made the Soviet economy turn over, if ever so poorly, was the system of personal relations that is known in Russian as *blat*. In Western writings it is sometimes referred to as bribes or corruption, but in the Russian context *blat* was so much more.[36] While it could include bribes, it was more of a social phenomenon, an obligation to help your friends (*svoim*). The outcome was an effective dissolution of the state, and the national economy, into a vast number of poorly interconnected networking groups, each of which would have its primary loyalty to the group. Self-evidently, this type of economy also has its rules and norms, but they will be very different from the universal and transparent rules normally associated with a market economy.

With these final impressions, we have arrived at a point where it may be time to return to what was said above about a clash of cultures, or of a fundamental institutional incompatibility between Russia and the EU. Are the features that have served to divide Russia from Europe possible to overcome, or should we simply learn to live with them? And what might the consequences be if Russia is indeed to be integrated, based on the ostrich strategy of simply refusing to see what does not agree with the preset agenda?

Rules versus influence

The main conclusion to be drawn from our digressions into Russian and European traditions is that, from a fundamental institutional perspective, we are encountering two distinctly different worlds. One rests on a set of common values that emphasize rule obedience, embodied in the rule of law and principles such as *pacta sunt servanda*. The other features norms and values that are based on rule-aversion, and in consequence promote and legitimate rule-evasion. In the former case, the state emerges as a legitimate enforcer of rules and rights. In the latter, the state is viewed as an alien force, which in practice dissolves into a maze of relations of protection and dependence. The former is transparent and accountable; the latter is opaque and unaccountable.

Since the real world will never be entirely black or white, we must recall what was said above about full Westernization as an 'aspirational ideal'. Much as true consumer sovereignty and genuinely free markets will never be encountered in real life, it should be recognised that the ideal of a market economy that is perfectly rooted in the rule of law will have to remain an ideal. This said, it is still the case that countries in the real world approximate one or the other of the two contrasting model worlds.

In the case at hand, Russia and the EU have proven to fall into two distinctly different categories. While Brussels is bent on rule-obedience, and on promoting the values that underlie such norms, Moscow is geared into hard bargaining and tough compromises with little if any interest in discussing universal norms and values. Can these two approaches be aligned with each other? From a policy point of view, this really is the pivotal question. Let us illustrate with the issue of external policy anchors.

Looking merely at the Central European and Baltic states, it is clear that the prospects of eventually winning membership in the EU – and in NATO – did serve to focus domestic politics, and thus to facilitate changes that might otherwise have been blocked by a host of special interests. Romani Prodi, the former chairman of the European Commission, claims that: 'By holding up the goal of membership we enabled these governments to implement the necessary reforms. Only this prospect sustained the reformers in their efforts to overcome nationalist and other resistance and fears of change and modernization.'[37] What remains to be asked is whether this example can be successfully transferred to the Russian case.

Since wishful thinking and political posturing have been such prominent features in the Russia–EU relation, it may be useful here to be specific. Let us look at two examples, which point to somewhat surprising conclusions. The first concerns Chechnya and the second the IMF, both representing conditions that may transform Russian behaviour.

As we may recall from above, when Russia was admitted to the Council of Europe, the first war in Chechnya was till ongoing. As it entailed gross violations of human rights, including the notorious 'filtration camps', Russian membership based on Council rules alone would have been out of the question. The argument that carried the day was based on the logic of an external policy anchor. If Moscow were to be admitted into the club, that would set such a high standard that Russian respect for human rights would be greatly improved.

Today we know that this view was wrong. The Kremlin cashed in on the benefits, and proceeded to renege on all implied obligations. With ever-louder voices calling for Russia to be expelled from the Council of Europe, we must conclude that it would have been better from the outset to abide by rather than bend the rules. All countries that live up to the standards of the Council should have a right to become members, and to enjoy the associated prestige. No exceptions.

The case of the IMF is just as clear. Up until the time when the Fund got involved with Russia, it had a clear and credible policy. Countries were given credits based on performance, including fulfilment of all obligations assumed as part of an agreement. When Russia became a member in 1992, and discussions on credits began, the IMF at first appeared reluctant to get involved. Soon enough, however, it caved in to political pressure and embarked on a programme of frivolous lending that ended only with the financial meltdown in 1998.

The crucial mistake was that of lending on promises rather than on performance. As would be the case with the Council of Europe, the Kremlin cashed in on the benefits and then proceeded to renege on its obligations. When the Fund decided in March 1996 to come up with $10 billion, representing the second largest commitment in its own history, even seasoned spin doctors had a hard time concealing that the money was provided in support of Boris Yeltsin's campaign for re-election. The Fund had thus been reduced to a player in Russian domestic politics. Seen as a whole, the story of IMF involvement in Russia forms a sordid tale of moral hazard, with a predictably unhappy ending.[38]

The moral of both of these illustrations concerns the policy implications of being forced to deal with actors that have a long history of rule-evasion and of reneging on obligations. The easy way out will be to assume the problem out of existence, to take promises at face value and proceed to ignore all evidence of growing malfeasance. While it offers tangible political rewards in the short term, in the sense of keeping a good ambiance at summit meetings, it also constitutes a recipe for major trouble down the road. In a sense, it may be compared to starting therapy for an alcoholic by pouring a stiff drink – just to make sure that we are both happy.

The fundamental distinction between the two stylized worlds that have been presented above lies in the fact that, in the absence of enforceable rules and rights, actors will have no choice but to engage in influence games, and to make sure that they hone their skills in playing such games. The games become path-dependent not least due to a process of negative selection, whereby those who are most skilled at bending or avoiding the rules will move closest to the top. Trying to abide by the rules will then be a sure way to lose.

During the initial stages of cooperation between Russia and the EU, the name of the game was to find areas of common interest, mainly in the realm of trade and investment. As it became more and more convinced of its own importance, the European Union also began to assume what the French would refer to as a *mission civilisatrice*. Instead of exploiting common interests, the relation was to be geared into formulating common values. Since the latter really is shorthand for transforming Russia into a Western society, it was a tall order.

If we do believe in such universal values that are associated with enlightenment ideals, then this must be seen as a laudable ambition. It does, however, also place a great deal of responsibility not only on the Russian side but perhaps even more so on Brussels. If Russian value systems are indeed to be changed, by some form of moral shock therapy, then it becomes of paramount importance that the doctor does not succumb to emulating the behavioural patterns of the patient; that is, the doctor should preferably not seek to cure alcoholics by engaging in binge drinking.

Overall, the Kremlin's strategy has been a logical and rational adaptation to that of the EU. When there is a problem in the relation, President Putin will deliberately avoid Brussels and prefer instead to seek out his 'friends' in Rome, Berlin, and Paris. A class act along these lines was played out when German Chancellor Gerhard Schröder responded to a question about Russian democracy by assuring that Putin is a 'dyed-in-the-wool democrat'.

As one commentator put it, while 'the uninitiated chuckled' insiders knew very well that 'the chancellor was simply indicating that he is not prepared to bite the hand that controls the valves of the pipelines that warm his country. Germany already gets 35 per cent of its oil and 40 per cent of its gas from Russia.' While it may have been politically expedient in the short term, it also meant serious moral hazard. As the head of a German government-affiliated think tank explained to the press, speaking on condition of anonymity: 'Given Moscow's history of strong-arming neighbours, we might want to think whether we really want to be in such a relationship.'[39]

From the Kremlin's point of view, it is a winning game that is being played. By first dangling promises of favourable business deals, it gets key Western governments to play down all criticism of 'democratic backsliding' and to join in the chorus praising a steadily improving Russian investment climate. Then it simply turns around and reneges on all promises, open or tacit. As a case in point, we may recall how Putin repeatedly promised that Yukos would not be destroyed, and that all would proceed according to the law. That was not quite the way in which it all ended, now was it? And has anyone complained?

The bottom line is that the games that are being played between Moscow and Brussels seem to be headed in a rather surprising direction. While the European Commission is publicly committed to universal values such as the rule of law and *pacta sunt servanda*, individual member states are busy emulating Russian-style rule-evasion. This not only applies to playing footsie with the Kremlin. Far more threatening for the European Union as such is the way in which crucially important rules on common economic policy are being broken.

One illustration may be found in the way in which some member states cooked their books in order to bypass the seemingly strict criteria that had been established for joining the euro. Another is the way in which both France and Germany remain in open and arrogant defiance of the once famed Stability Pact that was created to provide credibility for the euro.

Perhaps it is in moves of this kind that we see the real key to a future Russian membership in the European Union. As major players in Brussels become more and more involved in games of deceit and rule-evasion, and as the democratic legitimacy of the European Union as a whole becomes increasingly wobbly, the harder it will be for Brussels to lecture Moscow on transparency, accountability and – indeed – on what the Italians would call *mani puliti*. One Commission has already been brought down on charges of massive corruption, and it is not quite clear that the Augean stables have been properly cleaned.

Perhaps most amusingly of all, the Kremlin's current policy is playing straight into a deeply rooted European path-dependence. If there is one pattern that has been strikingly consistent over time, it is that of eternal infighting and of alliance-building where two actors gang up on a third. If Europeans had only been able to agree on a common policy, it must, for example, surely be the case that war in the Balkans in the 1990s could have been avoided. By reverting instead to their old ways of intrigue, they helped unleash a disaster.

The Marshall Plan was specifically designed to break this pattern, by forcing the Europeans to cooperate, and for a time it was highly successful. At present, however, Brussels shows all signs of reverting to proven old ways. The Stability Pact is a shambles, the attempt to ram through a European Constitution has run into a brick wall, and the big member states appear less able than ever to agree on vital matters of budget reform.

It is into this world of rule-evasion and personalized influence games that Russia is seeking entry. If admitted, the Kremlin will arrive with superior skills. Viewed from this perspective, it may be via Brussels that Russia will find its way back to superpower status. Would that not be a rather unexpected outcome of the glorious project of European integration?

Notes

*This chapter was written during a stay at George Washington University's Institute for European, Russian and Eurasian Studies. All the usual expressions of gratitude apply.

1   RECEP *Common Economic Space: Prospects of EU-Russia Relations* (Moscow: Russian-European Centre for Economic Policy 2002) 9 (emphasis in the original).
2   Rahr, A. 'Strategic Neighbourhood: EU-Europe versus EU-East', cited from *Johnson's Russia List*, 27 August (2004).

3   Erochkine, P. 'Common Economic Misconceptions', *The Moscow Times*, 14 April (2005).
4   *Vremya Novostei*, 18 April 2005 (cited from *Johnson's Russia List*).
5   The report was released on 20 April 2005, and may be found on www.coe.int
6   See further Wedel, J. R. *Collision and Collusion: The Strange Case of Western Aid to Eastern Europe 1989–98* (New York: St. Martins 1998), and Wedel, J. R. 'Tainted Transactions: Harvard, the Chubais Clan and Russia's Ruin', *The National Interest*, no. 59, spring (2000).
7   Erochkine, op. cit.
8   Cited by Goldman, M. *Piratizing Russia: Russian Reform Goes Awry* (London: Routledge 2003) 29–30.
9   See, for example, Lange, O. and Taylor F. M. *On the Economic Theory of Socialism* (Minneapolis, MN: University of Minnesota Press 1938).
10 Rosefielde, S. *Russia in the 21st Century: The Prodigal Superpower* (Cambridge: Cambridge University Press 2005) 56.
11 Kornai, J. *The Socialist System: The Political Economy of Communism* (Oxford: Clarendon Press 1992) esp. chapter 15.
12 Ibid., 361.
13 Kornai, J. *Economics of Shortage* (Amsterdam: North Holland 1980).
14 North, D. C. and Thomas R.P. *The Rise of the Western World: A New Economic History* (Cambridge: Cambridge University Press 1973).
15 In a highly condensed form, the central message of North's theory of institutional change is that the institutional matrix of a society consists of three different components. There are the formal rules, which may be changed overnight by political intervention. There are the informal norm systems, which change only gradually, and there are various mechanisms of enforcement, which make sure that the formal rules are upheld. It is the interplay between these three components that determines social change. See further North, D. C. *Institutions, Institutional Change and Economic Performance* (Cambridge: Cambridge University Press. 1990).
16 Olson, M. 'Autocracy, Democracy and Prosperity' in Zeckhauser R. J. (ed.), *Strategy and Choice* (Cambridge, MA.: MIT Press 1991) 135.
17 Terminology from Shleifer, A. and Vishny R. *The Grabbing Hand: Government Pathologies and Their Cures* (Cambridge, MA.: Harvard University Press 1998).
18 Olson, M. 'Why the Transition from Communism is so Difficult', *Eastern Economic Journal*, vol. 21, no. 4 (1995) 458.
19 This argument is presented in great detail in Hedlund, S. *Russian Path Dependence* (London: Routledge 2005).
20 See, especially, Pipes, R. *Russia under the Old Regime* (New York: Charles Scribner's Sons 1974).
21 Malia, M. *Russia under Western Eyes: From the Bronze Horseman to the Lenin Mausoleum* (Cambridge, MA: Belknap Press 1999).
22 Rosefielde, op. cit., 13.
23 Ibid.
24 Olson, M. 'The New Institutional Economics: The Collective Choice Approach to Economic Development' in Clague C. (ed.), *Growth and Governance in Less-Developed and Post-Socialist Countries* (Baltimore, MD and London: The Johns Hopkins University Press 1997) 50–51.
25 The following section has been pilfered, and adapted, from Hedlund, S. 'Property without Rights: Dimensions of Russian Privatization', *Europe-Asia Studies*, vol. 53, no. 2 (2001a).

26 Pipes, R. *Property and Freedom* (New York: Alfred A. Knopf 1999) 107–111.

27 Pipes, 1974, op. cit., 23.

28 Ibid., 50–51.

29 Crummey, R. O. *Aristocrats and Servitors: The Boyar Elite in Russia, 1613–1689* (Princeton, NJ: Princeton University Press 1983) 34.

30 Owen, T. C. 'Autocracy and the Rule of Law', in Sachs J. and Pistor K. (eds) *The Rule of Law and Economic Reform in Russia* (Boulder, CO.: Westview Press 1998) 24–25.

31 Pipes, R. 'Was There Private Property in Muscovite Russia?' *Slavic Review*, vol. 53, no. 2 (1994) 530.

32 Cited by Brabant, J. M. van *The Political Economy of Transition: Coming to Grips with History and Methodology* (London: Routledge 1998) 108.

33 North, D. C. *Structure and Change in Economic History* (New York: Norton 1981) 11.

34 For details, see Hedlund, S. *Russia's 'Market' Economy: A Bad Case of Predatory Capitalism* (London: UCL Press 1999).

35 See Hedlund, 2005, op. cit., ch. 8.

36 Ledeneva, A. V. *Russia's Economy of Favors: Blat, Networking and Informal Exchange* (Cambridge: Cambridge University Press 1998).

37 Sutela, P. '(Common European Economic) Space: Cold, Empty, Dark and Uninhabitable?' a paper presented to the AAASS National Convention, Boston, December (2004) 31–32.

38 See further Hedlund, S. 'Russia and the IMF: A Sordid Tale of Moral Hazard', *Demokratizatsiya*, vol. 9, no. 1. (2001).

39 *The Weekly Standard*, 7 February 2005.

13
Contingent Property Rights: The Cost to the EU of Russia's Accession

Steven Rosefielde

Introduction

Until 1987 the means of production including land were the collective property of the Soviet people. With minor exceptions, business and entre-preneurship were criminalized and asset management was vested in the communist party, the state apparatus, the planning mechanism, military industrial complex (VPK), secret police (KGB), red directors and various agrarian administrators.

This Stalinist order unravelled as president Mikhail Gorbachev and Boris Yeltsin replaced state ownership with contingent private property and usage rights that allowed managers to operate assets today for their personal benefit without any assurance about tomorrow. As late as July 2003, some scholars believed that insecure tenure and its inefficiencies were transitory aberrations; that contingent property rights had become inalienable, mak-ing Russia a normal economic system, until Mikhail Khodorkovsky was arrested and the gem of his Yukos empire, Yuganeftegaz, was transferred to Baikal Finance Group at a rigged bankruptcy proceeding.[1]

This event, the state's clear ambition to renationalize most of the petro-leum sector, its antipathy to democratic control of public programmes and the re-emergence of an authoritarian martial police state (a structurally militarized autocracy, where the secret police, not the Duma, impose presi-dential discipline), strongly suggest that property rights in Russia remain abnormal, precluding consumer sovereignty in the private sector and popu-lar democratic sovereignty in the public domain. Indeed, in this chapter I argue that renationalization is narrowing the scope of private property rights in Russia's natural resource sector and military industrial complex, and presidential and bureaucratic abuse is diminishing their quality, but-tressing Putin's authoritarian martial police state and increasing the poten-tial economic and political costs of any possible future accession of Russia into the EU. Russian property rights are trending back to the future, to Muscovy where the Tsar owned everything, and asset management was delegated to servitors, according to the sovereign's capricious command.[2]

Contingent property rights

Property rights are crucial to the performance of any economic system. They determine ownership of productive and personal assets, as well as usage rights, and derivatively the scope of production, consumption and public goods. For example, unless rights are comprehensive and inalienable, homeowners may be prohibited from using their houses for business, may be barred from selling them by restrictive covenants and may be forced to surrender them under eminent domain. In general, the greater the control individuals possess over their productive and personal assets, subject to the terms of a Lockean social contract, the greater the chances for their utility maximization (Pareto optimality). And, since social welfare depends heavily on the utility possibilities of each person, it follows that nations with comparatively inalienable ownership and property usage rights, given a democratic social contract, are likely to attain higher levels of collective well-being than twins operating in restrictive regimes.[3] The same arguments hold for democracy. Contingent property rights give autocrats leverage over rivals and discourage the establishment of well-functioning democratic processes.[4]

Russia, unlike the EU, is a state with severely circumscribed property rights, and the problem appears to be worsening. Since the rise of Muscovy in the 15th century it has been governed by the rule of men, understood as rent-granting autocracy (*samoderzhavie*), where the tsar, general communist party secretary, or president not only commands, but implicitly owns, all the property of the realm (productive and personal) and controls usage rights over grants and alienable property, with everyone else functioning as servitor, agent or servile labourer. Although there is a 'dictatorship of law', there is no rule of popularly legitimate law because courts are subordinate to the autocrat and his powerful servitors (oligarchs, bureaucrats, party officials, military and the secret police). And while the *vozhd* (leader) speaks about democracy, individual rights and national welfare, his will and the will of his insiders always take precedence over consumer and popular sovereignty. Muscovy, in the absence of inalienable property rights, creates privilege and disempowers individuals; the antithesis of the European Union.[5]

This gulf is likely to be a source of friction between fair Europa, operating under what Samuel Huntington calls the 'idea of the west',[6] and imperious Muscovy, especially so because Russia conceals its autocracy behind declarations of 'normalcy' that find a receptive audience in the EU.[7] Russian spokesmen characterize Muscovite autocracy as 'sovereign democracy', the martial police state as public protection, rent-granting as free enterprise and restricted rights as individual empowerment. These false claims have a veneer of plausibility because balloting isn't banned, militaries and secret police have some legitimate functions, rent-granting is easily conflated with profit maximization and, as Hegel insisted, discipline is required for people to freely actualize their potentials. The catch is that economic, political and societal processes are not Pareto self-regulating. Everything depends on the whims of the privileged. They fix inequitable rules of the game, revising them at their discretion, including contingent personal and productive property rights which give the system its superficial liberal lustre. People can behave 'normally' within the confines of their status, given the discriminatory rules, as long as their actions do not displease the autocrat and his inner circle. This allows them to posture as 'western'. But if offence is perceived, guilty parties are punished and the rules reformed from above. The approach is not totalitarian. Rent-granting does not require nano-control of underlings. The privileges and interests of the autocrat and his supporters are secured merely by power granting, subordination, administration and setting the requisite regulations.

Contingent property rights encompassing ownership, asset use, exchange and the acquisition of public goods are a flexible tool of autocratic governance. They allow the commander to relinquish some of his nano-authority to servitors and other segments of society in exchange for service and taxes, without empowering everyone in the Smithian sense to maximize the wealth of the nation. Russia's tsars place the maximization of their own welfare first, and the people's second.

The amount of power provisionally sacrificed depends on the *quid pro quo* and the state of political play. When tsars feel secure, rent-granting pays handsome dividends and contingent property rights tend toward irrevocability. When servitors' loyalty and usefulness are suspect, they are taught lessons, including the revocation of grants they mis-supposed had become inalienable property protected by the rule of law. The Muscovite system in this way tends to fluctuate between liberal and conservative autocracy as rulers struggle to adjust to shifting economic and political currents. They are sometimes willing to forego power for wealth, only to discover that their erstwhile supporters have become potential enemies, and then quickly reverse field. Viewed in historical perspective, the strategy is disadvantageous for the common man and the nation, and preferable for the privileged because its efficiency losses are asymmetrically distributed. Social welfare could be easily improved by replacing contingent property rights with secure possession and use required for Pareto efficient outcomes, but the sovereign and his circle would probably suffer. Similarly, Russia could dispense with its authoritarian martial police state if it became a 'normal' country, but its habituation to contingent property rights discourages it from doing so. Europa thus should be aware that her prospective groom is not what he pretends to be, and is not likely to be putty in her hands.

Misalliance: triumph of Europa over Muscovy?

This caveat does not contradict the World Bank's recent finding, based on an in-house computable general equilibrium study, that Russia would benefit from joining the WTO, and by extension the EU.[8] Transactors do not have to be Pareto efficient, enlightened or honest to benefit from market-widening. Nor is marriage precluded by a clash of civilizations. A union of Europa and Muscovy could survive. But would it be wise? There is no general answer to such questions. Much depends on the utility functions of the partners and the Bergsonian welfare functions of the judges.[9] However, in the spirit of Abram Bergson's conjecture that complex matters of this sort are amenable to rational discourse, let us suppose that the scope of benefits and stability of the misalliance are closely linked with the degree to which Muscovy approximates Meadean social democracy, where a competitive market form of social democracy provides optimal income and wealth transfers, together with the direct provision of popularly preferred public goods.[10]

The more Kremlin autocrats permit Paretian agency, including Arrow democracy, the better the prospects for Europa's and Muscovy's union, and *vice versa*. What can be inferred about the wisdom of the prospective misalliance from this rule of thumb? Is Russia ineluctably transitioning from autocracy to Meadean social democracy, as many advocates of Moscow's EU accession contend, or is the tide reverting toward a harsh authoritarian martial police state?

Shifting terms of compatibility

Prospects are disquieting as Putin's scheduled succession in 2008 draws near, despite the illusion of burgeoning prosperity created by the global petro-bubble. Russia seems headed for a period of turbulence after the bubble bursts, likely to result in a sterner and perhaps less economically efficient authoritarian martial police state, which could take diverse forms. It may verge toward renationalization and military resource mobilization; toward oligarchic indolence and complacency, or both; all undesirable from the standpoints of global security and Russia's EU accession.

Recent events confirm the validity of these concerns. The debate in the west has shifted from denying the failure of transition, decrying the emergence of *siloviki*-dominated authoritarianism, and celebrating Russia's growth prospects to a paradigm stressing the self-enfeebling character of hypercentralization,[11] waning post-bubble economic prospects and popular discontent. As usual, little mention is made of the darker interplay of Putin's military modernization drive, the reinvigoration of structural militarization or the harsh potential of an authoritarian martial police state that perceives itself under siege.[12]

Original sin in this new conception isn't autocratic rent-granting, structural militarization or secret police repression. Just as under Soviet communism, the disease is diagnosed more euphemistically as centralized bureaucracy, Muscovy in epaulets and bribes. Bureaucrats and the security services, in this context, are sympathetic to partial renationalization, administrative controls and stringent market regulation. They are venal, inefficient and anti-democratic. Whatever the private sector's rent-seeking defects, it is assumed that the further empowerment of conservative forces will make matters worse. Capital flight will accelerate,[13] the inflow of foreign direct investment will decline, business will be bureaucratically stultified, growth will decelerate, poverty reduction will falter,[14] global competitiveness will deteriorate, rent-seekers and small businessmen will become increasingly disgruntled and the people will grow restive. Bureaucratic hypercentralization, in short, must end badly, so Putin ought to save everyone a great deal of trouble by cashiering the *siloviki* and re-embracing liberalization *a la Rus*.

It would seem from this logic that, as a reasonable man, Putin has no choice. He should see the light and forsake his evil ways. Indeed, even if he believed in democratic free enterprise, which he does not,[15] this would be his only option. However, Yeltsin's Muscovy provides a third way, and on this score it is not obvious that a *siloviki*-dominated rent-granting order is worse than the oligarchic alternative.

The economy during the Yeltsin wild east era was catastroikic. Even though the military and KGB were downsized and downgraded, GDP fell 35 per cent from 1991 to 1998 (Table 13.1). Anything goes rent-seeking; corruption and swindling, which were the root causes of the financial crisis of 1998, seem to have been fatal to Russia's economic health.[16] The partial ruble devaluation-driven recovery which ensued in 1999 showed that

Table 13.1 Real GDP growth in the Russian Federation 1990–2005 (Percentage change over the preceding year)

Yeltsin Regime 1991–1999

1990	1991	1992	1993	1994	1995	1996	1997	1998	1999
−3.0	−5.0	−14.5	−8.7	−12.7	−4.1	−3.6	1.4	−5.3	6.4

Putin Regime 2000–2005

2000	2001	2002	2003	2004	2005
10.0	5.1	4.7	7.3	7.2	6.4

Sources: Economic Survey of Europe, 2005, No.1, Appendix Table B.1, p. 128. *Russian Economic Survey* (US-Russia Business Council, February 2006) p. 4.

Yeltsin's Muscovy was not entirely dysfunctional, but the rebound also coincided with the waxing fortunes of the FSB.

Moreover, the reinvigoration of Russia's Muscovite authoritarian martial police state, which gained momentum after its head Vladimir Putin succeeded Yeltsin to the presidency, did not destabilize the economy or send it into a tailspin. GDP rose rapidly under his tutelage, recovering more than half the ground lost since 1989 on official reckoning,[17] despite the strengthening of the federal bureaucracy, the centralization of authority, the prosecution of some oligarchs, the gathering power of the *siloviki* and the resurgence of arms production.[18] The restoration of some semblance of state power appears to have had a positive effect on Russia's economic performance compared with Yeltsin's shock 'therapeutic' rent-seeking *laissez faire*, a point often made by G-7 spokesmen until the spring of 2004, when it became evident that recovery and westernization were proving to be very different things.[19]

The west has grudgingly rediscovered, as the Third Reich once taught, that authoritarian martial police state-managed market economies which sometimes threaten international order are occasionally compatible with recovery, growth and patchwork prosperity. Although modern, closed, anti-competitive societies have obvious flaws, and have not stood the test of time,[20] some forms nonetheless can survive for decades, or centuries, and may be superior to degenerate alternatives like Yeltsin's wild east.

Aroused Muscovite regimes like those of Peter the Great, Catherine the Great and Stalin generate growth spurts by harrying rent-seekers. Stringent discipline, pressure, browbeating and punitive methods are routinely applied to overcome lethargy and corruption. History shows that Muscovite mobilization can be sustained for considerable periods of time under strong rulers, but the economic performance of weak Russian states has been comparatively poor because *laissez-faire* rent-granting is intrinsically anti-competitive.[21] The absence of the rule of contract law limits individual entrepreneurship, while lax oversight emboldens rent-grantees to consume the tsar's assets without managing them efficiently.

This poses a choice for Putin and a dilemma for the EU. Russia's president, if fully cognizant of the costs and benefits to society, can abandon his transiently successful, strong authoritarian martial police by switching sides or abdicating in favour of oligarchs. Alternatively, he can persevere holding the reins himself or pass the baton to his chosen *siloviki* successor to prevent a replay of Yeltsin's weak Muscovite regime, repress popular disorder and reinstall Russia as a superpower. Switching sides will provide Putin with relief from the post-petro-bubble migraines looming ahead, allowing him to shift blame for flagging growth as production approaches the 1989 capacity bound,[22] dodge responsibility when the petro-boom becomes a bust,[23] and deflect responsibility for CIS and domestic regional secessionist pressures,[24] insider factional intrigue, public discontent and youth agitation.[25] Oligarchs may also soothe his conscience with a golden parachute if he decides to exit early. However, abandoning the authoritarian martial police will not be easy. It will cut against the grain, requiring him to forsake superpower, jeopardize national security and his personal welfare should a dependable deal with his successors prove elusive. It will embolden unscrupulous rent-seekers, spur social unrest, risk a palace *coup d'etat* by his security service supporters of the sort that brought Putin himself to power,[26] and is probably unnecessary because he stands a reasonable chance of weathering the storm by being an artful dodger, talking like a westernizing liberal,[27] while acting like a Muscovite autocrat. Of course, the task would be simplified if Putin were determined to construct a well-functioning, self-disciplined, competitive society founded on the rule of law instead of the rule of men, but there is no evidence that he has the desire or know-how to do it, virtually assuring a drift toward structural militarization and repression.[28]

The challenge for the EU is more difficult. It has complex, inconsistent goals, papered over by the rhetoric of social democracy, that make it difficult for Brussels to sort out priorities behind lace curtains. The EU would like to see Russia transformed into a popularly sovereign social democracy, which is fully integrated into the global economy, stripped of structural militarization, superpower, secret police coercion, 'captive nations' like Chechnya, and other spheres of influence.[29] Many advocate achieving these objectives by promoting westernization. The approach would closely approximate the Cold War format against the Soviet authoritarian, planned, martial police state, but would assign a smaller role to 'strategic parity' and arms reductions. Hypercentralization in this updated version of containment policy replaces 'communism' and 'command economy' as Russia's Achilles' heel.

However, this wish list mischaracterizes the EU's choices, and the strategy is mute on tactics. Russia today and for the foreseeable future will remain wedded to the Muscovite rent-granting pattern, which encompasses a spectrum of possibilities from a Stalinist authoritarian martial police state to compassionate patriarchy. Masterly engaging Russia, including its accession to the EU, requires sorting out the Kremlin's future, determining which western policy goals are paramount, and what combination of Muscovite systems and incentives will yield the best results, even though the best may not be very good. For example, during Yeltsin's years the EU was content to abandon the practical goal of preserving Russian economic stability to promote the downgrading of the Russian military and secret police, some denuclearization, and the strengthening independence of Eastern Europe and former Soviet republics. This was easily accomplished because it accorded with Yeltsin's own priorities, although the economic and political fallout eventually contributed to the emergence of Putin's authoritarianism.

The problem today, however, has changed in three important respects. Putin and the EU no longer share the common cause of collaring the military, FSB and moving toward popular representative democracy. Also, although the Kremlin is making positive noise about the independence of the CIS, the possibility of a full-spectrum military resurgence during the next five years could easily bring about a reversal of polarity. The possibility of Russia's EU accession, accordingly, is dimming.[30] Consequently, the EU now has to decide on whether to hector Putin on these issues, focus on economics,[31] or foment regime change despite the risk that it could trigger a 'fortress Russia' reaction, if it wishes to do more than hide behind the counsel of perfection.[32]

Judging from past precedent, the EU can be expected to dither. Putin will be urged to 'restore' democracy, resist partial renationalization, fully privatize, open the economy, avoid hypercentralization, civilianize the bureaucracy, curb the FSB, modernize its military with restraint, acquiesce to the loss of its CIS sphere of influence, and foster equal opportunity in order to escape the menaces of economic growth retardation, popular discontent, political revolt, secession and regime change, without considering how the EU should respond if weakened central authority culminates in Hobbesian mayhem, or propels Putin toward 'fortress Russia'. Apparently, the EU is willing to gamble that the risk of haphazardly fostering regime change, instead of offering more thoughtful counsel, will be borne primarily by the Russian people as it was during the Yeltsin era, and that outcomes from the west's perspective will be net gains, an attitude presaging turbulence ahead.[33]

The better part of valour

This assessment augurs poorly for the success of a Europa–Muscovy union because of the inadequacies of both prospective spouses. The Muscovy evolving from communism is light years away from Meadean social democracy based on inalienable ownership and property usage rights, is trending away from consumer and popular sovereignty, and is subject to abrupt and destabilizing shifts within the autocratic paradigm. Renationalization in the natural resource sectors and military industrial complex is narrowing the scope of private property rights, while presidential reassignment of rent-grants and bureaucratic moral hazard degrade their quality. Both not only heighten the EU's business risk, but also buttress the autocratic and imperial features of the regime that social democrats abhor. Clearly, the current tilt toward a *siloviki*-dominated authoritarian martial police state can hardly be welcome news, but neither can EU leaders be cheered by the possibility of a return to Yeltsin-era rent-granting *laissez-faire*, hyperdepression, mass unemployment and rapid decline in life expectancy. Either way Muscovy's contingent property rights are incompatible with consumer and popular sovereignty. They depress efficiency and are prone to severe and unpredictable abuse. These negatives do not settle matters. It can always be argued that, since Russia is unlikely to discipline itself, it behoves Europa to break the impasse. If the Kremlin will not listen to reason as an outsider, perhaps it can be badgered into it as a member of the EU. But this is unlikely. The EU's inability to formulate an effective transition policy for Russia suggests that it will be no more successful in managing the relationship after accession. Blind faith is not likely to be the better part of valour.

Masters of illusion

The EU in this regard should consider whether its welfare is best advanced by acting as a good neighbour rather than as the overlord of the Eurasian economic space. It should pay close attention to the Russian model as it is economically and politically, rather than as EU idealists wish it to be, and should flexibly maximize social welfare accordingly. And if, in doing so, it chooses Russia's EU accession as an element of engagement, the EU should consider a prenuptial agreement, and be sure that there are provisions for amicable divorce.

Conclusion

Saint Simon prophesied that national enmities would someday vanish in a common European social democratic space from the Atlantic to the Urals. Reason would compel Russia to abandon the Muscovite authoritarian martial police state, foregoing rent-granting, great power rivalry and imperialism for the greater good. However, the Kremlin has steadfastly refused to relinquish the rule of men for the rule of law where private rights including freehold property take precedence over rulers' will. The Enlightenment, communism and counterfeit post-Soviet transition have not made Russia fitter for inclusion in the European Union than it was during the time of Ivan the Great.[34]

The stewards of the greater Europe project do not see it this way, however, even though many aspects of EU nation-building are going awry.[35] They still hope Moscow will have an epiphany, or can be rescued by geography and Euro-governance. Once Russia accedes to the *acquis communautaire*, they believe it will westernize. This is risky business. Muscovy is more likely to devour the EU by exploiting the rules than the other way around. Fortunately for Brussels, Vladimir Putin has rejected Russia's accession to the EU after a protracted flirtation, but the game is not over. Brussels may have another chance to tempt fate.

Notes

1 'Baikal is Shock Winner of Russia's YUKOS Auction', *Johnson's Russia List*, No. 8506, Article 1, 19 (December 2004); S. Rosefielde, 'Illusion of Transition: Russia's Muscovite Future', *Eastern Economic Journal*, 31(2) (2005) 283–296.

2 S. Hedlund, *Russian Path Dependence* (London: Routledge, 2005); S. Hedlund, 'The Property Rights Hurdle: Reconciling EU and Russia Traditions', paper prepared for the VII ICCEES World Congress, panel XI.24, Berlin, 28 July 2005; S. Hedlund, 'Vladimir the Great, Grand Prince of Muscovy: Resurrecting a Russian Service State', a paper presented at the American Association for the Advancement of Slavic Studies Conference, Salt Lake City, Utah, November 4 2005.

3 J. Meade, *The Just Economy* (London: George Allen and Unwin, 1978).

4 K. Arrow, *Social Choice and Individual Values*, 2nd edn (New York: Wiley, 1963); S. Rosefielde, *Comparative Economic Systems: Culture, Wealth and Power in the 21st Century* (London: Blackwell, 2002) chapter 1.

5 Cf. S. Hedlund, 'Professor Gerschenkron Goes to Brussels: Russian Catch-up Economics and the Common European Space', where he argues that EU governors in Brussels are as corrupt as the Russians. Perhaps Europa and Muscovy deserve each other.

6 S. Huntington, 'The West: Unique, Not Universal', *Foreign Affairs*, 75(6) (1996) 28–46; United Nations, 'Towards A New European Model of a Reformed Welfare State: An Alternative to the United States Model', in *Economic Survey of Europe*, 1 (2005) chapter 7, 105–114; cf. RECEP, *Common Economic Space: Prospects of EU-Russia Relations* (Moscow: Russian–EuropeanCentre for Economic Policy) 9.

7 A. Shleifer, *A Normal Country: Russia After Communism* (Cambridge, MS: Harvard University Press, 2005); cf. S. Rosefielde, 'Russia: An Abnormal Country', *The European Journal of Comparative Economics*, 2(1) (2005) 3–16; cf. S. Rosefielde, 'Russia: An Abnormal Country', *The European Journal of Comparative Economics*, 2(1) (2005) 3–16.

8 World Bank, *Russian Economic Report*, No. 10 (March 2005) 17–20. www.worldbank.org.ru.

9 A. Bergson, *Essays in Normative Economics* (Cambridge MA: Harvard University Press, 1966).

10 A. Bergson, 'Social Choice and Welfare Economics under Representative Government', *Journal of Public Economics*, 6 (1976) 171–190.

11 N. Buckley, 'Market Reformers and Former Spies', *Financial Times* (April 5 2005), reprinted in *Johnson's Russia List*, No. 9111, Article 9 (5 April 2005). Buckley cites Lilia Shevtsova to the effect that 'If Putin had alternative sources of information in Ukraine, in the benefits crisis, if he had an independent parliament and television, he would have known things were going wrong...It is hypercentralization backfiring.' Cf. L. Shevtsova, *Putin's Russia* (Washington DC: Carnegie Endowment, 2005); M. McFaul, N. Petrov and A. Ryabov, *Between Dictatorship and Democracy: Russia Post-Communist Political Reform* (Washington DC: Carnegie Endowment, 2004); S. Wagstyl, 'Economy: Liberals try to Lessen Grip of State', *Financial Times* (5 April 2005). Andrei Illarionov, Putin's economic adviser, German Gref, the Minister of Economics, and Alexei Kudrin, Minister of Finance, are faced with the growing strength of the statists in the administration, those who believe the state must play a leading role in managing the economy. On the issue of asset concentration see S. Guriev and A. Rachinsky,

'Ownership Concentration in Russian Industry' (October 2004) www.cefir.ru/download.php?id=136.

12 'Russia: Ivanov Says Defense Sector to Become Locomotive of Economy', Itar-Tars (June 14, 2006). 'The Russian Defense Minister is planning that defense firms will be manufacturing up to 70 percent of civilian industrial products by the year 2015'. 'Defense Minister: Russia Will Spend 50 Percent More on Weapons in 2006 Than 2005', *Johnson's Russia List*, Vol. 82, Article 16 (April 6 2006). V. Shlykov, 'Nazad v budushchee, ili Ekonomicheskie uroki kholodnoi voiny' [Back to the Future, or Cold War Economic Lessons], *Rossiia v Global'noi Politike* [Russia in Global Politics], 4(2) (March–April, 2006) 26–40.

13 United Nations, *Economic Survey of Europe 2005*, No. 1 (New York: United Nations, 2005) Chart 5.13, 63; cf. B. Grozovsky, 'We have a Gold Russia: Foreign Investment in Russia could reach 83 Billion dollars in 2005-2008', *Johnson's Russia List*, No. 9129, Article 17 (25 April 2005). 'Experts Predict Increased Capital Outflow from Russia', *Johnson's Russia List*, No. 9044, Article 12 (2006).

14 O. Solomonova, 'Nikolai Shmelev: The Swamp of Poverty' (Interview), *Johnson's Russia List*, No. 9119 (13 April 2005).

15 Putin infamously described his ideal as the 'dictatorship of law'.

16 S. Rosefielde, 'The Civilian Labor Force and Unemployment in the Russian Federation', *Europe-Asia Studies*, **52**(8) (2000) 1433–1447.

17 United Nations, *Economic Survey of Europe 2005*, No. 1 (New York: United Nations, 2005) Table B.1, p.128; GDP 1989–2003 fell 23 per cent, recovering from an official low of 45 per cent. GDP grew 6.8 per cent in 2004. See Table 5.2.1, p.65; cf. Alex Fak, 'Real GDP Figures are Anybody's Guess', *Johnson's Russia List*, No. 9132, Article 13 (27 April 2005).

18 J. Cooper, '*The Economics of Russian Defence Policy*', a paper presented at the conference on Russia under President Vladimir Putin: Towards the Second Term, European University Institute, Florence, 22–23 April 2004.

19 G. Tenet, 'The Worldwide Threat 2004: Challenges in a Changing Global Context', testimony before the Senate Select Committee on Intelligence, 24 February, Washington, DC, 2004.

20 J. Siegle, M. Weinstein and M. Halperin, 'Why Democracies Excel', *Foreign Affairs*, 83(5) (2004) 57–71.

21 A. Gerschenkron, *Economic Backwardness in Historical Perspective* (Cambridge MA: Harvard University Press, 1966).

22 S. Wagstyl, 'Economy: Liberals Try to Loosen Grip of State', *Financial Times* (5 April 2005). 'Economic data point to a decline in gross domestic product growth from the high level of 7.1 percent recorded last year. GDP rose just 4.4 percent in the first two months of 2005'. John Litwack, a World Bank economist, says that 'There is definitely a slowdown. The question is whether it will be a slight or a serious one.'

23 R. Arendt and W. Thompson, 'Stavki Sdelany: Optimizm bez Strakhovki' [Military High Command: Optimism with Reservations], *Vedomosti* [Russian Business Daily], No. 71 (21 April 2005).

24 A. Denison, 'One Russia for All: Citizens Believe that Russia May Collapse', *Vremya Novostei*, 25 April 2005. 'In recent polls, most respondents agree that the disintegration of Russia is a real threat. Over half agree that our society is facing urgent problems, which could in time cause disintegration. Most believe that specific forces are striving to break up Russia.'

25 Y. Bogatyreva, 'New Political Generation is Coming to Replace Yavlinsky and Zyuganov', *Johnson's Russia List*, No. 9111, Article 13 (5 April 2005). A wave of protests against benefits-to-money conversion swept Russian cities in January and February. Protests were organized by former beneficiaries, the Communist Party and activists from youth organizations, particularly numerous ones on the left.

26 S. Blank, 'The 18th Brumaire of Vladimir Putin', in Uri Ra'anan, ed., *Flawed Succession* (Roman and Littlefield, 2006).

27 N. Buckley and A. Ostrovsky, 'Russia Plans to Continue Liberal Reforms', *Johnson's Russia List*, No. 9111, Article 3 (5 April 2005). German Gref, Russia's economic development minister, has denied that the state aims to resume control of significant sectors of the economy, and he said that other liberal ministers had carte blanche to continue market-based reforms. 'Institutional Reform is Main Prerequisite for Russia's Economic Growth, Minister Says', *Johnson's Russia List*, No. 9111, Article 6 (5 April 2005). 'High-quality institutions and protection of investor rights are the key to creating more favorable conditions in Russia than in competitor countries.' All these liberal themes were featured in Putin's state-of-nation address on 25 April 2005. Russia, he said, was interested in an influx of foreign direct investment (despite Russia's levying a 1 billion dollar surprise tax last week on TNK-BP oil). He asserted that investors need stability rather than 'riddles and charades', and urged improved bureaucratic productivity in government, corporations and the Party. Putin set strengthening democracy as the highest priority, supported fortifying the rule of law and human rights, called for shortening the statute of limitations on reviews of controversial privatizations of state enterprises in the 1990s to ten years, and advocated a new 13 per cent flat tax rate on undeclared capital. He only drew the line on curtailing limits on stakes held by foreign investors in strategic Russian companies. Putin insisted that 'People had come to believe that the Russian people were somehow not suited to democratic government, rule of law and basic values of civil society. ... I would like to bring those who think like that back to reality', but qualified his remarks by observing that a 'special feature' of Russia's path to democracy was that it would not be undertaken at the expense of maintaining law and order and the stability required to attract investment. 'Strengthening of Democracy is Russia's Highest Priority: Putin,' *Johnson's Russia List*, No. 9129, Article 2 (25 April 2005). Cf., 'Putin Made State-of-Nation Address in Kremlin', *Johnson's Russia List*, No. 9129, Article 1 (25 April 2005); Richard Balmforth 'Putin Tells Taxman Don't Terrorise Investors,' *Johnson's Russia List*, No. 9129, Article 3 (25 April 2005).

28 S. Rosefielde, 'Russia 2084: The Treadmill of Muscovite Reform,' paper presented at the FOI Conference 'Whither Russia?' Stockholm, Sweden, 6–7 May 2004.

29 The EU version of this list requires Russia to relinquish power politics in the interest of Russian society, and to support European expansion under Brussels' auspices. See J. Hedenskog, V. Konnander, B. Nygren, I. Oldberg and C. Pursaiainen, *Russia as a Great Power* (New York: Routledge, 2005) and S. Rosefielde, 'Review of Russia as a Great Power', *Slavic Review* 65(2) (Summer 2006) 395.

30 'Europe Watchdog Attacks Russia on Rights, Democracy,' *Johnson's Russia List*, No. 9125, Article 15 (21 April 2005). Council of Europe, Report by Mr. Alvaro Gil-Robes, Commissioner of Human Rights, on his Visits to the Russian Federation, *Johnson's Russia List*, No. 9125, Article 16 (21 April 2005).

31 The goals here are opening markets to western commerce and investment, securing natural resource supplies, and secondarily fostering domestic Russian economic efficiency.

32 M. Yuriev, 'Krepost' Rossiia: Kontseptsiia dlia Presidenta' (Fortress Russia: Strategic Concept for President Putin), *Novaya gazeta*, No. 17 (March 15 2004) (http://2004.novayagazeta.ru/nomer/2004/17n7n17n-w44.shtml). S. Rosefielde, 'Russia 2084: The Treadmill of Muscovite Radical Reform,' BOFIT Working Paper, Helsinki (2005).

33 Anders Aslund has recently recommended that America should press democracy on Russia, while 'pragmatically pursuing common interests in non-proliferation and energy', because Putin's regime is on the verge of collapse. Bush should also urge Russia's integration into the global economy, and foment domestic anti-government disorder. This is a typical example of the counsel of perfection since it fails to consider the consequences of meddling and insurrectionary regime change, or the comparative merits of more focused policy alternatives. See A. Aslund, Policy Brief #41, Carnegie Endowment for International Peace, www. CarnegieEndownment.org (August 2005), reprinted in *Johnson's Russia List*, No. 9220, Article 3 (August 2005), and Aslund, 'Responses to Comments on "Putin's Decline and America's Response",' *Johnson's Russia List*, No. 9225, Article 2 (17 August 2005). Aslund is justified in denouncing Russia's 'mild' authoritarianism, and calling attention to the fragility of the post-Soviet Russian state, but as Sergei Roy asserts his policy analysis is journalistic, and his past prescriptions catastrophic. See S. Roy, 'Scenario for Russia or Provocation?' *Johnson's Russia List*, No. 9223, Article 16 (13 August 2005). Roy is particularly critical of Aslund's advocacy of American support (an ape playing with matches) for 'full scale civil war.' He considers it not just lunatic, but criminal. Edward Lozansky agrees. See Lozansky 'U.S. Should Rethink Its Policy Toward Russia,' *Johnson's Russia List*, No. 9231, Article 9 (24 August 2005).

34 S. Rosefielde, *Russia in the 21st Century: The Prodigal Superpower* (Cambridge, Cambridge UP, 2005); S. Rosefielde and S. Hedlund, *Russia since 1980* (Cambridge: Cambridge UP, 2008).

35 S. Rosefielde and Q. Mills, *Masters of Illusion: American Leadership in the Media Age* (Cambridge: Cambridge UP, 2007).

Selected Bibliography

Altvater, E., *The Future of the Market: An Essay on the Regulation of Money and Nature* (London: Verso, 1993).

Anderson, M. and E. Bort, *The Frontiers of the European Union* (New York: Palgrave, 2001).

Arrow, K., *Social Choice and Individual Values*, 2nd edn (New York: Wiley, 1963).

Ball, A.M., *Russia's Last Capitalists: The Nepmen, 1921–1929* (Berkeley: University of California Press, 1990).

Bandelin, O.J., *Return of the NEP: The False Promise of Leninism and the Failure of Perestroika* (Westport, CT: Praeger, 2002).

Boar, N., 'Assessing the Impact of the Carpathian Euroregion in the Maramureş Region' in J. Wendt et al., *Poland and Romania before Enlargement of European Union and NATO* (Warsaw: Carta Blanca, 2004) pp. 114–119.

Bondyrev, V.E., 'Dvoistvenyi kharakter NEPa v otnoshenii chastnika' [The double character of the NEP in terms of private capital], *Istoriia gosudarstva i prava: Federal'nyi zhurnal: nauchno-pravovoe izdanie* [History, state and right: scientific and legal publishing], 1 (2002) 15–21.

Bonin, J. and P. Wachtel, 'Financial sector development in transition economies: Lessons for the first decade,' *BOFIT Discussion Papers* 9/2002, http://www.bof.fi/bofit/fin/6dp/abs/pdf/dp0902.pdf (7 December 2006).

Borodkin, L.I. and E.I. Safonova, 'Gosudarstvennoe regulirovanie trudovykh otnoshenii v gody nepa: formirovanie sistemy motivatsii truda v promyshlennosti' [The government regulation of labour relations in the NEP years: shaping the system to motivate industrial workers] in L.I. Borodkin, ed., *Ekonomicheskaia istoriia: Obozrenie*, 5 [Economic History Review] (Moscow: Moskovskii gosudarstvenyi universitet, 2000) 23–46.

van Brabant, J.M., *The Political Economy of Transition: Coming to Grips with History and Methodology* (London: Routledge, 1998).

Bradshaw, M.J. and A.C. Stenning, 'The Progress of Economic Transition in East Central Europe' in J. Bachtler, R. Downes and G. Gorzelak, eds, *Transition, Cohesion and Regional Policy in Central and Eastern Europe* (London: Ashgate, 2001) pp. 11–31.

De Broeck, M. and V. Koen, *The 'Soaring Eagle': Anatomy of the Polish Take-Off in the 1990s* (Washington DC: International Monetary Fund, 2000).

Brown, G., *Global Europe: Full Employment Europe* (London: UK Department of the Treasury, 2005): http://www.hm-treasury.gov.uk/media/2/A/global_europe_131005.pdf

Chen, Y., *Chugoku no Keizai Kaihatsu to Chiiki Kakusa ni kansuru Jissho Kenkyu* [Empirical Study on Economic Development and Regional Differences: Examination on the City Cluster in Yangtze Delta] (PhD Dissertation, Hiroshima University, 2001).

CIBA Limited, *The Story of the Chemical Industry in Basle* (Lausanne: Urs Graf Publishers, 1959).

Clark, C.E., *Uprooting Otherness: The Literacy Campaign in NEP-era Russia* (Selinsgrove: Susquehanna University Press; London: Associated University Presses, 2000).

Clement, H., *Die neuen Nachbarn und die Europäische Union – Möglichkeiten und Grenzen der Integration am Beispiel Ukraine und Belarus* [The New Neighbours and the

European Union: Possibilities and Limits of Integration, the example of Ukraine and Belarus] (Osteuropa Institut: Munich, 2005), Working paper 256.

Commission of the European Communities, *European Neighbourhood Policy – Country Report for Moldova* (Brussels, 2004).

Conroy, M.S. 'Abuse of Drugs other than Alcohol and Tobacco in the Soviet Union', *Soviet Studies*, 42(3) (1990) 447–480.

Conroy, M.S., *In Health and In Sickness: Pharmacy, Pharmacists and the Pharmaceutical Industry in Late Imperial, Early Soviet Russia* (Boulder, CO: East European Monographs, 1994).

Conroy, M.S., 'Health Care in Prisons, Labour and Concentration Camps in Early Soviet Russia, 1918–1921', *Europe-Asia Studies*, 52(7) (2000) 1257–1274.

Conroy, M.S., 'Russian-American Pharmaceutical Relations, 1900–1945', *Pharmacy in History*, 46(4) (2004) 143–166.

Conroy, M.S., *The Soviet Pharmaceutical Business during Its First Two Decades (1917–1937)* (AUS. Series IX, History, 202; New York: Peter Lang, 2006).

Council of Ministers, *Polska 2025, długookresowa strategia trwałego i zrównoważonego rozwoju* [Polska 2025 – The Long-Term Strategy of Sustainable Development] (Warsaw: Council of Ministers, 2000).

Council of Ministers, *Narodowy Plan Rozwoju 2004–2006* [Poland National Development Plan 2004–2006] (Warsaw: Council of Ministers, 2003).

Council of Ministers, *Poland – National Strategic Reference Framework 2007–2013 in support of growth and jobs,* Initial Draft (adopted by the Council of Ministers on 14 February 2006).

Crummey, R.O., *Aristocrats and Servitors: The Boyar Elite in Russia, 1613–1689* (Princeton, NJ: Princeton University Press, 1983).

Davies, R.W., M. Harrison and S.G. Wheatcroft, eds, *The Economic Transformation of the Soviet Union, 1913–1945* (Cambridge: Cambridge University Press, 1994).

Demchik, E.V., 'Chastnyi kapital v gorodakh Sibiri v 1920-e gg.: ot vozrozhdeniia k likvidatsii' [Private capital in Siberia's cities, 1920: from rebirth to liquidations] (Barnaul: Izdatel'stvo Altaiskogo gosudarstvenogo universiteta, 1998).

Demchik, E.V., 'Chastnyi capital i gosudarstvennaia vlast'' v Sibiri: dialog serediny 1920-h gg.' [Private capital and state power in Siberia: dialogue about the mid-1920s] in B.A. Skubnevskii and V.N. Razgon, eds, *Predprinimateli i predprinimatel'stvo v Sibiri* [Businessmen and enterprise in Siberia], 3 (Barnaul: Izdatel'stvo Altaiskogo gosudarstvenogo universiteta, 2001) 91–105.

Dunford, M., 'Differential Development, Institutions, Modes of Regulation and Comparative Transitions to Capitalism: Russia, the Commonwealth of Independent States, and the former German Democratic Republic' in J. Pickles and A. Smith, eds, *Theorising Transition: The Political Economy of Post-Communist Transformations* (London: Routledge, 1998) pp. 75–111.

EBRD, *Transition Report 2003* (London: European Bank for Reconstruction and Development, 2004).

En'iuan, U, 'Nepmany, ikh kharakteristika i rol' [The Nepmen, their character and role], *Otechestvennaia istoriia* [National history] 5 (2001) 78–87.

Erturk, K. and N. Cagatay, 'Macroeconomic Consequences of Cyclical and Secular Changes in Feminization: An Experiment at Gendered Macromodeling', *World Development*, 23(11), (1995) 1970–1971.

European Commission, *Industrial Policy in an Open and Competitive Environment: Guidelines for a Community Approach* (COM (1990)) 556 final.

European Commission, Communication from the Commission to the Council and the European Parliament, *–Roadmaps for Bulgaria and Romania*. Brussels, 13.11.2002 (COM (2002a)) 624 final.

European Commission, *Industrial Policy for an Enlarged Europe* ((COM (2002b)) 714 final.

European Commission, 'Facing the challenge: The Lisbon strategy for growth and Employment', Report from the High Level Group chaired by Wim Kok, November 2004a.

European Commission, *Fostering Structural Change: An Industrial Policy for an Enlarged Europe* (COM (2004b)) 274.

European Commission, *Working Together for Growth and Jobs: A New Start for the Lisbon Strategy*, Commission of the European Communities (COM (2005)) 24 final.

European Commission, *Implementing the Community Lisbon Programme: A Policy Framework to Strengthen EU Manufacturing – Towards a More Integrated Approach for Industrial Policy* (COM (2005)) 474.

European Commission, *Implementing the Community Lisbon Programme: A Policy Framework to Strengthen EU Manufacturing – Towards a More Integrated Approach for Industrial Policy* (COM (2005)) 474 final.

European Commission, *Report on the Results of the Negotiations on the Accession of Bulgaria and Romania to the European Union*, prepared by the Commission's Departments, February 2005, 5859/05 25 DG Enlargement (2005).

European Commission, *Report from the Commission to the European Parliament and the Council on Romania's Progress on Accompanying Measures Following Accession*, Brussels, 27 June 2007 (COM (2007)) 378.

European Parliament, ed., *Report on Romania's Application for Membership of the European Union*, Committee for Foreign Affairs. Rapporteur: Pierre Moscovici (Strasbourg, 2005).

Fink, G., P. Haiss and S. Hristoforova, 'Bond Markets and Economic Growth', *EuropaInstitut Working Paper* 49, April 2003, http://fgr.wu-wien.ac.at/institut/ef/nexus.html (7 December 2006).

Fuszara, M., 'Women's legal rights in Poland and the process of transformation', in *Beyond Law: Stories of Law and Social Change from Latin America and around the World* (Latin American Institute of Alternative Legal Services, 1993), pp. 41–42.

Gimpelison, E.G., *NEP i sovetskaia politicheskaia sistema: 20-e gody* [The NEP and the soviet political system: 20th year] (Moscow: Institut rossiiskoi istorii RAN, 2000).

Gimpelison, E. G., *The NEP: The New Economic Policy of Lenina-Stalina. The Problems and Lessons (the 20 Years of XX century)*. (Moscow: Sobranie, 2004).

Gerschenkron, A., *Economic Backwardness in Historical Perspective* (Cambridge MA: Harvard University Press, 1966).

Goland, Y. 'Currency Regulation in the NEP Period', *Europe-Asia Studies*, 46(8) (1994) 1251–1296.

Goldman, M., *Piratizing Russia: Russian Reform Goes Awry* (London: Routledge, 2003).

Gomulka, S., 'Policy Challenges within the (Enlarged) European Union: How Can Economic Convergence be Fostered?' in G. Tumpel-Gugerell and P. Mooslechner, eds, *Economic Convergence and Divergence in Europe: Growth and Regional Development in an Enlarged European Union* (Cheltenham, Northampton: Edward Elgar, 2003), pp. 436–447.

Grik, N.A., *Sovetskaia ekonomicheskaia politika v 1921–1933 gg.: kriticheskii analiz* [Soviet economic policy, 1921–1933 (Critical analysis)] (Tomsk: Tomskii gosudarstvenyi universitet, 2002).

Grob, G. N., *The Deadly Truth* (Boston, MA: Harvard University Press, 2002).

Grzegorczyk, M., *Marketing bankowy* (Bydgoszcz – Łódź: Oficyna Wydawnicza Branta, 2004).

Haiss, P. and S. Marin, 'Options for Developing Bond Markets – Lessons from Asia for Central and Eastern Europe', *EuropaInstitut Working Paper* 63, January 2005, http://fgr.wu-wien.ac.at/institut/ef/nexus.html (7 December 2006).

Hall, D.E. and D. Danta, *Europe Goes East: EU Enlargement, Diversity and Uncertainty* (London: The Stationery Office, 2000).

Hayek, F.A., *The Road to Serfdom* (London: New York, 2001).

Harwood, A., *Building Local Bond Markets: An Asian Perspective* (IFC, 2000).

Hedenskog, J., V. Konnander, B. Nygren, I. Oldberg and C. Pursaiainen, *Russia as a Great Power* (New York: Routledge, 2005).

Hedlund, S., *Russia's 'Market' Economy: A Bad Case of Predatory Capitalism* (London: UCL Press, 1999).

Hedlund, S., 'Property without Rights: Dimensions of Russian Privatization', *Europe-Asia Studies*, 53(2) (2001) 213–217.

Hedlund, S., 'Russia and the IMF: A Sordid Tale of Moral Hazard', *Demokratizatsiya*, 9(1) (2001) 104–136.

Hedlund, S., *Russian Path Dependence* (London: Routledge, 2005).

Herring, R. and N. Chatusripitak, *The Case of the Missing Market: The Bond Market and What It Matters for Financial Development* (Wharton Financial Institutions Center, 2000).

Hessler, J., *A Social History of Soviet Trade: Trade Policy, Retail Practices, and Consumptions, 1917–1953* (Princeton, NJ: Princeton University Press, 2004).

Heywood, A., *Modernizing Lenin's Russia: Economic Reconstruction, Foreign Trade and Railways* (Cambridge: Cambridge University Press, 1999).

Hodgson, G.M., *Economics and Institutions: A Manifesto for a Modern Institutional Economics* (Oxford: Policy Press, 1993).

Hodgson, G.M., W.J. Samuels and M.R. Tool, eds, *The Elgar Companion to Institutional and Evolutionary Economics* (Hants: Edward Elgar, 1993).

Huntington, S., 'The West: Unique, Not Universal', *Foreign Affairs*, 75(6) (1996) 28–46.

Ilieş, A., *România intre milenii. Frontiere, areale frontaliere şi cooperare transfrontialiera* [Romania at the beginning of millennium. Borders, border regions and cross-border cooperation] (Oradea, 2003).

Ilieş, A., *România. Euroregiuni* [Romania. Euroregions] (Oradea, 2004).

Ilieş, G., 'The Eastern Limit of Maramureş Land and Its Status', in J. Wendt et al., *Poland and Romania before Enlargement of European Union and NATO* (Warsaw, 2004) pp. 111–113.

Ingham, M., H. Ingham and H. Domański, eds, *Women on the Polish Labour Market* (Budapest: CEU Press, 2001).

Jaworski, W.L., *Współczesny bank* [Contemporary Banking] (Warszawa: Poltext, 1999).

Karl, T.L. and P.C. Schmitter, 'Modes of Transition in Latin America, Southern and Eastern Europe', *International Social Science Journal* 128(43) (1991) 269–284.

Khaziev, R.A., 'Poslednie iz mogikan: krasnye kuptsy epokhi nepa': Materialy i dokumenty ob ural'skikh kommersantakh 1921–1928 godov* [Last of the Mohicans: red merchants of the NEP period: Material and the documents about the Urals merchant, 1921–1928] (Ufa: Bashkirskii gosudarstvenyi universitet, 2003).

Khaziev, R.A., ed., *Bubliki dlia respubliki: istoricheskii profil Nepmenov* [Bagels for the Republic: An Historical Profile of the NEPmen] (Ufa: Bashkir State University Press, 2005).

Knight, J. and L. Song, *The Rural-Urban Divide Economic Disparities and Interactions in China* (New York: Oxford University Press, 1999).

Kobrak, C., *National Cultures and International Competition: The Experience of Schering AG, 1851–1950* (Cambridge: Cambridge University Press, 2001).

Kornai, J., *Economics of Shortage* (Amsterdam: North Holland, 1980).

Kornai, J., *The Socialist System: The Political Economy of Communism* (Oxford: Clarendon Press, 1992).

Kowalska, A., *Economic Activity of Women and Their Position on the Labour Market* (Warszawa: Gus, 1996).

Lange, O. and F.M. Taylor, *On the Economic Theory of Socialism* (Minneapolis: University of Minnesota Press, 1938).

Ledeneva, A.V., *Russia's Economy of Favours: Blat, Networking and Informal Exchange* (Cambridge: Cambridge University Press, 1998).

Leiteritz, R.J. and L. Handrich, 'Post-Communist Transformation and Industrial Relations' in A. Hulsemeyer, ed., *Globalization in the Twenty-First Century: Convergence or Divergence?* (London: Palgrave Macmillan, 2003) pp. 68–82.

Lenin, V.I., *Ocherednye zadachi sovetskoi vlasti* (PSS) [The next goals of Soviet power], 5th edn, 36 (Moscow: Gosudarstvennoe izdatel'stvo poloticheskoi literatury, 1962).

Libenau, J., G.J. Higby and E.C. Stroud, *Pill Peddlers: Essays on the History of the Pharmaceutical Industry* (Madison, WI: American Institute of the History of Pharmacy, 1990).

Liutov, L.N., *Obrechennaia reforma: promyshlennost' Rossii v epokhu NEPa* [The doomed reform. Russian industry of the NEP period] (Ul'ianovsk: Ul'ianovskii gosudarstvenyi universitet, 2002).

Liutov, L.N., *Simbirskoe-Ul'ianovskoe Povolzh'e v gody nepa. (Ekonomika regiona). Uchebnoe posobie* [Simbirskoe – Ulianovskoe Povolzhie in the years of Nep (regional economy). Book] (Ul'ianovsk: Simbirskia kniga, 2005).

Malia, M., *Russia under Western Eyes: From the Bronze Horseman to the Lenin Mausoleum* (Cambridge, MA: Belknap Press, 1999).

Mandelson, P., *Global Europe.* http://ec.europa.eu/trade/issues/sectoral/competitiveness/global_europe_en.htm

McFaul, M., N. Petrov and A. Ryabov, *Between Dictatorship and Democracy: Russia Post-Communist Political Reform* (Washington DC: Carnegie Endowment, 2004).

Meade, J., *The Just Economy* (London: George Allen and Unwin, 1978).

Mencinger, J., 'Does Foreign Direct Investment Always Enhance Economic Growth?' *Kyklos*, 56(4) (2003) 491–508.

Ministry of Industry, *Industrial Policy – Plan of execution for years 1993–1995* (Warsaw: Ministry of Industry and Commerce, 1993).

Narskii, I.V., *Zhizn' v katastrofe: Budni naseleniia Urala v 1917–1922 gg.* [Life in catastrophe: Everyday life of the people of the Urals, 1917–1922] (Moscow: ROSSPEN, 2001).

North, D.C., *Institutions, Institutional Change and Economic Performance* (Cambridge: Cambridge University Press, 1990).

North, D.C. and R.P. Thomas, *The Rise of the Western World: A New Economic History* (Cambridge: Cambridge University Press, 1973).

North, D.D., *Structure and Change in Economic History* (New York: Norton, 1981).

Nugent, N., *The Government and Politics of the European Union* (London: Macmillan Press, 1999).

OECD, *Model Tax Convention on Income and on Capital* (Paris: OECD, 2003).

Olson, M., 'Autocracy, Democracy and Prosperity' in R. J. Zeckhauser, ed., *Strategy and Choice* (Cambridge, MA: MIT Press, 1991) pp. 131–157.

Olson, M., 'Why the Transition from Communism is so Difficult', *Eastern Economic Journal* 21(4) (1993) 437–461.

Olson, M., 'The New Institutional Economics: The Collective Choice Approach to Economic Development' in C. Clague, ed., *Growth and Governance in Less-Developed and Post-Socialist Countries* (Baltimore, MD and London: The Johns Hopkins University Press, 1997) pp. 37–64.

Orlov, I.B., 'Novaia burzhuaziia' v satire 20-h gg.' [New bourgeoisie] in S. Sekirinsky, ed., *Istoriia Rossii XIX–XX vekov: Novye istochniki ponimaniia* [XX century Russian history] (Moscow: Moskovskii obschestvenyi fond, 2001), 230–236.

Orlov, I.B., 'Obraz nepmana v massovom soznanii 20-h gg.: mify i real'nost' [The image of nepmen in twentieth-century mass consciousness: myths and reality], *Novyi istoricheskii vestnik* [New history bulletin], 1 (2002) 29–42.

Orlov, I.B., 'Grimasy nepa' v istoriko-revoliutsionnom fil'me 1920-kh godov' ['Grimasy nepa' in historical and revolutionary film in 1920], *Otechestvennaia istoriia* [National history] 6 (2003) 21–30.

Owen, T.C., 'Autocracy and the Rule of Law' in J. Sachs and K. Pistor, eds, *The Rule of Law and Economic Reform in Russia* (Boulder, CO: Westview Press, 1998) pp. 23–39.

Panaitescu, S., *An Assessment of Romania's Prospects of Accession to the European Union* (University of Oradea Publishing House, 2004).

Pavlínek, P., and A. Smith, 'Internationalization and Embeddedness in East-Central European Transition: The Contrasting Geographies of Inward Investment in the Czech and Slovak Republics', *Regional Studies* 32(7) (1988) 619–638.

Pejovich, S., *Economic Analysis of Institutions and Systems* (Dodrecht – Boston – London: Kluwer Academic Publisher, 1997).

Pickles, J. and A. Smith, eds, *Theorising Transition: The Political Economy of Post-Communist Transformations* (London: Routledge, 1998).

Pickles, J. and R. Begg, 'Ethnicity, State Violence, and Neo-Liberal Transitions in Post-Communist Bulgaria', Special Issue of *Growth and Change: Ethnicity, Violence, and Regional Change* 31(2) (2000) 179–210.

Pipes, R., *Russia under the Old Regime* (New York: Charles Scribner's Sons, 1974).

Pipes, R., 'Was there Private Property in Muscovite Russia?' *Slavic Review* 53(2) (1994) 524–530.

Pipes, R., *The Unknown Lenin* (New Haven, CT: Yale University Press, 1996).

Pipes, R., *Property and Freedom* (New York: Alfred A. Knopf, 1999).

Plummer, M. and R. Click, 'Bond Market Development and Integration in ASEAN', *International Journal of Finance and Economics*, 10(2) (2005) 133–142.

Rainnie, A., A. Smith and A. Swain, *Work, Employment and Transition: Restructuring Livelihoods in Post-Communism* (London: Routledge, 2002).

RECEP, *Common Economic Space: Prospects of EU-Russia Relations* (Moscow: Russian–European Centre for Economic Policy, 2002).

Reszke, I., *Wobec bezrobocia: opinie, stereotypy* [Facing Unemployment: Opinions, Stereotypes] (Warszawa: Scholar, 1995).

Rieser, H.H., Dezvoltarea economica in Euro-regiunea Dunare-Criş-Mureş-Tisa. La ce ne putem aştepta şi ce este de facut [Economic development in the euroregion Duna-Cris-Mures-Tisa] (Bucureşti: Romanian Office of the Friedrich Ebert Foundation, 2005).

Rieser, H.H., 'The DKMT-Euroregion as an Instrument for Cross Border Regional Development', *Romanian Review of Regional Studies*, 1(2005) 27–34.

Rieser, H.H., 'Die aktuellen Entwicklungen der Grenzregionen im südwestlichen Rumänien' [Actual developments of border regions in south-west Romania] in F.-D. Grimm, ed., *Grenzen und Grenzregionen in Südosteuropa* [Borders and border regions in South-East Europe], *Südosteuropa aktuell* 28 (1998) 102–110.

Rosefielde, S., *Comparative Economic Systems: Culture, Wealth and Power in the 21st Century* (London: Blackwell, 2002).

Rosefielde, S., 'Illusion of Transition: Russia's Muscovite Future', *Eastern Economic Journal*, 31(2) (2005) 283–296.

Rosefielde, S., 'Russia: An Abnormal Country', *The European Journal of Comparative Economics*, 2(1) (2005) 3–16.

Rosefielde, S., *Russia in the 21st Century: The Prodigal Superpower* (Cambridge, Cambridge UP, 2005).

Rosefielde, S. and S. Hedlund, *Russia since 1980* (Cambridge: Cambridge UP, 2008).

Rosefielde, S. and Q. Mills, *Masters of Illusion: American Leadership in the Media Age* (Cambridge: Cambridge UP, 2007).

Săgeată, R., 'The Role of the Double Settlements in the Euro-Regions Structure – A Case Study: The Romanian-Bulgarian Border Space in the Danube Sector' in J. Wendt et al., *Poland and Romania before Enlargement of European Union and NATO* (Warsaw, 2004) pp. 125–131.

Seppain, H., *Contrasting US and German Attitudes to Soviet Trade, 1917–1991: Politics by Economic Means* (New York: St. Martin's Press, 1992).

Shishkin, V.A., *Vlast'. Politika. Ekonomika. Poslerevoliutsionnaia Rossiia (1917–1928)* [Power, Policy and Economy in Post-revolutionary Russia, 1917–1928] (St. Petersburg: Dmitrii Bulanin, 1997).

Shleifer, A. and R. Vishny, *The Grabbing Hand: Government Pathologies and Their Cures* (Cambridge, MA: Harvard University Press, 1998).

Socha, M. and U. Sztanderska, *Strukturalne podstawy bezrobocia w Polsce* [Structural Unemployment in Poland] (Warszawa: PWN, 2000).

Smith, A. and A. Swain, 'Regulating and Institutionalising Capitalisms: the Micro-Foundations of Transformation in Central and Eastern Europe' in J. Pickles and A. Smith, eds, *Theorising Transition: The Political Economy of Post-Communist Transformations* (London: Routledge, 1998).

Waack, C., 'Das Städtepaar Giurgiu und Russe an der rumänisch-bulgarischen Grenze' [The twin city of Giurgiu and Rousse on the Romanian-Bulgarian border] in F.D. Grimm, ed., 'Grenzen und Grenzregionen in Südosteuropa', *Südosteuropa aktuell* (Munich) 28 (1998) 141–153.

Wagner, N., and D. Iakova, 'Financial Sector Evolution in the Central European Economies: Challenges in Supporting Macroeconomic Stability and Sustainable Growth', *IMF Working Papers* No.01/141, 2001 http://www.imf.org/external/pubs/ft/wp/2001/wp01141.pdf (7 December 2006).

Wallace, W., *Policy Making in the European Union* (Oxford: Oxford University Press, 1996).

Wedel, J.R., *Collision and Collusion: The Strange Case of Western Aid to Eastern Europe 1989–98* (New York: St. Martin's, 1998).

Weatherall, M., *In Search of a Cure: A History of Pharmaceutical Discovery* (New York: Oxford University Press, 1990).

Wilkin, J., *Jaki kapitalizm? Jaka Polska?* [Which Capitalism? Which Poland?] (Warszawa: PWN, 1999).

Williams, W.A., *American-Russian Relations, 1781–1947* (New York: Octagon Books, 1971).

World Bank, *World Development Report 1996: From Plan to Market* (New York and Oxford: Oxford University Press, 1996) p. 132.

World Bank, *China 2020 Series: Sharing Rising Incomes: Disparities in China* (Washington DC: World Bank, 1997).

World Economic Forum, *The Lisbon Strategy Review 2004 An Assessment Of Policies And Reforms in Europe* (Davos: World Economic Forum, 2004).

Worthen, D.B., *Pharmacy in World War II* (New York: Haworth Press, 2004).

Yeager, T.J., *Institutions, Transition Economies, and Economic Development* (Boulder, CO and Oxford: Westview Press, 1999).

Żukrowska, K., 'Klasyfikacja modeli transformacji gospodarczej' [Classification of models of transformation] in K. Żukrowska and D. Sobczak, eds, *Rozszerzenie strefy euro na Wschód* [Eastern enlargement of Euro-zone] (Warsaw, 2004) pp. 13–32.

Index